Venturi,
Scott Brown
& Associates

Buildings and Projects, 1986–1998

Venturi, Scott Brown

& Associates

Buildings and Projects, 1986–1998

Stanislaus von Moos

With project descriptions by
Denise Scott Brown and Robert Venturi
and an interview by Mary McLeod

THE MONACELLI PRESS

First published in the United States of America in 1999 by
The Monacelli Press, Inc.
10 East 92nd Street, New York, New York 10128.

Library of Congress Cataloging-in-Publication Data
Moos, Stanislaus von.
Venturi, Scott Brown & Associates : buildings and projects, 1986–1998 / Stanislaus von Moos ; with project descriptions by Denise Scott Brown and Robert Venturi and an interview by Mary McLeod.
p. cm.
ISBN 1-885254-97-0—ISBN 1-58093-001-8 (pbk.)
1. Venturi Scott Brown and Associates. 2. Architecture, Modern—20th century—United States. I. Title. II. Title: Venturi, Scott Brown and Associates.
NA737.V49M66 1999
720'.92'2—dc21   99-27063

Printed and bound in Italy

Designed by *Abigail Sturges*

Acknowledgments

Work on this book began around 1994, as a sequel to *Venturi, Rauch & Scott Brown: Buildings and Projects*, published in 1987, which itself was based on the comprehensive exhibition I was asked to prepare for the Museum für Gestaltung in Zurich in 1979. It has involved the know-how and patience of many people, both at the office of Venturi, Scott Brown & Associates in Philadelphia and at The Monacelli Press in New York. I wrote most of the introductory essay during a stay in the United States in 1996–97, first as a senior visiting fellow at the Center for Advanced Study in the Visual Arts in Washington, D.C., and then as the Jean Labatut Visiting Professor at Princeton University. At Princeton, a seminar titled "Venturi in Context" provided an opportunity to discuss some of the ideas that subsequently became the backbone of the text. Among the students, whose contributions were memorable, I would like to single out Sasha Sattar and Christy Schlesinger, and among colleagues, who shared their ideas with me, Robert Gutman and Carles Valhornat at Princeton, as well as Vincent Scully in Coral Gables, Florida. Special thanks are due also to Alan Colquhoun, Karin Gimmi, Thomas P. Hughes, Sarah Ksiazek-Williams, Mary McLeod, Frederic Schwartz, and George Thomas, who offered valuable advice on early drafts of the essay. So did Robert Venturi and Denise Scott Brown, whose lively participation in the genesis of the text has contributed greatly to its factual accuracy, although they cannot be blamed for imprecisions that remain—or for my European bias with regards to the work.

Among those most directly involved in the preparation and selection of the visual material, as well as in the editing of the various versions of the text (both the architects' and mine), were John Izenour of VSBA in Philadelphia and Jean-Noël Jetzer in Zurich. Working with Andrea Monfried, from The Monacelli Press, and with graphic designer Abigail Sturges has been a pleasure. I would like to mention two people with particular gratitude: the late Heinrich Klotz, who was one of the first European critics and historians to acknowledge the Venturis' importance for architecture today, and who brought me together with them during a conference held in Berlin ("Das Pathos des Funktionalismus," 1975); and Irène von Moos, my wife, who has actively shared and nurtured my curiosity about the Venturis' work for more than a quarter century.

—S.v.M.

Contents

7   Preface

STANISLAUS VON MOOS
Contextual Oscillations

11   *Penn's Shadow*

25   *Scenes of Learning*

35   *Secret Physiology*

47   *Tableaux*

57   *The City as Kimono*

DENISE SCOTT BROWN AND ROBERT VENTURI
Venturi, Scott Brown & Associates
Buildings and Projects, 1986–1998

75   *Urban Design*

121   *Civic Buildings*

217   *Institutional Buildings*

263   *Commercial Architecture*

283   *Houses*

301   *Renovations*

317   *Exhibitions, Interior Design, Decorative Arts*

MARY McLEOD
On Artful Artlessness: A Conversation

343   **On Artful Artlessness: A Conversation**

361   Bibliography

367   Photography Credits

Preface

The work shown in this book could be said to speak for itself. History, the source of many of its underlying formal ideas, has become a mass commodity, and issues of multiculturalism and ethnicity are prevalent. Yet while it is true that architectural discourse today relies to some degree on the ideas first heralded by Robert Venturi and Denise Scott Brown, and while their early work—the Vanna Venturi House, Guild House, some fire houses in Columbus, Ohio, and New Haven, Connecticut—belongs to the history of architecture as it is taught almost everywhere, the more recent buildings and projects have remained comparatively invisible. With the demise of postmodernism as the leading architectural fashion, an aura of mystery surrounds these architects, arousing in many critics curiosity as well as impatience, if not metaphysical disgust.

Clearly, the Venturis are subverting widely shared beliefs in the universe of architecture. They irritate, in professional quarters even more than elsewhere. And as a result, they are among the most written-about architects of their generation, despite and in addition to being prolific writers themselves.

This book inevitably reflects such a critical condition. Its bulk is devoted to the firm's buildings and projects since 1986, when I prepared *Venturi, Rauch & Scott Brown: Buildings and Projects*, which was published in 1987. The catalog section of the present volume has been prepared in collaboration with the architects, who also wrote the entries. As in the previous book, buildings and projects are grouped according to type and, within these categories, rough chronological order.

The project descriptions make clear that the architects' work is part of an evolving theoretical discourse. These texts both explain the buildings and projects at hand and serve as a guide through the work and its polemical implications. In the conversation at the end of the book, Mary McLeod, Denise Scott Brown, Robert Venturi, and I discuss in greater detail some of the firm's recent work as well as its underlying artistic procedures and theoretical preoccupations. My introductory essay, "Contextual Oscillations," attempts to review the oeuvre in light of its mature phase, purposely choosing a somewhat more detached view.

—S.v.M.

40 YEARS OF ARCHITECTURE

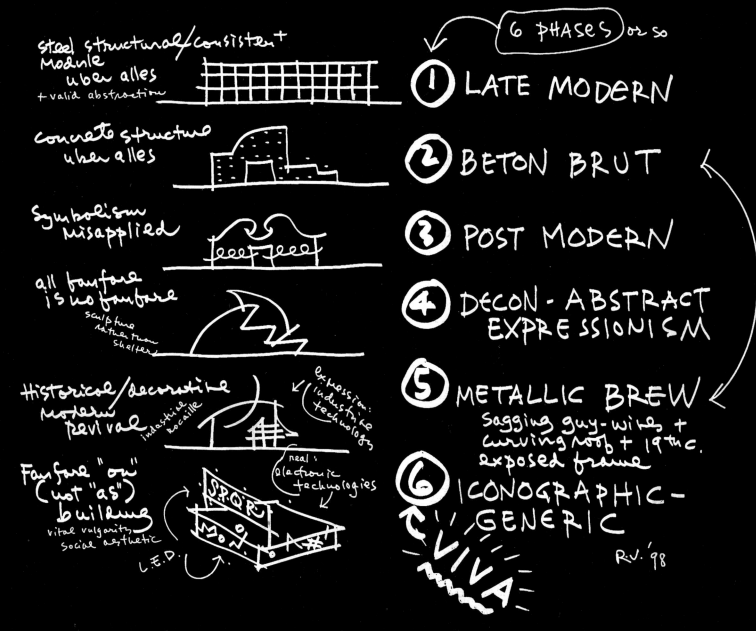

6 PHASES or so

steel structural/consistent
module
   uber alles
+ valid abstraction

① LATE MODERN

concrete structure
uber alles

② BETON BRUT

Symbolism
misapplied

③ POST MODERN

all fanfare
is no fanfare
sculpture
rather than
shelter

④ DECON - ABSTRACT EXPRESSIONISM

Historical/decorative
modern
revival
   industrial rocaille

expression:
industrial
technologies

real:
electronic
technologies

⑤ METALLIC BREW
Sagging guy-wires +
curving roof + 19 thc.
exposed frame

Fanfare "on"
(not "as")
building
vital vulgarity:
social aesthetic

SPQR MON

L.E.D.

⑥ ICONOGRAPHIC - GENERIC

VIVA
VIVA

R.V. '98

Contextual Oscillations

11   *Penn's Shadow*

25   *Scenes of Learning*

35   *Secret Physiology*

47   *Tableaux*

57   *The City as Kimono*

1. *Offices of Venturi, Scott Brown & Associates in a nineteenth-century loft building, Manayunk, Philadelphia, Pennsylvania.*

3. Charles Demuth, After All, *oil on composition board, 1933.*

2. *View from VSBA conference room toward Manayunk.*

Penn's Shadow

Looking out over the roofs of Manayunk, an old mill town northwest of central Philadelphia, "disfigured" by industrial "blight," one cannot help thinking of the brick structures, chimneys, painted signs, water tanks, and electric wires of Charles Demuth's mesmerizingly airy views from his home in Lancaster, Pennsylvania, painted between 1920 and 1933 (fig. 3). It is tempting to think that these paintings may have had a share in determining Robert Venturi and Denise Scott Brown's decision to move their office from its previous quarters on South Sixteenth Street, Philadelphia, to its present location in a loft building on the fringes of the city, thereby becoming part of what used to be the heart of industrial America.[1]

Main Street Manayunk, their present address, is a "real," not an idyllicized, Main Street (although it is currently undergoing its postindustrial recycling as a regional tourist strip), and so it recalls Venturi's "Is not Main Street almost all right?" of the 1960s. As for Demuth, one of his paintings carries the title *After All*. The source is apparently a stanza from Walt Whitman's *Leaves of Grass* (1855), entitled "Song of the Exposition":

> After all not to create only, or found only,
> But to bring perhaps from afar what is already founded,
> To give it our own identity, average, limitless, free,
> To fill the gross, the torpid bulk with vital religious fire,
> Not to repel or destroy so much as accept, fuse, rehabilitate,
> To obey as well as command, to follow more than to lead,
> These also are the lessons of our New World
> While how little the New after all, how much the Old, Old World![2]

Whitman at one point explicitly linked his poem about the "lessons of our New World" to his experience of the Philadelphia World's Fair of 1876. On the other hand, his lines are pregnant with concepts like collage, or readymade, and so they evoke a whole array of notions and images for twentieth-century Modernism to grasp. Filippo Tommaso Marinetti, Marcel Duchamp, Joseph Stella, and indeed Demuth himself appear to have picked up the thread.[3] And Whitman's insistence on the artist-poet as an interpreter rather than as an organizer or even creator of the primordial spectacles of modernity continues to reverberate even further down the history of Modern art—in the ironic realism of pop art as well as in the architecture of Venturi, Scott Brown & Associates.

Philadelphia's "official" architectural heritage offers no immediate precedent for the direction toward multicultural and multimedia "realism" taken by the Venturis; on the other hand, this heritage appears to be present—at least by implication—throughout their work. More recently, with projects like the Christopher Columbus Monument, the proposed Philadelphia Orchestra Hall, and Gateway Visitors Center and Independence Mall, all in Philadelphia, the city has again become an explicit theme (see pp. 96–101, 114–15, 196–203). In these projects, it appears to be the Venturis' aim to join this city's ideological inclinations toward patriotic romanticism, often veiled in neoclassical pomp, to the aesthetic challenge of the industrial and commercial sublime.

4. Postcard of Benjamin Franklin Parkway, Philadelphia.

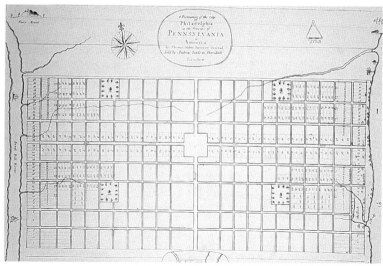

5. Thomas Holme, surveyor general of Pennsylvania, plan of Philadelphia, 1683.

6. Venturi, Rauch & Scott Brown, Welcome Park, Philadelphia, 1982.

National Shrine

To visitors who arrive in Philadelphia by train, at Thirtieth Street Station, and then take the subway into the city center (provided they can even find the metro station entrance situated in a nearby parking lot), Philadelphia's core, with its bombastic City Hall, still has panache (figs. 4, 8). From the roof terrace of the PSFS Tower, located only a few blocks east along Market Street, the colossal bronze statue of William Penn atop the tower of City Hall can still be experienced in its dual role as icon of the city founder, inviting the world to make Philadelphia a capital of trade, and as merciless height limit to the hubris of those who agreed to come. (Only during the Reagan years was the spell broken.)[4]

The driver who approaches Philadelphia from Interstate 95, however, finds downtown signaled laconically as "Independence Hall." The street map singles out the entire eastern section of the downtown area as Independence National Historic Park, thus identifying the city as a prime locus of American patriotism—with Independence Hall marking both the focus of the baroque *tapis verts* of Independence Mall *and* the transition to the scattered historic buildings of Society Hill (fig. 9).

The architecture of what once was called the Philadelphia school, which included Louis Kahn and Romaldo Giurgola, as well as Venturi, Rauch, Scott Brown & Associates, is profoundly attached to this historic area and its ethos. Here, in this national historic park and in the comfortable residential enclave of Society Hill, an area developed in the late 1950s and representing the initial step in a comprehensive program to revamp the center of the

city,[5] the visitor may stroll around exemplary buildings, evocative of both historic romance and architectural character. At the center is Independence Hall itself, arch-icon of the Red (brick) City of the revolutionary era, built from 1732 to 1756 and visible from a distance thanks only to its awkwardly proportioned steeple, which, notes Vincent Scully, is "widely out of scale on the garden side and in any distant view but falling into perspective from the street."[6] Next to Independence Hall, Independence National Historic Park begins, with William Strickland's Second Bank of the United States of 1817–24 (one of the nation's first public buildings in the Greek Revival style; fig. 25) as well as, further to the east, the Philadelphia Exchange of 1834, also by Strickland. Not every visitor realizes that the park is the result of a planning operation that dates back only half a century or so.[7] The operation had been heralded, in the 1920s, in a study of historic buildings undertaken by the Philadelphia chapter of the American Institute of Architects, the first of its sort, and, in the 1930s, Roy F. Larsen had proposed creating an open space around Independence Hall. But the idea was carried out only in the 1950s and 1960s, as a sequel, in part, to the "Better Philadelphia" exhibition of 1947, and clearly in an attempt to rival Benjamin Franklin Parkway, the city's Champs Elysées, built during and after World War I as a bold diagonal cut into the seventeenth-century grid (fig. 8). It was then, in the 1950s, that Independence National Historic Park became a display of carefully reconstructed historic buildings and gardens surrounded by open space and served by cobbled walkways, and that Society Hill, the portion of the central city closest to the Delaware River, was rede-

7. *Louis I. Kahn, Philadelphia Center Study, 1956; City Hall is at left with proposed new City Tower and Independence Mall at right.*

9. *Postcard of Independence Hall, Philadelphia.*

8. *Aerial view of the center of Philadelphia looking from City Hall toward Philadelphia Museum of Art.*

10, 11. Louis I. Kahn, "Market Street as a dock. Chestnut Street as a pedestrian way," 1952–53.

veloped as an exemplary case of historic preservation in the service of urban gentrification. Edmund N. Bacon, the long-time head of Philadelphia's planning commission, later described this operation as the "rebirth of Philadelphia."[8]

Kahn, Patriotism, and the Public Sphere

Louis Kahn's work toward the redevelopment of blighted neighborhoods, as well as his urbanistic proposals for Philadelphia, which Scully calls "grandiose and cataclysmic, like Le Corbusier's schemes,"[9] are all in a complicated way related to Philadelphia's mythic rebirth after World War II. Starting with a first tabula rasa plan of 1941, then culminating in a series of grand projects of around 1956–57, and also in a proposal of 1962, Kahn offered a whole set of plans, all focused on, among other things, disentangling pedestrian and automobile circulation. Between 1946 and 1954 he had himself been a consulting architect to the city planning commission; nevertheless, his actual projects all remained on paper.[10] The best known among them was published in *Perspecta* in 1955. It proposed a chain of giant cylindrical bodies, conceived as parking structures, encircling the city and capable of organizing both access to and departure from it. In terms of scale, the towers resemble the Colosseum in Rome, but the overall image is more reminiscent of the medieval enceinte of Carcassonne, thereby suggesting a somewhat ominous separation of the core, seen as a historic relic, from the rapidly decaying industrial sectors to the north and south[11] (figs. 7, 12).

What is most striking, from a contemporary viewpoint, is how much Kahn's projects, in their Capitoline monumentality, respond to the particular ethos of the city that has come to think of itself not only as a national shrine but also as the emblematic home of parliamentary democracy in an age of rampant anticommunism. Clearly, for Kahn, the issue of patriotism was inseparable from the idea of the public sphere, profoundly threatened, as he saw it, by the apocalypse of suburbanization and mass culture.[12] This became even clearer when later, in 1962, Kahn took Piranesi's map of the Campo Marzio, put a sheet of paper over it, and drew an updated version of his earlier plan, no longer featuring towers but with a heightened sense of the city's existing circulation pattern, and in particular with the system of freeways around the center redefined in terms of a viaduct. The elevation shows City Hall, which Kahn (like, incidentally, Paul Cret) had at one time proposed to eliminate, emphasized again in its emblematic outline and height-defining function (fig. 13).

When the king of Sweden was shown around Independence Hall after World War II, his guide, Roy F. Larsen, was shocked by the presence of a hotdog stand across the street. At that time, wholesale demolition in central Philadelphia had already begun, and so the hotdog stand was a significant anomaly. The planning ideal was a public sphere uncontaminated by commercial attitudes and interests. So the nearby neoclassical monuments were "liberated"—at the expense, symptomatically, of some valuable commercial structures from the nineteenth century, including landmarks like the Guaranty Trust and Safe Deposit Building by Frank Furness.

Robert Venturi's whole outlook, and certainly Denise Scott Brown's, went against this exclusivist approach; in fact, Venturi, in a recent comment, refers to the transformation of the area as "a vacuous Ville Radieuse" and a "postwar bomb site tarted up with landscaping." His relation to Kahn is another matter. Kahn was for Venturi something like "an architectural mother," as Scott Brown

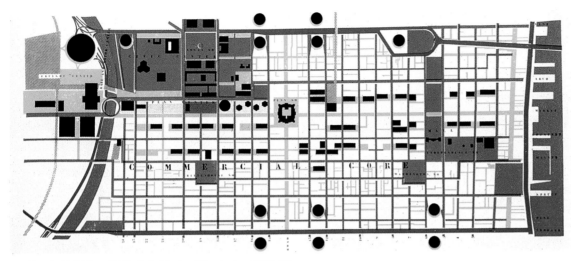

12. *Louis I. Kahn, Philadelphia traffic study, 1952–53.*

once wrote.[13] Venturi had known him since 1947. Later, in 1956–57, he worked at Kahn's office for nine months—the time when Kahn was working on his proposals for the Civic Center.[14] Kahn's increasing frustration with Philadelphia and its unwillingness to build any of his projects must be the background of a note sent to him by Venturi, which included a quotation about patriotism from a book by Albert J. Nock: "Burke touches this matter of patriotism with a searching phrase. 'For us to love our country,' [Burke] said, 'our country must be lovely' . . . Economism can build a society which is rich, prosperous, powerful, even one which has a reasonably wide diffusion of material well being. It cannot build one which is lovely."[15]

Complexity, the Civil Rights Movement, and the "Systems Approach"

In 1967, when Venturi and Scott Brown married, they moved into an apartment in I. M. Pei's elegant Society Hill Towers, so that historic Philadelphia literally lay at their feet.[16] Some of their firm's later works have since become a canonic part of this historic area: Franklin Court, Welcome Park (fig. 6), and the Columbus Monument, as well as the Benjamin Franklin Bridge with its imaginative lighting. If they had remained in this apartment, the Venturis might have been able to survey their contributions to the city's patrimony from their living room—or almost.

Venturi's first landmark building, Guild House, a home for the elderly sponsored by a Quaker community, located in another part of the city, can perhaps be seen as an artfully awkward demonstration of that striving toward the lovely (fig. 14). It also illustrates the intricate mix of attachment to and rebellion against Kahn, who at that time (around 1960) had just abandoned the geometrical-structural grandeur experiments carried out under the influence of Ann Tyng and Buckminster Fuller in favor of heroic abstract form.

Guild House shares with Kahn a commitment to the Red City of the fathers. It also relates to Kahn's obsession with the square box with a circular hole in it (an obsession that began at about this time, probably thanks to Venturi). But more important, what Kahn vis-

13. *Louis I. Kahn, Philadelphia Center Study with viaducts, 1962.*

14. *Robert Venturi in association with Cope and Lippincott, Guild House, Philadelphia, 1960–63; view from Spring Garden Street.*

15. *Guild House; view from community room toward Spring Garden Street.*

cerally rejected in modernity is here embraced. With the "commercial" sign above the entrance and the antenna above the main facade, mass culture is addressed as the prime architectural theme. Charged with visual references to the city—*this* city—and to the brick housing project and some older houses that were already there, Guild House is also deeply about yesterday's working-class Philadelphia, long gone.[17] And to that extent Guild House can also be seen as an act of symbolic resistance against policies of urban beautification that would manicure Independence Hall while destroying the neighborhood around it.

Unlike Kahn, the Venturis' way of celebrating the heritage of Philadelphia involves pop. Thanks to the lesson of pop art, the nostalgia in the design of Guild House is not so much of the "pride of place" kind—focusing on the Classical and the pretty; instead, it embraces the "ugly." The commercial vernacular (glorified in the

brash sign over the entrance and in the aluminum replica of the television aerial) has always been shocking, particularly to architects. Kahn thoroughly hated the antenna.[18] With its commercial symbols, Guild House locates the heroism of modern life in the bold iconography of advertising, as so many painters of the American school had done, Demuth being just one of them.

Yet these extravagant aesthetic complexities also interpret a political project. These were, after all, the great years of the civil rights movement. After Lyndon B. Johnson's 1964 victory over Barry Goldwater, and inspired by John F. Kennedy's New Frontier, coping with urban poverty and slums moved to the top of the American political agenda. With Johnson's Great Society, dealing imaginatively with the socioeconomic complexities of urban life, even using space-age technology in combination with a managerial "systems approach," became the new public rhetoric. The architec-

16. *Venturi and Rauch, South Street "Ruscha" (from "The Philadelphia Crosstown Community" study), 1968.*

ture of Guild House as well as the Venturis' subsequent interest in advocacy planning as a means of dealing responsively with social issues of urban renewal must be seen against the background of these new political imperatives. Venturi's very concept of "complexity," although distilled from aesthetic and literary theories, appears to relate to the "systems approach" then increasingly in vogue in American bureaucracy: "Everywhere, except in architecture, complexity and contradiction have been acknowledged, from Gödel's proof of ultimate inconsistency in mathematics to T. S. Eliot's analysis of 'difficult' poetry and Joseph Albers' definition of the paradoxical quality of painting."[19]

From South Street to Market Street

These broader ideological issues have their part in what is also, of course, a matter of cultural choice. *Learning from Las Vegas*, both the book of 1972 and the studies that preceded it, need not be discussed here. Nor is it necessary to address the fact that Rome, not Philadelphia, was the outpost that made Las Vegas look relevant to begin with (the Rome of Michelangelo, Bernini, and Borromini, *and* of Brasini, Pavesi, and Campari). On the other hand, Philadelphia was the place where the "lesson" was first applied. Early in 1968—some years after Guild House was built[20]—Scott Brown was approached by a consultant for the Crosstown Community in Philadelphia, a commercial strip threatened by an expressway. "If you can like the Las Vegas strip, we trust you not to try to neaten up South Street at the expense of its occupants."[21] Partly as a result of the study undertaken by Scott Brown, the freeway, another attempt to separate the wealthy from the poor, did not materialize (figs. 16, 17).

The operation that prevented South Street from undergoing the fate of Boston's West End was more than a question of professional doctrine. While addressing the very issues of the Great

17. Venturi and Rauch, view of South Street (from "The Philadelphia Crosstown Community" study), 1968.

Society, it also had a second dimension in that the Venturis were themselves involved in the neighborhood's destiny: "Bob Venturi, apart from being an architect, was a fruit merchant. He had inherited his father's business on South Street, so we were all threatened by the expressway."[22]

Other urban design and planning studies followed the South Street study. Urban preservation had moved to the core of the firm's interest in the Johnson era. Communities from far outside Philadelphia contacted them, and so did city councils faced with seeing inner cities fall into decay: Galveston, Texas, or Jim Thorpe, Pennsylvania. At times, the architects themselves went out to pin down endangered areas, such as the Art Deco district in Miami Beach, which also became the subject of a study that resulted in active preservation.[23]

19. *Venturi and Rauch, Franklin Court, Philadelphia, 1972–76.*

18. *Franklin Court, Philadelphia* (cover of American Architecture *by David P. Handlin; the photograph has been printed in reverse).*

20. *Postcard of Boathouse Row by night, Philadelphia.*

As for Philadelphia, the most important among VSBA's preservation projects involved new building as well: Franklin Court (figs. 18, 19). The site is part of the historic park that extends from Independence Hall to the Delaware River.[24] So it appears that Venturi, Rauch & Scott Brown was coopted by the very urban beautification that had transformed Philadelphia into a "bomb site." Yet for them, urban rehabilitation at a low economic level and renovation in the service of tourism turned out to be by no means mutually exclusive goals. The problem was how to make these two issues compatible. It is no coincidence that this project was commissioned by the National Park Service at about the time the idea to celebrate the Bicentennial with a World's Fair was definitively abandoned. So Franklin Court, ultimately, brings the fair to the city: it plays with the evocative mystery of the ephemeral architectural "sign" and sets it off against a context of urban permanence. What distinguishes Franklin Court from the other "shrines" in the nearby historic precinct is that it combines preservation and reconstruction with the magic of a fairlike installation, recasting Baroque scenography in terms of surrealism.[25]

Toward the Electronic Eiffel Tower

The Philadelphia tradition of celebrating itself in fairs and exhibitions began long before World War II. The 1876 World's Fair marked the peak of Philadelphia's industrial power; it not only brought hundreds of thousands of visitors to the city, but it also had a major impact upon its architectural culture. The Academy of Fine Arts, by Furness, was inaugurated at the opening of the exhibition.[26] It was the success of the fair that ultimately motivated the Philadelphia establishment to undertake the planning process that resulted in Benjamin Franklin Parkway and thereby transformed the old Georgian city into a showcase of the City Beautiful movement.[27]

In 1964, when Venturi handed in his Fairmount Park Fountain competition entry (fig. 21), a bold attempt to reinterpret the City Beautiful in terms of the moving automobile, Philadelphia was already knee-deep in preparation for the World's Fair of 1976.[28] Various sites had been envisioned. Kahn (who as a young architect had planned the buildings for the 1926 Philadelphia Exposition as a variation of Beaux-Arts moderne) had played an important role in the process, and his series of proposals, dating mainly from 1971–72, was among his last projects.[29] Like Kahn, and many other architects, the Venturis had made proposals for the 1976 Philadelphia Bicentennial World's Fair, which were at first no more successful. Yet predictably, and unlike Kahn, Venturi, Rauch & Scott Brown always visualized the event as a fair; in their eyes, the great thing that deserved to be celebrated was "people-to-people communications."

Since theirs was, in short, a vision of modernity inspired more by the views of Marshall McLuhan than by Modern architecture, their official project involved colossal signs and electronic message

21. *Venturi and Rauch in collaboration with Denise Scott Brown, Fairmont Park fountain project, Philadelphia, 1964; photomontage showing the proposed fountain at the foot of City Hall, with Penn Center office buildings.*

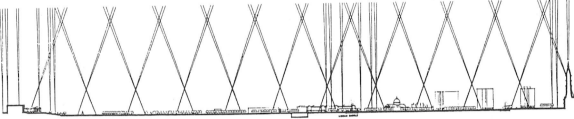

22. *Venturi, Rauch and Scott Brown, competition project for 1976 Benjamin Franklin Parkway Celebration, 1972.*

23. *VSBA, proposal for access avenue to the Magic Kingdom at Paris Disneyland, ca. 1989.*

boards for information and entertainment: "We use large and small spaces, large entrance ways, water areas, occasional piazzas, and especially important signs [that] function both emblematically as an identity image and traditionally as the symbolic value of an existing technology, our Crystal Palace or Eiffel Tower." Furthermore: "In McLuhan terms, the messages on the signs will provide interest and will take on importance as the message-media will, we believe, become a main forum for people-to-people communications."[30] While a deliberate tribute to Las Vegas, the project, perhaps unintentionally, harked back to earlier, constructivist fascinations with light spectacles. Its underlying theme, electronics and iconography as part of the urban environment, has been revived with vigor in the firm's more recent projects for public buildings, where monumentality meets with the ephemeral drama of the electronic sign (see pp. 166–71, 180–87, 196–203, 210–15, 312–15).

Rather than locating the American ethos in some realm of Jeffersonian political metaphysics, or in an idealist belief in the public realm as the locus of communal regeneration, these architects in their projects for the 1976 World's Fair bluntly addressed it in terms of America's claim to industrial leadership: the United States as the home no longer of steam engines and advanced electrical power equipment (as in the World's Fair of 1876) but of electronic communication.[31] Yet the project was not pursued further. Nor was the proposed Benjamin Franklin Parkway Celebration, also of 1972, which would have once again reframed the birth of the nation in terms of an ephemeral event, involving light shafts punctuating the sky and the flanks of the Philadelphia Museum of Art covered with electronic messages[32] (fig. 22).

Between Baroque Scenography . . .

The references to "old Philadelphia" may vacillate over time between variations on Baroque scenography on the one hand and explicit evocations of Holme's pragmatic seventeenth-century city plan on the other (fig. 5). The former strategy—playing with the Baroque—is epitomized by the Fairmount Park Fountain project. More recently, and in more explicitly scenographic ways, memories from Italy (the Ducal Palace in Venice, Palazzo Rucellai in Florence, an obelisk from Rome) are singled out to celebrate the glory of the Italian-American community in Philadelphia. The Christopher Columbus Monument, planned for a location on axis with Market Street but now unfortunately deprived of any grand access, honors Columbus while also responding to some exigencies of political correctness. Avoiding the pomp of a straight monument, being merely "almost" a piece of Beaux-Arts public art (is it an obelisk? or merely the mockup of an obelisk?), it somewhat laboriously reflects on the difficult status of public art today (see fig. 82 and pp. 116–17).

Even Benjamin Franklin Parkway at one point became a Venturian "theme." Venturi and Scott Brown know, of course, the emphatically Parisian origin of the parkway, which had explicitly been brought to Philadelphia as a "gift of France."[33] VSBA can be said to have returned the gift, proposing, in the early planning stages for Paris Disneyland, a grand access avenue connecting the subway station to the Magic Kingdom (fig. 23). Theirs is a Disneyesque Champs Elysées—with the Arc de Triomphe replaced by a magic castle. The Disney corporation rejected the idea. The axial view was in the end interrupted by a flamboyant hotel complex that obliterates the proposed "baroque" vista of the castle. Perhaps what worried the client even more than the grandiose

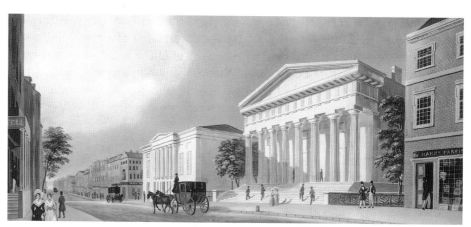

24. VSBA, Philadelphia Orchestra Hall, 1989; view of Broad Street Parade.

25. William Strickland (attrib.), view of Chestnut Street with the Second Bank of the United States on the right, Philadelphia, watercolor, early nineteenth century.

access avenue was the signage: instead of trees were two-dimensional mockups of Mickey, Minnie, Pluto, and the whole lot. Was the gesture perceived as not original enough or, rather, as too blatantly commercial? Be that as it may, as Venturi put it: "One can never hope to be more tasteful than the French in France, so one might as well be elegantly brash as only Americans in Paris can be."

. . . And Quaker Pragmatism

When, however, it comes to Philadelphia's "egalitarian" grid plan, irony is out of place—or almost. And this is certainly true in the context of a project that embodies much of the Philadelphia ethos to begin with, especially in its nobly restrained first version. For the project for the new Philadelphia Orchestra Hall, the Venturis had warned their clients that its aesthetic "would be that of a Pennsylvania Friends' meeting house rather than of a flamboyant baroque opera house" (fig. 24 and pp. 196–203).

Such restraint seemed inevitable in order to accommodate the stringent budget the client had imposed. Later, when it became clear that the official tendency was to upgrade Broad Street into a miniature Avenue de l'Opéra, VSBA countered with a revised project that subverted these Napoleonic temptations by celebrating the traditional American Main Street. The client hated the idea. Whether the current proposal for an altogether different opera house will finally be built remains to be seen.

Nevertheless, Venturi is rhapsodic as he writes about the "egalitarian" American gridiron plan that he sees exemplified by Philadelphia's layout: "One glory of our city as an urban whole is its gridiron plan . . . The city designed by William Penn represents the prototypical American city where urban quality and architectural hierarchy derive not from the special location of, but from the inherent nature of, individual buildings—as they sit in the grid and on the streets."[34] He continues: "The American gridiron city accommodates both unity and diversity by juxtaposing diverse architecture on a unified plan . . . The Academy of Music is not at the end of an *Avenue de l'Opéra:* and theoretically our mayor's house could sit across the street from a deli. Our buildings derive their hierarchical standing not from their ordained position but from their inherent character: our urbanism is egalitarian as well as diverse." In other words: "Let us design architecture for the real context, cultural and urbanistic, of pragmatic Philadelphia." Pragmatic Philadelphia—as opposed to, say, highfalutin Los Angeles, Frank Gehry's domain. Gehry's Walt Disney Concert Hall, Venturi says, "as a sculptural gesture looks good from a distance; our building via the quality of its detail looks good up close—and at eye-level. We love Los Angeles as the city of the

26. Robert Venturi, sketch showing view of Benjamin Franklin Bridge toward proposed "fanfare" skyscraper, Philadelphia, 1996.

27. Fragments of Statue of Liberty exhibited at the 1876 World's Fair, Philadelphia.

automobile but let us remain the city of brothers, not angels." In Welcome Park, a vestibule of sorts for those entering Independence National Historic Park from the nearby parking garage, Venturi built a moving tribute to the "city of brothers": a historic theme park in the shape of a garden. Its paving depicts Penn's original plan; a miniature bronze replica of Slate Roof House, one of Penn's temporary houses in the city, is mounted on a pedestal, at eye level; and in the middle, on a cylindrical base, stands Penn again, in bronze (fig. 6).

Revamping the National Shrine

Last and, in a literal sense, most spectacular among VSBA's proposals for the "national shrine" is the recent study of Independence Hall and the area around it, in view of possibilities of future development. The diagrams submitted to the Pew Charitable Trust—the institution that commissioned the study—ridicule the grandiloquent scale of the postwar schemes enacted by Edmund N. Bacon and others in the 1950s. Since there could be no question of reconstructing what is definitively lost, the firm devised an audacious compromise that involves historicist reconstruction *and* high-tech, nostalgia *and* multimedia "whammo" (see pp. 96–101).

Visitors arriving by bus along Market Street would be received by a portico to the historic site, as wide as a railway station. An LED program would occupy its partial vault, like a gorgeous electronic Tiepolo. In such a way, the fair and all it stands for, in terms of both mass spectacle and national symbolism, would once more

28. *Frank Furness, Provident Life and Trust Co. Building, Philadelphia, 1876–79.*

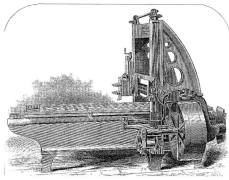

29. *Planing machine exhibited at the 1876 World's Fair, Philadelphia.*

return to the city, at a scale comparable (or almost) to that of the Manhattan Whitehall Ferry Terminal and its media facade glowing across the bay (see pp. 180–87).

Edmund Bacon's revenge against commercialism, highlighted by the sacking of Frank Furness's Guarantee Trust and Safe Deposit Building, would be compensated for by a bundle of commercial skyscrapers toward the northern end of the mall, crowned, in Venturi's sketch, by a flag. In such a way, Bartholdy's Statue of Liberty holding a torch is returned to Philadelphia, where, in a certain sense, it comes from (figs. 26, 27). And behind the portico that would replace the existing glass envelope for the Liberty Bell (designed by Romaldo Giurgola), visitors would find themselves once again in a "historic" setting—an urban square with two reconstructed houses along Chestnut Street that return to Independence Hall some of its long-lost eighteenth-century context and scale.[35] In the late 1990s, it seems unlikely any of this will ever be realized.

Philadelphia School

In the heyday of what at one time was referred to as the Philadelphia school, around 1960, Philadelphia could be said to have acquired the aura of an architectural mecca. In the meantime, other cities have taken over—Berlin, Barcelona, Los Angeles, to name but a few. As a result, some effort is required to envision the bygone glow.

Seen from afar and in retrospect, Philadelphia's sudden rise as a center of architectural thought, in the 1950s and 1960s, appears linked to the architectural sparkle of what Bacon had called the "rebirth of Philadelphia," including especially the visionary work of Kahn. The Philadelphia school emerged from the intellectual climate at the University of Pennsylvania, when, during the deanship of G. Holmes Perkins, the School of Architecture had become "a place of serendipitous meetings, paradoxical insights, and evolutionary ferment." From there, it appears to have "mounted a challenge to the rational and functional limitations of the modern movement by reintroducing issues of history, the urban context, and meaning."[36]

Kahn has always been seen as the school's leading spirit.[37] At the same time, with the Philadelphian George Howe becoming dean of the School of Architecture at Yale, and with Louis Kahn and later Robert Venturi and Denise Scott Brown teaching there, and above all with Vincent Scully becoming a prime interpreter of Kahn's and the Venturis' work, Philadelphia and Penn acquired a considerable aura, perhaps without ever really becoming aware of it. With Kahn's death in 1974, that aura quickly faded, surviving only in myth.[38] Some of its glow was bestowed upon Venturi, such as when Vincent Scully spoke of "the hoodlum from Philadelphia" as the true heir of Le Corbusier, thereby subverting the canonic line of descent that leads from Corbusier via Colin Rowe to the New York Five.[39]

All of that ran parallel to a shift in theoretical interests. Mannerism had moved to the center of academic attention, and the issue, as it turns out, is not without its links to Philadelphia's architectural past. Before and around 1950, Colin Rowe, at Cornell, had spoken about a mannerist tradition within the Modern movement itself, linking Le Corbusier to Palladio and Zuccari.[40] Slightly afterward, Venturi, toward the end of his 1954–56 tenure at the American Academy in Rome, discovered the relevance for him of the tradition of Italian mannerist architecture. His discovery of mannerism, to be sure, was framed not so much by an affinity to Le Corbusier but rather, as it appears, by his recently acquired familiarity with the American shingle style as studied by Vincent Scully. "Among the many things revealed in this now coherent group of houses [subsumed under the heading of shingle style] were their mannerist qualities," Venturi later affirmed.[41]

This conjuncture has provided Venturi with a vision that synthesized characteristics of Italian architecture of the sixteenth century and American architecture of the nineteenth. The Vanna Venturi House in Chestnut Hill is emblematic in that respect: it recalled Michelangelo's Porta Pia and Alessandro Vittoria's nymphaeum at Villa Barbaro as well as the Low House by McKim, Mead and White.[42]

Furness and Philadelphia "Mannerism"

Owing to the media success that followed the completion of the Vanna Venturi House and Guild House (lavishly published in the Yale journal *Perspecta*), and to Scully's immediate understanding of the magic of these works, Venturi became one of the leaders of the architectural avant-garde almost overnight. What was new with respect to Kahn was, among other things, the links that existed between these works and nineteenth-century eclecticism. The link became explicit when, in *Complexity and Contradiction*, Venturi made Frank Furness a key reference in his program of architectural complexity. Three years later, Scully went even further, presenting Furness as "the finest architect" of his age in America: "In his own way, Furness was the first great architect in America after Jefferson and certainly the most original American up to his time."[43]

Frank Furness had no doubt been the leading "Victorian" architect in Philadelphia (figs. 28, 30). His success within the industrial and entrepreneurial elite of that city was enormous.[44] But then, with the Chicago World's Columbian Exhibition of 1893, mainstream America was again sworn in on the Beaux-Arts grandeur of neoclassicism, and Philadelphia, with its Benjamin Franklin Parkway, did not escape the trend. As a result, Furness's architectural eccentricities, or "mannerisms," could be perceived only as deviations from the canonic rule. Furness's followers found themselves ridiculed in a series of articles, "Architectural Aberrations," that appeared at that time in *Architectural Record*.[45] And Talbot Hamlin wrote: "What should be small is big, and vice versa. Structural logic—the foundation of gothic—is forgotten. Stumpy polished granite columns; arches, cusped, pointed, and segmental; offsets, brackets and meaningless gigantic moldings are piled together in astonishing ways." As a result, Furness remained in limbo in American architectural consciousness until the 1960s, when his reappraisal as an architect began.[46]

In a recent article, Venturi has underlined how much Furness means to him: "My feeling for Furness is not hate-love; it is absolute unrestrained adoration and respect for his work; it elevates me by its quality, spirit, diversity, wit, tragic dimension." Yet he goes on to admit that his love "is a little perverse": "I can't help feeling it a touch kinky." For Venturi, what makes Furness interesting in a contemporary context is not just a matter of pure form, but a matter of form expressing the agony of the times: "He is a Mannerist as the anguished artist . . . evolving beyond the America of Manifest Destiny and Abolitionist idealism and toward the postwar realities of dynamic economic growth and uninhibited political corruption."[47] It is hard not to suspect an intention, on Venturi's part, to hint at analogies between the economic boom of the last fin de siècle and ours.

Venturi's fascination with this architect probably tells as much about his own conception of mannerism as about Furness's. On the other hand, there is a profoundly pragmatic side to Furness's "manners," and the same is probably true with Venturi's. Very plausibly, the unorthodox combinations of columns, pedestals, arches, bow windows, and so on in Furness's buildings have been interpreted as characteristic of a "harsh and honest realism" that uses striking combinations of materials and proportions in order to express function.[48] Seen in such a way, Furness's architectural manners emerge not so much as a nostalgic bricolage of historic memories but as a surrealist anticipation of twentieth-century machine aesthetics. Committed to the pragmatic ethos of the Philadelphia technician or engineer that made the city great, Furness turns out to be a true contemporary of the 1876 World's Fair that had inspired so much of his friend's, Walt Whitman's, vision of modernity.

30. Frank Furness, *University of Pennsylvania Library, Philadelphia, 1888–90 (illustration from* Harper's Weekly, *February 14, 1891).*

31. VSBA, *view of Dartmouth College, Hanover, New Hampshire, 1989.*

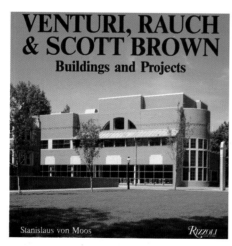

32. VSBA, *Gordon Wu Hall, Princeton University, New Jersey, 1980 (cover of* Venturi, Rauch & Scott Brown: Buildings and Projects).

33. *"The Founding of Dartmouth College by the Reverend Eleazer Wheelock, 1769," print, eighteenth century.*

Scenes of Learning

Venturi's career as an architect can be said to have begun with the design of a chapel to be inserted between two Victorian mansions—converted school buildings—of the Episcopal Academy in suburban Philadelphia (figs. 34, 35). With the choice of the topic and the site of his master's thesis, submitted at Princeton in 1950, Venturi took a direction that he never fundamentally revised.[1] The campus as an architectural challenge has been on his mind ever since, and, in the long run, it was in the American university—an "urbanistic world in itself," as Le Corbusier put it, with its "exquisite as much as extravagant gothic period environments"[2]—that the complexities of the Venturis' thoughts have found the most fertile response among clients.

Princeton and the University of Pennsylvania have been among the most committed of these institutional clients. Depending on the programs to be fulfilled and the sites to be occupied such buildings—Wu Hall and Fisher and Bendheim Halls at Princeton and the Bard College Library addition, among others—engage in dialogue with both the history of the building types to which they belong and the existing physical context. Like well-educated participants in a conversation, these buildings appear to socialize with their neighbors and to adapt to their manners. Some—like the Clinical Research Building at Penn—allude to the commercial fringes of the campus; others use a more erudite language. Some enact it in a restrained fashion, others in the somewhat talkative manner of one who has arrived a little late (see pp. 218–59).

The best example is Gordon Wu Hall at Princeton (fig. 32). Unlike its neighbors, Wu Hall demonstratively displays its difficult identity as an architectural hybrid, thereby incorporating *in miniature* the stylistic ambiguity characteristic of the campus at large. The two high, quasi-Elizabethan oriels on either side of the slab are a reminder of those at McCosh *and* of some English country houses by Lutyens. The sign above the entrance combines medieval and mannerist forms—as some of the best neo-Elizabethan and neo-Jacobean houses on campus do. But the "ideal," abstracted, planar, and floating character of this screen is a tribute both to Josef Albers and, in its general pop character, to Roy Lichtenstein (see figs. 76–79).

Yet the forms in the end recede as mere semantic and symbolic inflections within a system that is determined by three typological themes: the neo-medieval dining hall, the International Style exterior (including the window pane set flush to the facade and the pilotis), and the thermal window that unifies the composition and gives it a scale appropriate for this location (almost on axis with the Princeton train station at the other side of the tennis courts). So what the building conveys is not a particular historical style but stylishness itself. At the same time, the building's raison d'être may be perceived as a way to organize and orchestrate pedestrian flow at a critical point.

Together with the firm's numerous other campus buildings, and in particular with Fisher and Bendheim Halls and the Bard College

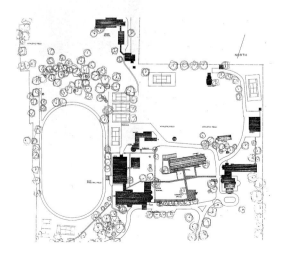
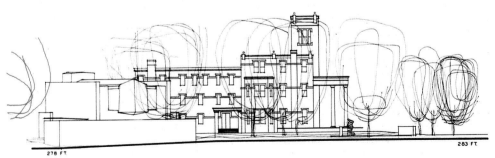

34, 35. Robert Venturi, chapel at the Episcopal Academy, Merion, Pennsylvania, 1950; site plan and elevation (MFA thesis project, Princeton University School of Architecture).

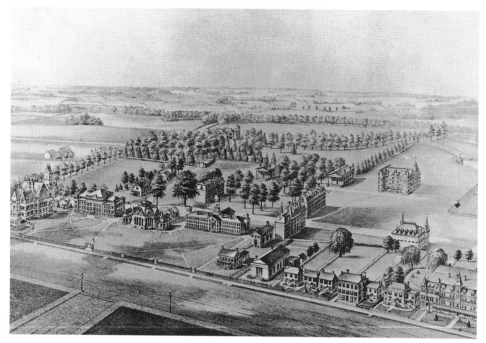

37. Cope & Stewardson, Blair Tower and adjacent college buildings, Princeton University, 1880s; railroad tracks are in the foreground.

36. College of New Jersey, Princeton, New Jersey, 1875; Nassau Hall is in the center (lithograph by C. O. Hudnut).

Library addition, it is architecture that follows the scenario of an erudite conversation: the more amiable it gets, the better the chance for a joke—such as when the architects decide literally to bend the facade of Bendheim Hall. Or when, as at Bard College, the pronaos of an Ionian temple is reflected in a brash porcelained aluminum facade that translates the Classical icon into a pop billboard (see pp. 220–29).

Symmetry and Picturesque "Erosion"

Unlike the University of Virginia at Charlottesville, the unified monument to Thomas Jefferson's passion for ancient Rome, the Princeton campus is a site of considerable complexity, being the result of a succession of conflicting strategies of campus design, each of them reflecting the ambitions of its time. In its eighteenth-century beginnings, Princeton (or the College of New Jersey, as the university was then called) restricted itself to building a large, multifunctional structure surrounded by a wide open space. In such a way, Nassau Hall, North America's largest building in 1753, sitting proudly in the field that expands southward from the small town,[3] represents the principle of open planning on the basis of large, independent structures surrounded by greenery as opposed to the traditional English model of the enclosed quadrangle (fig. 36).

The two Greek Revival pavilions of Whig and Cliosophic Halls,

added like two symmetrically arranged satellites in 1837, suggest Nassau Hall as the focus of an axial composition that extends southward, but soon after, with Prospect House, the president's residence, built in 1849, the erosion of this symmetrical campus layout began. Deliberately set off center, at the highest point of a picturesque garden, the Italianate mansion, typical of the mid-Victorian era, started to redefine the campus as an irregularly shaped landscape. Later additions either enhanced the axial setup or broke it, emphasizing the romantic garden concept, as with Alexander Hall, by William A. Potter.

This was the situation in 1896, when the College of New Jersey at Princeton proclaimed itself Princeton University, thereby initiating a period of rapid expansion. Princeton, favoring a conservative ethos, headed toward the English quadrangle system—a model that some years earlier had been adopted at Yale and, with more architectural precision, at Trinity College in Hartford, Connecticut (1872)—and decided to use the Gothic style for its new dormitories. The architects Cope & Stewardson gave Princeton's new dormitories a loose shape meandering down the slope on the western flank of the campus, forming a long dividing wall between the community of scholars and the public that was interrupted only by the massive tower of Blair Hall[4] (fig. 37 and pp. 106–9).

Structures of an Educational Landscape

Venturi has given a synthesis of what this evolution means in terms of design: "Campus planning at Princeton has historically combined, balanced, and integrated two approaches that can be distinctly defined. The first is characterized by the original Nassau Hall complex of buildings, which projects unifying axes and balancing symmetry among Classical forms as points in space; the second is characterized by the Holder-Hamilton Hall complex, where picturesque and continuous form directs and encloses space and is perceived as evolving over time . . . it is important to note and remember that the various combining of these two distinct ways in the history of the overall planning of the Princeton campus has been pragmatically rather than grandiosely directed." He then adds a quote from Ralph Adams Cram, the architect Princeton had hired in 1906 to develop a general plan for the campus. In a 1908 talk to alumni, Cram, a fervent promoter of the English quadrangle system, went as far as attributing a moralizing function to that kind of complex design: "One of the most essential elements in all education is that the students should feel themselves surrounded . . . by definite . . . law, from which there is, however, a way out into the broadest and highest freedom. This must absolutely be shown in the material form of the university."[5]

As a result, Cram's master plan proposed to enhance the intricate combination of symmetrical and open planning. That the Princeton buildings followed a distinctly ideological agenda had already become apparent when Woodrow Wilson, upon assuming the presidency of Princeton in 1902, proclaimed that "by the very simple device of building our new buildings in the Tudor Gothic Style we seem to have added to Princeton the age of Oxford and Cambridge; we have added a thousand years to the history of Princeton by merely putting those lines in our buildings which point every man's imagination to the historic traditions of learning in the English-speaking race."[6] Princeton's architecture is thus perceived by its patrons as illustrating those architectural ideals thought to be appropriate to the specifically Princetonian ideology of higher learning and collegiate club life. Via historic reference, the campus illustrates the pedagogical program.

Examined more closely, the idea of a university as an architectural theme park is as old as the concept of the "academical village." In a letter to the architects William Thornton and Benjamin Latrobe, Thomas Jefferson had written, in 1817, concerning the University of Virginia at Charlottesville (fig. 38), that he planned to give the pavilions of his university "a variety of appearance, no two alike, so to serve as specimens for the Architecture lecturer."[7]

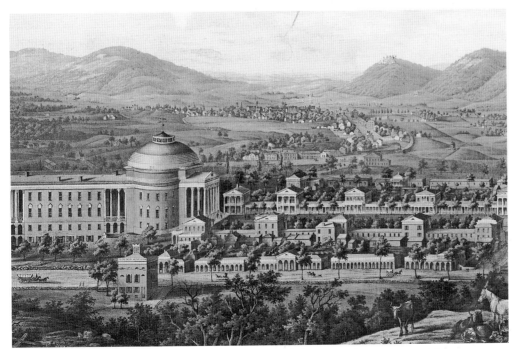

38. *Thomas Jefferson, University of Virginia, Charlottesville, 1817–26; view from the west with library at left and teachers' houses along the green (lithograph by F. Sachse & Co, 1856).*

39. *Ralph Adams Cram, Art and Architecture Building (McCormick Hall), Princeton University, 1923.*

In 1923, when Ralph Adams Cram planned and built McCormick Hall, the Art and Architecture Building at Princeton, this concept of architecture as built lesson in history appears to have been important (fig. 39). In fact, that building, situated in the near center of the campus and now somewhat damaged by two more recent additions, originally housed both the Department of Art and Archeology (until the late 1960s) and the School of Architecture. In terms of architecture, it epitomizes the aura of academic art history: "The building . . . , rising high in the middle of the low, spreading, Collegiate Gothic Princeton campus, was Italianate in style and stuccoed in red and yellow in contrast to the gray, green, and purple of the surrounding fieldstone dormitories. It was all the more remarkable for being designed by the unbending Gothicist (who was also the university architect), Ralph Adams Cram."[8]

The "Princeton System"

To view McCormick Hall as an acknowledgment, on Cram's behalf, of the increasing interest of American art history in the Italian Renaissance, typical of the age of Bernard Berenson, would prob-

ably overdraw the point.[9] Yet architecture at Princeton was more intricately connected to the practice of art history than anywhere else: the Princeton School of Architecture was the only one in the United States to be directed by a historian rather than an architect, and students there were from the very beginning required to take the entire basic offerings of the Department of Art and Archeology in architectural history, plus various courses in figurative art. This strong bias in favor of history, and of history's role in the genesis of a project, was "based on the belief that an architect should have a well-rounded education in liberal studies, [and] that he should understand and appreciate the other arts in their relation to architecture."[10] After World War II, when Venturi became a student there, the Princeton system had not changed, even if, in the studio, Modern architecture occupied center stage. Other schools had at that time proceeded much further in their strategy to sever history from design. Their success in the world of architecture resulted in marginalizing Princeton. As Venturi put it: "In the forties when we were here, the Princeton school of architecture was considered *passé*; in the common view it was an architectural back-

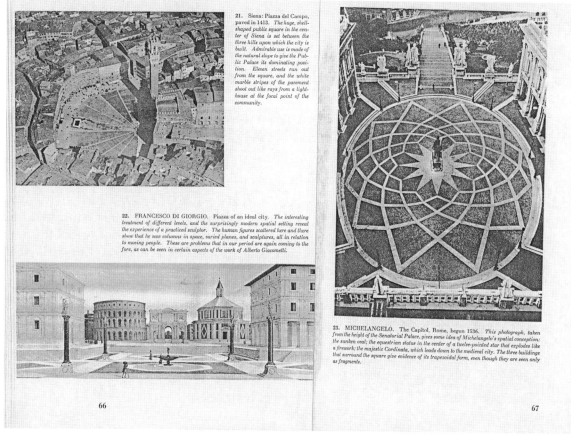

41. Max Abramovitz, Wallace K. Harrison, Philip Johnson, and Eero Saarinen, Lincoln Center for the Performing Arts, New York, 1957–66.

40. Double-page spread from Space, Time and Architecture *by Sigfried Giedion, 1941 (1954 edition).*

42. *Louis I. Kahn in collaboration with Douglas Orr, Art Museum and Gallery, Yale University, New Haven, Connecticut, 1951–53; farther along Church Street is the Arts and Architecture Building by Paul Rudolph, 1958–62.*

43. *Giambattista Piranesi, view of the Forum of Nerva, eighteenth century (from* Vedute di Roma, *ca. 1745).*

water—dominated by Jean Labatut who was a graduate from the Ecole des Beaux-Arts. Harvard was the place."[11]

At that time, the School of Architecture was still located in McCormick Hall. Jean Labatut, the most distinguished architect on Princeton's faculty, had studied under Laloux at the Ecole des Beaux-Arts in Paris. Modern architecture, to him, represented not an ideological program but a set of rules to work from pragmatically, that is, according to the specific demands of program and site and, if necessary, in combination with traditional architectural modes.[12] As for Donald Drew Egbert, the art historian, Venturi's most important teacher at Princeton, he was not only the first historian of the Ecole des Beaux-Arts but also one of the first American scholars to have analyzed the ideological roots of functionalism.[13]

The Issue of "Context"

"I took Donald Drew Egbert's course on the History of Modern Architecture four times," Venturi wrote. "I sat in on it as a freshman, was the slide projectionist as a sophomore, took it for credit as a junior, and taught in it as a graduate student teaching assistant."[14] When Venturi made his first trip to Rome in 1948, he must have been familiar with most of the buildings he saw there from slides or illustrations in books. Among the sites he appears to have considered particularly evocative was the Campidoglio. A year later, working on his master's thesis at Princeton, he returned to the subject, examining the Campidoglio's complicated fortune as a

site and as an urban composition.[15] At about the same time, Sigfried Giedion had revisited Rome, trying to add historical perspective to his concept of the "new tradition" of Modernism. The Capitoline area appeared like an anticipated response to the then pressing concern for the "humanization" of city life[16] (fig. 40). For Giedion, the Campidoglio was a token of the "social imagination" innate in the architectural genius Michelangelo. Somewhat later, Max Abramovitz, Pietro Belluschi, Gordon Bunschaft, Wallace K. Harrison, and Philip Johnson built their own Campidoglio in New York: the Lincoln Center for the Performing Arts[17] (fig. 41).

Venturi, in short, was at that time not alone in his fascination with this site, yet his reading of it did not concentrate on civic symbolism. The issue was "Context in Architectural Composition," as the title of his 1950 thesis indicates. Venturi had spotted the term in an article on Gestalt psychology studied at Eno Hall, then Princeton's psychology department.[18] What interested him concerning the Campidoglio and what was illustrated with the help of a collection of historic prints, photographs, and maps was primarily the change of meaning the site has undergone as a result of the accidents of its building history and as a result of its surroundings—from the late Middle Ages to the early twentieth century when the colossal monument to Vittorio Emmanuele II threatened almost to crush it. Seen in such a way, context appears to be more a magnetic field, by definition open to change, than a given situation that needs to be frozen into permanence.

44. Paul Rudolph, Yale University Arts and
Architecture Building, New Haven, 1958–62.

45. Eero Saarinen, Morse and Stiles Colleges,
Yale University, New Haven, 1962.

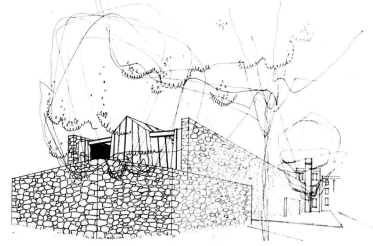

46. Robert Venturi, chapel at the Episcopal Academy, Merion,
Pennsylvania, 1950; perspective (MFA thesis project, Princeton
University School of Architecture).

More recent and more dogmatic applications of "contextualism" have considerably narrowed the concept, especially where it has become almost an equivalent of law for architects working in existing neighborhoods and for design review boards in charge of keeping them under control. As a result, Venturi finds that context has by now become an "often misunderstood and ultimately misapplied" concept—an opinion that no doubt irritates the ecological fundamentalists among his friends: "Let us achieve authentic quality by enhancing reality rather than embalming sentiment," he says.[19] In fact, while bureaucratic contextualism is primarily dictated by the will to prevent change, Venturi's intention is to understand and control its effects, and to deal with them responsibly. Seen in such a way, his theory of context in architectural composition turns out to be more a set of criteria to keep in mind than a set of rules to obey. But since it is rules that count with design review boards, it is easy to imagine the resulting conflicts—such as when, at Princeton, the Venturis advocate a design approach that is recessive vis-à-vis the given context,[20] while at Penn, they stand up polemicizing against what they call "devious members of preservation squads" eager to embalm historic environments that are often not worth it.[21]

Yale

Innovation versus preservation is a classic issue in university building, and the history of campus planning is the history of how to get away with the contradictions involved. By the 1950s, Yale had become the most prolific laboratory of American campus architecture. In some ways, it was also a laboratory for the Philadelphia school, whatever its pedigree. Unlike Princeton at the time of Cram, Yale had decided that architectural coherence of the campus as a whole was no longer crucial.[22] Yet at the same time, while the archi-

47. *Venturi and Rauch, Yale Mathematics Building Addition, New Haven, 1969; model view.*

CONTEXT AND HISTORY **We are seldom now in America the first building on the block. Context is significant.**

An architect who ignores context is a boor; an architect who considers only context is a bore.

We now go from sensitivity to context to a diverse aesthetic: context leads to anti-universalist architecture.

Acknowledgement of context does not mean the new building has to be like the old ones. Harmony can derive from contrast as well as analogy - look at the Piazza San Marco. It's a question of appropriateness.

Context promotes meaning. Change in context promotes change in meaning. The new design is conditioned by context, and conditions context and enhances it

We tend to forget how recent our acknowledgement of historical architecture is. Alas, the pendulum has swung too far, from intolerant progressive Modernism to sanctimonious historicist restoration where we are contemptuous of new buildings and evolving settings.

48. *VSBA, "Context and History" panel from Institute of Contemporary Arts exhibition, Philadelphia, 1992–93.*

tecture turned away from the familiar panoplies of architectural historicism, it did so in a way that itself seemed increasingly pregnant with history. Kahn's new Yale Art Gallery is symptomatic in that respect[23] (fig. 42). The story of the building is also the story of its critical reception: the presence of highly valued historicist buildings in the neighborhood—Swartwout's Fine Arts Gallery next door, built in 1927, the most distinguished among them—had forced Kahn into a dialogue with the existing structures along the street. He acknowledged this situation in terms of massing and rooflines.

Kahn had received the commission while he was architect in residence at the American Academy in Rome, and that appears to have had an inspiring impact upon his critics. As a result, the building was later invested with an aura that placed it on the threshold of postmodernism. The high, blind wall of the Yale Art Gallery facing Church Street with its *marcapiani* was by some seen as an echo of the wall of the Forum of Nerva as seen by Piranesi (fig. 43). In reality, the crux of the building was elsewhere, since Kahn's interests at that time focused on issues of geometry and the possibilities of space frames; imperial Rome preoccupied him only later.[24]

Paul Rudolph's Art and Architecture Building across the street from the Art Gallery, completed during Rudolph's 1958–65 tenure as the chairman of the School of Architecture, can serve as an additional example (fig. 44). Not by coincidence, the building appears to have been on Nikolaus Pevsner's mind when he uttered his famous warning against "the return of historicism."[25] Vincent Scully, while recognizing its Corbusian sculptural power, praised the building for being "splendidly designed for its corner site and in relation to the pre-existing university buildings along Chapel Street."[26] George Hersey, Scully's colleague in the art history department, saw Rudolph's "brutalist" language pregnant with "renewed signs of free replication": "Before it was completed, Walter McQuade warned that Rudolph's Art and Architecture Building might wind up as a locomotive crash between Wright and Le Corbusier." Hersey continues by explicitly linking this kind of stylistic eclecticism to that of Richard Upjohn, a first-generation Gothic Revivalist: "Such a combination of two entirely heterogeneous architectural languages is comparable to Upjohn's use of High Victorian Gothic and Second Empire. Indeed, Rudolph goes further than Upjohn, for his building has not only a Larkin aspect, and a

Richards Medical aspect, but a Kenzo Tange aspect, a Georges Vantongerloo aspect, and even a Sir John Soane aspect."[27]

So much for eclecticism. Other new Yale buildings referred to further distant pasts. Around 1964, shortly before Venturi began to teach at Yale, Philip Johnson completed his forceful Kline Biology Tower at some distance from the center, a building wrapped with vertical profiles that recall a neoclassical colonnade. And even earlier, in 1962, Eero Saarinen had built Stiles and Morse Colleges across the street from the collegiate Payne Whitney gymnasium, built in the 1920s (fig. 45). With its two towers and its passageways offering scenic vistas of the nearby "gothic" spires, Saarinen's contextual approach went clearly beyond Kahn's and Rudolph's. Saarinen practiced a technique of direct formal reference to the given context. The aim was a symbiosis of old and new and was, as Scully put it, "a beginning toward picking up that dialogue with the past which architecture is all about."[28]

Although Saarinen's interest in historicist paraphrase, and in particular his fascination with texture and color—the yellow Min-nesota Dolomite stone that recalls the tans of earlier buildings at Yale—appears to foreshadow aspects of the Venturis' own contextualism, Saarinen's solution was too much of a "fishing village" to make sense for them.[29] But even so, Saarinen's use of formal paraphrase, as well as Kahn's ambivalent attitude to both geometry and history, Rudolph's brutalist eclecticism, and, above all, the critical reception of these phenomena in the writings of Scully and Hersey, set the stage on which the Venturis' own theorizing and work could unfold and be perceived as meaningful.

The Rhetoric of "Learning"

In its breathtaking intellectual and cultural horizon (from literary theory to anthropology, from art history to architectural theory, from Italian mannerism to rococo, from Vanbrugh to Aalto, and so on), *Complexity and Contradiction* may be said to represent the intellectual ferment of Princeton. Yet Yale, as it turned out, offered an intellectual context particularly responsive to its message. Here, Vincent Scully became Venturi's closest ideological

49. VSBA, *Institute of Contemporary Arts exhibition, Philadelphia, 1992–93.*

50. VSBA, competition project for National Museum of Scotland, Edinburgh, 1991.

ally. He wrote the enthusiastic preface to the book, while Marion Scully helped edit the text. Venturi's first project in the genre of campus architecture was thus designed not for Princeton but for Yale: the addition to the Yale Mathematics Building of 1969 (fig. 47). It was Charles Moore, a Yale colleague, who wrote the most perceptive analysis.[30] And inevitably the campus was involved in the way the Venturis subsequently wrote about their work, such as when, for *Perspecta*, they set their own "ugly and ordinary" Guild House in Philadelphia against the "heroic and original" Crawford Manor in New Haven, by Paul Rudolph, then chairman of the School of Architecture, thereby underscoring the disjunction that, as they see it, separates their work from that of the preceding avant-garde.

The Venturis like to use the work of their colleagues in order to clarify issues of theory: by way of this comparative method the reader is led (or perhaps misled) to understand their buildings as exemplars of a position.[31] On another level, the strategy of comparison is part of a stubborn rhetoric of "Learning": with "Learning from Levittown" (still unpublished) and "Learning from Lutyens," with "Learning from Las Vegas"—a study that started, after all, as a Yale studio—and (predictably) "Learning from Philadelphia," not to mention "Learning the Right Lessons from the Beaux Arts" (and "Learning the Wrong Lessons from the Beaux Arts"), they inaugurated and practiced a new genre of architectural writing, and that genre appears to have stayed with them since.

As Vincent Scully said in 1973: "They have been made to talk so much . . . they have probably stiffened in their didactic role."[32] The often embittered undertone their diatribes have more recently acquired appears to prove him right. In fact, the more they retire from the academe that made them great, the more they tend to charge the presentations of their work with didactic admonitions, positional claims, and sarcastic "sweet and sour aphorisms," called "mals mots"[33]—often spread monumentally across the walls like newspaper headlines, provocatively turning the exhibition gallery into a classroom and the visitor into a college student who has come to learn (figs. 48, 49).

On the other hand, why should the effect of their theorizing (reflected in the snowballing of theory courses in architecture schools) not unnerve them—as does the triviality of some of the criticism leveled against their work? Do we need to see these installations as tokens of an imaginary Penn-Yale axis of architectural "scholasticism"[34] that keeps itself alive via a technique of agit-prop, shooting back at some Columbia or Princeton brahmins (who may not even notice)? Or should we be content to view the "mots" as having to do with the fun of puns? Or merely as ornamental "language games" suggesting old as well as new ways of invigorating architecture as art (fig. 50)?

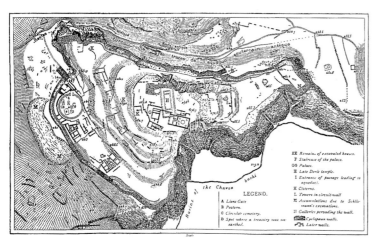

51. *Citadel of Mycenae (from* Art in Primitive Greece *by Perrot and Chipies).*

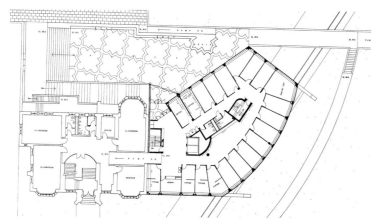

52. *Venturi and Rauch, Yale Mathematics Building Addition, New Haven, 1969; first-floor plan.*

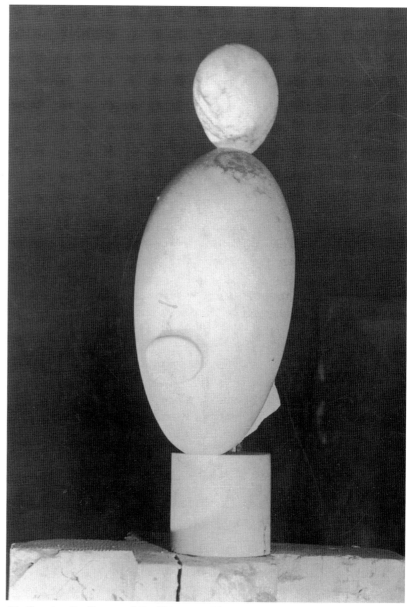

53. *Constantin Brancusi,* La Négresse Blanche, *1923 (photograph by Brancusi).*

Secret Physiology

Functionalism is generally seen as serving the logic of the plan: a diagram of functions, visualized in a sketch, determines the distribution of spaces. This is the way form is generated according to the functionalist agenda. Even Le Corbusier, the rationalist, speaks of the *plan dictateur*—although his suggestive bubble metaphor implies the third dimension: "A building is like a soap bubble. This bubble is perfect and harmonious if the breath has been evenly distributed from the inside. The exterior is the result of an interior."[1]

With the rediscovery of context in architectural design, the emphasis has shifted again toward the facade. As a result, plans are a subject that architects today seldom write about. But while, for the Venturis, such concerns have come to lie outside the area of their polemical interests,[2] this theoretical abstinence has not prevented them from putting as much skill and energy into the design of those footprints as they do into their preciously crafted facades and renderings. In fact the plans of many of their projects appear to have something in common, something that, while it cannot be described in terms of stylistic reference, is pertinent to *their* style.

More than other "contextualist" architects of today, Venturi, Scott Brown & Associates has made extensions to existing buildings the focus of their art. Because "we are seldom now in America the first building on the block,"[3] that pairing of buildings—old and new—is generally conceived as forming a dialogue that involves both assimilation and contrast, mimicry and inversion. The proposed 1969 addition to the Yale Mathematics Building is emblematic in that respect. Seen in plan, it appears like the disproportionately large head of an embryo in relation to the body as a whole, or like a meticulously lined case containing the building's "private parts" (fig. 52). In his discussion of this project, Colin Rowe attributes the artfully clumsy juxtaposition of old and new to Venturi's failure to deal successfully with the problem of bulk imposed by the brief; but I like to suggest that this "failure" should perhaps be seen instead as part of an aesthetic program.[4]

Forms that mushroom sideways from an existing body have since become a key theme in VSBA's projects for museum extensions. In the proposed Museum für Kunsthandwerk in Frankfurt of 1979 (later built according to a design by Richard Meier), the "fungus" has become so big that it drags the old museum building—the Villa Metzler—along like the cocoon of a previous state of museology, or like a snail shell that has become too small a house for the fast growing museum-animal (fig. 54). Above all, there is the Sainsbury Wing of the National Gallery in London, with its contours that passively follow the existing rooflines and street pattern and at the same time respond to the conflicting needs of the program (fig. 55). The new wing can perhaps best be described as an appendix to William Wilkins's neoclassical museum building, echoing some of its formal elements while turning them into a "soft" configuration, a body without bones—like Claes Oldenburg's *Soft Plugs* or other appliances of the early 1960s (fig. 56).

Whether full like a person with a weight problem who tries to remain decorous (as in the Museum für Kunsthandwerk) or wrinkled like an organ excessively strained by use (as in the Sainsbury Wing), these additions are applied to their cores in artfully whimsical ways. Or is it possible to speak of "paedomorphic inversions" of architectural form toward an unsuspected archetypal primitivism?[5] Should these egg- and embryo-shaped forms be read in a Freudian way as metaphors of the creative act from which any work of art originates? These are, after all, themes fundamental to the history of Modern art; Brancusi is merely a reminder (fig. 53).

Based on the vital issues of space and circulation, this secret physiology appears to represent the "body language" of the firm's architecture, as opposed to its more codified forms of symbolic communication via facade design and ornamentation. Referring to a Venturian formula, it is tempting to see it as yet another "forgot-

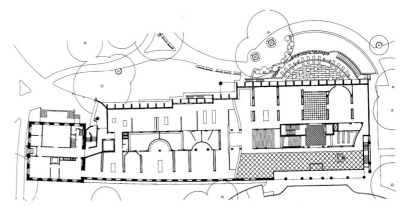

54. *Venturi, Rauch & Scott Brown, competition project for Museum für Kunsthandwerk, Frankfurt-am-Main, 1979.*

ten symbolism of architectural form": not so much based on explicit symbolic convention but suggestive of a personal attitude toward form that is itself part of an aesthetic tradition.[6] In fact, the formal principle that structures the physiology of these extensions appears to be an "organic" one in that viewers are encouraged to read the overall forms as results of a growth process often originating from an old kernel.[7] It is enough to say that the footprints of these public buildings are a topical part of the rhetoric of visual seduction practiced by these architects—and that, to the degree that this is so, they subvert the firm's own theorizing, focused as it is on iconography and a "definition of architecture as shelter with decoration on it."[8]

Weather Charts and "Fluid" Cities

One key to the quasi-organic undercurrent of the work lies in the way VSBA has come to look at urban space. Scott Brown and Venturi believe planning and urban design have more to do with understanding the city as it is than with dictating what it ought to be like.[9] Their politics of "understanding" the city in its broad social, economic, and cultural complexity, and their willingness to "learn" from it, relate to that conviction. "Understanding," as they see it, involves the capacity to grasp not just the physics of built form but the generally hidden or at least not immediately manifest social, economic, and technological dynamics at work within it (fig.

57). As urbanists, they believe in confronting the city as a set of complex, interrelated systems, and in taking an incremental approach to its planning.

Architecture, seen against this program, tends to become a means of both discovering and interpreting the nature of a given situation in "an urban context that is broader than the physical," as Denise Scott Brown puts it. The Sainsbury Wing of the National Gallery in London is particularly evocative of that procedure. Its site plan highlights the area's circulation pattern: the graphics underscore the character of the new wing and its own circulation pattern as an extension to the existing city fabric rather than as a mere addition to the museum (fig. 55). As for the facades of the new building, they can be read as a variously modified reflection of what was already there in terms of urban context[10] (see pp. 122–39).

In such a way, architecture takes part in the nursing and nurturing of the city *as it is*. As a design attitude, this strategy departs from the idealist imposition of progress and order upon a society often not suited for it, as practiced in general by high Modernism. It is of a programmatically recessive, responsive kind. Few images convey this approach to the city as succinctly as the group portrait showing Alison and Peter Smithson together with Nigel Henderson and Eduardo Paolozzi sitting in a street in Bethnal Green, London—urban medicine men, grieving, as it appears, over Modernism's failure to understand what the city *really* is

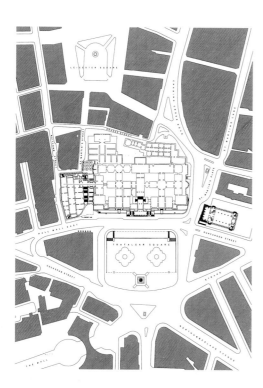

55. VSBA, Sainsbury Wing of the National Gallery, London, 1987; site plan with Trafalgar and Leicester Squares.

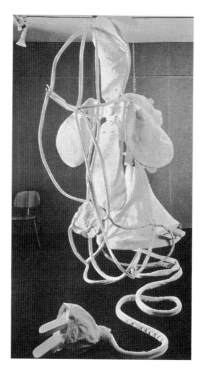

56. Claes Oldenburg, Giant Soft Fan, *1967.*

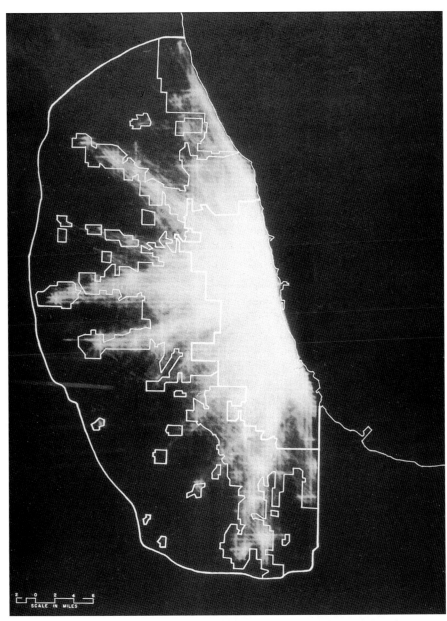

57. *"Desire Lines of Internal Person Trips" (from* Chicago Area Transportation Study, *vol. 1, 1959).*

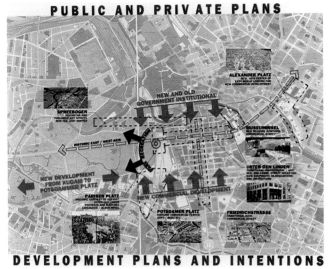

58. VSBA, *urban planning analysis of Berlin, 1995.*

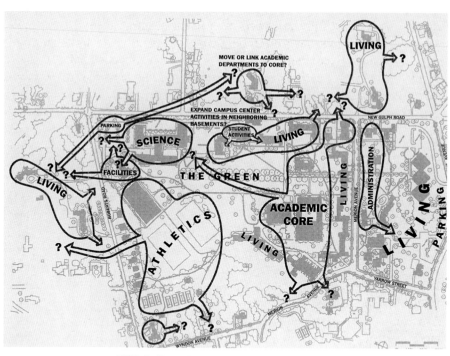

59. VSBA, *Bryn Mawr College future growth study, Pennsylvania, 1996–97; diagram showing anticipated future trends.*

60. *Peter Smithson, Eduardo Paolozzi, Alison Smithson, and Nigel Henderson in Bethnal Green, London (from* The Independent Group *by David Robbins).*

about (fig. 60). Among the phrases Scott Brown, who studied in London in the early 1950s, inherited from the Smithsons, "active socio-plastics" is perhaps the most evocative.[11]

Since 1960, when she joined the faculties of architecture and planning at the Graduate School of Fine Arts at the University of Pennsylvania, Scott Brown has developed a systematic approach to these matters. She inaugurated what she calls the "FFF studios." "Form, forces, and function" suggest what others later called an "ecological model of the urban environment": "The thesis was that the physical form of the city depends as much upon the forces within the environment, the society and its technology as it does on 'functions' as architects define them."[12] At the time Scott Brown taught at Penn, similar thoughts were in circulation at Harvard; for example, Fumihiko Maki wrote: "We must now see our urban society as a dynamic field of interrelated forces. It is a set of mutually independent variables in a rapidly expanding infinite series. Any order introduced within the pattern of forces contributes to a state of dynamic equilibrium—an equilibrium which will change in character as time passes." And, in general: "Our cities are fluid and mobile."[13]

In order to make responsible design choices, an architect needs first to feel the pulse of the given situation. This is why the planning studies later produced by the firm include so many maps and charts, often beautifully rendered in spectral shades, or keyed with sweeping arrows, nervously pulsating circles, or alarmingly swelling bubbles that indicate the pressures and trends that shaped the place over the years, also suggesting the most likely future congestions and expansions. In such a way, the sites at hand (be they campuses or cities at large) are diagnosed with the help of "weather charts," as it were. Rather than as architecture, they are defined in terms of trends, of lines of force—like the "desire lines" on the maps of the *Chicago Area Transportation Study* of 1959, which Denise Scott Brown says were particularly evocative for her[14] (fig. 57). Only after such a diagnosis does the next phase of this sociocultural nurturing begin: design. And with VSBA, these diagnostic perceptions are often directly reflected in the formal makeup of the resulting plans.

Visual Peristalsis and Empathy

While the footprints of many among Venturi, Scott Brown & Associates' recent buildings can to a certain degree be read as metaphors of processes and movements, the circulation within, or rather the ease of circulatory movements, becomes their prime architectural theme. A comparison of the Sainsbury Wing to the 1977–84 addition to the Staatsgalerie in Stuttgart by Stirling and Wilford almost speaks for itself (figs. 61, 62). The program and function of the two buildings are to a large degree analogous.[15] Visitors, upon entering the buildings at street level, must follow a complicated route before finally arriving at the galleries, traversing a maze of shops, cashiers, information stands, and cafeterias. It is in the implementation of the program that the difference between Stuttgart and London becomes all the more striking: Stirling and Wilford construct the path from the street to the museum entrance, and then on the inside, through the passageways skirting the edge of the rotunda, or across the labyrinthine ramps and small corridors that escort visitors to the galleries, by using complicated detours as an intricate obstacle course; Venturi and Scott Brown gather the crowd in the lobby in order to draw it almost magnetically to the "baroque" stairwell that connects the lobby to the gallery floor (see pp. 122–39).

The Sainsbury Wing is, among other things, a circulation and digestion apparatus attached sideways to the old building; its physiological coding is directly attributable to its function. The main stair, reminiscent of Castel Drogo, with its slightly conical configuration that makes it look shorter than it actually is when seen from below and longer when seen from above, is itself an intestine—and its disquieting visual peristalsis is accentuated in the processional that follows via the false perspective that cuts laterally through the gallery and is arrested in front of Cima da Conegliano's *Incredulity of St. Thomas*.

At the Sainsbury Wing, this "physiological" treatment of circulation relates directly to the needs of museums to handle crowds; volume of flow affects the shape of those passages as it does the form

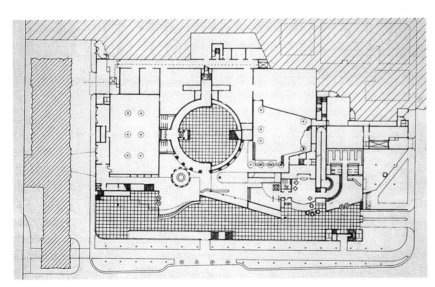

61. *James Stirling and Michael Wilford, Staatsgalerie, Stuttgart, 1984; ground-floor plan.*

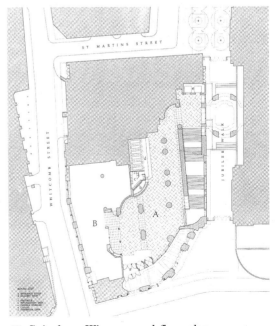

62. *Sainsbury Wing; ground-floor plan.*

63. VSBA, *Fisher and Bendheim Halls, Princeton University, 1986–90; entrance.*

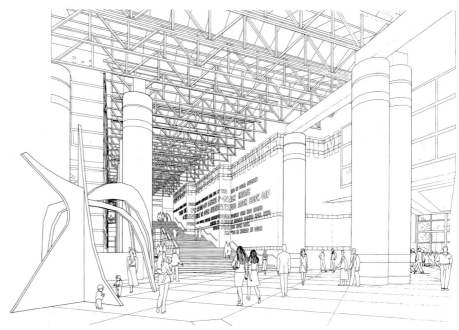

64. VSBA, *competition project for Stedelijk Museum addition, 1992; view of great hall.*

of streets. Other projects illustrate the procedure at a more intimate scale. In the addition to the Bard College Library, the flow of pedestrian traffic expected to trickle down from the hillcrest is first gathered in a vesicle-shaped forecourt, where it is turned sideways and then pumped, as it were, toward the interior. In such a way the building, which at first glance may almost be reduced to the colorful yellow and white curtain wall that emerges to the side of the old Ionic peripteros, turns out to be essentially a mouth, or the architectural representation of a gulp (see pp. 224–29).

In other instances, especially in the campus buildings, where the architects work with the generic typologies of office and laboratory space, these circulation dynamics are relegated to the margins: they affect the no-man's-land between inside and out, between "private" and "public" space, so that the edges become part of the intricate system of arcades, footpaths, and stairwells that connect the buildings to themselves and to the main arteries of pedestrian flow on campus. The archetype, within the firm's work, is the proposal for North Canton Town Center of 1965, and in particular the community center, with its open arcade oriented toward the church[16] (fig. 71). More recently, at Princeton, in Fisher and Bendheim Halls, as well as in the George LaVie Shultz Laboratory, the architecture looks as if it wants to suck the campus footpaths inside. And at Fisher and Bendheim Halls (as had already been the case at Gordon Wu Hall), a processional way is arranged tangentially, parallel to the main body, intricately tying

the architectural object into the system of circulation forces that constitutes the campus as a whole (fig. 63).

With all these examples, the margins between inside and out are defined as literally flowing, and their configuration can take the form of a sidewalk, a gallery, or an arcade arranged to serve as a link between buildings. The first-floor plan of the Gordon and Virginia MacDonald Medical Research Laboratories at the University of California, Los Angeles, for example, consists of a simple rectangle whose edges are rounded off, suggesting a prism swimming in the channels of pedestrian circulation like a fetus in a mother's womb (fig. 65). Here the intricately woven network of footpaths, which are partly sunken into the grass as if to emphasize their directional thrust, merges toward the street into a wide stair. Through its position at the edge of the building, the "arch" that forms the climax of the stairs indicates that the steps not only serve the building itself but also the neighboring institutions, which may be reached by the pathway that runs by the flank of the building (see pp. 220–23, 234–39).

Body Metaphors in History

Venturi, Scott Brown & Associates' plans often freeze movement through space and time into planar ornament, as in some works of Art Nouveau. Sullivan, even Van de Velde, comes to mind, and some ferns photographed by Karl Blossfeldt (fig. 66). Issues of function and movement become meaningful as art only through the combined powers of empathy and design. Geoffrey Scott in *The Architecture of Humanism* asserts that the basis of creative design in architecture is defined as "the tendency to project the image of our functions into concrete forms."[17] For art, Scott says, addresses us "through immediate impressions rather than through the process of reflection, and this universal metaphor of the body, a language profoundly felt and universally understood, is its largest opportunity." In order to communicate the vital values of the spirit, architecture, he insists, "must appear organic like the body."[18]

The city as a "living organism" has been an idée fixe in the theory and history of urban design ever since the Renaissance. R. D. Martienssen's study on space in Greek architecture, known to Scott Brown as a student in Johannesburg, is a case in point.[19] Martienssen at one point refers to the "Greek attitude to the city as a pure projection of human effort," and he goes on to explain how the city, unlike its Assyrian and Egyptian precedents, was thought of in Greece "as being a union of persons rather than a group of buildings," or even "more of a person and less of a place."[20] Other passages in Martienssen's book appear to be even more immediately evocative in view of Scott Brown's interests, such as when he describes how "in very early times, whether under the influence of Babylon or not, the idea of a generous processional way seems to have been established in Greece and her colonies."[21]

Martienssen was by no means the only source from which an architect could have drawn the concept of a city as an organism. Such ideas were much discussed in the 1950s—and also much criticized in planning circles. Kahn himself liked to visualize the city as a circulation apparatus (see fig. 12). When Philip Johnson writes that "architecture is surely *not* the design of space, not the massing or organizing of volumes," and that these are merely "auxiliary to the main point which is the organization of procession," he appears to draw on a view similar to that expressed by Martienssen. As he continues, it becomes clear that ancient Greece, once again, is the ultimate reference: "It is known to the veriest tourist how much more he enjoys the Parthenon because he has to walk up the Acropolis, how much less he enjoys Chartres cathedral because he is unceremoniously dumped in front of it."[22] At the time Johnson wrote these words for *Perspecta*, in 1965, Le Corbusier's Carpenter Center for the Visual Arts at Harvard was barely finished, and Johnson could not help seeing it as "a beautiful study in processional excitement" (fig. 68): "The shifting, rising, declining, turning path that [Le Corbusier] forces on us gives varied, solemn, laughable Coney Island experiences that please the stomach."[23]

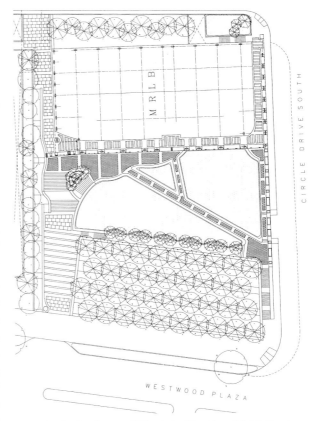

65. VSBA, Gordon and Virginia MacDonald Medical Research Laboratories, University of California, Los Angeles, 1986–91; site plan with system of paths.

66. Karl Blossfeldt, Ferns, *photograph, 1928.*

Not by coincidence, the Carpenter Center again recalls the campus as the key theme in the architecture of Venturi and Scott Brown—and so does Johnson himself, when he presents his Kline Biology Tower at Yale as his prime example of a processional organization of space. When Le Corbusier visited Harvard in 1959, he is said to have been fascinated with the movement of students along the diagonal paths crisscrossing Harvard Yard. With its spectacular ramp joining Prescott and Quincy Streets, the Carpenter Center can be said to celebrate—rather than accommodate—the idea of the campus as a system of circulation arteries. In doing so, it appears to have opened up a whole cycle of projects and buildings for American campuses organized around the idea of circulation.[24]

Passages and Galleries: From Nolli to Fourier

All of this does not mean that the city as seen by Venturi and Scott Brown can be understood as a mere system of processional ways. Nor can the buildings most charged with urban metaphors be explained in terms of mass circulation alone. The bloodstream merely serves the living tissue that makes up the substance of it all. Throughout, circulation needs to be seen as a tributary to the more static and permanent aspects of the house and the city. And permanence is organized in terms of a generic plan, based on a grid (in the city, Greek or American) or on a simple, rhythmic structural bay and an even pattern of windows (such as in a lab or classroom building with a plan that allows for hundreds of changes of use to come). Scott Brown writes, "Out of this generic loft evolve the rhythms of the building's facade—the regular beats, which are then syncopated or made dissonant for the exceptions that occur

for functional reasons (a main doorway) or iconographic ones (an inscription, a sign, or a representation)."[25]

Not by coincidence, the Sainsbury Wing consists of various different types of traffic patterns at once: the worm-shaped ground-floor lobby and the stair fit the form of a moving crowd, while the rectangular grid of the top-floor gallery spaces fits the needs of the individual visitor. Yet the key—and an element that appears to have received particular attention on the drawing board—is the main stair with its "Miesian" glass facade, which is arranged so that it offers views of the open walkway that runs alongside it and of Trafalgar Square beyond. Within the Venturian oeuvre, the main precedent for this stair is the lobby of the Humanities Building at Purchase, an interior street in the form of a *grande galerie* that runs parallel to the outdoor walkway and is separated from it by a glass pane (fig. 70). While in one way duplicating the public space outside, this interior street is transformed into a ritual passage that leads toward the stairwell at the end of the hall and thereby signifies direction and hierarchy.

In recent years, variations on the theme of the "symbolic street" have multiplied in VSBA's work, and there are various lines of typological affiliation. Unlike some British architects who, in the 1960s and 1970s, returned to the street as a "continuous built form" while avoiding any direct historicist reference,[26] VSBA enters into a dialogue with the entire panoply of historic precedents, including lakeside boardwalks, palatial stairwells from the Renaissance, Tintoretto's *Finding the Corpse of St. Mark*, Nolli's plan of Baroque Rome, Fourier's phalanstery, and even the covered arcades of nineteenth-century London or Paris (figs. 69, 73). Seen in retrospect, the open portico that runs alongside the proposed YMCA at North Can-

67. Aerial view of Princeton University with diagonal footpaths and Nassau Hall toward left.

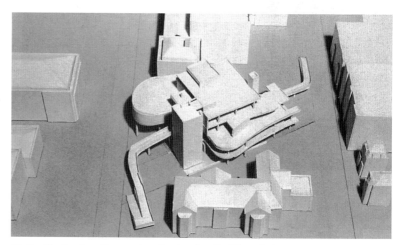

68. Le Corbusier, Carpenter Center for the Visual Arts, Harvard University, 1960; presentation model (from Le Corbusier at Work by E. F. Sekler and W. Curtis).

69. Passage Jouffroy, Paris, 1847.

70. Venturi & Rauch, Humanities Building at New York State University at Purchase, 1968; entrance hall.

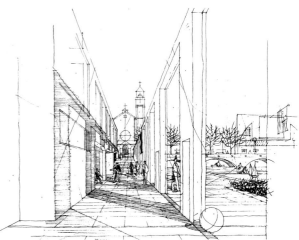

71. Venturi & Rauch, North Canton Civic Center project, 1965; view through "arcade" in front of YMCA looking toward church (drawing by Robert Venturi).

ton of 1965 is a particularly suggestive image. An urbanistic hybrid (half urban arcade, half lakefront promenade), the portico illustrates Venturi's fascination with long, directional spaces (fig. 71). The solution is echoed, much more recently, in the proposed "Disney Boardwalk" at Disney World in Orlando, Florida, with tree-shaped trellises replacing the screen made of walls and openings,[27] and at the Berry Library at Dartmouth and the Frist Campus Center at Princeton (see pp. 252–58).

The Sainsbury Wing and the Seattle Art Museum stairways, with their broadening and narrowing contours shaped to accommodate lateral and longitudinal access, are urbanistic in character. They recall streets on Nolli's plan of Rome. Directional spaces on an urban scale, equipped with stairs, also come to mind—in Rome, on the Campidoglio, or at Rouen or Tarragona, near the cathedral. At the same time, more specifically architectural precedents must be considered, too, such as palatial stairwells, preferably from the Renaissance or the era of neoclassicism, or walled, single-run interior stairs in fifteenth-century *palazzi*. Among the examples referred to by the Venturis is the stair behind the Porta della Carta, in the courtyard of the Doge's Palace in Venice—again a

hybrid, both public and private, both urbanistic and palatial.

As for the more linear variations on the theme, they are also referred to by the architects as "symbolic streets." As a form, such streets descend from the classic gallery type, that is, the covered walkways that in the palatial architecture of Italy and France served as links between parts of the residences and/or as covered or even closed loggias from which to enjoy views into the countryside. From the sixteenth century on, these spaces were often used for the display of art, such as at Fontainebleau, the Uffizi, or Sabbioneta.[28] Then came Versailles, with its Grande Galerie overlooking the park. And with Victor Considérant's project for a Fourierist phalanstery, the *grande galerie* has finally entered the architectural imagery of utopian socialism.[29]

How does this long tradition become part of an architectural language of today? Venturi appears always to have been aware of the tradition of the gallery, especially as it was occasionally revived in Modern architecture.[30] The Sainsbury Wing and the Seattle Museum of Art are direct variations on the theme. With the student center at the University of Delaware, the meaning of the symbolic street has shifted toward that of a commercial mall,

72. *Jacopo Tintoretto,* Finding the Corpse of St. Mark, *sixteenth century.*

73. *Venturi & Rauch, competition project for the Football Hall of Fame, 1967; interior view (collage and drawing by Gerod Clark and Robert Venturi).*

highlighting and collecting the multitude of functions, social and commercial, that make up this large building. The facade toward the campus, with its vertical glass panes, recalls industrial or commercial architecture (as had already been the case with the courtyard facade of Fourier's phalanstery in the well-known drawing by Victor Considérant). By turning Considérant's parti inside out, arranging the multistory gallery along the building's main facade (rather than toward a nonexistent courtyard), VSBA has built a miniature shopping mall (not far, incidentally, from a real one)[31] (see pp. 230–33).

Large-Small and Vice Versa:
Houses as Cities in Miniature

In a sense, the way these symbolic streets organize the flow of people through space, often—as at the University of Delaware Student Center—providing a sense of place as well as direction by slight bends or lateral expansions, is urbanistic rather than architectural; yet that kind of "urbanism" appears to be, at least in the Venturis' minds, the very essence of what makes the floor plan of a house work. So at first sight, the reference for these symbolic streets is the Baroque city of Rome as documented on Nolli's eighteenth-century plan and the Las Vegas Strip. Nolli's plan proposes the abolition of the traditional distinction of interior and exterior public space: the naves of the churches of Rome are as public as the streets that lead up to them.[32] At the same time, the irregular shapes of these directional spaces also recall solutions Venturi had found for the circulation—functionally undetermined or partially residual spaces (streets)—in his early houses. This is why the symbolic streets can perhaps best be explained in terms of the small individual residences designed by Venturi as exercises in miniature of how to juxtapose serving and served spaces (fig. 74). The stair of the Vanna Venturi House in Chestnut Hill is no less urbanistic in its spatial symbolism than the concave volume of the chimney that frames the living room in a way similar to the Palazzo Pubblico on the Piazza del Campo in Siena. Similarly, in the Trubek House, on Nantucket, the stairwell generates a brightly lit spatial interstice between inside and out, with a large window separating the children's bedroom on the upper floor from the narrow but high "communal" space of the stairwell. Seen in retrospect, it is the Sainsbury stairwell in a nutshell[33] (fig. 75).

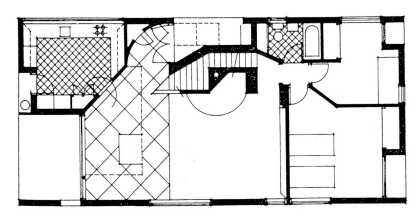

74. *Venturi & Short. Vanna Venturi House, Chestnut Hill, Pennsylvania, 1961; first-floor plan.*

75. *Venturi & Rauch, Trubek House, Nantucket Island, Massachusetts, 1970; view from stairs toward the living room.*

76. *Roy Lichtenstein,* Magnifying Glass, *1963.*

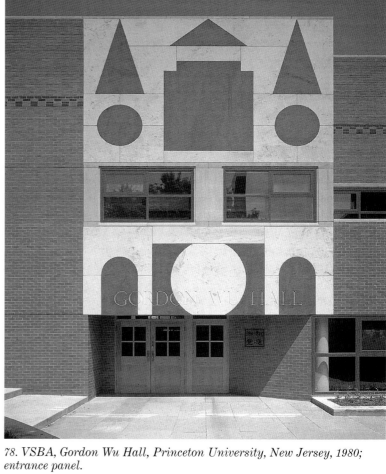

78. *VSBA, Gordon Wu Hall, Princeton University, New Jersey, 1980; entrance panel.*

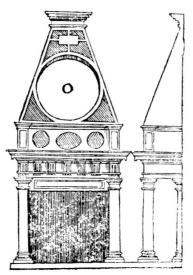

77. *Sebastiano Serlio,* Chimney mantelpiece, ca. 1537 (from *Settimo libro di architettura).*

79. *Wooton Lodge, England, ca. 1600; portal.*

Tableaux

Simulation, or trompe l'oeil, has always pursued two ends: to fool the eye and/or, in doing so, to capture the mind through the elaborateness of the artifice. While the naïf is fooled, the sophisticate admires. The tension that exists between these two responses is inherent in any architectural revivalism, from Hadrian's Villa in Tivoli to the themed shopping environments of today. And it is one aspect that makes American architecture a tricky subject. Its "bastardy," its obsession with "replicated replications," its ingeniously pragmatic attitude toward dematerializing, propping up, and recycling the prototypes of historic architecture in altered circumstances and utilitarian contexts, have often been discussed, mostly—from Le Corbusier to Umberto Eco—with a satirical bent. George L. Hersey, speaking of the University of Virginia at Charlottesville, and of the way the Pantheon in Rome with its massive walls is there reduced to a thin shell superimposed upon a honeycomb of offices and corridors, compared Jefferson's "sweetened restatement of the Pantheon" to "Fragonard adapting an antique Venus" (figs. 80, 81). He is content with acknowledging the facts. American country houses of the eighteenth century, with their facades decked out in the "shrunken trappings of a much larger European prototype" (such as Mount Vernon), appear to him characteristic of a constituent element of the American architectural past. If Hersey is correct, imitating larger prototypes at a smaller scale and/or for uses different from those of the original, thereby obliterating "the European distinctions between building types," is as typically American as the opposite procedure, which resulted in the tower of St. Marks in Venice reproduced as a skyscraper in New York.[1]

The work of Venturi, Scott Brown & Associates appears to be particularly involved in these American preoccupations. With it, levels of reality as well as types of historic reference seem constantly intertwined. Imagery appears to be projected upon buildings in various degrees of abstraction and in ways that at times are hardly noticeable, and then again celebrate aggressive theatrical make-believe. On some occasions the architects are content with spreading bold graphic ornament across a mere shed; at other times they indulge in three-dimensional carvings that compete with the realism of Disneyland. Such things make the Venturis hard to digest.[2]

On the other hand, there is also too much aesthetic nerve in their

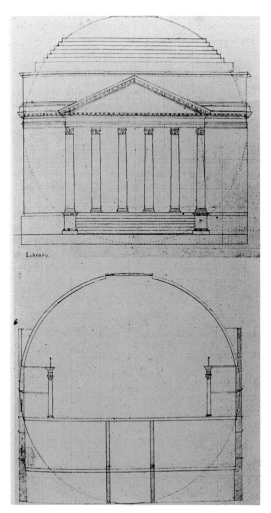

80. Thomas Jefferson, Rotunda, University of Virginia, Charlottesville, ca. 1820; facade and cross section.

81. Giambattista Piranesi, view of the Pantheon in Rome (from Vedute di Roma, ca. 1745).

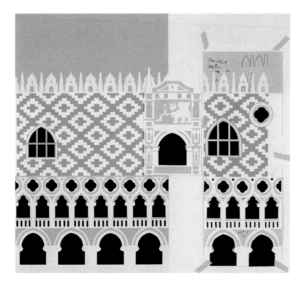

82. VSBA, Marconi Plaza Monument, 1985; collage.

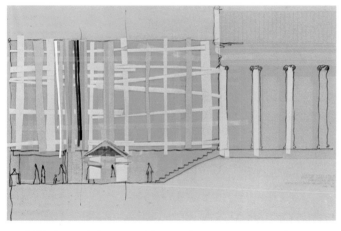

83. VSBA, Bard College addition, Annandale-on-Hudson, New York, 1990; facade study.

84. VSBA, competition project for U.S. Embassy, Berlin, 1995.

work to make it acceptable in contexts where head-on historicist illusion is all that counts. In their "historicist" work, Venturi and Scott Brown like to present the observer with the gap that exists between the model chosen and the replication or reproduction of it proposed in the new building. With a "twisted smile" (Robert A. M. Stern), they like to make art from deconstructed architectural make-believe, an art that draws attention not so much to the result of the replacement as to the mechanism of replacement as such.[3] Although figurative and not abstract, this art is therefore also *about* abstraction in that it displays the procedure by which an original becomes its duplicate. As Denise Scott Brown has written: "Contextual borrowings should never deceive; you should know what the real building consists of beneath the skin. For this reason our allusions are representations rather than copies of historic precedents. The deceit is only skin deep."[4]

Built Gaps; or, Architecture and "De-Familiarization"

Bertolt Brecht long ago postulated a similar strategy for what he called the "epic theater" of today. His aim was a rhetoric whereby the actor stands back from the role he or she performs so that the spectator is not overwhelmed or taken in by the plot.[5] Although Brecht has never been an explicit reference for the Venturis, their work could be said to have aestheticized this model. What they refer to as their irony in the use of historic or pop imagery could be said to be a counterpart to Brecht's strategy of "de-familiarization" (*Verfremdungseffekt*), by which he forces the spectator into a critical distance from the events on stage.

The ghost house in Franklin Court is a case in point (see fig. 19). Its purpose is not to act "as if" Franklin's House were still in place. Its theme is the gap that exists between the house that may have existed there at one time and its absence now.[6] In a similar vein, the theme of the entrance facade of Gordon Wu Hall at Princeton is the gap—the difference—that exists between the obelisks and decorative panels drawn by Serlio or built in some Elizabethan mansion and the use that is here made of such sources (figs. 77–79). The impact and the meaning of this entrance panel result from the joint techniques of flattening out and blowing up, or rather zooming in, that generated the work.[7]

Similarly, the theme of the two proposed facades for Marconi Plaza in Philadelphia is the gap between the three-dimensional volumes of the Doge's Palace in Venice and some Florentine palazzo on the one hand and their flattened reproductions here; furthermore, in the reproductions of the Doge's Palace it is the gap between the symmetrical composition of the "true" facade and the asymmetrical composition of the proposed scenographic replica (fig. 82). In such a way, the facade joins a whole panoply of parodizing variations on

85. VSBA, *proposed Stardust Hotel for Paris Disneyland, ca. 1989; facade study.*

an architectural classic—with Venturi's 1979 reinterpretation of Mount Vernon as the best-known example. In the Bard College Library addition, the theme is once again the gap that separates the "authentic" Ionic peripteros of the old library building from, first, the symbolic miniature propylon below and, second, the "abstract" aluminum facade next door—which in itself represents a whole progression of tectonic abstractions from solid masonry on the left to Miesian transparency on the right (fig. 83). Or should the gap be described as a link? In the library addition the colorful, two-dimensional curtain wall works as a paraphrase (not really a parody) of its three-dimensional neighbor.[8] In order to achieve harmony with its environment, it is contrast that is here underscored, not analogy. Furthermore, the equation between old and new is approximate and metaphorical, not literal.

In the Sainsbury Wing, however, or the proposed American Embassy in Berlin, the opposite strategy is used: what strikes first is the overall analogy between old and new; contrast hits the eye only at second glance. In London it is the syncopated rhythm of columns, the fully glazed side wall, and the big dark hole of the entrance that break the order imposed on the site by the buildings that were already there (see pp. 122–29). In the Berlin project the intention was again to evoke the historic character of the site—Pariser Platz as it existed before the war—while avoiding the banality of a mere historicist reconstruction. While the solution may at first appear conventional, the inflated scale of the windows and then the LED panel in the halfway hidden entrance forecourt, glowing toward Pariser Platz like a red silk lining underneath a Brooks Brothers suit (fig. 84 and pp. 210–15) considerably blur the first effect of unproblematic serenity.

Seen as pure form, such variously manipulated references endow the architecture with that aura of mannerist complexity that long ago became characteristic of the firm's work. Yet, measured against the standard of the imagery evoked, the status of the "symbol" begins to vacillate with the widening gap between the original and the replica.[9]

In the process of these instrumental recyclings, forms and signs are subjected to intriguing semantic transformations. On the facade of the proposed Stardust Hotel at Paris Disneyland, the huge decorated prop no longer stands for the sinister machinations of yesterday's gambling world but for a Las Vegas that has become

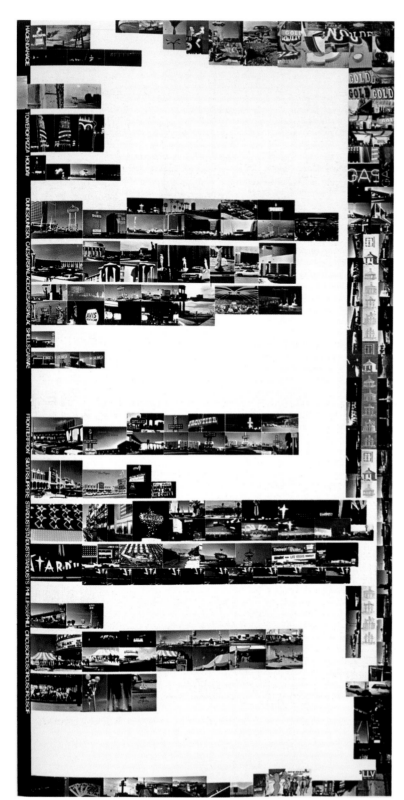

86. "Strip communication images," 1972; series of photographs from Las Vegas study.

87. Postcard of Zytglogge clock tower, Berne, Switzerland, sixteenth century.

88. VSBA, competition project for Whitehall Ferry Terminal, New York, 1992.

an entertainment park for the family at large (fig. 85). The proposed Whitehall Ferry Terminal in Manhattan implies a similar process of symbolic neutralization. Once again, the theme is the gap that exists between the real clock that might be built there (were it not obsolete at a time when everybody carries a wristwatch) and the colossal, electronically generated jumbotron image of a clock. The Venturis appear to believe that by virtue of the mere substitution of the real clock by its electronic surrogate the image's atavistic symbolism of authority and order—in short, of control by the state—will be neutralized (fig. 88).[10] They believe the postindustrial public will increasingly consume such "outdated" symbols as entertainment. The tourists who today gather around the colossal mechanical clocks at Venice, Strasbourg, and Berne, deciphering the astronomical symbols displayed around them and awaiting the procession of the heraldic animals and figures generated by the clockwork at certain times, support that kind of reasoning[11] (fig. 87).

Pictorial Architecture

In painting, photography, and film, architecture does not need to be "good" in order to look good. A boring shed, a miserable hut, a ruin, rusting signs along the highway, or even "bad" architecture can be powerful subjects (fig. 89). Venturi argues that architects should not forget this simple truth. In *Complexity and Contradiction in Architecture*, discussing Peter Blake's book *God's Own Junkyard*, Venturi argues: "The pictures in this book that are supposed to be bad are often good. The seemingly chaotic juxtaposition of honky-tonk elements express an intriguing kind of vitality and validity, and they produce an unexpected approach to unity as well." As if to limit the potential damage of such aestheticizing irony, he goes on: "It is true that an ironic interpretation such as this results partly from the change in scale of the subject matter in photographic form and the change in context within the frames of the photographs."[12]

The next step was *Learning from Las Vegas*, a study that frames the "seemingly chaotic juxtaposition of honky-tonk elements" in one of the world's flamboyant sites of greed and commercialized vice. Throughout, the "frames of the photograph" work as a means of redeeming aesthetically what everybody agrees to be "bad," commodifying in such a way "the experience of everyday life for a high cultural market."[13] In that respect, *Learning from Las Vegas* explicitly draws on the tradition of pop art. Ed Ruscha, in particular, serves as a direct reference.[14]

This emphasis on photography as a means to document and analyze urban form is not limited, in the work of the Venturis, to the genre of the architecture book. It is also an aspect of the design work. Photography is used both as a tool of investigation and as a

89. *American strip (from* God's Own Junkyard *by Peter Blake; reprinted in* Complexity and Contradiction in Architecture *by Robert Venturi).*

90. *Sebastiano Serlio, comic scene (from* Primo libro di Architettura, *1545).*

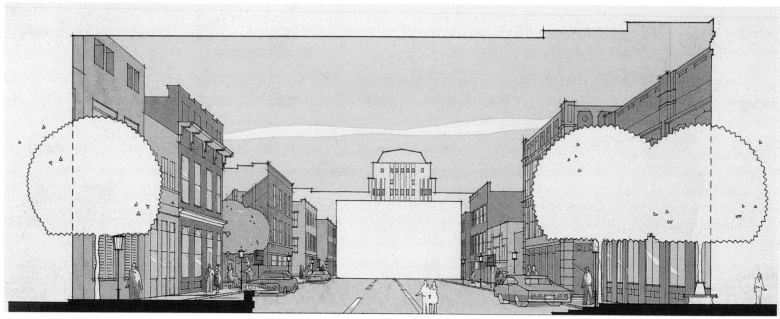

91. *Venturi, Rauch & Scott Brown, Galveston development project, Texas, 1974; view of the "Strand."*

support for design. Their projects are generally accompanied by renderings (more recently computer renderings) that show a culture of draftsmanship that recalls the Ecole des Beaux-Arts of Labrouste's time. In fact the eclecticism of the firm's graphic styles is a subject of its own: some of the renderings, like the drawings for the Westway Study of 1978–85, are reminiscent of Jacques Gréber's renderings of Benjamin Franklin Parkway. Others draw explicitly on graphic styles of early-twentieth-century artists like Maxfield Parrish.[15]

Once built, the Venturis' projects are again subjected to meticulous photographic documentation by a photographic crew headed by Steven Izenour, and at times by such artist-photographers as Stephen Shore. In such a way, architecture is continually chased by the camera, be it the given context that needs to be learned from or the final project artfully rendered in situ.

Osmotic Transfers

In the late 1990s, with the scenic landscapes of Disneyland as built illustrations of episodes from movies, such osmotic transfers between artistic genres are more readily seen as characteristic of the postmodern culture industry than as what they also are: an atavism of Western art. Since Masaccio and Brunelleschi, architecture and urban design have drawn from concepts developed and imagery proposed in the visual arts. The picturesque garden was modeled on paintings by Claude Lorrain, Gaspard Dughet,

and Salvator Rosa. As Alexander Pope put it, "All gardening is landscape-painting. Just like a landscape hung up."[16] With Modern architecture the situation is admittedly blurred: Le Corbusier rejected the pictorial concept of urban design he had inherited from Camillo Sitte, replacing it with a concept where "art" at first sight determines not so much the looks as the structural conception of the built artifact. On another level, however, he continued to use and develop it, first, by subjecting the building and the city to the logic of the *promenade architecturale;* second, by frequently abandoning or subverting Classical formality in favor of irregular (functional) arrangements; and third, by incorporating the landscape as a component of architectural form.[17]

This ambiguity is eloquently mirrored in the negative twist given to the term *picturesque* in *Complexity and Contradiction in Architecture.* "I make no special attempt to relate architecture to other things," Venturi says.[18] In general, he locates picturesqueness at the opposite end of what complexity and contradiction are about: "An architecture of complexity and contradiction . . . does not mean subjective expressionism," much less "an architecture of symmetrical picturesqueness which Minoru Yamasaki calls 'serene.'"[19] More recently, Venturi even suspects that deconstruction is infected by the virus of breaking orders not on the grounds of circumstance, as it should be, but "for . . . picturesque or arty reasons."[20]

Clearly, the picturesque is here seen as spurious license—as it might have been by any straight Modernist. Yet rejecting a concept is one way of learning from it. At second glance, the analogies that link the Venturis' position to the picturesque appear to be stronger than the differences.[21] Many of their aesthetic concerns, their attitude to issues like contrast, variety, shifting scales, even to the issue of control (that is, the idea that architects need to accept that there is a limit to their control), are closer to the picturesque tradition than might appear to them. The principles of mixture, of abrupt variation, of contrast; the consideration of "things rough and careless in aesthetic matters," even "shifts of scale," have become central in their art.[22]

A consideration of the roots of the picturesque aesthetic in rhetoric strengthens the point, for even though the picturesque relates to pictures, painting is not its ultimate reference. Elements of the picturesque garden that serve diversion, variety, or even fun also relate to the Classical theory of the stage, as it is depicted in Sebastiano Serlio's woodcuts of the tragic and, more important here, the comic scenes[23] (fig. 90).

The Townscape Movement and Its Legacy

With the hopes of social redemption once associated with Modern architecture thoroughly compromised, traditional concepts of place and space have seen a renaissance. In the 1950s, this trend started to thoroughly subvert the doctrine of the Modern movement. With it came a reassessment of cities and neighborhoods that had resisted modernization.

In England and America, such revivalist concern, as well as the

92. *Walt Disney checking a model of Main Street, Disneyland, Anaheim, California, ca. 1950.*

93. *Robert Venturi in association with Cope and Lippincott, Guild House, Philadelphia, 1960–63; view from Spring Garden Street.*

94. *Advertising brochure for apartment homes in Washington, D.C., ca. 1995.*

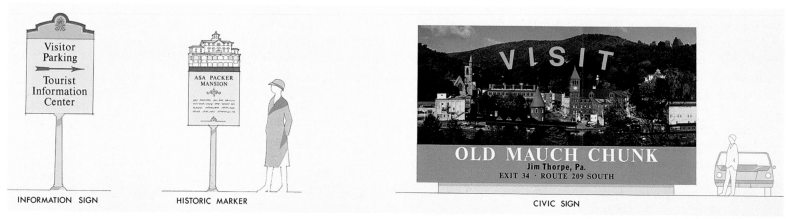

INFORMATION SIGN   HISTORIC MARKER   CIVIC SIGN

95. *Venturi, Rauch & Scott Brown, visitor information sign for Jim Thorpe, Pennsylvania, 1977.*

dogmatism that often comes along with it, is in part a legacy of the townscape movement, whose origins can be located in the pages of *Architectural Review* in the late 1940s and early 1950s. Here is a description of its ingredients: "A perhaps wholly English taste for topography; a surely Bauhaus-inspired taste for the pregnant object of mass production—the hitherto unnoticed Victorian manhole, etc.; a feeling for paint, the texture of decay, eighteenth century folly and nineteenth century graphics; representative titles of all this include: 'The Seeing Eye or How to Like Everything'; 'Eyes and Ears in East Anglia—a schoolboy's holiday tour by Archibald Abus aged 14 ½, etc." Colin Rowe and Fred Koetter, who wrote these lines, argue that "much of present-day activity is incomprehensible unless we are prepared to recognize the ramifications of townscape's influence."[24]

Be that as it may, with the urban upheavals of the 1960s, with the civil rights movement, the Great Society of the Johnson era, and with advocacy planning, the discourse of urban design turned toward pictorial and scenographic demonstrations, abandoning the rhetoric of abstract form. At the time of Herbert Gans's *The Urban Villagers* and Jane Jacobs's *The Death and Life of Great American Cities*, this reconsideration of traditional modes of life gained significant political momentum as a project, in general terms, of the left. Yet at the same time, the aesthetic charm and wit of early postmodernist work, as well as its antagonism to the monotony of worn-out corporate styles, and also its apparent complicity with pop, made the movement attractive to the elite, so that it ended up being swiftly coopted by the cultural and political mainstream: "With amazing rapidity, postmodernism became *the* new corporate style, after Philip Johnson's notorious Chippendale top for AT&T instantly convinced patrons of its marketability and prestige value."[25] In the meantime, the once emancipatory return

to pictorial and scenic visualizations of public space have been taken over by urban design review boards, architects, and developers alike (fig. 94).

City Tableaux: Outline of a Typology

At least three emblematic types of "city tableaux" currently appear to be universally shared as models: first, the wholesale preservation of historic neighborhoods (Plaka in Athens, the Marais in Paris, the old city of Berne); second, contextual zoning of districts whose historic ambiance is considered worthy of protection by design guidelines, however strict or loose; and third, the creation of scenic enclaves in places where ambiance is not to be preserved but to be created from scratch, such as theme parks, including Disneylands and Disney Worlds.[26] Like other architects of their generation, Venturi and Scott Brown have been involved in all three types of architectural revivalism, but unlike most, the concerns involved in these enterprises have been central to their work from the beginning.

Even their early professional training pointed in that direction. Denise Scott Brown has spotted the impact of the new brutalism and the work of Team X as part of her London education.[27] On the other hand, she claims that her and her husband's "Learning from . . ." studies of the 1960s did not develop from the townscape movement or from a latter-day modernist emphasis on "good manners," as derived from the once influential book by Trystan Edwards.[28] By so explicitly referring to this legacy she at least suggests that she was thoroughly familiar with it.

The work of VSBA unfolds between the relative extremes of advocacy planning (in the 1960s and 1970s) and planning for the needs of tourism and mass entertainment (in the 1980s and 1990s); numerous projects for academic and cultural institutions fall between these endpoints. The firm's work encompasses, in other words, the entire spectrum of strategies within which populist attitudes have been considered appropriate, including the more erudite historicism of the traditional American campus. As preservationists, VSBA has fought for the survival of existing neighborhoods, such as South Street in Philadelphia and the Art Deco district in Miami Beach, while more recently, state-of-the-art restorations for Ivy League institutions—the Furness Building at the University of Pennsylvania, Memorial Hall at Harvard—have become a special focus (see pp. 306–9, 312–15). On the other hand, some form of contextual zoning has been implicit in most of their housing schemes, beginning with Guild House. It is also a key idea behind the Sainsbury Wing and the San Diego Museum of Contemporary Art exteriors, museum complexes that explicitly respond to design guidelines derived from context, adopting existing rooflines as well as motifs and materials already in use in buildings next door or nearby (see pp. 172–77). In the category of scenic enclaves, VSBA has made proposals in the form of murals that depict urban monuments,[29] or in the form of public spaces furnished with miniature reproductions (models, in fact) of topical buildings in their respective locations (Copley Square, Boston; Western Plaza, Washington, D.C.; or Welcome Park, Philadelphia; figs. 6, 96).

As high culture variations on a vernacular theme, the environments relate not only to what Umberto Eco described as the American trend toward the "crèche-ification of the bourgeois universe," they are part of it.[30] That such scenic enclaves should attract and entertain children as well as adults has been a stated claim of the Venturis.[31] While in those miniature environments architecture is reduced to the scale of the toy, elsewhere, such as at Franklin Court—not to mention the Big Apple proposed for Times Square, New York—visitors themselves become miniaturized as they stroll about the inflated environments (fig. 97).[32] Through the variously applied techniques of shrinking and blowing up given forms, the spectator is turned first into Gulliver among the Lilliputians, and then into Gulliver amid the Brobdingnagians.

96. Venturi, Rauch & Scott Brown, Western Plaza, Washington D.C., 1977.

97. Venturi, Rauch and Scott Brown, Times Square Plaza design with Big Apple, New York, 1984.

100. *Japanese prints made by an unidentified artist, shown at the Paris World's Fair, 1887.*

98, 99. Roof lanterns of Tokyo taxis.

The City as Kimono

As a result of the Venturis' first trips to Japan in 1990, Tokyo and Kyoto joined Rome and Las Vegas as places to learn from. Rome had been the motor behind *Complexity and Contradiction in Architecture*, Las Vegas the subject of *Learning from Las Vegas*, but now, with time more scarce—the office was booming—the ideas were summarized in a short essay rather than in a full-fledged treatise.[1]

Even so, their position on Japan once again goes right to the heart of their ambivalent relation to Modernism: "We put off going to Japan for many years, despite the fact that we are Modern architects—or perhaps *because* of the ways Modern architects, from Bruno Taut through Wright, Gropius, and others, promoted the classic architecture of Kyoto." In such a way, Japan, and the impact it made on Western architecture, lays bare the generational conflict that appears to be one of their inescapable themes: "Each generation of Western architects has seen in Japan what it wanted to see. The interpretation our generation was exposed to was extra-selective; it corresponded to the minimalist, structuralist, modular purity of early Modern architecture and focused on the villas and shrines of Kyoto." That was enough to postpone, for a while, any plans for trips to the Far East. On the whole, the Modernist view of Japan "made this architecture seem irrelevant to us," they argue, and thus their curiosity stayed West, in Italy and England, instead of wandering East, to Japan.[2]

Kimono and Building

The most surprising part of the Venturis' comments on Japanese architecture is their view of the kimono, the landscaped garden, and the market as part of the building. When they criticize their Modernist forebears for having limited their curiosity to the "sublime simplicity" of the structural system, ignoring the movement of colorful garments and clothes "the architecture acted as background for," they imply a notion of architecture that includes the *repoussoir*. And when Venturi and Scott Brown think that the decorative foreground is as much a part of the configuration to be perceived and understood as the structural system that defines the space, they seem to have in mind more the genre pictures of Hiroshige than the structural rationality celebrated by European Modernism (fig. 100). Theirs is an explicitly inclusivist view of the Japanese temple: "Unlike our purist predecessors, we needed to

101. *New Palace and Lawn, Tokyo (from* Katsura: Tradition and Creation in Japanese Architecture *by T. Shinoda).*

103. Robert Venturi, "Japanese Architecture as Elemental Shelter," felt-pen sketch, 1991 (from Two Naifs in Japan).

102. World's Columbian Exposition, Chicago, 1893; Japanese Pavilion (Ho-o-den) is in foreground.

see the building with the kimonos," they argue. And the color and variety of the kimonos "upon the pure and apparently simple architectural convention of the temple . . . must be included and envisioned in the aesthetic equation."[3]

In such a way, the Japan of Modern architects—from Taut to Gropius, from Mies to Neutra—is rejected in favor of another ideal. The minimalist (or structuralist) view is substituted by a pictorialist one, one that includes the temples' decoration, and even the volatile foregrounds made from the garments of the visitors—which is not to forget the visual complexity of the "markets beyond their gates."[4] The Japan thus perceived, in short, resembles the japonisme of painters like Whistler, Manet, and Monet (fig. 106).

American versus European Japonisme

The intricate ways in which, from the late nineteenth century onward, "East Asian Art became intertwined with modernism, with avant-garde Western painting," and the ways in which "each prepared the way for the other"[5] have often been analyzed. The origins of French impressionism coincide with the impact made by

the arts and crafts from the Far East at the first International Exhibitions. It is by no means only a French phenomenon. In fact, when Edouard Manet turned to Oriental prints for inspiration and reference, James McNeill Whistler, the American painter in Paris, had already preceded him with paintings that celebrate Japan by way of its silk fabrics and pottery. At VSBA's recently completed hotel and spa complex in Nikko, Kirifuri, Japan, it might even be argued that it was Whistler's theme of ornamental drapery in closed interior spaces that surfaced as a theme, rather than the somewhat later European japonisme of Van Gogh, Toulouse Lautrec, Bonnard, and many others, with their preference for a linear and two-dimensional language of forms[6] (see pp. 270–79).

As for the more specifically architectural aspects of the Venturis' japonisme, their lack of interest in those aspects of Japanese architecture that concerned the Modernists—structural purism and Zen or Shinto spirituality—seems once again to merge with a specifically American tradition. Japan had been on the minds of American architects since the World's Fairs in Philadelphia and Chicago (1876 and 1893, respectively), when the first reconstructions of Japanese houses and palaces sparked an interest in Japanese building art. The Chicago exposition contained a reconstruction of the Ho-o-den, a twelfth-century Buddhist temple in Kyoto, prominently located on an otherwise bare island in the middle of a lake next to George B. Post's huge Manufactures and Liberal Arts Building (fig. 102).[7] In the years following the Chicago exposition, many leading American architects—Bruce Price, Ralph Adams Cram, even McKim, Mead and White and later the Greene brothers—absorbed elements of traditional Japanese architecture and made them part of their language.[8] To most of these architects, Edward Morse's book of 1886, *Japanese Houses and Their Surroundings*, was probably as important as the Ho-o-den itself.

Even Frank Lloyd Wright, who insisted he had not been influenced by Japanese building (although he made no secret of his admiration for it) would probably have agreed with Morse, the first American scholar of Japanese architecture, that "it was primarily through its roof that the Japanese house derived its distinctive character."[9] Be that as it may, it is with these architects, and in particular with Greene and Greene and Frank Lloyd Wright, that the familiar image of the Japanese house entered the iconography of a specifically American tradition of architectural Modernism, that is, it became Americanized.

Gropius and Japan

The European Modern movement gave the Western view of Japanese building a radical twist, and it is interesting that the Venturis, in their writing, should so emphatically dissociate themselves from the European view of Japan while making no explicit reference to their American antecedents. In fact, the architecture of Mies, Gropius, Stam, Duiker, and, later, Neutra is so singularly centered on ideas of structural logic and modular seriality that one scholar went so far as to speculate about a "basic *japonisme*" of which these protagonists may not even have been conscious.[10]

As Walter Gropius put it in an essay of 1960 on the Katsura Palace in Tokyo (Gropius had visited Japan only in 1954): "I had

104. Marc-Antoine Laugier, primitive hut (from Essai sur l'architecture, 1755).

105. Ludwig Mies van der Rohe on the building site of the Farnsworth House, Plano, Illinois, ca. 1946–50.

found, if only in illustrations, that the old hand-made Japanese house had already all the essential features required today for a modern prefabricated house, namely, modular coordination—the standard mat, a unit of about 3' x 6'—and moveable panels. It deeply moved me, therefore, to come finally face to face with these houses."[11] Perhaps predictably, Gropius's enthusiasm for the "cult of utter simplicity and austerity," for the "noble poverty" of Japan's building prejudiced him against buildings where other qualities were brought to the fore, such as the famous Tokugawa mausoleum at Nikko.[12] The beautiful illustrations of the book in which Gropius's essay appeared show the problem in a nutshell: throughout, the abstract geometry of patterns and structural frames is emphasized. The geometrically intricate roofs are almost always cut away, reducing the architecture to an agglomeration of black-and-white rectangular, modular units juxtaposed on the intricately laid-out gardens around them, where mounds of grass are interspersed with lumps of granite[13] (fig. 101).

Japan and the Western Primitive Hut

In rejecting the European view of Japan as the paradise of modular rationality, Venturi and Scott Brown focused on the roof as the distinctive sign of the Japanese house (fig. 103). In so doing, they also echoed, perhaps unconsciously, the early American perception of the Japanese house as it was epitomized in Morse's remark that its "distinctive character" came primarily from the roof. Like others before them, the Venturis were stunned by the ubiquity of decorative and symbolic roofs in the sacred precincts of Japan (and of Korea, where Venturi traveled in the early 1990s): "Roofs are everywhere. A gate is a roofed shelter as well as an entrance; a garden wall has a little roof to act as coping; roofs are sometimes eloquently redundant, as in the vertical stacks of roofs of a pagoda or in the accommodations to clerestories."[14]

The essay in which these remarks were made, "Two Naifs in Japan," begins with a reference to Abbé Laugier and then rather precipitously introduces the Vanna Venturi House in Chestnut Hill as a modern counterpart to Laugier's elemental symbolism.[15] That Japan should in the Venturis' eyes turn out to be a memento of the Vitruvian primitive hut comes as somewhat of a surprise: the structuralist definition of the primitive hut as given by Laugier is perhaps more likely to suit the cause of the purist interpreters of Japan than their own. Mies's Farnsworth House is, after all, a more plausible heir to Laugier's hut than Venturi's mother's house[16] (figs. 104, 105). But then, the Farnsworth House cannot seriously be connected to Japan other than by formal association. Mies may have been aware of traditional Japanese building at an early time, but to speak of an influence would mean to miss the point of his art.[17]

Bruno Taut, Mies's contemporary, is another matter. Taut had traveled to Japan in 1933 and stayed there for a number of years, studying traditional Japanese culture and criticizing the Japanese propensity toward adopting Western lifestyles. He too, like Gropius after him, favored the puritan architecture of the imperial villas and the Shinto temples over the lavishly ornamented Buddhist temples, particularly those built under the Shoguns "as a deliberate architecture of power."[18] Taut may be said to have introduced an antithetical view of Japanese building that was to become typical of Modernist interpretations for decades. The lessons drawn from this antithesis (through Katsura "towards the good society, or *via* Nikko towards Kitsch, swamp, conflict, and towards Japan's decline") were the very crux of Taut's pedagogical activity in Japan. Yet the hope that his vision would materialize dwindled under the pressures of the country's rapid industrialization and militarization. Booming Tokyo appeared to him as a monstrosity: "There can be nothing more nauseating than the area around Ginza."[19]

The City as a Kimono

What made Taut sick enchanted the Venturis half a century later. Among the themes that dominate their view of Japan is the particularly Japanese nature of urban density: "Tokyo has its act together—though granted it is a chaotic act. But is not this a convincing chaos or an order that is not yet understood? Or an ambiguity without anguish?"[20]

What appears to strike them most are the dense juxtapositions of village dwellings and corporate high-rises, the side-by-side existence of macro- and microbusinesses, the combination of small urban shrines and international corporate headquarters, all topped or wrapped by exhilarating neon signs and LED screens: "then the taxis, always immaculate, whose roof lanterns, in a variety of forms, symbols, graphics, and colors, identify the over 200 companies they are associated with and reflect the diversity, spirit, and wit of the whole scene"[21] (figs. 98, 99). In short, what fascinates is Tokyo's outrageous amalgamations of cultures and technologies, ranging from the local to the global, from rural craft to high tech, including high design architecture from abroad: "contemporary buildings that we liked in Tokyo or Kyoto that we could not accept elsewhere."

All that visual turmoil—Tokyo's "chaos"—makes for "cockeyed configurations . . . in an urban infrastructure of straight streets and wide avenues lined with trees or regiments of commercial signs; or crooked lanes lined with utility poles draped with myriad wires."[22] In one of his colorful felt-tip pen sketches, Venturi compares the chaos of Tokyo to the hidden order of a kimono pattern (fig. 107).

106. *Claude Monet*, La Japonaise
(Camille Monet in Japonaise costume),
oil on canvas, 1876.

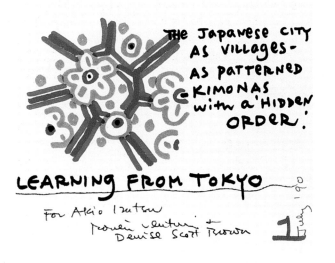

107. *Robert Venturi, "Learning from Tokyo,"*
felt-pen sketch, 1990 (from Two Naifs in Japan).

"Venturi Shops" and an East-West Spa

As the Modernists had done earlier, and in the best of colonial traditions, the Venturis adjust the impact of traditional Japanese
building to a Western, or rather American, agenda. In that respect,
they can be compared to Greene and Greene as well as to Wright,
except that the Venturis' reception of Japan was neither architec-
tural-motific nor monocultural, but pictorial and multicultural. So is
their interest in Japanese bric-a-brac, as documented in the "Venturi Shops" exhibition. With a myriad of little objects brought home
from their trips, they orchestrated yet another of their lessons
addressed to the design profession: "dolls, dishes, balls, boxes,
boxes-in-boxes, hairpins, statues, chopsticks, chopstick holders,
comic books, and idols, made of, among other things, plaster, porcelain, paper, bamboo and lacquered wood, all skillfully crafted and
colored";[23] a Japanese flea market, in short, made of collectibles
that belong in the cultural no-man's-land between the toy and the
cult object, the throwaway gadget and the votive gift. In the
museum display, written comments spread over the walls in bold

type, referring to the "skill," "charm," "wit" of anonymous Japanese
design, highlight the visual enchantment proper to these small
items. Unable, as outsiders, to discern exactly which objects belong
to the daily rituals of eating and celebrating around the family table
and which bear explicit religious symbolism, the architects add a
caveat, making clear that they did not intend to violate any religious
precepts (see pp. 320–21).

This American interpretation of the Japanese everyday would
be no more than an incident in the long history of East-West cultural osmosis were it not made material in one of the firm's
important architectural projects. The resort hotel in Nikko, Kirifuri, completed in 1997, can certainly not be described in terms
of the Venturis' *japonisme* alone. Nor can it be seen as an interpretation of the opulently ornamental and therefore ill-reputed
Buddhist sanctuaries of Nikko. It summarizes the Venturis'
position with respect to functionalism at large, and with respect
to the rituals of privacy and publicity as they structure life in a
big hotel and spa. And finally, it demonstrates their obsession

*108. Peter Thumb, St. Marien
Pilgrimage Church, Neu Birnau,
Germany, eighteenth century.*

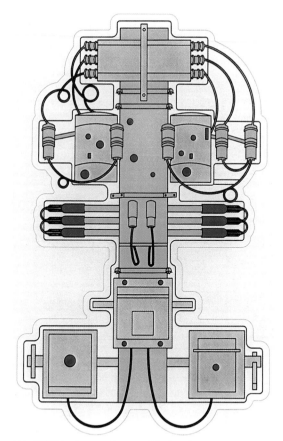

*109. VSBA, decorative motifs for the "symbolic
street" in the Hotel Mielparque Resort Complex,
Nikko, Kirifuri, Japan, ca. 1994.*

with multicultural symbolism through graphic representation (figs. 109, 110, and pp. 270–79).

The colored renderings of the spa building recall, first of all, Frank Lloyd Wright. What distinguishes Wright and the Venturis from the austerity of traditional Japanese building (as epitomized in the tea houses and imperial villas) is the Western notion of comfort. As Americans, their view of the house as an envelope suitable for moments of rest involves the notion of upholstery—physical and symbolic. Nikko is not a sports club; it is a health facility for people who want to relax. It is also a hotel in a landscape; the way the pavilions are set into the mountain site recalls Wright. And the "fake," decorative aluminum rafters of the symbolic roof, rather than referring to Japanese temples, seem to greet the carefully crafted wooden ones of Greene and Greene's Gamble House in Pasadena.[24]

The rest is an American, post–Las Vegas appliqué of Japanese motifs to an architecture that, besides its overall organic feel, is itself conventionally Modern, in fact, International Style—as are all new hotels in Japan. The Mondrian pattern on the entrance facades is an East-West pun, based on the Venturis' perception that Mondrian's art may be linked to European ideas about Japanese building—an idea difficult to sustain on the level of formal influence but not altogether unlikely in the context of Western theosophical thought and its interest in the religious traditions of the Far East. As for the orgiastic decoration of the symbolic street that serves and connects the different parts of the complex, it is a wild projection of the honky-tonk of a traditional Japanese shopping street (perhaps even with a reminiscence from Main Street, Manayunk) interspersed with flattened representations of paper flowers, electric wiring, and decorative banners based on patterns from historic kimonos found in the National Museum in Kyoto. Here, the architecture dissolves into a wild stage set, its symbolic volatility defeated only by the threat of its actual permanence. This is what happens when the nave of Neu Birnau encounters the city center of Osaka on a mountain in Japan.

110. VSBA, "symbolic street" in the Hotel Mielparque Resort Complex.

Notes

Penn's Shadow (pages 11–23)

1. Robert Venturi and John Rauch became partners in 1964. Denise Scott Brown was Venturi's colleague at the University of Pennsylvania from 1960 on, joined the firm in 1967, and became a partner in 1969.

2. As cited in Betsy Fahlman, *Pennsylvania Modern: Charles Demuth of Lancaster* (Philadelphia: Philadelphia Museum of Art, 1983), 67.

3. See Dickran Tashjian, *Skyscraper Primitives: Dada and the American Avant-Garde, 1910–1925* (Middletown, Conn.: Wesleyan University Press, 1975), as well as Patrick C. Stewart, "Charles Sheeler, William Carlos Williams, and Precisionism," *Arts Magazine* 58 (November 1983): 100–114.

4. On Philadelphia urbanism see Werner Hegemann, *Amerikanische Architektur und Stadtbaukunst* (Berlin: Wasmuth, 1925); John W. Reps, *The Making of Urban America: A History of City Planning in the United States* (Princeton, N.J.: Princeton University Press, 1965); and, more recently, David B. Brownlee, *Building the City Beautiful: The Benjamin Franklin Parkway and the Philadelphia Museum of Art* (Philadelphia: Philadelphia Museum of Art, 1989).

5. M. Christine Boyer, *The City of Collective Memory: Its Historical Imagery and Architectural Entertainments* (Cambridge, Mass.: MIT Press, 1994), 396.

6. Vincent Scully, *American Architecture and Urbanism* (New York: Praeger, 1996), 44. At the time of its origin, the State House was among the largest buildings in the American colonies. Since then, it has become a symbol of American independence. When Walter Gropius was asked to design the Pennsylvania pavilion at the New York World's Fair of 1939, he agreed to have the state represented by a full-scale replica of Independence Hall. See Winfried Nerdinger, *Walter Gropius* (Gebr. Mann Verlag, 1985), 200ff. However, the interior was organized according to modern, "functional" exhibition strategies.

7. See Edmund N. Bacon, *From Athens to Brasilia* (New York: Viking Press, 1967), 243–71; Constance M. Greif, *Independence: The Creation of a National Park* (Philadelphia: University of Pennsylvania Press, 1987); and Boyer, *City of Collective Memory*, 392–96.

8. Bacon, *From Athens to Brasilia*, 243–71; see also, Edmund N. Bacon, "Urban Design of Today: Philadelphia," *Progressive Architecture*, August 1956, 108–9. The socioeconomic raison d'être of this operation is not at stake here, nor the architecture of Penn Center, highly publicized at one time. Due to the action of the federal government, one million dollars had been allotted to Philadelphia in 1956 in order "to create a new urban environment." That not only triggered a certain amount of neighborhood planning (following, in part, Kahn's work in the Mill Creek area of around 1953–55), it also made it possible to rethink the plan of central Philadelphia as a financial and services center.

9. Scully, *American Architecture and Urbanism*, 224.

10. See Vincent Scully, *Louis I. Kahn* (New York: Braziller, 1962). On Kahn's work for Philadelphia see Peter S. Reed, "Philadelphia Urban Design," in *Louis I. Kahn: In the Realm of Architecture*, ed. David Brownlee and David DeLong (New York: Rizzoli, 1991), 304–11, as well as, more recently, the comprehensive study by Sarah Williams Ksiazek, "Critiques of Liberal Individualism: Louis Kahn's Civic Projects, 1947–57," *Assemblage* 31 (1997): 57–79.

11. Louis I. Kahn, "Order and Form," *Perspecta* 3 (1955): 47–59. See also Venturi's evocative comments on this project: "If Kahn's urban planning acknowledged existing fabric—as opposed to that of Frank Lloyd Wright . . . —Kahn's intrusions within the urban fabric could be nevertheless heroic and utopian, as in monumental public parking garages resembling the turrets of medieval fortresses." See Venturi, "Thoughts about Evolving Teachers and Students," *Iconography and Electronics upon a Generic Architecture: A View from the Drafting Room* (Cambridge, Mass.: MIT Press, 1996), 86, 89.

12. See Sarah Williams Ksiazek, "Architectural Culture in the Fifties: Louis Kahn and the National Assembly Complex in Dhaka," *Journal of the Society of Architectural Historians* 52, no. 4 (1993): 416–35.

13. Denise Scott Brown, "A Worm's Eye View of Recent Architectural History," *Architectural Record*, February 1984, 72. See Venturi's own tribute to

Kahn: "Louis Kahn Remembered: Notes from a Lecture at the Opening of the Kahn Exhibition in Japan, January 1993," *Iconography and Electronics*, 87–92.

14. At about the same time, in 1958, Denise Scott Brown arrived at the University of Pennsylvania, coming from the Architectural Association in London together with her husband, Robert Scott Brown. Before joining the AA, Scott Brown had studied at Witwatersrand University in Johannesburg. She had been advised by Peter Smithson that Penn was the place to study planning; at the same time, she also hoped to study with Kahn. See Denise Scott Brown, "Between Three Stools: A Personal View of Urban Design Pedagogy," *Urban Concepts: Architectural Design Profile* 83 (London: Academy Editions, 1990): 9–20.

15. Albert J. Nock, *Memoirs of a Superfluous Man* (New York, 1943); quotation from an undated letter by Venturi to Kahn as cited in Ksiazek, "Architectural Culture in the Fifties," 424.

16. This was after a few months of living at the Vanna Venturi House in Chestnut Hill. It was in 1972 that they moved to their beautiful Medary house in West Mount Airy, arguably the only Art Nouveau residence in Philadelphia, or even in the United States.

17. Not by coincidence, one of the corridors of Guild House is decorated with a ceramic mural that celebrates the city through its architectural landmarks, including, predictably, Independence Hall. While my earlier discussion of Guild House (in *Venturi, Rauch & Scott Brown: Buildings and Projects* [Fribourg: Office du Livre; New York: Rizzoli, 1987], 22–31) has emphasized the connections with Kahn, the significance of Guild House in terms of urban design still awaits an in-depth analysis. On VSBA's strategy of urban design and its sources, see *Venturi, Rauch & Scott Brown*, 77–85.

18. Later Kahn appears to have come around, admitting that "there is truth in Las Vegas"; see Venturi, "Thoughts about Evolving Teachers and Students," 86.

19. Robert Venturi, *Complexity and Contradiction in Architecture* (New York: Museum of Modern Art, 1966), 16. Denise Scott Brown recalls being more directly influenced by Great Society systems thinkers than Robert Venturi was. "Crane helped me to relate systems thinking to urban design" (communication to the author, June 1998). That there is a correspondence between Venturi's notion of "complexity" and the "systems approach" has been pointed out to me by Thomas P. Hughes, who also allowed me to consult the chapter on the "systems approach" in his forthcoming book *Rescuing Prometheus* (New York: Pantheon, 1998).

20. Guild House, it should be remembered, predates the Venturis' interest in Las Vegas.

21. Denise Scott Brown, "The Rise and Fall of Community Architecture," *Urban Concepts*, 34. See also von Moos, *Venturi, Rauch & Scott Brown*, 90.

22. Von Moos, *Venturi, Rauch & Scott Brown*, 35. In fact, the freeway represented a threat to the Venturi fruit store (designed first by Phineas Paist and redesigned by G. Edwin Brumbaugh). The redevelopment of the West End in Boston, as is well known, had become a key case of recent urban history thanks to the sociologist Herbert Gans, with whom Denise Scott Brown had studied at the University of Pennsylvania. See Herbert Gans, *The Urban Villagers: Group and Class in the Life of Italian-Americans* (Toronto: Free Press/MacMillan, 1962).

23. See von Moos, *Venturi, Rauch & Scott Brown*, 122–25 (Galveston and Jim Thorpe) and 110–15 (Miami Beach). See also Scott Brown, "Rise and Fall of Community Architecture," 31–39. Concerning Miami, Scott Brown has given the "full story" in "My Miami Beach," *Interview*, 1986, 156–58. See also, in this context, Barbara Baer Capitman, *Deco Delights: Preserving the Beauty and Joy of Miami Beach Architecture* (New York: Dutton, 1988), 42ff.

24. Of the row of houses that once formed the edge of the site owned by Benjamin Franklin on Market Street only the party walls and fragments of the street facades appear to have survived. John Milner was the architect of the reconstruction (communication by George L. Thomas). On the significance of Franklin's lost original house see also G. B. Tatum, *Penn's Great Town: 250 Years of Philadelphia Architecture* (Philadelphia: University of Pennsylvania Press, 1961), 34.

25. Von Moos, *Venturi, Rauch & Scott Brown*, 104–9.

26. A good pictorial record of the fair is given in Robert F. Looney, *Old Philadelphia in Early Photographs, 1839–1914* (New York: Dover Publications, 1976), 195–223. On the importance of the fair in relation to industrial culture at the time, and more specifically the architecture of Furness, see George E. Thomas, "Frank Furness: The Poetry of the Present," in *University of Pennsylvania Library: Frank Furness*, ed. Edward R. Bosley (London: Phaidon, 1996), 4–24.

27. Brownlee, *Building the City Beautiful*, 16 and passim.

28. On the Fairmount Park Fountain project see Venturi, *Complexity and Contradiction*, 122–23; Robert A. M. Stern, *New Directions in American Architecture* (New York: Braziller, 1969), 51ff.; and von Moos, *Venturi, Rauch & Scott Brown*, 86ff. For a more thorough discussion of the Fairmount Park Fountain project in terms of political symbolism and of its contribution to the recent history of public sculpture see my forthcoming book on built art.

29. Louis Kahn, "I Love Beginnings," *A+U: Louis I. Kahn* (commemorative issue), 1975, 278–86; on "The Forum of Availabilities," see Romaldo Giurgola and Jaimini Mehta, *Louis I. Kahn* (Zurich: Artemis, 1975), 241, and Brownlee and De Long, *Louis I. Kahn*, 112–25 and passim. Later, once the World's Fair idea and the selected site to the south of the city had been abandoned in favor of a more local event—owing to the lack of federal funds—Kahn proposed a large, T-shaped hall to be built at Independence Mall. None of these projects had come through by 1974. On the latter project see Marc Philippe Vincent, "Bicentennial Exposition," in Brownlee and DeLong, *Louis I. Kahn*, 414–17. Even the Mikveh Israel Synagogue, which, according to one of Bacon's concepts, was to conclude the perspective of Independence Mall, finally remained unbuilt (see Giurgola and Mehta, *Louis I. Kahn*, 44–47).

30. Von Moos, *Venturi, Rauch & Scott Brown*, 303.

31. The model of this approach was the Pavilion of the Czecho Slovak Republic at the Montreal World's Fair of 1967: "An architectural and structural nonentity, but tattooed with symbols and moving pictures . . . The show, not the building drew the crowd. The Czech pavilion was almost a decorated shed." Robert Venturi, Denise Scott Brown, and Steven Izenour, *Learning from Las Vegas*, (Cambridge, Mass.: MIT Press, 1972; rev. ed., 1977), 151.

32. Von Moos, *Venturi, Rauch & Scott Brown*, 98ff. The concept of monumentality implied by this project has a telling precedent in a comment by Jean Labatut, Venturi's teacher at Princeton. In his article "Monuments and Memorials," in *Forms and Functions of Twentieth Century Architecture*, ed. Talbot Hamlin (New York, 1952), vol. 3, 523–33, Labatut writes: "Great memorials and monuments intended merely to last for comparatively short periods of time—a few years, months, hours, or even minutes—have been and will continue to be built to celebrate certain great occasions." He goes on to describe the "architectural air space made by beams of light" at certain occasions glorifying peace after World War I in Paris. "They are a type of ephemeral architecture, but they are monuments nevertheless."

33. The French architect Jacques Gréber, responsible for the Benjamin Franklin Parkway as it was finally carried out, had described it as a "gift" of France expressing its gratitude for the American invasion at the end of World War I: "I am glad to say that, if by this work the city of Paris may be enabled to bring to its sister in America the inspiration of what makes Paris so attractive to visitors, it will be the first opportunity of Paris to pay a little of the great debt of thankfulness for what Philadelphia and its citizens have done for France during the last three years"; as cited in Brownlee, *Building the City Beautiful*, 34.

34. Robert Venturi and Denise Scott Brown, "The Hall and the Avenue: Thoughts Concerning the Architectural and Urban Design of the Philadelphia Orchestra Hall (etc.)" (1993; revised 1995, *Iconography and Electronics*, 173ff.). It is interesting, in this context, that Venturi explicitly associates Kahn with this American tradition of the gridiron plan in his "Protest Concerning the Extension of the Salk Center," reprinted in *Iconography and Electronics*, 81ff.

35. A comparable solution for this square was proposed by Jacques Gréber in his projected Memorial Court of Independence (1930). I am grateful to Maria Lindenfeldar for having pointed out to me the thesis by Madeline E. Cohen,

where these and related projects are discussed: "Postwar City Planning in Philadelphia: Edmund N. Bacon and the Design of Washington Square East" (Ph.D. diss., University of Pennsylvania, 1991). Upon publication of the Venturis' scheme, Philadelphia newspapers ran numerous articles both pro and con. Edmund N. Bacon, in his eighties at the time, was the most vocal critic of the Venturis' scheme: Edmund N. Bacon, "Keep the View, Revitalize the Mall," *Philadelphia Inquirer*, June 9, 1996.

36. The first quote is from Mimi Lobell, "Postscript: Kahn, Penn, and the Philadelphia School," *Oppositions* 4 (October 1974): 63ff.; the second from John Lobell, "Book Review," *American Institute of Architects Journal* 7 (1976): 176–77. The term "Philadelphia school" was introduced by Jan Rowen, "Wanting to Be: Philadelphia School," *Progressive Architecture*, April 1961, 130–63.

37. Romaldo Giurgola's work as an architect and writer may have a share in this fame. John Lobell goes as far as stating that Giurgola and Mehta, with their *Louis I. Kahn*, closed the circle opened by the school's challenge, "bringing the discussion of architecture to the fullest limits of human experience"; "Book Review." See also, in this context, Denise Scott Brown who, speaking of "the real Philadelphia school," emphasizes the particular role of the School of Planning for her own work; "Between Three Stools," 15.

38. Its protagonists vehemently denied there was a Philadelphia school, and recently, even G. Holmes Perkins questioned whether it existed; *Drawing Toward Building: Philadelphia Architectural Graphics, 1732–1984* (exh. cat., Philadelphia: Pennsylvania Academy of Fine Arts, 1986). I am grateful to Peter Reed for having alerted me to this reference.

39. Vincent Scully, *The Shingle Style Today or the Historian's Revenge* (New York: Braziller, 1974), 40.

40. Colin Rowe, "Mannerism and Modern Architecture," *Architectural Review*, 1950, 289–99, reprinted in Rowe, *The Mathematics of the Ideal Villa and Other Essays* (Cambridge, Mass.: MIT Press, 1976).

41. See "Homage to Vincent Scully and His *Shingle Style*, with Reminiscences and Some Outcome," *Iconography and Electronics*, 41ff. See also Vincent Scully, *The Shingle Style: Architectural Theory and Design from Richardson to the Origins of Wright* (New Haven: Yale University Press, 1955); later republished as *The Shingle Style and the Stick Style: Architectural Theory from Downing to the Origins of Wright* (New Haven: Yale University Press, 1971). Mannerism as perceived by Colin Rowe and as previously defined by Nikolaus Pevsner and, in particular, John R. Summerson was also a legacy Denise Scott Brown brought to the office from her years as a student in London.

42. It should be added that, in its broken Classicism, combined with an unabashed acceptance of the poverty of means available, the Vanna Venturi House also shares preoccupations of certain European work of its time—designs by Luigi Moretti, Vittorio Gregotti, Gae Aulenti, Vittorio Raineri, and others. See in particular G. Raineri, "Casa a Superga," *Casabella* 219 (1958): 17–19, as well as "Casa per 'week-end' in Brianza," where Gae Aulenti and Luisa Castiglioni propose an interesting synthesis of Kahn and the gabled roof: *Casabella* 241 (1960): 32–37. Of those works, Moretti's Casa Girasole in Rome, which had been reproduced in Venturi's *Complexity and Contradiction*, can be considered a direct influence.

43. Scully, *American Architecture and Urbanism*, 92ff.

44. Between the end of the 1860s and the end of the 1880s, Furness built no fewer than three hundred buildings; see George E. Thomas, Michael J. Lewis, and Jeffrey A. Cohen, *Frank Furness: The Complete Works* (New York: Princeton Architectural Press, 1991).

45. [Montgomery Schuyler?], "Architectural Aberrations no. 7: The Fagin Building," *Architectural Record*, April–June 1893, 470–72.

46. This reappraisal began with Venturi's *Complexity and Contradiction in Architecture*. The quote is from Talbot Hamlin, *The American Spirit in Architecture* (New Haven: Yale University Press, 1926), 160.

47. Robert Venturi, "Furness and Taste," in Thomas et al., *Frank Furness*, 5ff.

48. George E. Thomas, "Frank Furness' Red City: Patronage of Reform," in *Frank Furness*, 62, 69. See also Thomas's more recent article, "Frank Furness: The Poetry of the Present," 4–51.

Scenes of Learning (pages 25–33)

1. Robert Venturi went to school at the Episcopal Academy in Merion, Pennsylvania, between the ages of eight and seventeen. The two Victorian mansions had been designed by William L. Price (1861–1916), a pupil of Frank Furness and designer of the protomodern Traymore Hotel in Philadelphia and the Marlborough-Blenheim Hotel in Atlantic City, for which the Venturis later designed an addition. See George E. Thomas, "W. L. Price: Builder of Men and of Buildings" (Ph.D. diss., University of Pennsylvania, 1975); on the proposed addition see Stanislaus von Moos, *Venturi, Rauch & Scott Brown: Buildings and Projects* (Fribourg: Office du Livre; New York: Rizzoli, 1987), 223–25. Venturi's master's thesis is referred to in von Moos, *Venturi, Rauch & Scott Brown*, 80, 146ff., where several plates are shown. The thesis includes the theoretical study "Context in Architectural Composition" (1950), of which a revised version is published in Robert Venturi, *Iconography and Electronics upon a Generic Architecture: A View from the Drafting Room* (Cambridge, Mass.: MIT Press, 1996), 335–74.

2. Le Corbusier, *Quand les cathédrales étaient blanches* (1937; rev. ed., Paris: Gonthier, 1965), 154, 106 (translation by the author).

3. The term *campus* was coined here, or rather first used for university complexes, probably around 1770. The classic study of campus planning is Paul Venable Turner's *Campus: An American Planning Tradition* (New York: Architectural History Foundation; Cambridge, Mass.: MIT Press, 1984); but see also Robert A. M. Stern, *Pride of Place: Building the American Dream* (Boston: Houghton Mifflin Company; New York: American Heritage, 1986), 41–85. Nassau Hall measured 190 by 50 feet in the original plans; see Turner, *Campus*, 17, 47–50. A good survey of the architecture at Princeton is given by Constance Greif et al., *Princeton Architecture: A Pictorial History of Town and Campus* (Princeton: Princeton University Press, 1967).

4. This idea draws on Cope & Stewardson's work at Bryn Mawr (as George E. Thomas pointed out to me). Later, the additions by the Philadelphia architects Day and Klauder, more stylistically "correct" and at the same time more loose and suburban in configuration and scale, continued this picturesque interpretation of Tudor and Jacobean collegiate architecture at Princeton. See Turner, *Campus*, 215ff.

5. The Cram quote is from Donald Drew Egbert, *The Architecture and the Setting* (New York: Princeton University Press, 1947). On Cram and his role at Princeton, see Turner, *Campus*, 217, 230–35, and passim.

6. *Princeton Alumni Weekly*, December 13, 1902; as quoted in Turner, *Campus*, 227.

7. Turner, *Campus*, 83.

8. David van Zanten, "The 'Princeton System' and the Founding of the School of Architecture, 1915–20," in *The Architecture of Robert Venturi*, ed. Christopher Mead (Albuquerque: University of New Mexico Press, 1989), 34.

9. Cram had submitted three alternative projects in different styles for McCormick Hall, and what appears to have determined the choice was, perhaps more important than any ideological reason, the presence of the neo-Romanesque buildings in the immediate neighborhood. See van Zanten, "The 'Princeton System,'" 43 n.5.

10. From the university catalog of 1920–21, as quoted in van Zanten, "The 'Princeton System,'" 38.

11. Venturi, *Iconography and Electronics*, 93.

12. On Labatut see van Zanten, "The 'Princeton System,'" 40ff.

13. Venturi has repeatedly documented his indebtedness to Egbert. See, in particular, Robert Venturi, "Tribute," in Donald Drew Egbert, *The Beaux-Arts*

Tradition in French Architecture (Princeton: Princeton University Press, 1980), xiii, and Venturi, "Learning the Right Lessons from the Beaux-Arts," in Robert Venturi and Denise Scott Brown, *A View from the Campidoglio: Selected Essays, 1953–1984* (New York: Harper & Row, 1984), 70–95.

14. Venturi, "Tribute," xiii.

15. Robert Venturi, "The Campidoglio: A Case Study," *Architectural Review*, May 1953, 333ff.; reprinted in Venturi and Scott Brown, *View from the Campidoglio*, 12ff.

16. See the chapters "Perspective and Urban Design" and "Sixtus V and the Planning of Baroque Rome" added to the tenth edition of Giedion's influential *Space, Time and Architecture* (1941; 10th ed., Cambridge, Mass.: Harvard University Press, 1954). CIAM (Congrès Internationaux d'Architecture Moderne) had at that time invested considerable energy in the problem of the urban "cores"; see Jacqueline Tyrwhitt, José Luis Sert, and Ernesto N. Rogers, eds., *The Heart of the City: Towards the Humanization of Urban Life* (New York: Pellegrini and Cudahy, 1952). The "rebirth of Philadelphia," discussed in "Penn's Shadow," is very much part of the same story.

17. Lincoln Center, together with other works of the late 1950s, swiftly attracted Giedion's verdict against "playboy architecture." See the introduction to the 1964 edition of *Space, Time and Architecture*, xxxii.

18. What the actual source may have been is not known to me. In *Venturi, Rauch & Scott Brown*, I have tried to sketch some of the theoretical implications of Venturi's theory of context and contrast (15ff. and passim).

19. "The Preservation Game at Penn: An Emotional Response," in Venturi, *Iconography and Electronics*, 145. Regarding the "often misunderstood and ultimately misapplied" definition of context, the full quote goes as follows: "It's nice when a daring idea becomes an accepted idea but it hurts a little—especially as it is often misunderstood and ultimately misapplied" ("Introduction to My M.F.A. Thesis," in Venturi, *Iconography and Electronics*, 333ff.). On the issue of preservation, see also "From Las Vegas to Artfulness." As a term, *contextualism* is certainly more recent than the design approach it stands for. In a footnote to a recent article on context, Denise Scott Brown summarizes as follows: "The term 'context' came into general use in the 1970s. Robert Venturi used it in the title and text of his masters thesis, 'Context in Architectural Composition,' at Princeton in 1950"; "Talking About the Context," *Lotus*, 1992. On the whole, contextualism, as it came to be referred to in the 1970s, appears to be an amalgam of various sources, old and new. Thomas Schumacher sees the phenomenon primarily in relation to Colin Rowe and Fred Koetter's "Collage City"; "Contextualism: Urban Ideals plus Deformations," *Casabella* 359–60 (1971): 78–86. Stuart Cohen, who claims to have been the first to use it programmatically, develops it within his analysis of the Venturis' early work; "Physical Context/Cultural Context: Including it All," in *Oppositions* 2 (1974): 1–40. John Lobell, in turn, sees a concern for context as the common denominator of Kahn's and Venturi's work; "Kahn and Venturi: An Architecture of Being in Context," *Artforum*, February 1979, 46–52. Venturi lectured widely in the 1960s, most likely also involving the notion of context. On the other hand, in the only portion of his thesis published prior to 1986 ("The Campidoglio: A Case Study"), the actual term *context* does not occur.

20. "These buildings that are workplaces and dignified at the same time must not be architecturally trendy, but rather . . . generic, and therefore most likely to extend harmony within their campuses and to acknowledge context via analogy, not via contrast . . . It is ironic that most of the work of our office consists of institutional-civic buildings that often pertain to campuses and require contextual analogy over contextual contrast; we are thereby out of step in terms of the sensibility of our time which is hyped—listen to loud music, look at the padded shoulders, watch the commercial sound-bites"; Robert Venturi, "Some Words Concerning Designing for Architecture on American Campuses," *Iconography and Electronics*, 74.

21. Venturi, "Preservation Game at Penn," 145.

22. Turner, *Campus*, 262ff.

23. It had been the Philadelphia architect George Howe, chairman of the Yale School of Architecture since 1950, who had suggested Kahn as the architect of the new Art Gallery building. On George Howe and on the vicissitudes of the Yale School of Architecture between 1950 and 1965 in general, see Robert A. M. Stern, "Yale 1950–1965," *Oppositions* 4 (1974): 35–62. In his introductory note to the article, P.D.E. (Peter Eisenman) refers to the "strangely placid" aura characteristic of Yale, "disengaged equally from polemics and theoretical speculation"; it appears that by the mid-1960s that condition had significantly altered.

24. See Sarah Williams Ksiazek, "Critiques of Liberal Individualism: Louis Kahn's Civic Projects, 1947–57," *Assemblage* 31 (1997): 57–79. For a recent assessment of the Yale Art Gallery's "Roman" quality, see Kurt W. Forster, "The Historian between the Architects: Scully, Kahn, Rudolph and Venturi at Yale in the 1960s" (unpublished ms., 1996).

25. Nikolaus Pevsner, "The Return of Historicism," *Journal of the Royal Institute of British Architects* 68 (1961); reprinted in *Studies in Art, Architecture and Design, Victorian and After* (Princeton, N.J.: Princeton University Press, 1968), 242–59. See also his "Address Given at the Opening of the Yale School of Art and Architecture, 1963," *Studies in Art*, 260–65.

26. Vincent Scully, *American Architecture and Urbanism* (New York: Praeger, 1996), 202ff.

27. George L. Hersey, "Replication Replicated: Notes on American Bastardy," *Perspecta* 10 (1965): 228. Philip Johnson, in turn, can't help seeing "a mannerist (do we dare use the word Mannerism?) play of spaces" at work in the building; "Whence and Whither: The Processional Element in Architecture," *Perspecta* 9–10 (1965): 169.

28. The quote is from Vincent Scully's conversation with Robert A. M. Stern in Stern, *Pride of Place*, 79, where Stern gives a useful account of the architecture of Yale.

29. Communication to the author by Denise Scott Brown, August 1997. Saarinen's interest in texture and color has been pointed out to me by George E. Thomas.

30. Charles W. Moore and N. Pyle, *The Yale Mathematics Building* (New Haven: Yale University Press, 1974), 68–85.

31. The Venturis vigorously insist that such, indeed, was never intended. Guild House cannot be adequately understood in terms of its antagonism to Rudolph's Crawford Manor alone, nor, incidentally, the Thomas Lewis Microbiology building in Princeton in terms of its emphatic rebuttal of Kahn's Richard's Medical Towers at Penn.

32. Vincent Scully, "Foreword," in John W. Cook and Heinrich Klotz, *Conversations with Architects* (London: Lund Humphries, 1973), 7.

33. See Venturi, "Mal Mots: Aphorisms—Sweet and Sour—By an Anti-Hero Architect," *Iconography and Electronics*, 299–329. It is symptomatic that Venturi's last book opens with two diagrams in the form of timetables, comparing the firm's position on topical architectural issues to the positions, as Venturi sees them, of other contemporary architectural movements.

34. See Tom Wolfe, *From Bauhaus to Our House* (New York: Farrar, Straus & Giroux, 1981), 103–23.

Secret Physiology (pages 35–45)

1. Le Corbusier, *Vers une architecture* (Eng. ed., *Towards a New Architecture*, trans. Frederick Etchells), 146.

2. This was not always the case; see Venturi's comments on the plans of his Guild House as well as of the Vanna Venturi House in *Complexity and Contradiction in Architecture* (New York: Museum of Modern Architecture, 1966), 116ff., 120ff. In *Learning from Las Vegas*, Venturi, Scott Brown, and Izenour write: "Please do not criticize us for primarily analyzing image . . . Along with most architects, we probably spend 90 percent of our design time

on these other important subjects [process, program, structure, social issues, etc.] and less than 10 percent on the questions we are addressing here; they are merely not the direct subject of this inquiry." Robert Venturi, Denise Scott Brown, and Steven Izenour, *Learning From Las Vegas* (Cambridge, Mass.: MIT Press, 1972; rev. ed., 1977), 90ff.

3. The firm made this statement under the heading "Context and History," in one of the programmatic phrases displayed in the ICA Exhibition of 1993–94.

4. Colin Rowe, "Robert Venturi and the Yale Mathematics Building," *Oppositions*, fall 1976, 11–19. I have proposed an interpretation of VSBA's plans as art elsewhere and in greater detail: "Body Language and Artifice: On Some Recent Designs by Venturi, Scott Brown & Associates," *A+U*, June 1990, 121–30, and "Fussspuren," *Archithese*, June 1995, 40–44. The buildings mentioned are documented in Stanislaus von Moos, *Venturi, Rauch & Scott Brown: Buildings and Projects* (Fribourg: Office du Livre; New York: Rizzoli, 1987), 172–76 (for the Yale Mathematics Building Addition).

5. The phrase "paedomorphic inversions" is borrowed from Thomas A. P. van Leeuwen's interpretation of American architecture in *The Skyward Trend of Thought* (s'Gravenhage: AHA Books, 1986), 63.

6. *The Forgotten Symbolism of Architectural Form* was added as a subtitle to the second, paperback edition (1977) of Venturi, Scott Brown, and Izenour, *Learning from Las Vegas*. In this book, the authors reject the kind of physiognomic expressionism or "biotechnical determinism" characteristic of the symbolic practices in high Modern architecture (and, as I am arguing here, even for parts of their own work). They quote passages from Alan Colquhoun as well as from Ernst H. Gombrich in support of their position (see "Theories of Symbolism and Association in Architecture," 131–34). Elsewhere in the same book, they refer to the difference between "denotation and connotation" in architectural symbolism, thereby implicitly suggesting a possible base for a discussion of their "organic" style as well.

7. I am using the notion of the "organic" in architecture in an empirical way, thinking of Frank Lloyd Wright and Alvar Aalto, for example, although not necessarily along the lines their work has been interpreted by authors like Sigfried Giedion or Bruno Zevi (see in particular Bruno Zevi, *L'architettura organica* [Turin: Einaudi, 1945]). The philosophical and theoretical implications the term had within the Vitruvian tradition and beyond are not relevant here. These implications have been studied exhaustively by Caroline van Eck in *Organicism in Nineteenth-Century Architecture: An Inquiry into Its Theoretical and Philosophical Background* (Amsterdam: Architecture & Natura Press, 1994). A particularly interesting study on organic expression in architecture by Donald Drew Egbert appeared while Venturi was a student at Princeton: "The Idea of Organic Expression and American Architecture," *Evolutionary Thought in America* (New Haven: Yale University Press, 1950), 336–96. Egbert sees the concept of "organic expression" as an important ideological root of functionalism.

8. On the "decorated shed" as an alternative to the late Modern "duck" see Venturi, Scott Brown, and Izenour, *Learning from Las Vegas*, 63–72 (in the original edition), as well as, more recently, Robert Venturi, "A Definition of Architecture as Shelter with Decoration on It, and Another Plea for a Symbolism of the Ordinary in Architecture," *A+U*, January 1978, 3–14. In the description of many among their recent works, the architects insist on a conceptual separation of "decoration" from "shed." Most critics and historians have since rather uncritically adopted that notion as a key to the firm's work, and my own study is no exception: see von Moos, "Anatomy of a 'Decorated Shed,'" *Venturi, Rauch & Scott Brown*, 22–31. In a comment on an early draft of this essay, Denise Scott Brown insists that "the 'shed' has its own art—it's the art that hides art—second glance architecture" (August 1997).

9. The theoretical precedents and roots of VSBA's urbanistic thought have been variously discussed in articles by Denise Scott Brown, which will be referred to below. For some general information see von Moos, "Urban Design," *Venturi, Rauch & Scott Brown*, 77–85.

10. At one point, Scott Brown is quoted as having visualized the general form of the building as an extrapolation of the surrounding structures and cornice heights "long before Bob was to draw a single line"; Andrea Gabor, *Einstein's Wife: Work and Marriage in the Lives of Five Great Twentieth Century Women* (London/New York: Penguin Books, 1995), 215.

11. Denise Scott Brown, "Between Three Stools: A Personal View of Urban Design Pedagogy," *Urban Concepts: Architectural Design Profile* 83 (London: Academy Editions, 1990): 9.

12. Scott Brown, "Between Three Stools," 13.

13. Fumihiko Maki, *Investigations in Collective Form* (St. Louis: Washington University School of Architecture, 1964). See also Lucius Burckhardt and Walter M. Förderer, *Bauen ein Prozess* (Niederteufen: Niggli, 1968). Speaking of the urban theories of architects like Kevin Lynch, David Crane (the link between Penn and Harvard), and Maki, Scott Brown at one point says that "none were as useful as we hoped they would be" ("Between Three Stools," 13).

14. Oral communication to the author, August 1997.

15. This comparison has been proposed elsewhere in greater detail: Stanislaus von Moos, "Venturi, die Kunstgeschichte und das 'Princeton System': Zum neuen Erweiterungsbau der National Gallery in London (1986–1991)," *Künstlerischer Austausch/Artistic Exchange: Akten des XXVIII Internationalen Kongresses für Kunstgeschichte Berlin, 15–20 Juli 1992* (Berlin: Akademie Verlag, 1993), 15–34. On Venturi's ideas on the Sainsbury Wing (and on museum architecture in general), see Robert Venturi, "From Invention to Convention in Architecture (The Tenth Thomas Cubitt Lecture at the Royal Society of Art)," *RSA Journal*, January 1988, 89–103. On the Staatsgalerie in Stuttgart, see Francesco Dal Co and Tom Muirhead, *I Musei di James Stirling Michael Wilford and Associates* (Milan: Electa, 1990).

16. The project is documented in summary in von Moos, *Venturi, Rauch & Scott Brown*, and in greater detail in "Venturi & Rauch: Oeffentliche Bauten," *Werk. Archithese* (special issue) 7–8 (1977): 25–28.

17. Geoffrey Scott, *The Architecture of Humanism: A Study in the History of Taste* (1914; New York: Norton Library, 1974), 159. Scott goes on to say that "the tendency to recognize, in concrete forms, the image of those functions is the true basis, in its turn, of critical appreciation."

18. Scott, *Architecture of Humanism*, 161, 164. Scott himself is fully aware of his indebtedness to theories of empathy that had been developed in the years before 1900 by Lipps and others; see *Architecture of Humanism*, 159.

19. R. D. Martienssen, *The Idea of Space in Greek Architecture, with Special Reference to the Doric Temple and Its Setting* (Johannesburg: Witwatersrand University Press, 1964).

20. Martienssen, *Idea of Space*, 21; the latter phrase is quoted by Martienssen from P. Gardner, *The Principles of Greek Art*.

21. Martienssen, *Idea of Space*, 19. According to Scott Brown, Martienssen's discussion of Greek urbanism in relation to procession is itself influenced by constructivist theories of movement through space (communication to the author, August 1988). It is worth noting that the ideas of "passage" and of "eternal wandering" have played a major role in Sigfried Giedion's understanding of the architecture of ancient Egypt, as discussed in his *The Eternal Present II: The Beginnings of Architecture*, vol. 2 of W. A. Mellon Lectures in the Fine Arts (Princeton: Princeton University Press, 1963), esp. 282, 349–360, 396, 398 ("Ritual Processions in Egypt, Mesopotamia, and Greece"). The role played by processions and pilgrimages as factors both of urban form and of sacred architecture in the subsequent centuries of Christian architecture has been studied more recently by Adolf Reinle, *Zeichensprache der Architektur* (Zurich: Artemis, 1976), esp. 289ff., "Symbolik der Treppen" ("symbolism of stairs").

22. Philip Johnson, "Whence and Whither: The Processional Element in Architecture," *Perspecta* 9–10 (1965): 167.

23. Johnson, "Whence and Whither," 167. On the Carpenter Center, see Eduard F. Sekler and William Curtis, *Le Corbusier at Work: The Genesis of the*

Carpenter Center for the Visual Arts (Cambridge, Mass.: Harvard University Press, 1978).

24. See Paul Venable Turner, "Movement and the Urban Model," *Campus: An American Planning Tradition* (New York: Architectural History Foundation, Cambridge, Mass.: MIT Press, 1984), 267–80.

25. Denise Scott Brown, written communication to the author, August 31, 1997.

26. Kenneth Frampton, "The Generic Street as a Continuous Built Form," in *On Streets*, ed. Stanford Anderson (Cambridge, Mass.: MIT Press, 1978), 308–37. Of course, the idea of the "symbolic street" also has canonic Modernist premises in Le Corbusier (Plan Obus, Unité d'habitations, etc.) as well as in the work of the Smithsons (Golden Lane Housing, etc.) and of Team X.

27. As a lakefront promenade lined with "trees," the Disney Boardwalk project is also a variation of the F.D.R. Memorial Park proposal of 1960; see von Moos, *Venturi, Rauch & Scott Brown*, 79.

28. On the linear gallery type, see Nikolaus Pevsner, "Museums," *A History of Building Types* (London: Thames & Hudson, 1976), 111–38, and also Wolfram Prinz, *Die Entstehung der Galerie in Frankreich und Italien* (Berlin: Gebr. Mann, 1977).

29. On Fourier and Considérant, see Franziska Bollerey, *Architekturkonzeptionen der utopischen Sozialisten* (Berlin: Ernst & Sohn, 1977, 1991).

30. One example is O. R. Salvisberg's Machine Laboratory of the ETH in Zurich, built around 1935. During a visit to Zurich in 1977, Venturi seemed particularly impressed by the corridors from which visitors look out into the machine hall ("like from the Grande Galerie in Versailles toward the park," as he remarked). The symbolic street at Purchase had been completed several years earlier. As for the Machine Laboratory, currently that view is unfortunately blocked by more recent additions. See Stanislaus von Moos, "Architektur auf den zweiten Blick," in "O. R. Salvisberg," *Werk. Archithese* (special issue) 10 (1977): 3–6.

31. In her perspicacious critique of the American mall, Margaret Crawford has already made the link with the utopian tradition, interpreting the mall as "an ironic reversal of the redemptive design projects imagined by 19th century utopians such as Fourier and Owen, who sought unity through collective productive activity and social reorganization . . . rather than . . . consumption"; Crawford, "The World in a Shopping Mall," in *Variations on a Theme Park: The New American City and the End of Public Space*, ed. Michael Sorkin (New York: Noonday Press, 1992), 6. Concerning the architecture of public indoor spaces at Las Vegas, Venturi, Scott Brown, and Izenour point to the fact that new construction techniques have made the "high, lit and windowed" monumental space altogether obsolete, creating a new roadside monumentality that is emphatically "low" and "glittering in the dark" (*Learning from Las Vegas*, 54ff.). Fortunately for architecture, in their own symbolic streets they returned to the premodern (as well as high Modern) preference for traditionally scaled, high "naves" (without sacrificing the effects of glittering—in some cases, as at the University of Delaware Student Center). By returning—at least halfway—to the nave, their preference ostensibly meets with that of the designers of more recent American shopping malls.

32. At the time of their discovery of Nolli, Scott Brown and Venturi were primarily intrigued by the analogy of this situation to that of the Las Vegas Strip, "where the public space goes right through the casinos and into the patios beyond" and where even the parking lots "are ritualized and given a ceremonial function" (*Learning from Las Vegas*, 77).

33. See von Moos, *Venturi, Rauch & Scott Brown*, 256–59, esp. the illustration on 258.

Tableaux (pages 47–55)

1. George L. Hersey, "Replication Replicated: Notes on American Bastardy," *Perspecta* 10 (1965): 215, 216. This article is among the references quoted in the Venturis' *Learning from Las Vegas*. See also Hersey's studies on architectural associationism: "J. C. Loudon and Architectural Associationism," *Architectural Review*, August 1968, 88–92; later integrated in Hersey, *High Victorian Gothic: A Study in Associationism* (Baltimore: Johns Hopkins University Press, 1972). The panoply of writings on the moral vicissitudes of the "true" and the "false" in architecture needs not be listed here; the most recent contribution is by Ada Louise Huxtable, *The Unreal America: Architecture and Illusion* (New York: New Press, 1997).

2. Although scenography is central to Venturi and Scott Brown's architectural thinking, it has only recently been addressed head-on by them—in response to criticism. See Robert Venturi, "J'Adore St. Paul's," *AD Profile*, September–October 1993, viii–xii; reprinted in *Iconography and Electronics upon a Generic Architecture: A View from the Drafting Room* (Cambridge, Mass.: MIT Press, 1996), 287–95. See my own earlier discussion of scenography in "The City as Stage," *Venturi, Rauch & Scott Brown: Buildings and Projects* (Fribourg: Office du Livre; New York: Rizzoli, 1987), 60–70.

3. Umberto Eco describes the full-scale model of the Oval Office in the Lyndon B. Johnson Library in Austin, Texas, as an example of the opposite procedure, where the "completely real" becomes identified with the "completely fake," that is, where the "sign aims to be the thing, to abolish the distinction of the reference, the mechanism of replacement"; *Travels in Hyperreality* (San Diego/New York/London: Harcourt Brace, 1986), 6ff.

4. Denise Scott Brown, "Talking about the Context/A proposito del contesto," *Lotus* 74 (1992): 125–28.

5. Among the numerous texts by Bertolt Brecht on the theory of *Verfremdung* see his "Kurze Beschreibung einer neuen Technik der Schauspielkunst, die einen Verfremdungseffekt hervorbringt," *Gesammelte Werke* (Frankfurt: Suhrkamp, 1967), 341–48.

6. "Gap" is here intended not merely as the "gap between the building and its decoration [that] gets wider with each new technology of communication," as Mark Wigley has discussed it ("The Decorated Gap," *Ottagono* 94 [1990]: 36–47), but more generally as the abyss that inevitably exists between an original and its representation.

7. As far as this visual strategy is concerned, Wu Hall relates to the Columbus Fire Station specifically in the way its facade is made of two overlapping facades (one real, one virtual, that is, suggested by paint); beyond that, the Princeton project can be said to refer to Palladio's church of S. Giorgio Maggiore in Venice. Speaking of the "cardboard architecture" characteristic of the "neo-avant-garde," Robert E. Somol has described the visual strategy at hand as the technique of building structure "from the point of view of its reproduction": Somol, " 'Les Liaisons Dangereuses,' or 'My Mother the House,' " *Fetish* 4 (1992): 63.

8. And beyond that, as a paraphrase of the entire history of architecture. Deborah Fausch has linked the design of the Bard College Library addition, as well as other projects and buildings by VSBA, to the theme of architecture as clothing ("Architektur als Bekleidung") as formulated by Gottfried Semper and later, in the early twentieth century, reinterpreted in the work of Otto Wagner. See Fausch, "Towards 'An Architecture of our Times': Scaffold and Drapery in the Work of Venturi, Scott Brown and Associates," in *Architecture: In Fashion*, D. Fausch, P. Singley, and R. El-Koury (New York: Princeton Architectural Press, 1994), 344–61. See also, in this context, the conversation with the Venturis on fashion in this same book ("Fabrication: Cycles of Taste in Architecture, In Conversation with Robert Venturi and Denise Scott Brown," 362–75). The dress analogy was first proposed as a paradigm in Modern architecture by Mary McLeod in "Undressing Architecture: Fashion, Gender, and Modernity," in *Architecture: In Fashion*, 38–123. See also Mark Wigley's essay in the same book ("White Out: Fashioning the Modern") as well as his *White Walls, Designer Dresses* (Cambridge, Mass.: MIT Press, 1996). In light of Wigley's analysis, Fausch's reading of the Venturian paradigm of "scaffold and drapery" looks more intricately connected to the Modern movement than the

theatrical implication of her thesis appears to suggest, but that line of thought cannot be pursued here.

9. The changing nature of this gap has been the subject of Denise Scott Brown's and Robert Venturi's study of "hot" and "cool" borrowings in developer housing. Although their "Learning from Levittown" study has been excerpted (V. Carroll, D. Scott Brown, and R. Venturi, "Styling, or 'These Houses Are Exactly the Same. They Just Look Different,'" *Lotus International*, February 1975, 162–71, 234ff.), the bulk of it still awaits publication.

10. The symbolism of "control" appears to have played a certain role in the discussions of this project by Staten Island politicians, at least in the sense that they used it as an argument against the design.

11. It is interesting that Paul Klee, who was born in Berne in 1879, should have felt so strongly about the atavistic symbolism of the sixteenth-century Berne clock tower (Zytglogge) that he carefully avoided including it in any of his numerous early drawings of the city's skyline. See Osamu Okuda, "Reflektierender Blick auf Bern: Paul Klee und seine Heimatstadt," *Georges Bloch—Jahrbuch des Kunstgeschichtlichen Seminars der Universität Zürich* (1995), 146–62. On the symbolism of public clocks see Stanislaus von Moos, *Industrieästhetik (Ars Helvetica)* (Disentis: Desertina, 1992), vol. 11, 23–32.

12. Robert Venturi, *Complexity and Contradiction in Architecture* (New York: Museum of Modern Art, 1996), 102.

13. Wigley, "The Decorated Gap," 38ff. Since Wigley interprets *Learning from Las Vegas* as "an artwork" offered to the "gaze of a traditional reader," it may be added that the design of the original edition, published in 1972, was not done by the Venturis. In fact, they declare that the "latter day Bauhaus design of the book," its "'interesting' Modern styling . . . belied our subject matter." They appear to be happier with the "ordinary" paperback edition done a few years later; Robert Venturi, Denise Scott Brown, and Steven Izenour, *Learning From Las Vegas* (Cambridge, Mass.: MIT Press, 1972; rev. ed., 1977), xv.

14. See Ed Ruscha, *Every Building on the Sunset Strip* (1966), or others among his photographic scrapbooks, like *Twentysix Gasoline Stations* (1963) or *Nine Swimming Pools and a Broken Glass* (1968).

15. See Denise Scott Brown, "Zeichnen für den Déco-Distrikt," *Archithese*, March 1982, 17–21. On the relation between graphic and photographic image-making and design, see also my "Architektur als Bilderbogen: Graphik und Photo-Graphik bei Venturi und Rauch," *Jahrbuch für Architektur*, ed. Heinrich Klotz (Braunschweig/Wiesbaden: Vieweg, 1980), 95–112

16. Susanne Lang, "The Genesis of the English Landscape Garden," *The Picturesque Garden and Its Influence Outside the British Isles*, ed. Nikolaus Pevsner (Washington, D.C.: Dumbarton Oaks, 1974), 1–29. On the subject of the picturesque garden, see Adrian von Buttlar, *Der Landschaftsgarten: Gartenbaukunst des Klassizismus und der Romantik* (Cologne: DuMont, 1989).

17. See Richard A. Etlin, *Frank Lloyd Wright and Le Corbusier: The Romantic Legacy* (Manchester/New York: Manchester University Press, 1994), 112ff. ("Le Corbusier Defines the Architectural Promenade"), 143ff. ("The Reasoned Picturesque"), and passim. Many of these design procedures are themselves related to Le Corbusier's techniques of manipulating photographic imagery. See Beatriz Colomina, *Privacy and Publicity: Modern Architecture as Mass Media* (Cambridge, Mass.: MIT Press, 1994).

18. Venturi, *Complexity and Contradiction*, 20.

19. Venturi, *Complexity and Contradiction*, 25.

20. Robert Venturi, "Notes for a Lecture Celebrating the Centennial of the American Academy in Rome Delivered in Chicago," *Iconography and Electronics*, 51.

21. The Venturis' theoretical antagonism to "picturesqueness" deserves a more thorough analysis than can be attempted here. In their theoretical statements, they emphasize the conflict that may exist between the "picturesque" and "function," such as when Denise Scott Brown insists that qualities such as those just described are legitimate only if they emerge from the given prob-

lem or program, rather than as applications adapted for the sake of being picturesque (communication to the author, August 31, 1997). While much current architecture may be characterized by such a conflict, the picturesque as a theoretical position in history primarily represents an attempt to give function its dignity and place in aesthetic theory. Seen in such a way, the Venturis' own work is hardly imaginable outside the picturesque tradition.

22. Sidney K. Robinson, *Inquiry into the Picturesque* (Chicago/London: University of Chicago Press, 1991), 4. Robinson perhaps somewhat overstates the aspects of the picturesque tradition that would connect it to postmodernist sensibility. Stephen Copley and Peter Garside found it "disconcerting" to see how Robinson had stressed the proto-postmodern sides of the picturesque: "Indeed his presentation and celebration of the Picturesque movement's eclecticism, refusal of fixity and authority, and exploitation of marginality, sometimes makes it sound disconcertingly like a program for architectural Postmodernism"; Stephen Copley and Peter Garside, eds., *The Politics of the Picturesque: Literature, Landscape and Aesthetics since 1770* (Cambridge: Cambridge University Press, 1994), 4.

23. Serlio's views had a profound impact on the theory of landscape painting by the seventeenth-century Italian painter Lomazzo—which in turn serves as a link from Serlio to the eighteenth-century concept of the picturesque. See Susanne Lang, "Genesis of the English Landscape Garden," 2–3. Serlio's woodcut of the comic stage is explicitly referred to in Colin Rowe and Fred Koetter, *Collage City* (Cambridge, Mass.: MIT Press, 1979), 14, and also implicitly, as I have tried to argue, in Venturi's *Complexity and Contradiction* (see von Moos, *Venturi, Rauch & Scott Brown*, 60–69). More recently, M. Christine Boyer has challenged this interpretation, attributing the "failures of architecture as a narrative gesture," among other things, to the "false comparison" of the tragic and the comic scenes as drawn by Serlio; M. Christine Boyer, *The City of Collective Memory: Its Historical Imagery and Architectural Entertainments* (Cambridge, Mass.: MIT Press, 1994), 124ff.

24. Rowe and Koetter, *Collage City*, 34ff. Among what was influenced by the townscape movement the authors include Jane Jacobs and the "allegedly scientific notational systems of Kevin Lynch," as well as "Pop-inspired appraisals of the Strip at Las Vegas and enthusiasm for the phenomenon of Disney World."

25. Mary McLeod, "Architecture and Politics in the Reagan Era: From Postmodernism to Deconstructivism," *Assemblage* 8 (1989): 29.

26. M. Christine Boyer, "Cities for Sale: Merchandizing History at South Street Seaport," in *Variations on a Theme Park: The New American City and the End of Public Space*, ed. Michael Sorkin (New York: Noonday Press, 1992), 181–204. The concept of the tableau is also central in Boyer's more recent treatise *The City of Collective Memory*, 46ff. ("The City of Spectacle") and 59ff. ("The Politics of Representational Forms"). On the politics and design of Disneyland, see Sorkin's "See You in Disneyland," *Variations on a Theme Park*, 205–32, as well as, more recently, Beth Dunlop, *Building a Dream: The Art of Disney Architecture* (New York: Harry N. Abrams, 1996).

27. Denise Scott Brown, "Learning from Brutalism," in *The Independent Group: Postwar Britain and the Aesthetics of Plenty*, ed. David Robbins (Cambridge, Mass.: MIT Press, 1990), 203–6; see also her earlier study, "Team 10, Perspecta 10 and the Present State of Architectural Theory," *Journal of the American Institute of Planners*, January 1967, 223–32. The London avant-garde was not alone in fighting for a revision of functionalist doctrine in urbanism. Similarly vocal was the Dutch Forum group with Aldo van Eyck as the most radical critic of established CIAM urbanism, as well as Ernesto N. Rogers, the editor of *Casabella*. Among his perspicacious editorials at least two should be noted here: "La responsabilità verso la tradizione," *Casabella-Continuità* 202 (1954): 1–3, and "Le preesistenze ambientali e i temi pratici contemporanei," *Casabella-Continuità* 204 (1955): 3–6. The ideas proposed by Rogers were later reworked by Aldo Rossi, at that time a young architect and critic working for *Casabella;* see, for example, Aldo Rossi, "Il passato e il presente nella nuova architettura," *Casabella* 219 (1958): 16.

28. Scott Brown, "Talking About the Context," 125–28; *Good and Bad Manners in Architecture* is the title of a book by A. T. Edwards (London: Alec Tiranti, 1944).

29. Von Moos, *Venturi, Rauch & Scott Brown*, 113.

30. Eco, *Travels in Hyperreality*, 10.

31. In their unpublished comments on the Edison project, a program for prototypical schools, they write: "We think that, just as little children like to play with doll houses, so older children will like to be in a doll's town, so to speak, as they work and live all day in this new school that is an institution as well as a community."

32. See von Moos, *Venturi, Rauch & Scott Brown*, 88ff. (Copley Square), 116–21 (Western Plaza), 138–40 (Welcome Park), and 104–9 (Franklin Court).

The City as Kimono (pages 57–62)

1. Robert Venturi and Denise Scott Brown, "Two Naifs in Japan," *Architecture and Decorative Arts: Two Naifs in Japan* (Tokyo: Kajima Institute Publishing Co., 1991), 8–25; reprinted in Robert Venturi, *Iconography and Electronics upon a Generic Architecture: A View from the Drafting Room* (Cambridge, Mass.: MIT Press, 1996), 109–18.

2. Venturi and Scott Brown, "Two Naifs in Japan," 8–21.

3. Venturi and Scott Brown, "Two Naifs in Japan," 10.

4. The Venturis' comments on their rugs for V'soske are apt. The discussion of "pictorialism" is also important.

5. Warren I. Cohen, *East Asian Art and American Culture: A Study in International Relations* (New York: Columbia University Press, 1992).

6. For a recent survey of *japonisme* in Modern art see *Japonisme* (Paris: Musée d'Orsay; Tokyo: National Museum of Occidental Art, 1988). Among Whistler's paintings that illustrate his fascination with Japanese textiles, *Purple and Rose* (1864) is perhaps the best known. German art developed its own *japonisme*, as the beautiful painting by Adolf Menzel, *Le magasin japonais* (1885) shows.

7. See Kevin Nute, *Frank Lloyd Wright in Japan: The Role of Traditional Japanese Art and Architecture in the Work of Frank Lloyd Wright* (New York: Van Nostrand Reinhold, 1993), 16ff., 48–72; see also *Japonisme*, 330–35.

8. Decades before the Chicago World's Columbian Exposition, in the late 1870s, even Frank Furness had a brief, "Victorian" *japonisme* phase, inspired by a Japanese painter living with him on Locust Street in Philadelphia (communication from George L. Thomas, August 1997).

9. Edward Morse, *Japanese Homes and Their Surroundings* (1886; 2nd ed., London: Fleet Street, 1888), 77; see also Nute, *Frank Lloyd Wright in Japan*, 42.

10. Karin Kirsch, *Die Neue Wohnung und das Alte Japan: Architekten planen für sich selbst; Edward William Godwin, Frank Lloyd Wright, Charles Rennie Mackintosh, Walter Gropius, Egon Eiermann, Toyo Ito* (Stuttgart: Deutsche Verlags Anstalt, 1996), 7.

11. Walter Gropius, "Architecture in Japan," in Toko Shinoda, *Katsura: Tradition and Creation in Japanese Architecture* (New Haven: Yale University Press, 1960), 203. Gropius does not give a date for his early discovery of Japanese houses in European illustrations. On Gropius's discovery of Japan, see Kirsch, *Die Neue Wohnung und das Alte Japan*, 155ff.

12. Speaking once again of Katsura in Tokyo, Gropius said: "Strangely enough, this attitude of restraint had, during the same period, its counterpart in the ostentatious display of the mausoleum of the powerful Tokugawa Shoguns at Nikko. Tremendous skill in craftsmanship was misused here by the Shoguns to glorify themselves with an overbearing profuseness of ornament and decoration which destroys the clarity of the architectural composition as a whole and leaves an impress of conceit and self-praise": Gropius, "Architecture in Japan," 207. At a closer look, even Katsura shows regrettable "signs of decline" in Gropius's view: added ornamental elements, "all too ornamented bronze-hardware on and above the sliding doors, the purely decorative ramma panels, too-elaborate shelves and cabinets."

13. This "abstract" view of Japanese architecture is best visualized in houses designed by Kenzo Tange in the 1950s, which were swiftly acclaimed by Giedion as "another example of the new regionalism"; Sigfried Giedion, *Architecture, You and Me: The Diary of a Development* (Cambridge, Mass.: Harvard University Press, 1958), fig. 35. Tange had in fact contributed a historical analysis of Katsura to Shinoda's *Katsura*, and it is this book that Alison and Peter Smithson may have had in mind when they wrote that "Fundamentally both the Modern Movement in its heroic phase and our ideas of that time used as their measure traditional Japanese architecture as understood through photographs seen in Europe," in *Without Rhetoric: An Architectural Aesthetic, 1955–1972* (Cambridge, Mass.: MIT Press, 1974), 4.

14. Venturi and Scott Brown, "Two Naifs in Japan," 12.

15. Venturi and Scott Brown, "Two Naifs in Japan," 9.

16. On the Farnsworth House as "primitive hut," see Fritz Neumeyer, *Mies van der Rohe: Das kunstlose Wort; Gedankrn zur Baukunst* (Berlin: Siedler Verlag, 1986), 168ff.

17. Mies must have seen the publication of a Japanese tea house in Wasmuth's *Monatshefte der Baukunst* in 1921–22 but he never visited Japan. At any rate, when Werner Blaser showed him his book *Tempel und Teehaus in Japan* (1956), he had no objections to the equations Blaser made between Japanese architecture and Mies's work. On Mies and Japan, see Kirsch, *Die Neue Wohnung und das Alte Japan*, 12ff. In an interesting paper, "The Bauhaus and Japan: Unification or Opposition?," Akio Izutsu has recently discussed Mies's affinity to Japanese architecture from a Japanese point of view (unpublished ms., VSBA archives, Philadelphia).

18. Kurt Junghanns, *Bruno Taut 1880–1938* (Berlin: Elefanten Press/ Henschel Verlag, 1983), 107. See Bruno Taut, *Houses and People of Japan* (Tokyo: Sanseido, 1937). The best summary of Taut's Japanese experience is by Joshio Dohi, "Bruno Taut, sein Weg zur Katsura-Villa," in *Bruno Taut 1880–1938* (Berlin: Akademie der Künste, 1980), 120–28. See also Heinrich Taut, "Bruno Taut in und über Japan," *Bruno Taut*, 129–36. The political contradictions involved in Western interpretations of Japanese architecture cannot be discussed here. Gropius himself was surprised to see that younger Japanese architects were unable to share his enthusiasm for the imperial villas and the principle of modular planning realized there because they saw them as a symbol of feudalist tyranny, whereas conservative Japanese saw the same forms as expressive of patriarchal virtues. See Kirsch, *Die Neue Wohnung und das Alte Japan*, 156.

19. "Tokio—Scheusal von Geschäftsstadt. Es kann gar nichts ekelhafteres als die Ginzagegend geben"; Taut, "Bruno Taut in und über Japan," 133.

20. Venturi and Scott Brown, "Two Naifs in Japan," 16.

21. Venturi and Scott Brown, "Two Naifs in Japan," 21.

22. Venturi and Scott Brown, "Two Naifs in Japan," 18.

23. Venturi and Scott Brown, "Two Naifs in Japan," 10, and Robert Venturi, "Venturi Shops," *Iconography and Electronics*, 119–21. When the director of the Philadelphia Museum of Art saw the collection spread over the dining table at the Venturis' house, she decided to include it as part of an exhibition on Japanese design in 1994. "Venturi Shops" has since been shown in various European museums.

24. Esther McCoy, *Five California Architects* (New York: Praeger, 1975), 103–47.

Venturi, Scott Brown

& Associates

Buildings and Projects, 1986–1998

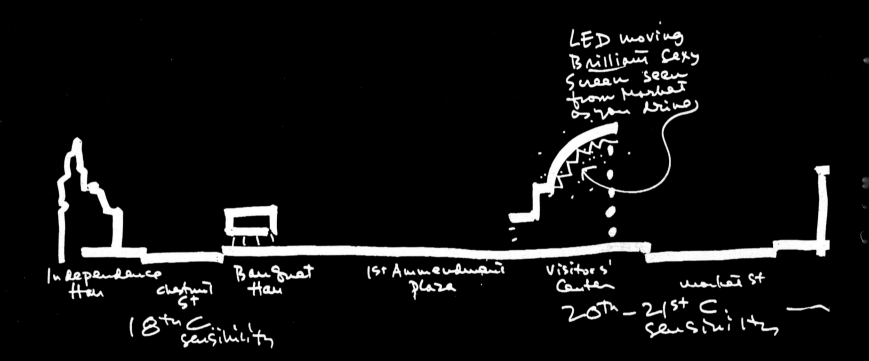

LED moving
Brilliant Sexy
Screen seen
from Market
as you drive

Independance
Hall
chestnut
St

18th C.
sensibility

Banquet
Hall

1st Ammendment
Plaza

Visitors'
Center

Market St

20th – 21st C.
sensibility

Urban Design

76 *Memphis Center City Development Plan*

80 *Berlin Tomorrow Competition*

84 *Battery Park City*

86 *Houston Museum of Fine Arts*

88 *Denver Civic Center*

92 *Columbus Gateway Study*

94 *Perris Civic Center*

96 *Gateway Visitor Center and Independence Mall*

102 *Dartmouth College Campus*

106 *Princeton Train Station Gateway*

110 *Perelman Quadrangle*

112 *Bryn Mawr College Concept Plan*

114 *Benjamin Franklin Bridge Lighting*

116 *Christopher Columbus Monument*

118 *National World War II Memorial*

1 Memphis Center City Development Plan

Memphis, Tennessee, 1984–1987

Venturi, Rauch & Scott Brown was selected by the Center City Commission to head an interdisciplinary planning team to develop a concept plan for downtown Memphis, the historic (and present) center city that stands on the Chickasaw Bluff above the Mississippi River floodplain. Over the past twenty-five years office and retail growth in east Memphis caused historic downtown to become the western boundary of the city; but in the 1980s rehabilitation and new building recommenced in the area overlooking the Mississippi.

Fearing intense development could erode the amenity of the city-river connection, the Center City Commission called for a comprehensive development strategy, an overview that would address the area's problems, develop policies, and implement programs to encourage development, while at the same time preserving the beauty of the bluffs and the view over the river, prime attractions for economic development. The twenty-two volumes of the plan consider the role and potential of the downtown and its surroundings in a broad economic, cultural, and regional context. Future markets for housing, office, and retail uses were investigated; recommendations were made for the role of Memphis's cultural institutions, historic fabric, and inner-city neighborhoods in the city's regeneration; and regional transportation initiatives were critiqued.

The urban design plan concentrated on the juxtapositions of scale between old and new that would occur with development. It emphasized Memphis's cultural and historical richness as the city of cotton, the blues, rock and roll, W. C. Handy, and Elvis Presley, and also as an American tribute to the capital of the pharaohs, incorporating these identities yet broadening its vision in approaching the future. A balance was sought between long- and short-term and large- and small-scale recommendations.

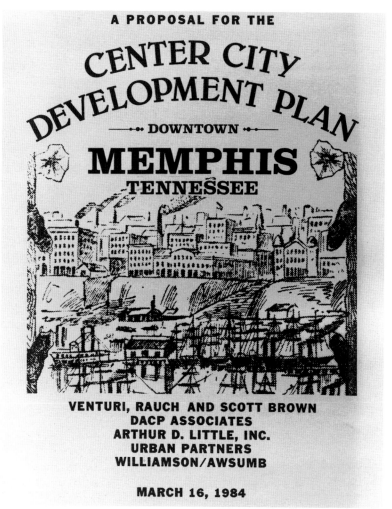

Cover of report

Principal in charge:
Denise Scott Brown
Project managers: Gabrielle London,
James Williamson
With: Catherine Consentino,
David Schaaf
In association with: Killinger Kise
Franks Straw; Arthur D. Little, Inc.;
Urban Partners; Williamson/Awsumb
Architects; Tennessee Valley Center;
Robert L. Morris, Inc.

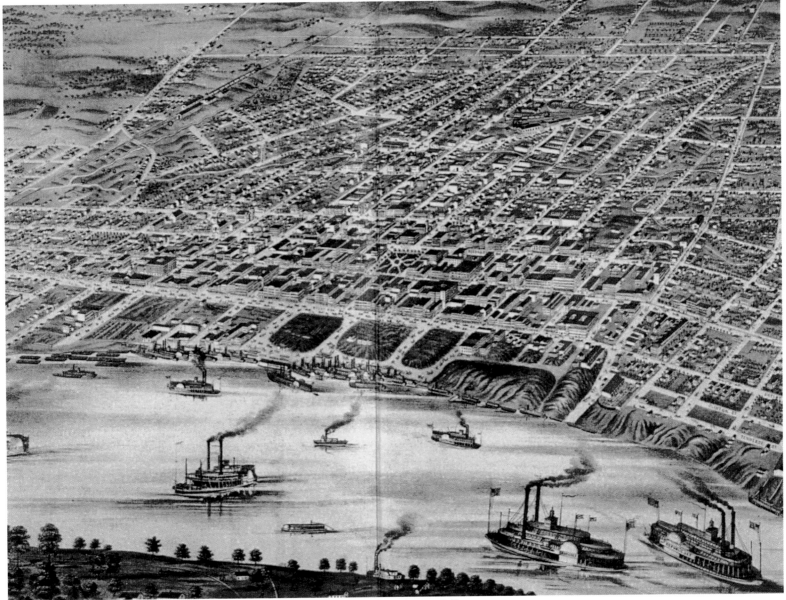

View of historic downtown Memphis with Mississippi River (nineteenth-century print)

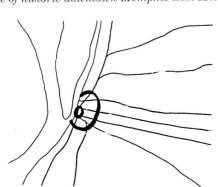 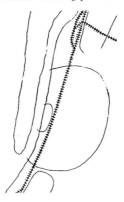 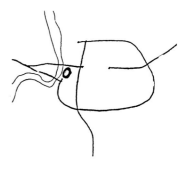

Historic links between the city center and its surrounding areas

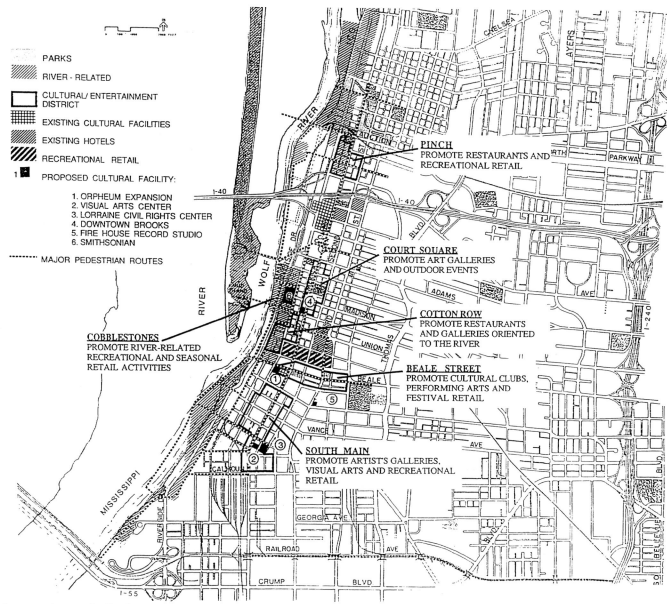

Legend

- **PARKS**
- **RIVER - RELATED**
- **CULTURAL/ ENTERTAINMENT DISTRICT**
- **EXISTING CULTURAL FACILITIES**
- **EXISTING HOTELS**
- **RECREATIONAL RETAIL**
- **1** PROPOSED CULTURAL FACILITY:

  1. ORPHEUM EXPANSION
  2. VISUAL ARTS CENTER
  3. LORRAINE CIVIL RIGHTS CENTER
  4. DOWNTOWN BROOKS
  5. FIRE HOUSE RECORD STUDIO
  6. SMITHSONIAN

- .... MAJOR PEDESTRIAN ROUTES

PINCH
PROMOTE RESTAURANTS AND
RECREATIONAL RETAIL

COURT SQUARE
PROMOTE ART GALLERIES
AND OUTDOOR EVENTS

COTTON ROW
PROMOTE RESTAURANTS
AND GALLERIES ORIENTED
TO THE RIVER

COBBLESTONES
PROMOTE RIVER-RELATED
RECREATIONAL AND SEASONAL
RETAIL ACTIVITIES

BEALE STREET
PROMOTE CULTURAL CLUBS,
PERFORMING ARTS AND
FESTIVAL RETAIL

SOUTH MAIN
PROMOTE ARTIST'S GALLERIES,
VISUAL ARTS AND RECREATIONAL
RETAIL

Proposed cultural and economic uses for the downtown area

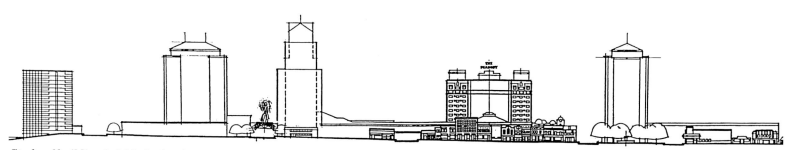

Study of building heights in the city center

PEABODY PLACE

ELVIS
ON BEALE STREET

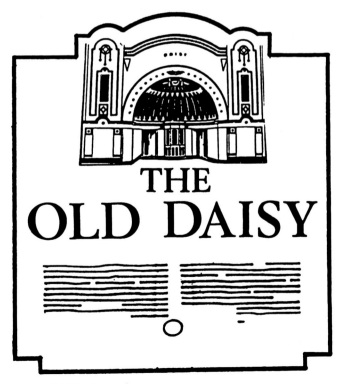

THE
OLD DAISY

MID-AMERICA
MALL SHUTTLE

Suggested historic markers

2 Berlin Tomorrow Competition
Planning Study and Proposed Monument for Berlin

Berlin, Germany, 1990

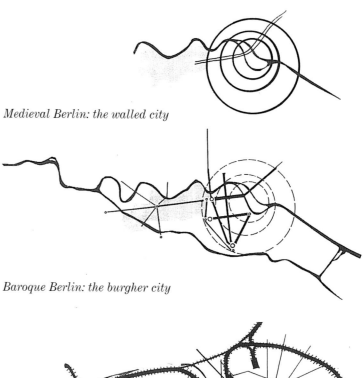

Medieval Berlin: the walled city

How should Berlin be planned now that the wall is down? This historic event has transformed the city by establishing (and reestablishing) connections between the eastern and western sectors, thereby opening up opportunities for governmental and commercial development. Through a study of maps of the city's past and present, VSBA architects and planners have tried to understand the effects, physical as well as symbolic, of removing the wall. Walls have come down in Berlin before, and patterns of use and infrastructure have altered as a result. To suggest directions for Berlin tomorrow, the study charts the city's beginnings and subsequent history, limns out some patterns of "city physics" likely to prevail when barriers are gone, and posits ideas for future growth.

Baroque Berlin: the burgher city

Reading History from the Map

Over its history, Berlin has grown as a set of patterns on patterns. With the postwar political stand-off, Berlin became a symbol for the Cold War. The capitalist city massed its commercial and financial activities along Kurfürstendamm, taking its hold from the prewar commercial activities around Breitscheidplatz. To the east, socialist planning was demonstrated in housing along the Stalinallee, in the redesign of the great urban places destroyed by bombs, and, at the local level, in a cellular pattern of retail and community facilities related to housing enclaves. These vast changes took place primarily through the adaptation of what remained of the historic urban patterns.

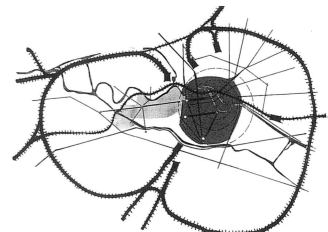

The railroad city

"City Physics" and the Urban Stress Diagram

At any one time, Berlin's inherited infrastructure has been differentially weighted, as a reflection of the different intensities of use of its sectors. The city's road and rail systems form a stress diagram whose vectors vary according to changes within the sectors and also in the connections between them. The removal of the Wall will give rise to changes in population movement, the daily journey to work, street uses and configurations, development patterns, and urban infrastructure, vastly redistributing the pattern of stresses on the city.

Visionaries for Berlin today must be good "physicists," understanding how the urban stress diagram is likely to shift. Welcome pressures for change should be channeled in directions believed to be desirable for the city; others should be resisted. For example, Unter den Linden is an area where large-scale change would be hurtful

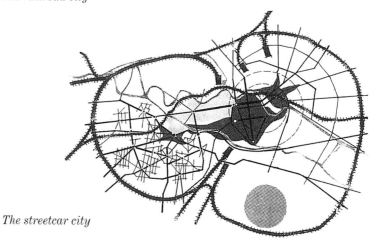

The streetcar city

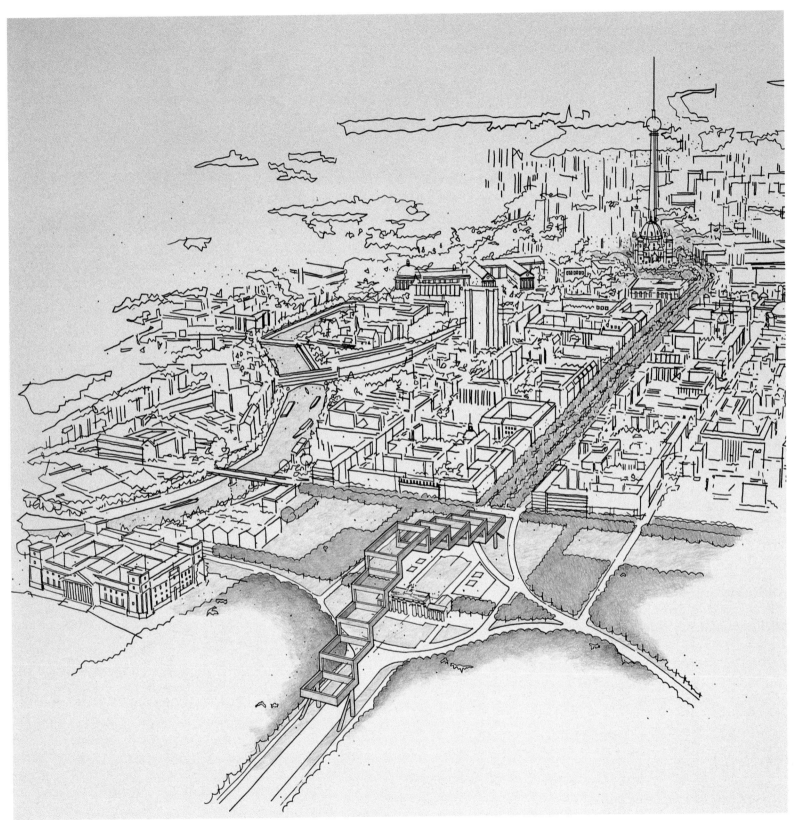

Brandenburg Stairs and Pariser Platz looking toward Unter den Linden

and should be resisted. *Directly south is, we suspect, an area likely to change, given the probable growth around the airport and between Potsdamer Platz and Checkpoint Charlie. The area south of the Tiergarten between the Wall and Kurfürstendamm appears to be suitable for large-scale change; it could be important to the reestablishment of connections between west and east. Defining patterns of change and permanence within the city will require good knowledge of how city systems work.*

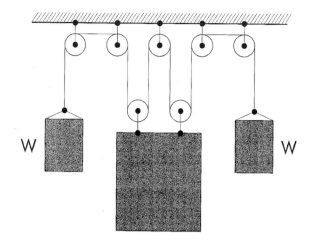

Stress diagram

New Threads in an Old Web: South of the Tiergarten

As a bold step in reknitting the fabric of Berlin, we suggest linking Kurfürstendamm with Alexanderplatz via a grand avenue along the south edge of the Tiergarten. The new connection would provide not only a physical link but also a civic artery steeped in historical significance.

Curving north toward the Brandenburg Gate and Unter den Linden, the avenue should acknowledge the ghost of Potsdamer Platz and Leipziger Platz while integrating with the older Berlin of cultural, institutional, and civic importance. It should be an auspicious vehicular and pedestrian route lined by buildings that look onto the park, with residential enclaves between the civic and institutional buildings. This planning approach would reestablish a continuity and create a bridge among various architectural spaces, historical and political eras, and functional zones.

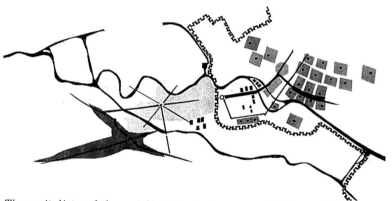

The capitalist and the socialist cities before removal of the wall

Berlin's Public Spine

Removing the Wall at the Brandenburg Gate will reunite the spine of parks and institutions that runs from the Tiergarten in the west through the Brandenburg Gate to Unter den Linden and the Stalinallee. This was the fame of prewar Berlin.

The main axis through the Tiergarten is probably safe from destruction owing to its location, but the fate of Unter den Linden is less assured. Through whatever forces of history, this is one of the few institutional streets in Europe that does not have a major commercial component. We feel it should remain that way.

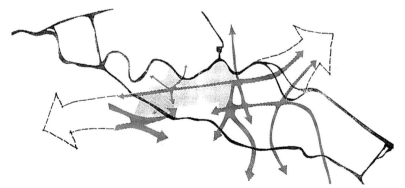

Growth trends for the period following the removal of the wall

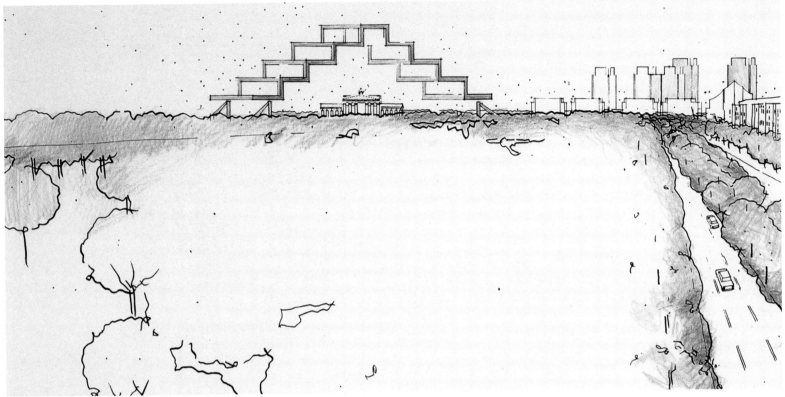

Proposed Brandenburg Stair monument

Brandenburg Stair

This is perhaps the most symbolic location for the removal of the Wall. Here, where no building should be, we have recommended a second gateway to link east and west, old and new. The structure itself is raised above eye level to permit the Brandenburg Gate to maintain its own spiritual and symbolic function.

The symbol expresses bridging, coming together, surmounting problems. It spans the Brandenburg Gate, reinforcing the passage through at the pedestrian level and over at the gestural level. A structural tour de force rather than an elegant structure, the bridge-as-stairs is an immediate, memorable image—explicit, joyous, and beautiful.

Principals in charge:
Denise Scott Brown, Robert Venturi
Project managers: Nancy Rogo Trainer,
Steven Wiesenthal
With: David Schaaf

3 Battery Park City
North Neighborhood Plan

New York, New York, 1992–1993

On the Hudson, near Manhattan's southern tip, Battery Park City is one of the world's great urban opportunities. The Battery Park City Authority asked VSBA to reexamine aspects of its North Neighborhood Plan, considering land use, architectural character, zoning, and possible uses for specific sites.

Working within the overall master plan, we considered the height and massing of buildings to preserve views from the river edge; relationships between development and the park at the western edge of the project; transitions from commercial to residential areas; and use of New York City references, specifically Riverside Drive, for Battery Park City's riverfront buildings.

Working at several scales, we discussed options for subareas and individual blocks, defining possible patterns of land use circulation, building massing, and open space for residential and commercial areas and, suggesting their relation, to lower Manhattan, the riverfront, and North Park.

Principal in charge:
Denise Scott Brown
Project architect: John Forney
With: Robert Venturi, Catherine Bird,
Jason Brody, Stephanie Christoff,
Douglas Hassebroek, Michael
Haverland, Steven Izenour,
Susan Lockwood, Amy Noble,
David Rosenberg, David Vaughan
In association with:
Anderson/Schwartz Architects

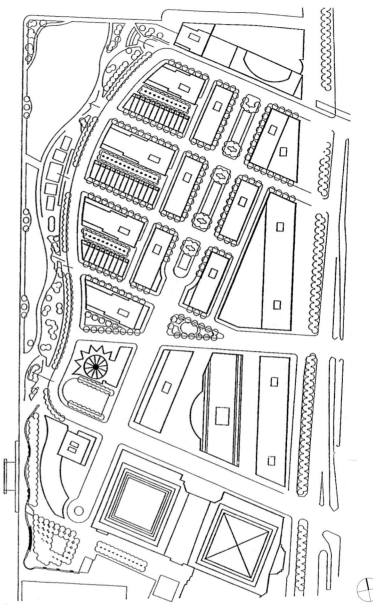

Proposed VSBA scheme for River Terrace

View of Battery Park City from the northwest about 1980

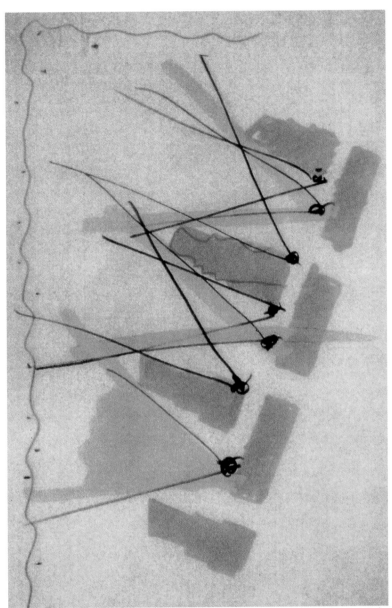

Study of the views from the proposed towers

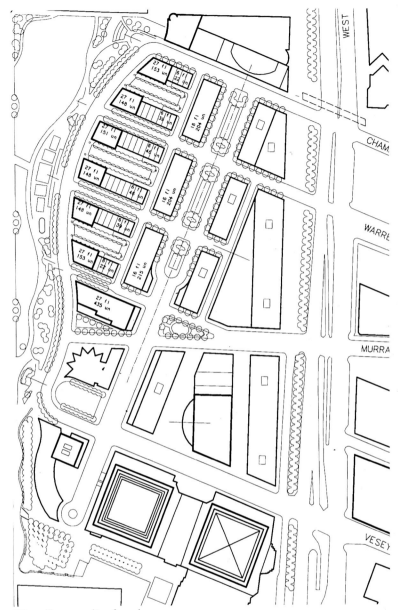

River Terrace site plan A

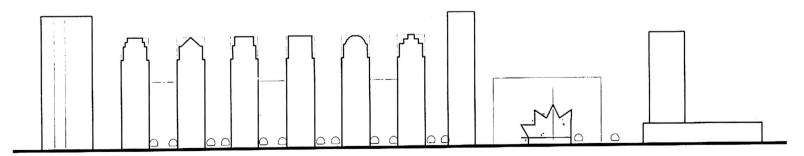

Study of building heights according to Site Plan A

4 Houston Museum of Fine Arts
Master Plan

Houston, Texas, 1989–1990

The planning process for the five-block Houston Museum of Fine Arts complex required VSBA to play these roles: as urban planners, we represented the institution's requirements before city agencies; as urban designers, we defined a civic realm and the experience of city inhabitants and visitors within such a realm, and handled zoning and aesthetic review issues; and as architects, we programmed uses, arranged spaces and circulation sequences, analyzed regulatory codes, and proposed preservation and aesthetic requirements.

The museum lies between several urban centers and precincts, on and near important arterial and throughway routes. The main museum building, including the Mies van der Rohe addition, contains about 110,000 square feet of space. The plan was to double the museum's area, strengthen its identity and image, and create a public sector within a coherent museum campus. The plan would include landscaped pedestrian sequences leading to the museum's front entrances, opportunities for safe and convenient parking, and appropriate signage.

VSBA examined several options for development and recommended the "inflected" option. This would create new buildings on two blocks east of the existing museum, linking these to the curve-fronted Mies addition by a sweep of facades placed not quite parallel to the city grid. The nonrectilinear, inflected geometry of the campus's three major buildings suggested a civic rather than a commercial identity and reinforced Bissonnet Street as a civic cross-axis to Main Street.

Principal in charge:
Denise Scott Brown
Project managers: Nancy Rogo Trainer, Malcolm Woollen
With: Robert Venturi, Catherine Bird, James Bradberry, Michael Haverland, Timothy Kearney, Adam Meyers, David Schaaf, Kenneth Wood

Proposed museum additions along Binz Street in the "inflected" option with Mies van der Rohe building (far right on facing page)

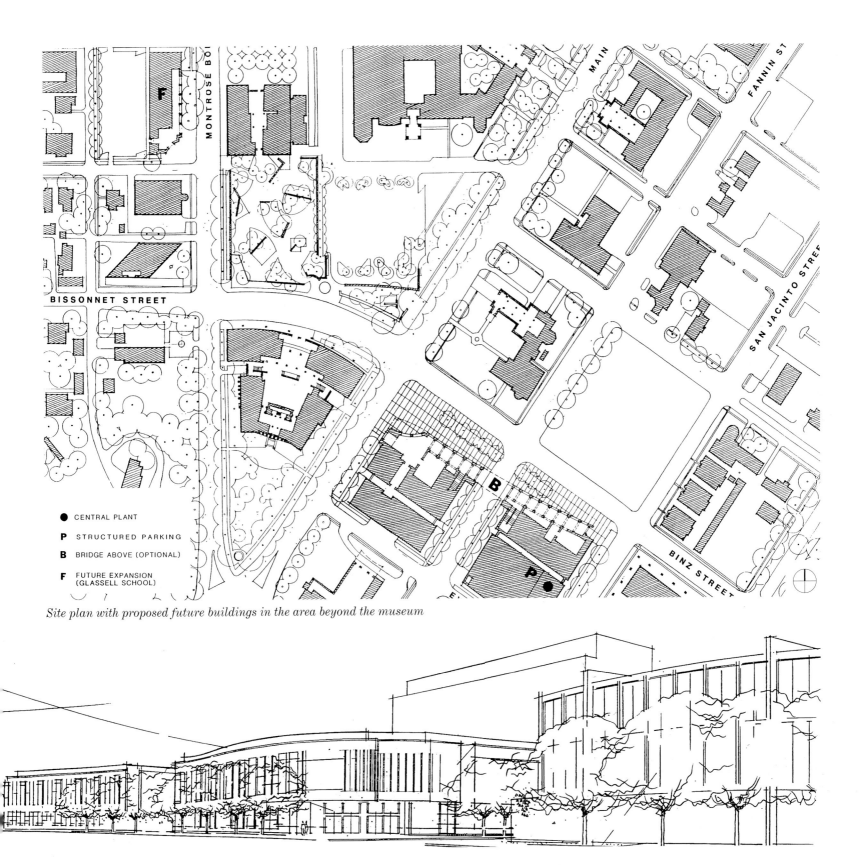

Site plan with proposed future buildings in the area beyond the museum

CENTRAL PLANT

P STRUCTURED PARKING

B BRIDGE ABOVE (OPTIONAL)

F FUTURE EXPANSION
   (GLASSELL SCHOOL)

5 Denver Civic Center
Cultural Complex

Denver, Colorado, 1991–1995

The Denver Art Museum, Public Library, and Colorado Historical Society at the southern perimeter of the Civic Center form the hub of several overlaid patterns, urban and architectural, cultural and symbolic, at the edge of the downtown.

The institutions commissioned VSBA to help plan a cohesive, memorable, and accessible Civic Center Cultural Complex with members sharing collections and programs, a common landscape, and possibly future facilities. The concept plan defined a joint vision of a new Center for Western American Culture.

The primary focus was on two city-owned blocks directly south of the complex, but the study also considered the role of the institutions regionally and city-wide and made proposals for the development of surrounding neighborhoods and the downtown to support the cultural complex. Recommendations included an arc-shaped urban forecourt, which would embrace the three institutions and, through its curve, contrast with the rectilinear Denver city grid, thus suggesting that three blocks of Thirteenth Avenue are civic rather than commercial.

The first increment of the plan shows trees and obelisk-like verticals that define points along the Arc. These stand on their own as civic sculpture but can also act as foreground for future buildings. Although widely spaced, they are strong enough to define the forecourt as the first shared identity of the cultural complex. Seen obliquely from Thirteenth Avenue, the separate verticals overlap to suggest a curved and filigreed screen, with a delicacy and transparency that do not obstruct views of the mountains or city.

Phase I
Principal in charge:
Denise Scott Brown
Project manager: Nancy Rogo Trainer
With: Robert Venturi, Brian LaBau,
Felisa Opper
In association with: DHM, Inc.; Planners, etc.; Robert L. Morris, Inc.
Phase II
Principal in charge:
Denise Scott Brown
Project manager: John Bastian
With: Robert Venturi, Jason Brody,
Amy Noble, Felisa Opper
In association with:
Pouw & Associates, Inc.

The location of the cultural complex in the city and the greater metropolitan area

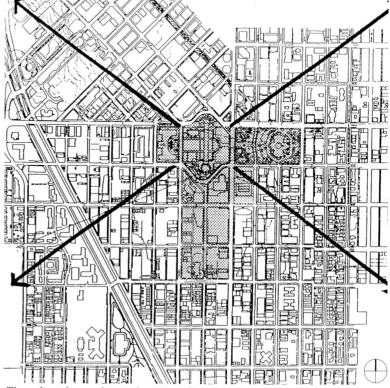

The cultural complex and surrounding neighborhood

Proposed differentiation of function in the center of Denver (blue is institutional; red is commercial; yellow is residential; orange is administration)

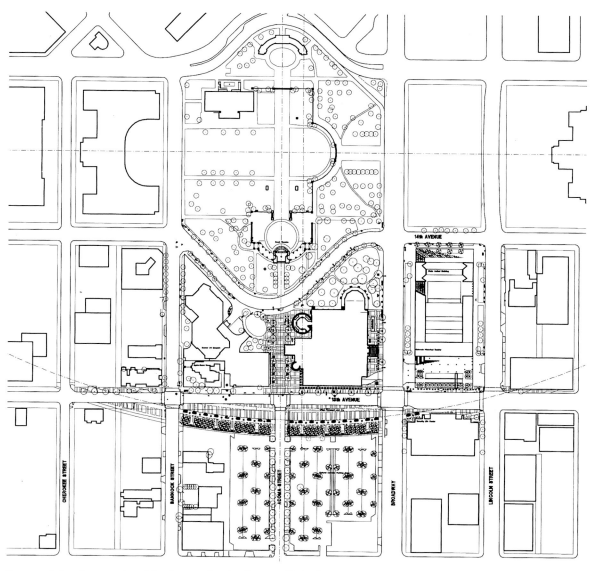

Proposed Arc forecourt and landscape for the Denver Civic Center Cultural Complex

Views of existing Denver Civic Center

Perspective view looking west with proposed Arc forecourt and existing library building (by Michael Graves)

6 Columbus Gateway Study

Columbus, Indiana, 1991–1993

The Columbus Gateway Study was a federal demonstration project for the design of a new entrance to the city of Columbus, Indiana. Like most small cities located just off the interstate highway system, Columbus needs to identify itself from the outside and to attract the driver-by into the city.

In defining ranges of graphic, lighting, and landscape options for Route 46 and Interstate 65, the challenge was to find a way to project a civic image within the traditional commercial context of a Holiday Inn, a McDonald's, and a Shell gasoline station at the edge of town. Finding a workable and effective solution to this problem was considered important, not only in the context of our work but by the federal agencies involved, for the continuing economic health of Main Street America. It was appropriate that the designs proposed be generic and applicable to other cities across the United States.

Part of our proposal included a series of street lights along the median strip of the road leading to the town from the federal highway that were themselves conventional in their design but unconventional in their varicolored surfaces and their rhythmic sequence. Seen obliquely from a moving car, these objects would create an animated rainbow—both during the day and, via carefully adjusted lighting, at night.

Principal in charge: Steven Izenour, Robert Venturi
Project manager: Timothy Kearney
With: Denise Scott Brown, Michael Haverland
In association with: Pflum, Klausmeier & Gehrum Consultants; Woolpert; Michael Van Valkenburgh and Associates, Inc.; Storrow Kinsella Partnership, Inc.

Overall plan of western entrance to Columbus with project areas indicated

Western commercial area by night (photomontage)

Proposed gateway

7 Perris Civic Center
Competition

Perris, California, 1991

The competition design for the center of Perris, California, derives from the traditional American urban grid plan, which accommodates and celebrates the pragmatic and egalitarian ideals characteristic of the United States. In the landscape of the Perris Civic Center an urban grid is abstracted, by reducing the scale, and symbolized, by making of it an urban garden.

The existing historic, architectural, and natural elements (buildings and trees) on the site have been maintained so that they act as counterpoints and exceptions within the grid. The Civic Center grid is indeterminate at the edges as it meets the grid of the city: it is independent in its relation to the buildings on the site. A profusion of boulders of another age (in erratic configurations characteristically found in the valley beyond the town) juxtaposes itself upon the almost miniature-scale grid pattern, which is itself defined by a parterre of varying plants and paving. This kind of landscape permits easy circulation for pedestrians and, where appropriate, vehicles within its grid throughout the site. The large central gathering space is demarcated by subtle material changes that follow the grid pattern, but it functions as one uninterrupted level area.

View of model

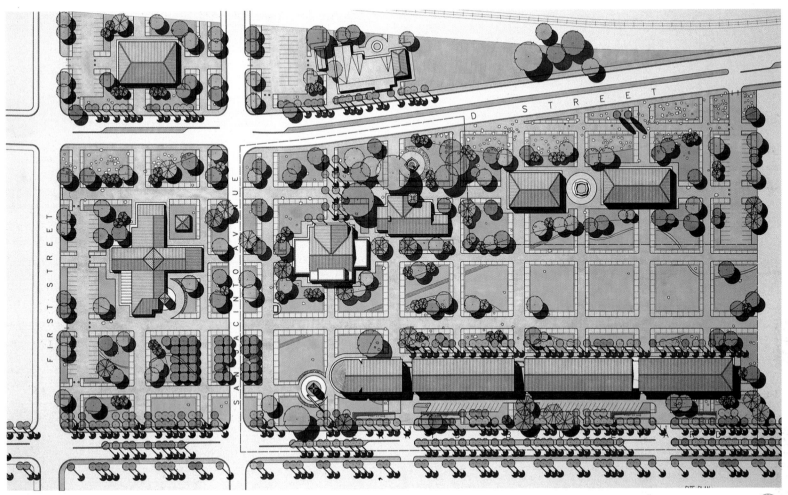

Site plan

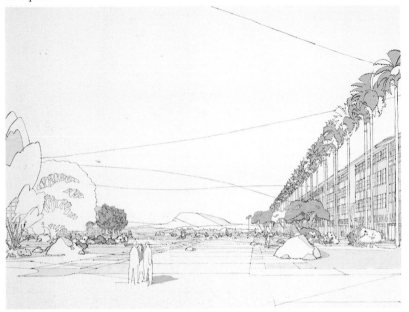

Perspective view looking west to public plaza through Civic Center entrance

Principals in charge:
Robert Venturi, Steven Izenour
Project managers: Ian Adamson,
John Forney
With: Denise Scott Brown
In association with:
Anderson/Schwartz Architects; Quennel Rothschild Associates

8 Gateway Visitor Center and Independence Mall

Planning for Independence National Historic Park

Philadelphia, Pennsylvania, 1996

One challenge of the planning project for the Gateway Visitor Center and Independence Hall was to rectify the architectural, urban, and symbolic debasement inflicted forty years ago on Philadelphia's historical Independence Hall precinct— the demeaning, perceptual and symbolic, of Independence Hall by patriotically souping up its delicate urban context and the deadening, perceptual and actual, of its urban setting via pretentious city-planning impositions. In its new context, the original modest Georgian hall became an inadequate baroque palace pathetically terminating a pompous Beaux-Arts axis called the Mall, a Versailles-on-the-Delaware, whose spatial dimensions exceed those of Trafalgar Square and the piazza of St. Peter's. And the urban fabric became a vacuous Ville Radieuse, symbolically a postwar bomb site tarted up with landscaping. What an irony—a heroic Ville Radieuse and an autocratic baroque axis imposed upon the prototypical American gridiron city plan of Philadelphia, created by William Penn (not a Roi Soleil) as explicitly nonhierarchical and egalitarian in its content and effect, its order sublimely combining variety with unity!

The project involved a redesign of the urban fabric as a revived context within this historical precinct and the design of a new visitor center appropriate in location and architectural quality to Independence Hall—a State House in a Quaker city whose Georgian detail should be approached obliquely from close up along a street rather than frontally from a distance as the termination of an axis.

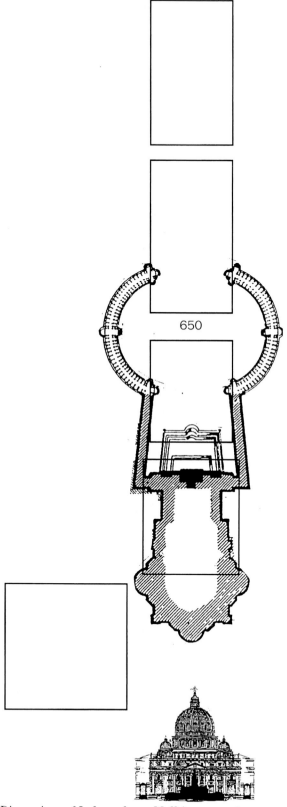

Dimensions of Independence Mall in comparison to the piazza of St. Peter's in Rome

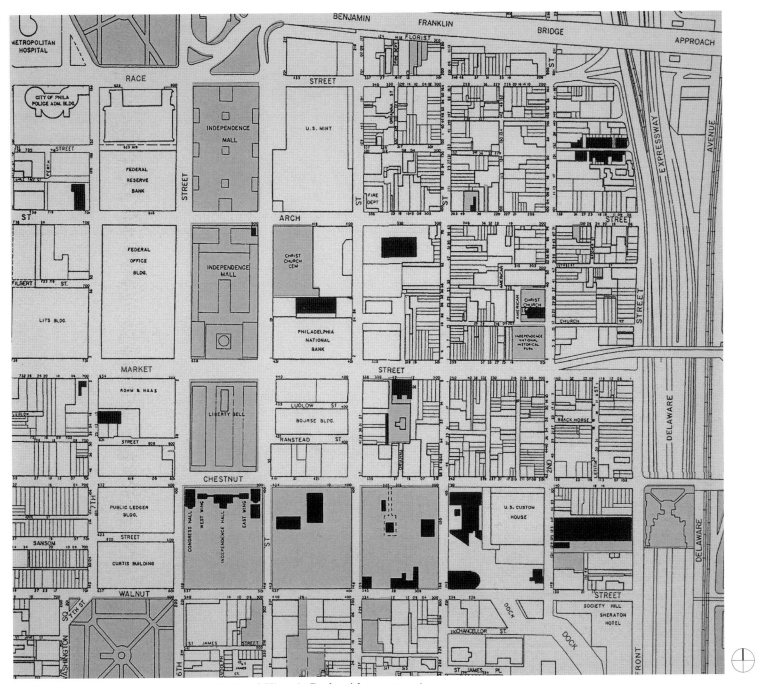

Independence Mall and Independence National Historic Park, with monuments

Principals in charge:
Denise Scott Brown, Robert Venturi
Associate in charge:
Daniel McCoubrey
Project manager: Heather Clark
With: Diane Golomb, Nathalie Peeters

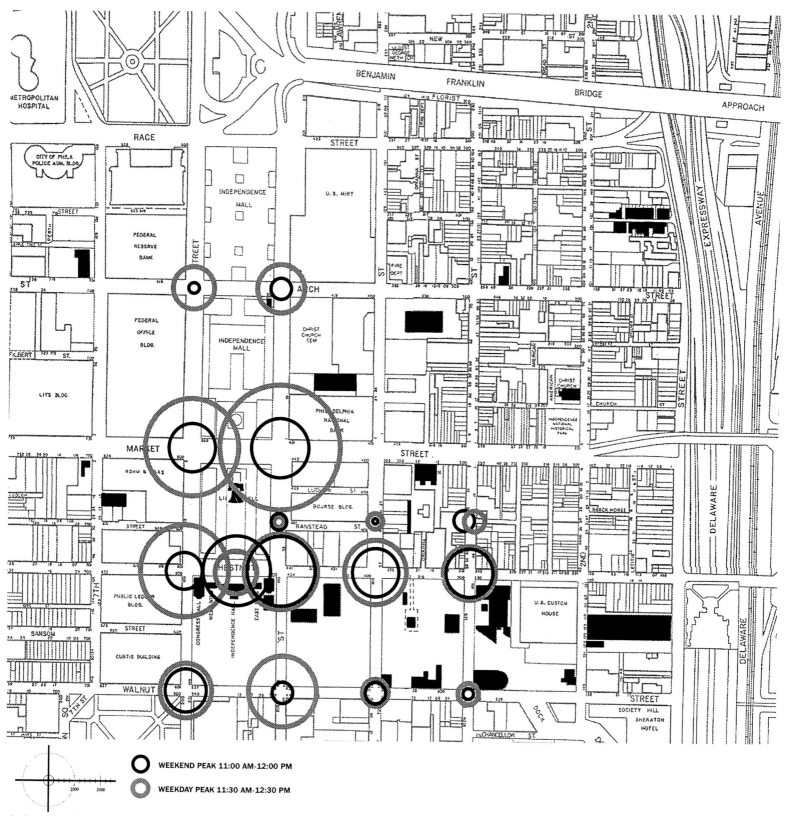

Pedestrian circulation densities in Independence Mall

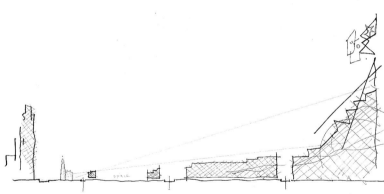

Proposed infill of Independence Mall (drawing by Robert Venturi)

Jumbotron and Historic Context

Our conceptual designs were preceded by an analysis that surveyed original intentions and design alternatives for the future and considered existing urban conditions, including land use, vehicular and pedestrian circulation, and regional urban influences, that would act as realistic and inspiring determinants within the ultimate design process.

The Gateway Visitor Center on the south side of Market Street presents an eighteenth-century-scale facade toward the south, defining a modest square to accommodate "first amendment activities" before Independence Hall. The north facade's twentieth-century scale and its length help reinforce spatial and retail continuity along Market Street. Across the road, vertical pylons, seen obliquely by pedestrians or passengers, create a perceptual solid, thereby maintaining the directional and spatial quality of the street. Spaces between the pylons form civic niches suitable for outdoor exhibitions.

Inside, the visitor center combines layers or zones of generic parallel spaces. The north layer is an open covered arcade behind which is a grand glassed-in gallery containing a large mural in its vault—an urban Jumbotron billboard, seen from Market Street through the arcade, that in its LED screen recalls the tesserae of Byzantine mosaic murals but that has changing pixel images, ornamental and informational, that create memorable twentieth-century-scale iconographics for day and night. A southern layer contains secondary spaces and, behind, a small-scale arcade facing Independence Hall. Across these layers, at the center of the block, is a cross-axis containing and proclaiming the Liberty Bell.

One block north, the former Independence Mall is filled with twentieth-century-scale uses—parking garages, tourist drop-off and waiting areas for buses, and a proposed Constitution Center building. North of that, the third mall block is reserved for further development—presumably for denser, larger uses at a

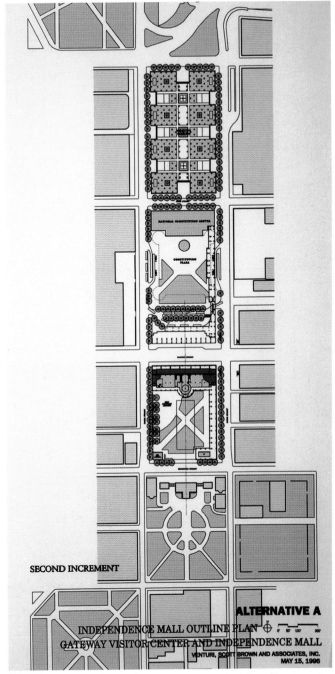

Independence Mall with proposed Gateway Visitor Center

Proposed glassed gallery with LED screen (sketch by Robert Venturi)

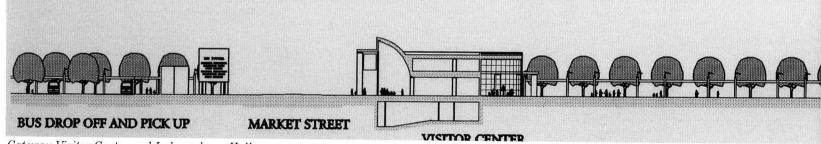

BUS DROP OFF AND PICK UP   MARKET STREET   VISITOR CENTER

Gateway Visitor Center and Independence Hall

twenty-first-century scale, whose imagery will be seen from the Benjamin Franklin Bridge as one enters the city by car. So both sensibility and scale go from eighteenth to twentieth to twenty-first century as one moves north.

This design reinforces the spatial and retail continuity of Market Street east and west and also helps to define Fifth and Sixth Streets north and south by infilling the mall with cityscape. Fifth Street, in particular, can be narrowed once again to its original dimension, because tourist and school buses will drop off within the mall and then move out. Urban retail activity can return to both sides of this street in existing buildings and in exterior stalls that will teem with things appealing to American and foreign consumers (such stalls characterize pilgrims' ways to shrines worldwide). The original architect of the mall, it is said, was humiliated to find a hotdog stand across from Independence Hall. We hope for many such stands to grace and enliven a real urban context for our national shrine.

Unfortunately, few shared our views on the extent to which the mall and the Independence Hall area should be redensified, and a design alternative that we had recommended against was chosen.

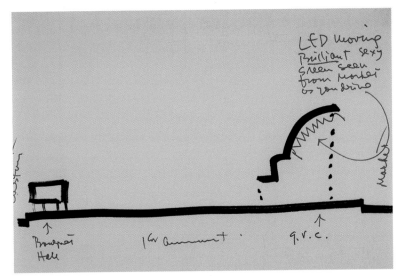

Proposed glassed gallery with LED screen (sketch by Robert Venturi)

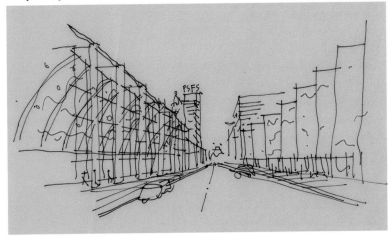

View of Market Street toward PSFS building and City Hall, with proposed Gateway Visitor Center to the left

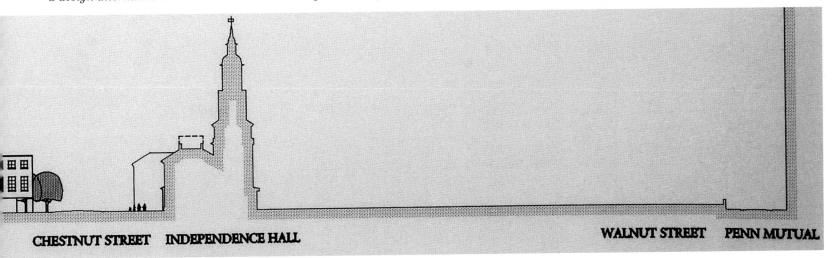

CHESTNUT STREET   INDEPENDENCE HALL   **WALNUT STREET   PENN MUTUAL**

9 Dartmouth College Campus
Concept Plan for Extension

Hanover, New Hampshire, 1989–1993

When Dartmouth College acquired the former Mary Hitchcock Memorial Hospital and medical school site and facilities directly north of the present campus, the size of the complex brought into question the future nature of an institution that has stoutly maintained its status as a college. What would become of the college if it inherited scientific buildings in such large number?

The concept plan approached a spectrum of concerns ranging from long-term academic goals to problems of snow removal. Although the plan is intended to help shape the campus for the next two to three decades, its first built increment could, if strong, permanently affect the Dartmouth ethos and guide the growth of the campus over the next hundred years.

"Learning from Dartmouth"

After an analysis of the college's educational goals and growth potential, a study of the capacity of its land and buildings, and a survey of its architecture and landscape, we proposed several alternative plans based on different assessments of the college's options and aspirations. The alternative chosen by Dartmouth established the new area for primarily academic growth. Some administrative functions could be decentralized into smaller, older hospital buildings at the perimeter of the site, but the major part of the newly available land was planned to take care of Dartmouth's academic, departmental, and classroom growth for the foreseeable future, the first uses being psychology and a large north extension for Baker Library.

Our study suggested principles to guide the growth of the new complex. Although New Hampshire is rural, Dartmouth is in a small New England town; its famous Green, the college's major symbol, was once the town commons. Dartmouth's earliest buildings, including Dartmouth Hall, are located directly opposite the Green to the east. This first building group established the major identity of the college and its lifelong relation to the Green. In the 1920s, Baker Library was sited at the northern edge of the Green, reorienting the campus complex and suggesting a second major identity. A third large addition, behind Baker Library, would define one more identity.

Another theme at Dartmouth was the immediacy of wilderness. The town is urban but wooded hills and a harsh climate suggest the nearness of wild land, which, in fact, penetrates the campus, almost reaching the Green. Wild landscape and cold weather have given the

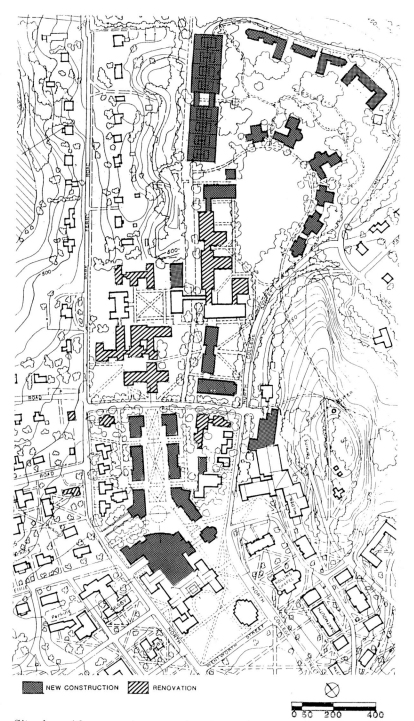

NEW CONSTRUCTION   RENOVATION

0 50 200 400

Site plan with proposed new construction and renovation

Front lawn on the Green

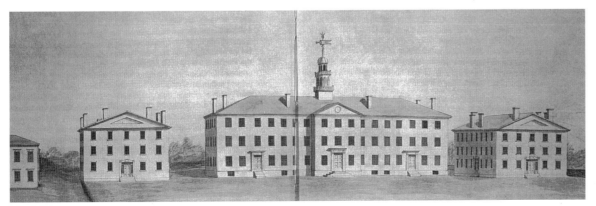

Nineteenth-century view of Dartmouth College buildings

Principal in charge:
Denise Scott Brown
Project managers: Malcolm Woollen,
Daniel McCoubrey
With: Michael Peters, David Schaaf,
Steven Wiesenthal

Quadrangle with proposed new structures looking south toward proposed Baker Library extension

Dartmouth community a strong outdoor ethos and a penchant for skiing. Nevertheless, the faculty want their automobiles beside their classrooms, citing the long cold winters as the reason, and the administration suggests that most activities on campus be kept within a ten-minute walking distance of each other.

Existing buildings at Dartmouth provided important input to the plan. The earliest were generous relatively wide structures in plan, with gracefully spaced windows and structural rhythms suitable for varied uses over the years. These generic, loftlike buildings, lightly ornamented to suggest their academic purpose, seemed useful models for the design of new classroom and department buildings on campus.

On either side of College and Main Streets, grassy, treed areas and their bordering buildings defined another memorable element of the Dartmouth image. In particular, the block north of (that is, behind) Baker Library, the first site for expansion, was edged with separate, small-town buildings and contained at its center the remains of a declivity that had once run diagonally across the campus. We recommended that major academic growth for the foreseeable future be handled by a new quadrangle set in this block. This would be a workaday place. Along it would be simple, mainly brick buildings, with openings onto the quadrangle. The order of their building should be related to campus priorities. At the southern end of the quadrangle would be a major extension to Baker Library. The northern end would be open to the land of the former medical school.

A four-story height limit would be mandated, but a setback of all buildings at the third story would be encouraged to help maintain the existing Dartmouth character of moderately low, sturdy buildings. As a model for these buildings we suggested our addition to the western end of the Thayer Building on the campus. By keeping its width relatively narrow (120 feet across), the whole quadrangle could be built within the center of the block; existing buildings and views west and east would not be disturbed. Pedestrians would walk northward along College and Main Streets to reach the quadrangle. The first building of the quadrangle, the psychology building at its northwest edge, is the first project to follow the guidelines of the plan. We are working on the extension of the library, the centerpiece of the new quadrangle, and on a plan to convert Webster Hall, on the Green, to a special-collections library (see pp. 256–58).

10 Princeton Train Station Gateway
Gateway for Princeton University Campus

Princeton, New Jersey, 1995

The objective of the Princeton Train Station Gateway project is to restore and renovate the existing Princeton railroad station buildings and to renew the area they dominate via urban, architectural, lighting, and landscape design. The place is to become an explicit gateway—formal and symbolic—to the university, acknowledging civic as well as institutional character.

The "book" works as a sculptural sign and a symbolic image—a means of identifying this place from afar and close-up. Other elements of the design include a bold sign announcing Princeton University above the existing station canopy; the enhancement of the historic fabric of the station buildings via renovation and restoration; ground-plane improvements, including new and varied paving; a new stairway that via its curved plan reinforces a sense of connection to the campus; and a series of light poles that direct circulation paths.

Law and Freedom
Campus planning at Princeton has historically combined, balanced, and integrated two approaches that can be distinctly defined. The first is characterized by the original Nassau Hall complex of buildings, which projects unifying axes and balancing symmetry among Classical forms as points in space; the second is characterized by the Holder-Hamilton Hall complex, where picturesque and continuous form directs and encloses space and is perceived as evolving over time.

Both ways are dear to Princetonians since they richly acknowledge and tensely juxtapose the ideal and the pragmatic, the Classical and the Romantic, the formal and the picturesque. But it is important to note and remember that the various combinations of these two distinct ways in the history of the overall planning of the Princeton campus have been pragmatically rather than

Principal in charge: Robert Venturi
Project manager: James Wallace
Project architect: Mindy No
With: Diane Golomb, Timothy Mock, Karen Pollock

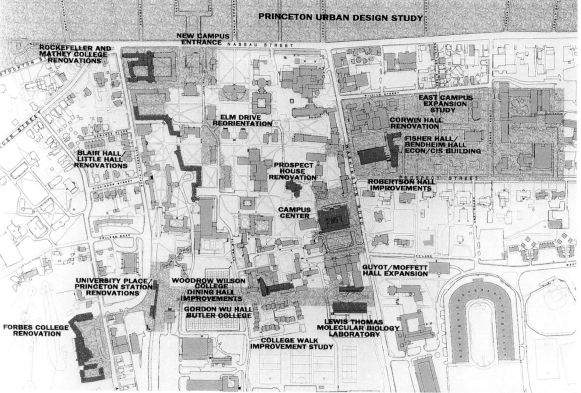

Site plan of the Princeton campus, with VSBA projects in red

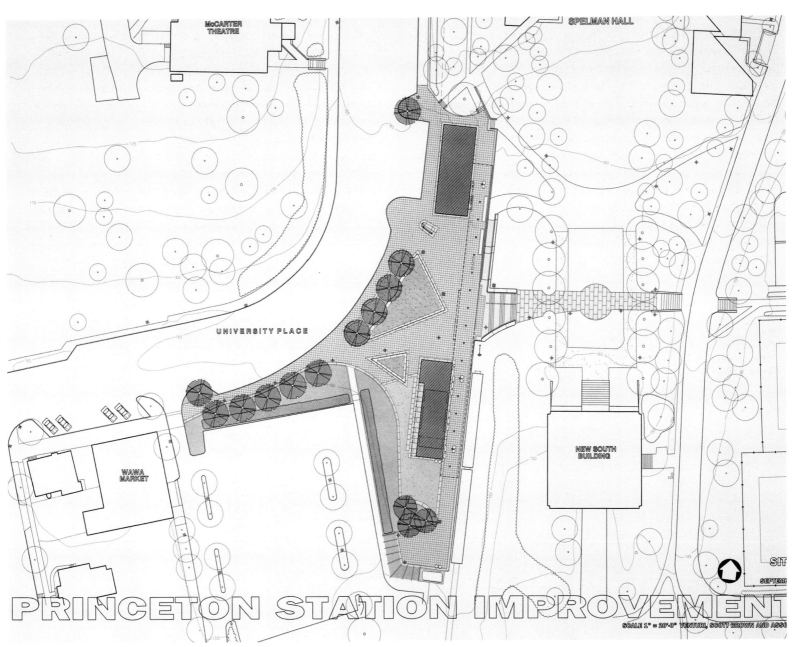

Site plan of train station

General view of Princeton Campus about 1920

grandiosely directed. Does this make of the campus plan a kind of incomplete and therefore ironical whole at any one time?[1]

The architectural-urban relationship between town and gown at Princeton has also evolved over time. The original relationship represented—perhaps established—the classic American configuration in which the college and town are explicitly identifiable and distinctly separate. In this paradigm Main Street, or Nassau Street, was poignantly urban-commercial on one side and rural-institutional on the other—a form of segregation often certified by a ceremonial gate to the campus. Currently this distinction between town and gown is diminishing physically and symbolically, and boundaries are becoming ambiguous. For example, Forbes College is in a former inn separated from the central campus by a regional convenience chain store (Wawa), a regional theater (McCarter), and the train shuttle itself. The design of the station complex, which is both on- and off-campus, works in a parallel way as it combines various and complex combinations of connections, uses, forms, and symbols—institutional and civic.

The idea of the gateway has various precedents at Princeton: the explicit Fitz-Randolf Gate on Nassau Street and the gateway to McCosh Walk on Washington Road; the Gothic Revival arches at Holder, Hamilton, and '79 Halls. Both kinds of gateway explicitly mark the boundary of the campus and celebrate an entrance. Blair Arch, the most imposing entrance of all—considered as an aesthetic

part of its original context—represents in one way the most relevant precedent for the Princeton Station entrance.

The foreground of the grandly Gothic arch was originally dominated by the then Princeton Station, thus creating an immediate juxtaposition between new and old—the realistic railroad-industrial and the stylized monastic-medieval—that, as illustrated in old photos, is dynamic and poignant. Because the idea of boundary is diminished in our new complex, the picturesque sense of place and the implicit expressions of direction derive from explicit signs rather than from a functional and symbolic arch-as-gate. Jean Labatut referred to a "maximum of effect with a minimum of means." This is what we are attempting to achieve—literally (cost-wise) and figuratively (aesthetics-wise)—while creating a complex, rich, and ambiguous effect appropriate for a late-twentieth-century place that connects, or even merges, university and community.

1. Ralph Adams Cram said, in a talk to alumni in 1908: "One of the most essential elements in all education is that the students should feel themselves surrounded . . . by definite . . . law, from which there is, however, a way out into the broadest and highest freedom. This must absolutely be shown in the material form of the university." Quoted in Donald Drew Egbert, *The Architecture and the Setting*, (Princeton, N.J.: Princeton University Press, 1947).

Princeton Station with "book"

SIGN ELEVATION

View of Princeton Train Station from parking lot

11 Perelman Quadrangle
Campus and Architectural Plan for a Student Center,
University of Pennsylvania

Philadelphia, Pennsylvania, 1995–

The University of Pennsylvania's Houston Hall was the first student union constructed in America. The late-nineteenth-century building, set adjacent to College and Logan Halls and across from the dormitories on Spruce Street, complemented the academic, administrative, and residential functions of the university; but as the campus expanded, this student-centered coherence was lost. In choosing Penn's historic heart as the site of the Perelman Quadrangle, the university is restoring and adapting its most loved and best remembered buildings to define a new center that is a precinct rather than a palace.

The concept evolved during a series of master-planning studies by VSBA. The functions of the student center are expanded beyond Houston Hall, across its adjoining plaza (redesigned as Wynn Commons), into College, Williams, and Logan Halls and Irvine Auditorium. This Perelman Quadrangle will reestablish the importance the student union once held. Wynn Commons, lined by Collegiate Gothic and High Victorian buildings set with shade trees and enriched with seating, signs, and her-

aldry, will provide a sense of arrival, place, and enclosure as the quadrangle entrance. Gateway markers will announce the quadrangle within the campus. An amphitheater and rostrum at opposite ends of the commons and low walls at the edges will complement new building entries and encourage gathering and sitting. Inscriptions, images, and applied pattern will add further interest.

Inside, the buildings will be restored to their former grandeur. Houston Hall will remain the focal point of the student-center community. Irvine Auditorium will be adapted and restored as a performance hall with capacities ranging from 400 to 1,200 seats. College Hall's commons entrance, sealed for decades, will be reopened to focus the Office of Admissions onto the commons, making Perelman Quadrangle the first destination of many prospective students. Heavily used spaces, including student art galleries, auditoriums, coffee shops, meeting rooms, and twenty-four-hour study lounges, are planned for the ground level on or near Wynn Commons.

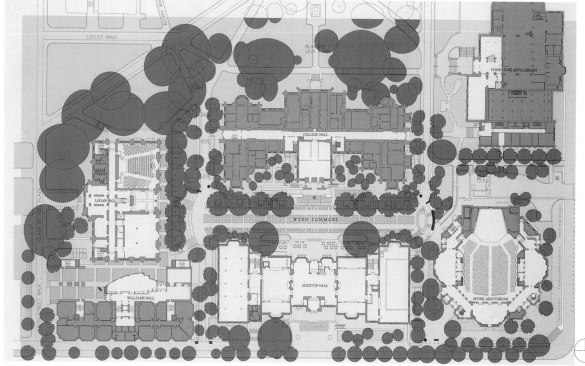

Site plan

Perspective looking east

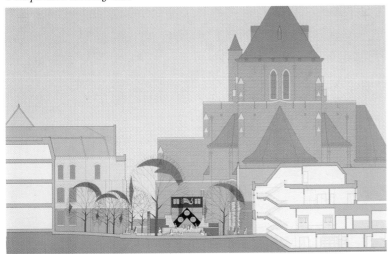

Section through Wynn Commons and Houston Hall

Master Planning, Programming, and Preliminary Design Phase
Principal in charge:
Denise Scott Brown
Project manager: David Marohn
With: Stephanie Christoff, Ronald Evitts, Elizabeth Hitchcock, Agatha Hughes, Susan Lockwood, Meredith McCree, Mark Stankard, Joy Yoder

Design Phase
Principals in charge: Robert Venturi, Denise Scott Brown
Project manager: John Hunter
Project architects: John Hunter, Susan Lockwood, Richard Stokes, Jon Wagner

With: Hideano Abe, Courtney Anspach, John Bastian, Stephanie Chistoff, Ronald Evitts, Eliabeth Hitchcock, Jake Hokanson, Kathleen Kulpa, James Liebman, Jeffrey Lewis, Adam Meyers, Timothy Mock, Julie Munzner, Mindy No, Felisa Opper, Eric Oskey, Cynthia Padilla, Ahmed Patash, Matthew Seltzer, Andrew Thurlow, Howard Traub, Kenneth Wood, Jeffrey Wyant, Aaron Young

12 Bryn Mawr College Concept Plan

Bryn Mawr, Pennsylvania, 1996–1997

Bryn Mawr College's campus core was shaped by Calvert Vaux, Frederick Law Olmsted, Ralph Adams Cram, Cope and Stewardson, Louis Kahn, and others. The orthogonal patterns of the landmark Collegiate Gothic early campus are set in beautiful contrast with the undulating topography of the Romantic valley landscape to the west. Outside its planned core, the college has grown incrementally by annexing former private residences across peripheral streets. Over time, patterns of use, circulation, and entrance on campus have shifted out of line with each other and with the college's changing needs and expanded boundaries.

VSBA's concept plan outlines several ways of considering the physical character and development of the campus, then suggests principles and strategies to help realign present patterns with present and future needs. Recommendations for meeting near-term goals are related to long-range options. Possible first increments of development include new campus gateways outside the traditional core. The recommendations attempt to make these first projects compatible in spirit and scale with the delicate, loosely woven landscape of the campus *fuori le mura*.

Sixteenth-century map of Bruges, Flanders showing dense core and less developed fuori le mura

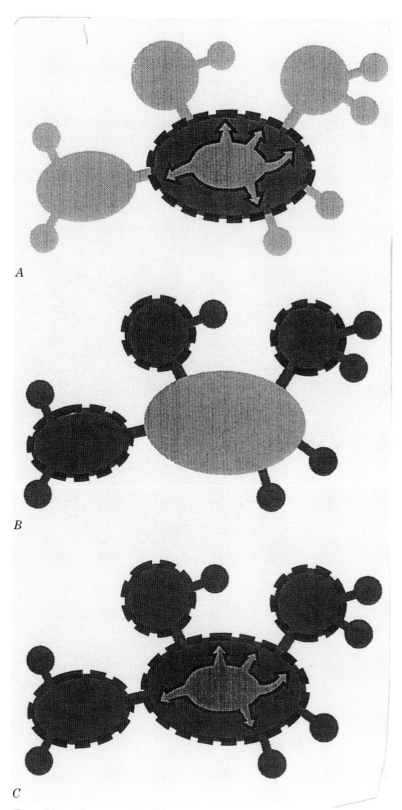

A

B

C

Bryn Mawr Campus. Possible strategies for physical development: consolidation at the core (A), emphasis on satellites (B), emphasis on core and satellites (C)

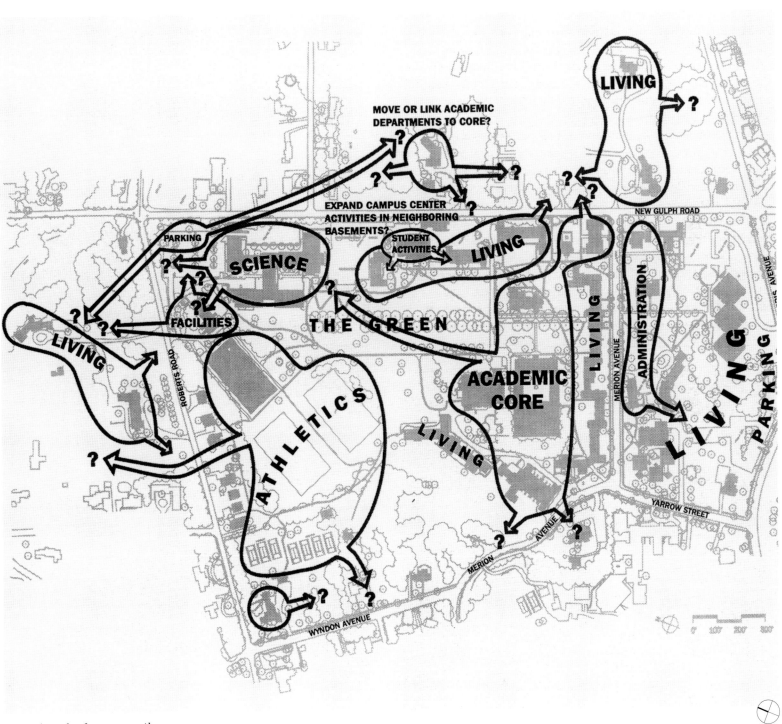

Principal in charge:
Denise Scott Brown
Project manager: Nancy Rogo Trainer
With: Robert Venturi, Linna Choi,
Stephanie Christoff, Jeffrey Lewis,
Matthew Seltzer

LIVING

?

MOVE OR LINK ACADEMIC
DEPARTMENTS TO CORE?

?

?

?

?

?

?

?

NEW GULPH ROAD

EXPAND CAMPUS CENTER
ACTIVITIES IN NEIGHBORING
BASEMENTS?

PARKING

STUDENT
ACTIVITIES

SCIENCE

LIVING

?

?

LIVING

?

?

?

FACILITIES

THE GREEN

?

MERION AVENUE

ADMINISTRATION

LIVING

PARKING

ROBERTS ROAD

ATHLETICS

ACADEMIC
CORE

LIVING

LIVING

?

?

YARROW STREET

?

MERION

AVENUE

?

?

?

WYNDON AVENUE

Directions for future growth

13 Benjamin Franklin Bridge Lighting

Philadelphia, Pennsylvania, 1986–1988

Our design was the winning entry in an open competition to develop a lighting design for the Benjamin Franklin Bridge, the suspension bridge that spans the Delaware River as it connects Philadelphia and Camden, New Jersey. Unlike conventional bridge and architectural lighting, which tends to emphasize large structural elements such as piers and roadbeds, this design highlights the suspension cables themselves to create a glowing curtain of light across the river.

Inventive technology was required because a suspension bridge is mostly air with very little structure or surface to reflect light. To address this challenge, the design solution was based on techniques learned from Las Vegas signs, where there is little form or structure and where moving, animated lights attract the eye. Conventional metal halide lights, located at the base of the suspension cables for ease of maintenance, illuminate the catenary cable above. An innovative dimming circuit developed by George Izenour allows rapid on-and-off sequencing of each light, creating a sense of rapid movement and a shimmering effect from shore to shore; the lighting permutations are triggered by the frequent passages of commuter trains over the bridge.

Principal in charge: Steven Izenour
With: John Andrews, Adam Anuszkiewicz, Kairos Chen, Miles Ritter, Matthew Schottelkotte
In association with: George C. Izenour

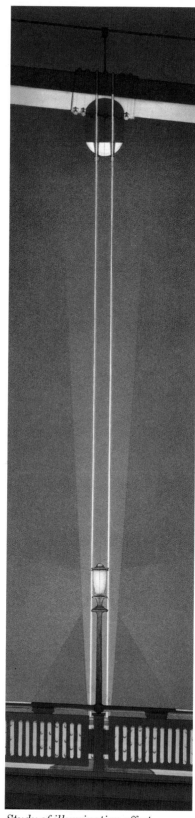

Study of illumination effect

Benjamin Franklin bridge at night

14 Christopher Columbus Monument

Philadelphia, Pennsylvania, 1988–1992

The Christopher Columbus Monument is a sculptural form that was designed to look good close-up—in the quality of its detail and its friendly scale—and to read well from a distance—in its vivid imagery and bold scale. This form also works as a symbol; it refers to the obelisk as a traditional and accepted urban device, American and Italian. But it is an obelisk in modern form, in both the lightness of its structure and materials—cantilevered stainless-steel sheets that work as diaphragms—and the light it emits between its "mortar joints," which effects a lantern at night and allows the structure to become a twenty-four-hour monument.

The base of this form and the surrounding paving are made up of granite with patterns and color inscriptions. As a monument it is virtually maintenance-free (except for the lighting) and it is pigeon-resistant. It is designed both to adapt to and to enhance its particular context along the Delaware River in Philadelphia.

Principal in charge: Robert Venturi
Project manager: Timothy Kearney
With: Ian Adamson, Steven Izenour, Maurice Weintraub, David Schaaf

Base

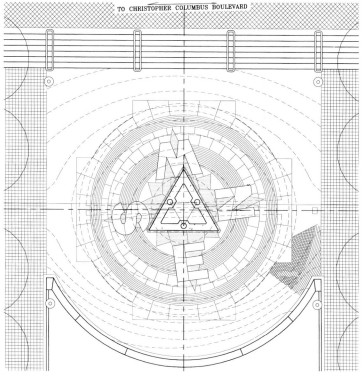

Plan

View toward Delaware River

15 National World War II Memorial
Competition Entry for a Memorial on the Mall

Washington, D.C., 1996

VSBA agreed with the designated siting of the World War II Memorial within the principal axis of the nation's capital—in line with the Capitol Building, the Washington Monument, and the Lincoln Memorial. The design does not intrude on but works within this significant configuration—by day, its iconographic-monumental wall, seen from close-up, is juxtaposed with the base of the Lincoln Memorial; at night, seen from a distance, its rays of arc lights produce a V-for-victory image at a great scale in the sky among the other important monuments.

This design acknowledges individual scale and civic scale; the former accommodates an iconographic dimension as the viewer "reads" the map of the world and the inscriptions, and the latter accommodates a symbolic dimension as the V-for-victory image is perceived as lighting. The small-scale quality is manifest via traditional masonry bas-relief, and the large-scale quality is manifest via advanced technology as projected against the sky. The monument integrates with its context via analogy in its traditional location and via contrast in its symbolism and technology.

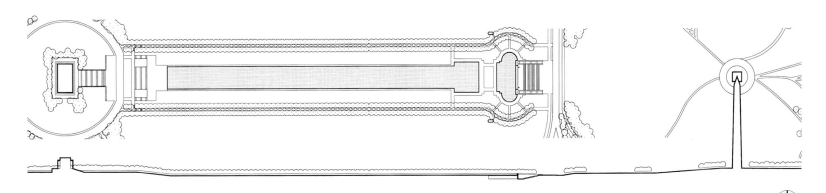

Washington Mall with proposed World War II Memorial on axis with the Lincoln Memorial

Study of lighting effect

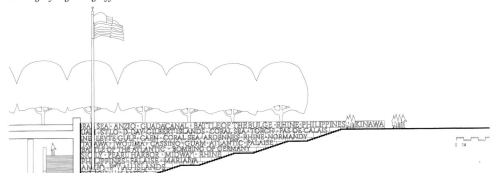

Section with masonry bas-relief

Principals in charge: Robert Venturi, Steven Izenour
Project manager: Nancy Rogo Trainer
With: Angelina Chong, Adam Meyers, Delano Shane

Early Facade Sketch, Philadelphia Orchestra Hall
R.V. '87

Graphics

Civic Buildings

122   *Sainsbury Wing*

140   *Seattle Art Museum*

148   *Children's Museum, Houston*

154   *National Museum of Scotland Addition*

156   *Peabody Essex Museum Addition*

158   *Ames Library Addition*

160   *National Museum of the American Indian*

162   *Expo '92 Pavilion*

166   *Stedelijk Museum Addition*

172   *Museum of Contemporary Art, San Diego*

178   *Junipero Serra Shrine*

180   *Whitehall Ferry Terminal*

188   *Battery Park Band Pavilion*

190   *Celebration Bank,*
       The Walt Disney Company

192   *Fire Station,*
       The Walt Disney Company

194   *Trenton Fire Station Extension*

196   *Philadelphia Orchestra Hall*

204   *Hôtel du Département de la Haute-Garonne*

210   *Berlin U.S. Embassy*

16 Sainsbury Wing
Addition to the National Gallery

London, England, 1986–1991

Built on the last open space on Trafalgar Square, the Sainsbury Wing houses one of the world's foremost collections of early Italian and Northern Renaissance paintings. Stylistically, the 120,000-square-foot wing was designed to relate to the original building (by William Wilkins, 1832–38) while maintaining its own identity as contemporary architecture. It is constructed of the same Portland limestone and observes the cornice height of the original.

Classical elements from the Wilkins facade, including its characteristic pilasters, are replicated on the new building, but they are used in new and unexpected ways, alongside elements that contrast with the older building—for example, large square-cut openings to accommodate late-twentieth-century museum attendance and small metal columns to create small-scale interest at eye level. The chief elements of the facade, especially the pilasters, create a jazzy rhythm that calms down as it evolves toward Pall Mall South. It is significant that this evolution, from the Wilkins building to the street line of Pall Mall South, is read as a kind of undulating billboard that is visually distinct from the other facades of the wing, side, and rear; thus the historical elements of the facade are expressed not as authentic but as symbolic and referential.

This "mannerist" composition of architectural elements old and new aims at creating harmony within its urban context via analogy and contrast. The wing is designed as a fragment of a greater whole in its inflection toward the Wilkins building and Trafalgar Square. A new and generous entry gives access to the entire National Gallery.

Inside are major museum facilities, such as a lecture theater, temporary exhibition galleries, a museum shop, a restaurant, and conference rooms, as well as an interactive computer information center for the public. On the east side, a stair, at the scale of a typical civic exterior, is located behind a large glass wall that affords an oblique view of the Wilkins building and Trafalgar Square. The stair leads from the lobby to the third-floor permanent galleries, which are at the same level as the major gallery floor of the Wilkins building and accessible to and from it; the painting collection is displayed on this floor. The galleries, laid out en suite with a gently implied hierarchy of small, medium, and large rooms, are lit by a balanced combination of natural and artificial light. Some galleries contain windows that overlook

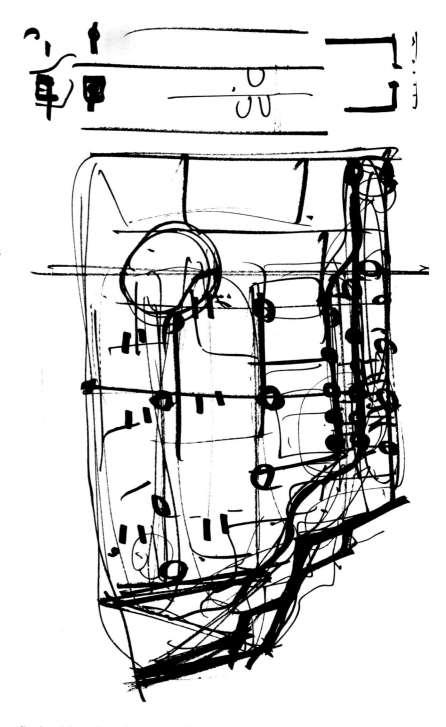

Study of the gallery floor of the Sainsbury Wing (sketch by Robert Venturi)

View toward the National Gallery (from Duncannon Street) with Sainsbury Wing at center

other interior spaces and offer glimpses of the outside, allowing visitors to orient themselves within the building. Windows are important to substantiate the setting as conventional more than original and suggestive of the original environments of the paintings. Clerestories with an elaborate system of sensor-operated louvers allow filtered light into each gallery space for optimal viewing conditions and energy efficiency, while also providing the visitor a welcome sense of the ever-changing light outside.

The new wing is separated from the Wilkins building by Jubilee Walk, a redesigned pedestrian way that connects Trafalgar and Leicester Squares. A bridge between the two buildings provides views toward both squares and connects galleries in the new wing and the original building. The remaining public museum spaces are located on four levels below the main gallery level. All spaces are related to either the upper or lower grand processional stair.

Principals in charge: Robert Venturi, Denise Scott Brown
Project directors: David Vaughan, Steven Izenour
Project managers: John Chase, John Hunter
With: William Algie, Edward Barnhart, Britt Brewer, Andrew Erstad, Steven Glascock, James Kolker, Jeffrey Krieger, Perry Kulper, Brian LaBau, Robert Marker, Richard Mohler, Thomas Purdy, George Ross, Mark Schlenker, Garreth Schuh, David Singer, Richard Stokes, Nancy Rogo Trainer, Mark Wieand, Maurice Weintraub
In association with: Sheppard Robson Architects

Elevation of Trafalgar Square facades of Sainsbury Wing (at left) and National Gallery (at center); St. Martin-in-the-Fields is at right

View of the Sainsbury Wing

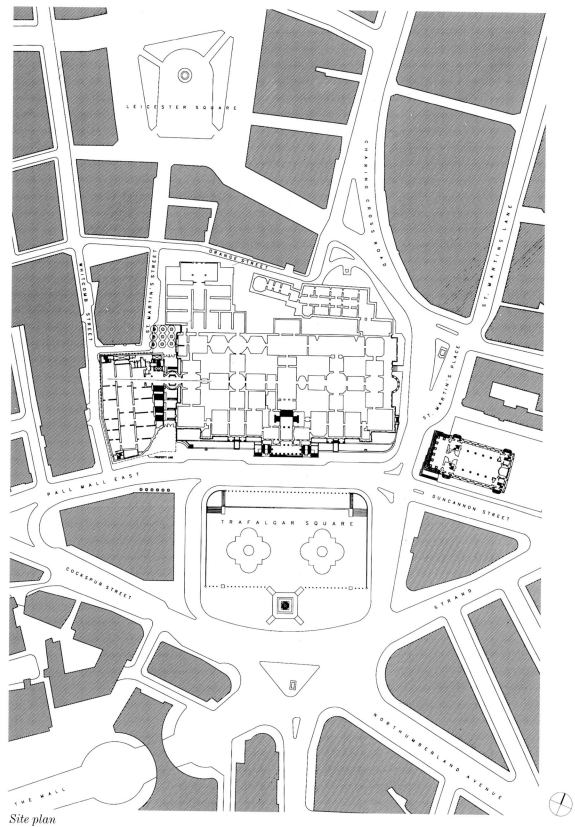

Site plan

View along Sainsbury Wing toward main building by Wilkinson

South elevation

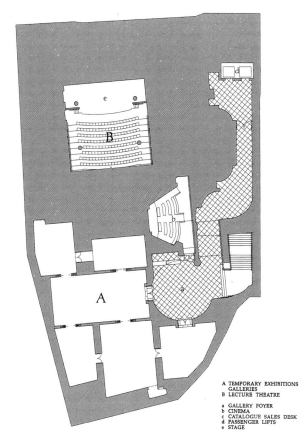

A TEMPORARY EXHIBITIONS
  GALLERIES
B LECTURE THEATRE

a GALLERY FOYER
b CINEMA
c CATALOGUE SALES DESK
d PASSENGER LIFTS
e STAGE

Basement plan

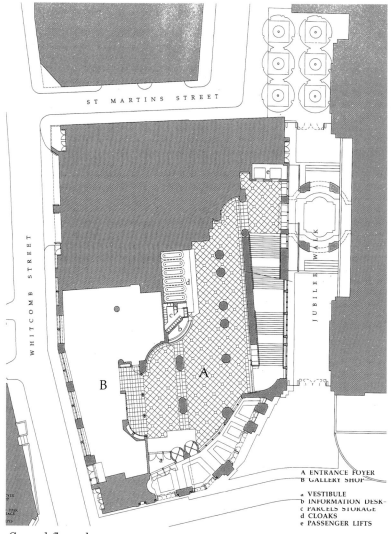

ST MARTINS STREET

WHITCOMB STREET

JUBILEE WALK

A ENTRANCE FOYER
B GALLERY SHOP

a VESTIBULE
b INFORMATION DESK
c PARCELS STORAGE
d CLOAKS
e PASSENGER LIFTS

Ground-floor plan

Details of Trafalgar Square facade

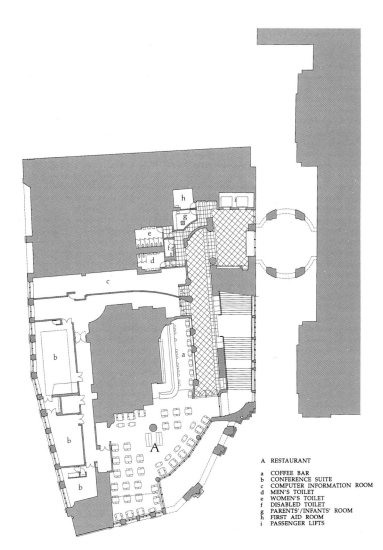

A RESTAURANT

a COFFEE BAR
b CONFERENCE SUITE
c COMPUTER INFORMATION ROOM
d MEN'S TOILET
e WOMEN'S TOILET
f DISABLED TOILET
g PARENTS'/INFANTS' ROOM
h FIRST AID ROOM
i PASSENGER LIFTS

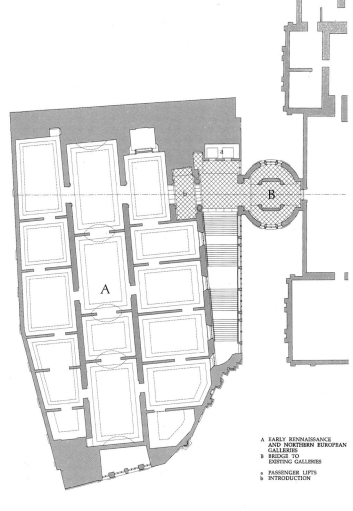

A EARLY RENNAISSANCE
    AND NORTHERN EUROPEAN
    GALLERIES
B BRIDGE TO
    EXISTING GALLERIES

a PASSENGER LIFTS
b INTRODUCTION

Mezzanine (restaurant floor) plan   *Gallery-floor plan*

View from main stairwell to Trafalgar Square

View of Trafalgar Square from Jubilee Walk

View of Jubilee Walk from Trafalgar Square

Exterior view of stairwell

Detail of iron gate

View of Sainsbury Wing from Trafalgar Square

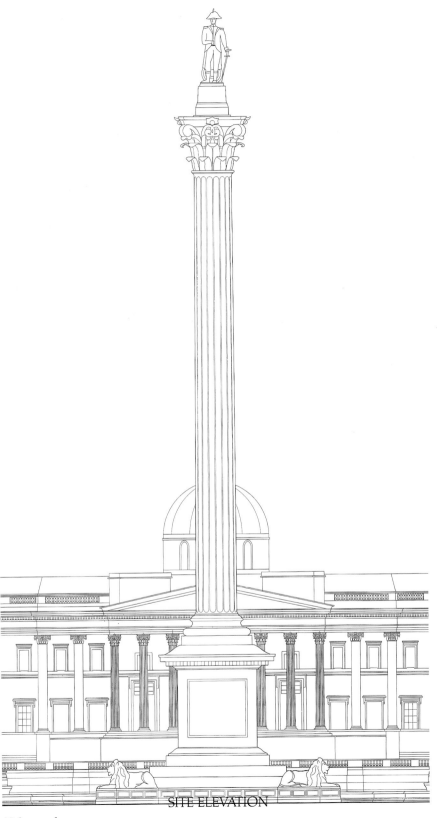

SITE ELEVATION

Nelson column

Entrance lobby with view toward main stair

View up main stair

View down main stair

View down main stair

Detail of main stair

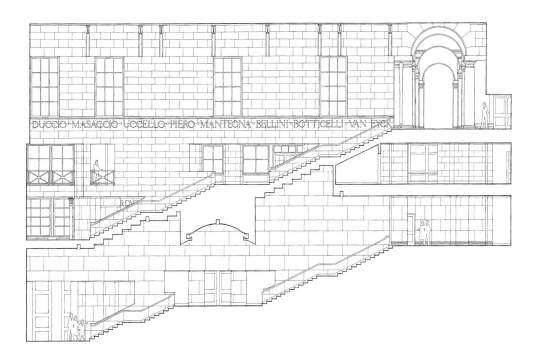

Section through main stair

View into gallery space

Views of gallery floor

GALLERY LEVEL

MEZZANINE LEVEL

STREET LEVEL

BASEMENT MEZZANINE LEVEL

BASEMENT LEVEL

Section through Sainsbury Wing

QUOTES FROM CRITICS
PRO

**THE SAINSBURY WING
NATIONAL GALLERY
TRAFALGAR SQUARE
LONDON**

"The finest new art gallery in Europe..."
LEAD EDITORIAL, The Times (London), July 9, 1991

"It is a triumph, a dazzling display... It revives architectural humanism."
SIMON JENKINS, The Sunday Times (London), April 19, 1987

"The Sainsbury Wing...is a marvel...a building which both sustains a presence across a large square and fits comfortably into the adjacent streetscape."
SIMON JENKINS, The Sunday Times (London), May 4, 1991

"The collection as a whole has never looked more compelling or more beautiful; the permanent galleries of the Sainsbury Wing set new standards for the world of art."
MARINA VAIZEY, The Sunday Times (London), June 30, 1991

"Let there be no doubt about it, the wing's top floor galleries are an unmitigated triumph."
JOHN RUSSEL TAYLOR, The Times (London), July 9, 1991

"...the finest galleries of the 20th century."
NEIL MACGREGOR, Director, The National Gallery, May 1991

"...at home in the 20th and the 16th century, as relaxed with Mies as with Brunelleschi."
CHARLES JENCKS, Financial Times, July 9, 1991

"The marriage between building and masterpieces is exhilarating..."
LORD SAINSBURY of Preston Candover, May 1991

"...some of the most beautiful galleries built in Europe since the war."
TANYA HARROD, The Independent, June 30, 1991

"...a building that evokes the sacred spaces for which much of the art that it houses was made."
ANDREW GRAHAM-DIXON, The Independent, July 9,1991

"...For once, an architect has stepped back and placed his own ego second to the display of works of art...it represents philanthropy, architecture, and museum professionalism all working together in the service (first) of the pictures, and then of the public."
RICHARD DORMENT, Daily Telegraph, July 28, 1991

"Art and architecture fuse in an unforced yet sublime union."
RICHARD CORK, The Sunday Times Saturday Review, June 22, 1991

"These galleries...are among the finest of recent museum history, bathed in natural light and elegantly detailed."
MANUELA HOELTERHOFF, The Wall Street Journal, July 8, 1991

"The Sainsbury Wing...is not just Britain's building of the year or even the decade. It is also Venturi and Scott Brown's masterpiece.
This is a rich and profound piece of architecture, a virtuoso demonstration of space, light, volume and proportion brought together through the consummate understanding of a designer with great instincts reinforced by great learning."
MARTIN FILLER, House and Garden, April 1991

"The Sainsbury Wing stands apart from, and above, its counterparts in the primacy it gives the encounter with art."
THOMAS HINE, The Philadelphia Inquirer, July 14, 1991

QUOTES FROM CRITICS
CON (British)

**THE SAINSBURY WING
NATIONAL GALLERY
TRAFALGAR SQUARE
LONDON**

"After the erection, the anti-climax...a shallow triumph of well-mannered pastiche over thrusting originality.
...more post office than Post Modern.
...a dull, cowardly edifice designed not by an architect but an exterior decorator."
HENRY PORTER, The Independent, March 21, 1991

"...we are to be given a vulgar American piece of Post-Modern mannerist pastiche."
EDITORIAL, Architectural Review, 1987

"...it delights in perversity, irrationality and awkwardness...An insult both to the National Gallery and to London.
The National Gallery extension is the cruellest disappointment I have ever suffered as an architectural critic."
GAVIN STAMP, The Times, May 4, 1991

"...some coloured Egyptianish columns which look as though they wandered down from Carnaby Street in the sixties and are too stupid to find their way back."
RICHARD BOSTON, The Guardian, June 28, 1991t

"...picturesque mediocre slime."
PETER DAVEY, Architectural Review, December 1988

"Mr. Venturi has come to the land of Good Queen Bess, Sir Christopher Wren and the Prince of Wales like a camera-toting middle-aged mid-American tourist. If he had come riding high, spurs shining, guns blazing, he might have created a starlet of a building that we could have loved."
JONATHON GLANCY, The Independent, June 26, 1991

"At the National Gallery, Venturi displays all the nervousness of an untutored foreigner at a Buckingham Palace banquet. He is grossly deferential - mealy-mouthed - and when he cracks a joke it is a polite but unfunny one."
KENNETH POWELL, The Daily Telegraph, June 26, 1991

"...a building that will inspire neither awe nor affection; outside it is all clever clowning, as short-lived and tiresome as a pun; inside it is confused, ugly and incompetent."
BRIAN SEWELL, The Evening Standard, June 28, 1991

"The exterior of the Venturi building is certainly not a carbuncle - it is more like a skin graft."
DERWENT MAY, Elan, June 28, 1991

"...one of the greatest disappointments on the London architectural scene this century..."
KENNETH POWELL, Sunday Telegraph, May 1991

"...After the much publicized attempt to find a suitable architect through an open competition, Venturi's offering is surely the runt of the litter."
ROBERT TORDAY, Connoisseur, August 1991

"And Ruth Ettinger, an art student, said: 'It's just nothing. It doesn't catch the eye at all. Do you know the architects were an American couple and they're really old?'"
IAN KATZ, The Guardian, July 9, 1991

"What do Bob Venturi, the Sainsbury's and Mrs. Thatcher have in common? They all come from families of grocers!"
SCORPIO, Building Design, June 26, 1991

Critical reactions to the Sainsbury Wing: the "Second Battle of Trafalgar"

View of gallery sequence from lateral axis

17 Seattle Art Museum

Seattle, Washington, 1984–1991

The complex program for a modern museum must serve a heterogeneous community; house educational, administrative, and commercial activities; and provide support space for services, storage, and conservation, as well as offer the primary space for the exhibition of art. All these can be accommodated by means of the generic loft system promoted in the design for the Seattle Art Museum. The flexibility of the loft space allows the museum's various and growing collections to be displayed within cultural and physical contexts appropriate to particular artworks and to the museum's diverse audiences.

Variations in structural bay size provide a three-zone organiza-tion on all levels of the building. The longer spans paralleling the north facade house bigger, more flowing sequences of spaces. Bays along the south facade suit installations requiring smaller, more enclosed spaces. The intermediate zone accommodates services and circulation and, at each end, windows where visitors can orient themselves to the city and see natural light. Vistas across the parallel series of rooms provide opportunities for cross-cultural comparisons and visual contrasts.

The curve at the corner of the building breaks the loft system inside as well as out, creating an exception to the orthogonal order and generating visual and spatial tension within the spaces.

Main entrance with feet of Jonathan Borofsky's Hammering Man

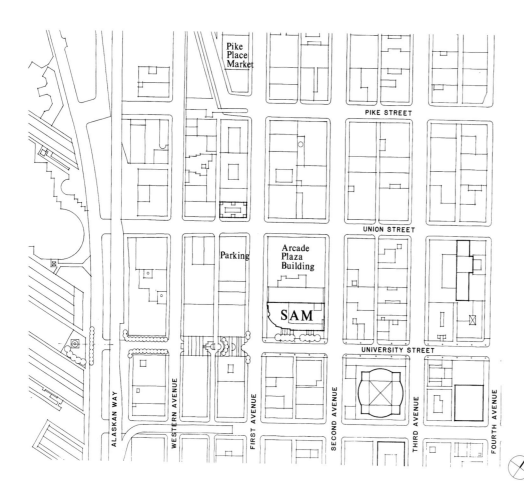

Site plan

View of entrance facade with Hammering Man

The Museum as a Work of Art

This building was designed to be a work of art, yet one that does not upstage but instead serves as a background for the art inside. It does not conform to the current trend of the museum as articulated pavilions but to an older tradition—going back to the adapted palaces and grand museums of the nineteenth century and the original Museum of Modern Art in New York— of the museum as generic loft.

Acknowledging its downtown context—in an American city, within a grid plan, placed along a street like any other building—it derives its civic quality not by means of a special location (at the end of a boulevard for instance) but through a combinations of scales—big and little. Though a relatively small building, it holds its own among the larger buildings around it through its scale.

The play of small- and large-scale elements helps make the building friendly from the outside despite its overall lack of windows. (The client wanted galleries that admitted no natural light.) This is further enhanced at eye level through the building's openness and its lyrical rhythms, color, and ornament. The rectangular order of the loft is broken at the First Avenue and University Street entrance, where the corner is rounded to generate exterior civic space and accommodate the sculptural figure by Jonathan Borofsky. Thus the museum is both civic and civil. Civic scale penetrates the interior by means of the grand stair, which is visible from and corresponds to the sidewalk stair outside and which makes the building feel open and accessible.

Detail of main facade

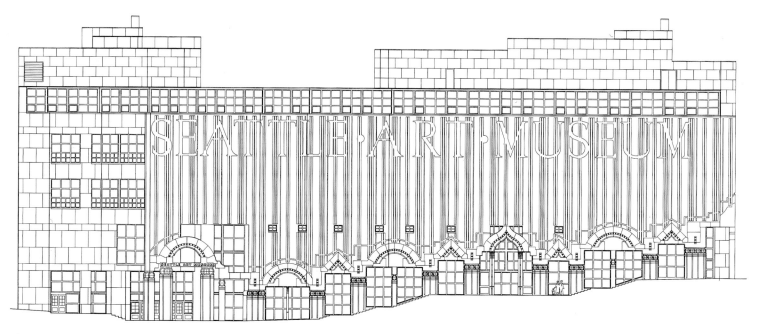

Southeast elevation

Principal in charge: Robert Venturi
Project managers: James Bradberry,
John Pringle
Project architects: John Bastian,
Ann Trowbridge
With: Denise Scott Brown,
Daniel Borden, John Forney,
Gary Griggs, Brian LaBau,
Matthew Schottelkotte,
Douglas Seiler, Mark Stankard,
Mark Wieand, James Winkler
In association with: Olsen/Sundberg
Architects

Rear entrance

Entrance lobby

View of main concourse from rear entrance

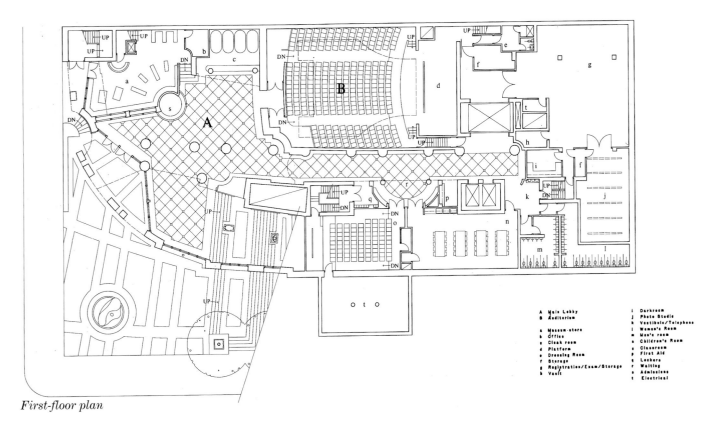

First-floor plan

A Main Lobby
B Auditorium

a Museum store
b Office
c Cloak room
d Platform
e Dressing Room
f Storage
g Registration/Exam/Storage
h Vault

i Darkroom
j Photo Studio
k Vestibule/Telephone
l Women's Room
m Men's room
n Children's Room
o Classroom
p First Aid
q Lockers
r Waiting
s Admissions
t Electrical

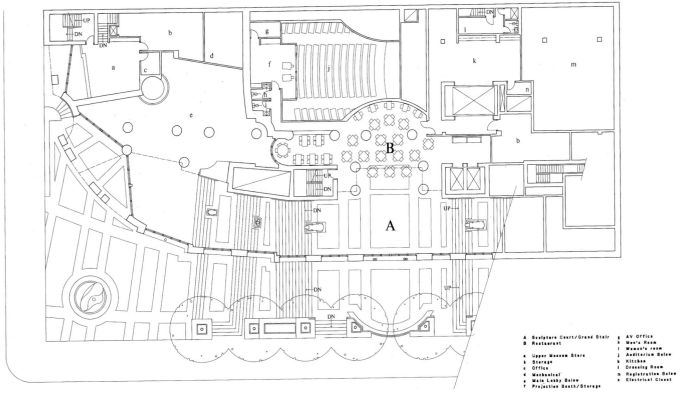

Mezzanine plan

A Sculpture Court/Grand Stair
B Restaurant

a Upper Museum Store
b Storage
c Office
d Mechanical
e Main Lobby Below
f Projection Booth/Storage

g AV Office
h Men's Room
i Women's room
j Auditorium Below
k Kitchen
l Dressing Room
m Registration Below
n Electrical Closet

View along circulation way

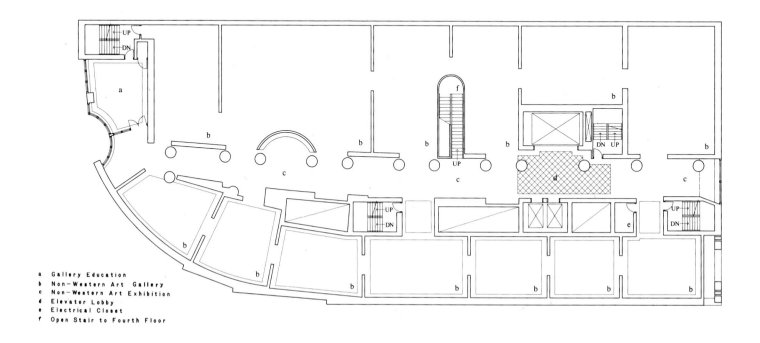

a Gallery Education
b Non-Western Art Gallery
c Non-Western Art Exhibition
d Elevator Lobby
e Electrical Closet
f Open Stair to Fourth Floor

Third-floor plan

View of gallery

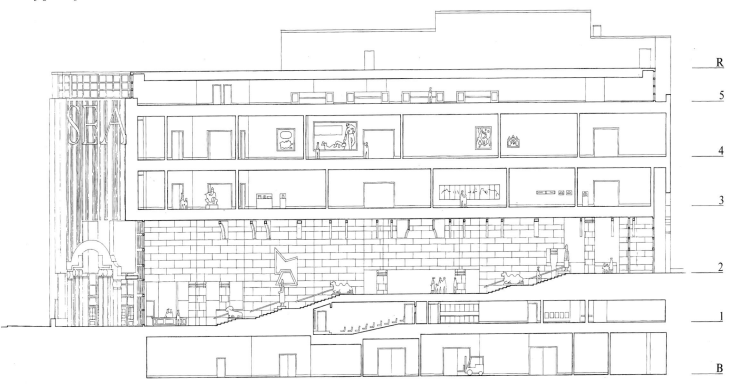

Section looking north

18 Children's Museum

Houston, Texas, 1989–1992

The design for the Children's Museum of Houston acknowledges, indeed exploits, the inherent dichotomy of the museum's requirements—generic exhibition areas that accommodate flexibility, on one hand, and permanent spaces that evoke the memorable character of this particular institution, on the other hand. The Kids' Hall, with its rainbow-colored arches and rhythmic arcade, provides an imageable counterpoint to the flexible and changing exhibition spaces beyond it.

Along Binz Street is the permanent, institutional part of the building; toward the back and interior of the site is the shedlike exhibition area. The shop spaces for producing and maintaining exhibitions are located in a separate building, economical in construction and remote from the main building to make its dust and noise less obtrusive. In between is a play garden.

The main facade adapts a symbolism deriving from monumental institutions typical of the adult world. The colonnade along the Binz facade and the brightly painted "caryakids" along the side facade playfully refer to traditional Classical architecture. The large scale of the columns is complemented by small-scale, decorative detail at child height. The symbolism is adult-monumental-museum but the detail is a playful, friendly, colorful arabesque on the adult norm for museums. The other parts of the building are modern and utilitarian (and economical—they are carefully modified prefabricated buildings—Butler Buildings) and are designed to accommodate the flexible uses within. This building resembles, in a light-hearted way, the Houston Museum of Fine Arts up the street, with its juxtaposed original masonry Classical facade and Mies van der Rohe Modern facades.

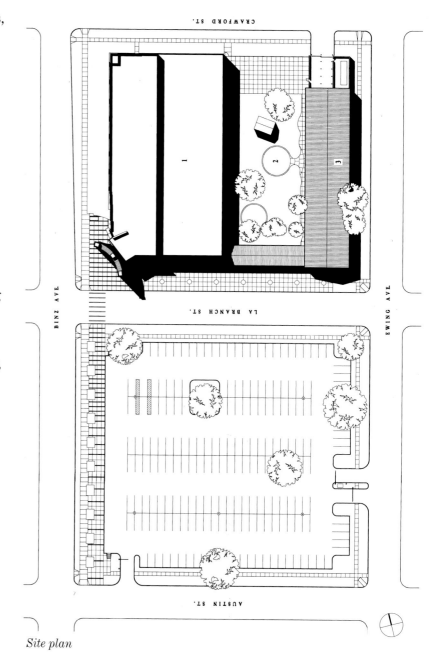

Site plan

Views across parking lot

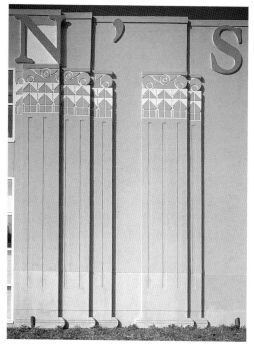

Detail of north facade

Principal in charge: Robert Venturi
Project manager: David Schaaf
With: Denise Scott Brown, Jeannie
Adams, Steven Izenour, Timothy
Kearney, Nancy Rogo Trainer
In association with: Jackson and
Ryan, Architects, Inc.

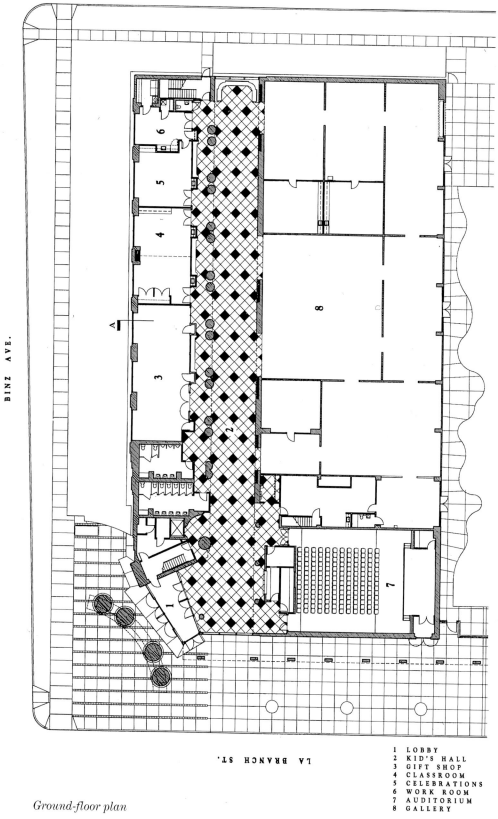

Ground-floor plan

BINZ AVE.

LA BRANCH ST.

1 LOBBY
2 KID'S HALL
3 GIFT SHOP
4 CLASSROOM
5 CELEBRATIONS
6 WORK ROOM
7 AUDITORIUM
8 GALLERY

Kid's Hall ceiling decoration

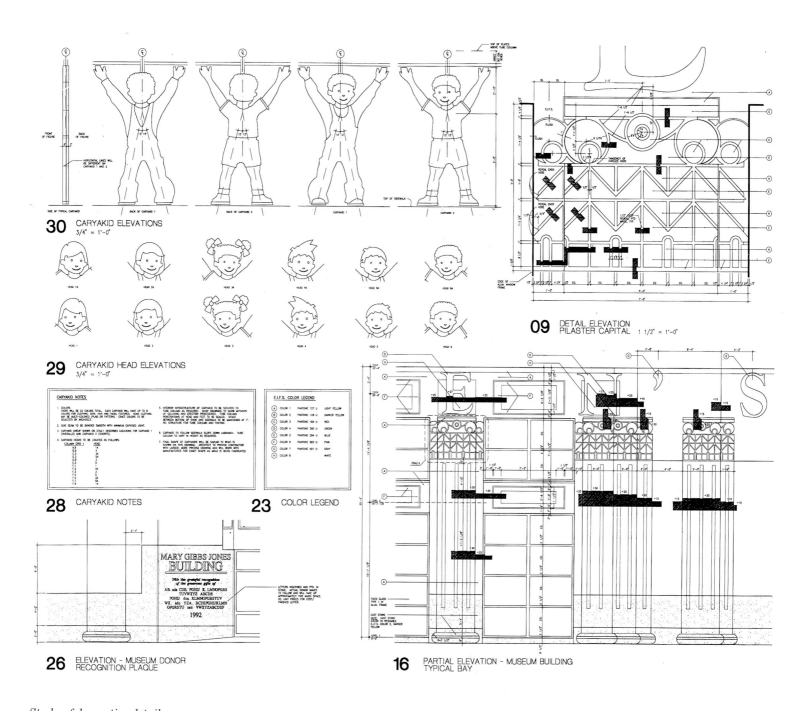

30 CARYAKID ELEVATIONS
3/4" = 1'-0"

29 CARYAKID HEAD ELEVATIONS
3/4" = 1'-0"

28 CARYAKID NOTES

23 COLOR LEGEND

09 DETAIL ELEVATION
PILASTER CAPITAL   1 1/2" = 1'-0"

26 ELEVATION – MUSEUM DONOR
RECOGNITION PLAQUE

16 PARTIAL ELEVATION – MUSEUM BUILDING
TYPICAL BAY

Study of decorative details

View from Kid's Hall toward entrance porch

Children's Museum **153**

19 National Museum of Scotland Addition
Competition Entry

Edinburgh, Scotland, 1991

The design for an addition to the National Museum of Scotland projects in the interior a continuation of the large-scale atrium axis of the original building while connecting all exhibition levels with a monumental stair that promotes flowing space. This main axis ends on a cross-axis in the new wing; the cross-axis parallels a street and is simultaneously a double-height exhibition space containing large exhibits visible from that street. Like some other museum buildings, where wall and space are more important than windows, most of the exterior facades are ornamented by large-scale incised graphics—here depicting the names of famous Scotsmen and -women in the manner of the front facade of Henri Labrouste's Bibliothèque Ste. Geneviève in Paris. Another more sculptural-symbolic gesture on the side elevation articulates a lighthouse.

Principals in charge: Robert Venturi, Steven Izenour
Project manager: John Chase

Perspective view of proposed addition

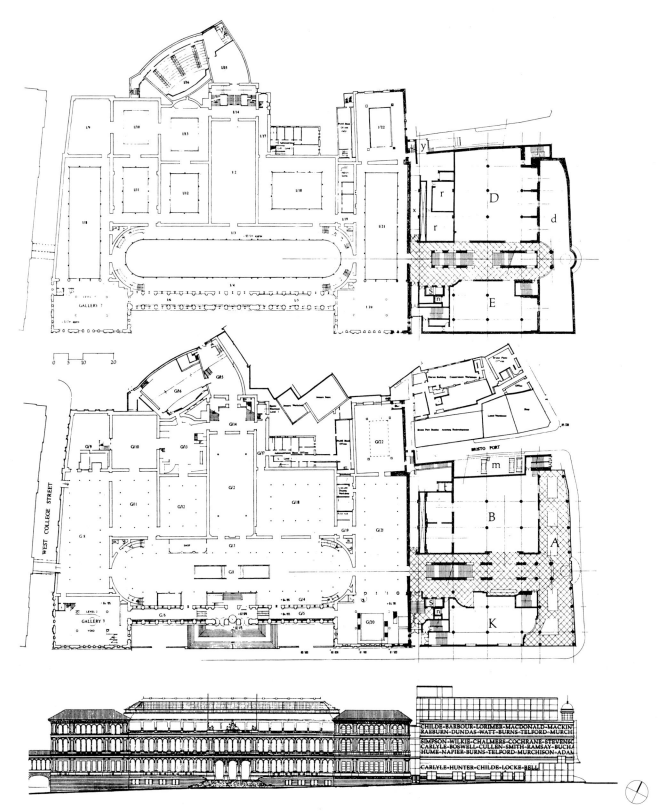

First- and ground-level plans; elevation with original building at left

20 Peabody Essex Museum Addition
Competition Entry

Salem, Massachusetts, 1996

The Peabody Museum is situated on two blocks diagonally across from one another within the gridiron plan of the historic harbor city of Salem. The main building consists of many wings attached to each other over many years that have led to a variety of styles outside and a spatial maze inside. We designed the extension of this building to involve a minimum of demolition of the old fabric, because adding to demolished segments of an existing building is both very complex and expensive. By proposing only a small amount of demolition, we approached the challenge in a realistic and positive way, acknowledging the existing architectural configuration not as a negative mess but as a positive maze, intriguing and picturesque, and thus expressing historical evolution within a historical museum.

The Museum as a Maze

We solved the important issue of rational and perceptible circulation routes within a museum—even a museum as a maze— via a system of what we called "beacons." These elements occur at each turning point within the major circulation system through the galleries so that from any point a visitor can see the next beacon on the route. Of course, it is possible to ignore the beacon-oriented circulation system and have the fun of being lost among the exhibits. The beacons, symbolizing lighthouses, are made to be seen from a distance, but at close range the small-scale graphic and computer-driven elements work to supply information about the immediate area of the museum.

Certain parts of the design involve new additions to (not substitutions within) the original fabric, so there is admittedly not a grand hierarchical procession of spaces within, but at the corner entrance is a new substituted wing—a lobby that carefully establishes the building and its image as an institution inside. From this hall the maze begins. The exterior along the old urban streets looks like what it is—a series of connected buildings—but, again, around the entrance is new architecture that identifies the institutional whole via iconography in the form of a big sculptural element and a big mural as a sign. Along the streets beyond the entrance are the equivalent of retail shop windows that contain interesting exhibits and make vital the urban quality of this place.

We lost the competition because the institution wanted grand architecture in the manner of old museums; we thought this would strain the budget.

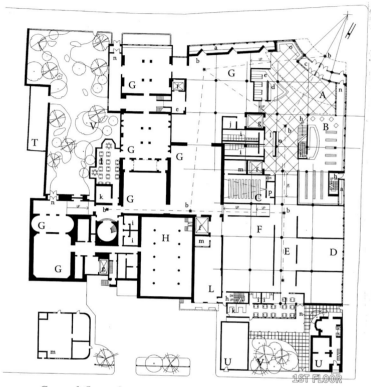

Ground-floor plan

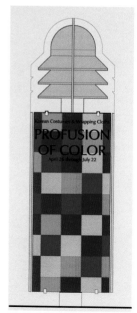

"Beacon" serving as information board

Principals in charge: Robert Venturi, Denise Scott Brown, Steven Izenour
Project managers: Ann Trowbridge, Nancy Rogo Trainer
With: Angelina Chong, Claudia Cueto, Diane Golomb, Timothy Kearney, James Kolker, Jeffrey Lewis, Matthew Seltzer, Delano Shane, Linh Tran

Facade details

East elevation

21 Ames Library Addition

North Easton, Massachusetts, 1996

VSBA designed an addition to a most distinguished historic building, the Oliver Ames Free Library by H. H. Richardson in the town of North Easton, Massachusetts. The exterior and interior of the original building have been well maintained and its original uses have essentially been retained, except in the basement. The new wing was designed to relate to the natural context of the rural site and to the architectural form of the original building and to be recessive, in its proposal for a generic loft in the grand tradition of New England mills. This type of space works well for the flexible interior uses of a modern library.

Harmony between new and old in this design is achieved via analogy and contrast among the elements of the composition, architectural and natural: the gentle curve of the new wing contrasts with the orthogonal forms of the original building but acknowledges and adapts to the gentle configurations of the topography; the flush surfaces of buff bricks and pink granite of the new wing are analogous in color and partially identical in material but contrasting in texture to the old wing; and the exterior scale and compositional rhythms of each, the old and the new, are bold, although the symbolism of the original building refers specifically to French Romanesque architecture while that of the new wing refers generically to New England mills.

Principal in charge: Robert Venturi
Project managers: Daniel McCoubrey, Richard Stokes
With: Hideano Abe, Susan Lockwood

View of addition with existing building by H. H. Richardson (1877–78)

Site plan

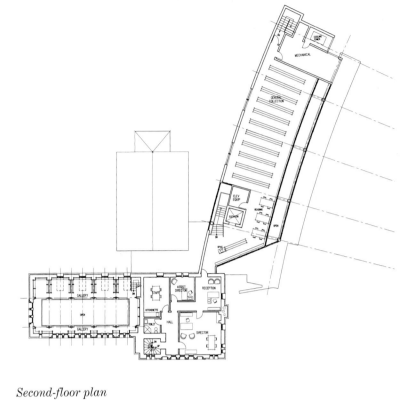

Second-floor plan

Ground-floor plan

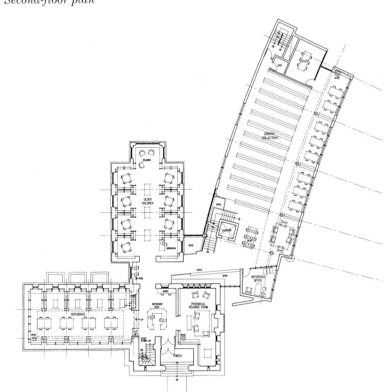

First-floor plan

22 National Museum of the American Indian

Facilities Program of Requirements for the Smithsonian Institution

Washington, D.C., 1991–1993

The first national museum for Native Americans of the Northern and Southern Hemispheres, to be built on the last remaining site on the Mall in Washington, D.C., and at the Smithsonian's storage and research facility in Suitland, Maryland, is to be a center for cultural activity, outreach, education, and study, and an environment for display of Indian objects in the context of the cultures that made them.

After intensive consultation with Native American communities, constituencies, and experts, we developed "The Way of the People." Its volumes contained programs for spaces; criteria for function, quality, and relationships of spaces; predesign studies; technical services guides; and construction and operating cost estimates for the museum. The report also includes comments by participants in the consultations to convey the flavor of the programming process and to help satisfy the goal that Native American values and voices determine the program and design of the museum.

The program recommended guidelines for building siting, massing, and materials; discussed cultural symbolism in architecture and the character of ceremonial and performing-arts space; and made suggestions for the qualities of indoor and outdoor space, the visual connection between elements, and the division of space between Washington and Suitland, Maryland. Criteria were defined for display and care of objects to accord with tribal traditions and for incorporation of technical systems to meet museum outreach, exhibition, and research requirements.

Principal in charge:
Denise Scott Brown
Project manager: Ann Trowbridge
Project architects: James Kolker,
Ronald Evitts
With: Catherine Bird, Stephanie
Christoff, Tom Jones, Adam Meyers

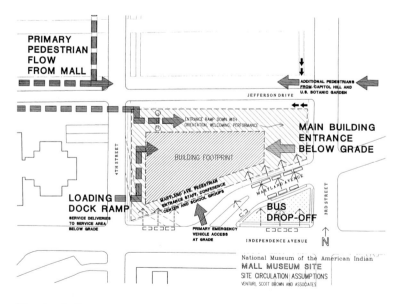

Site circulation

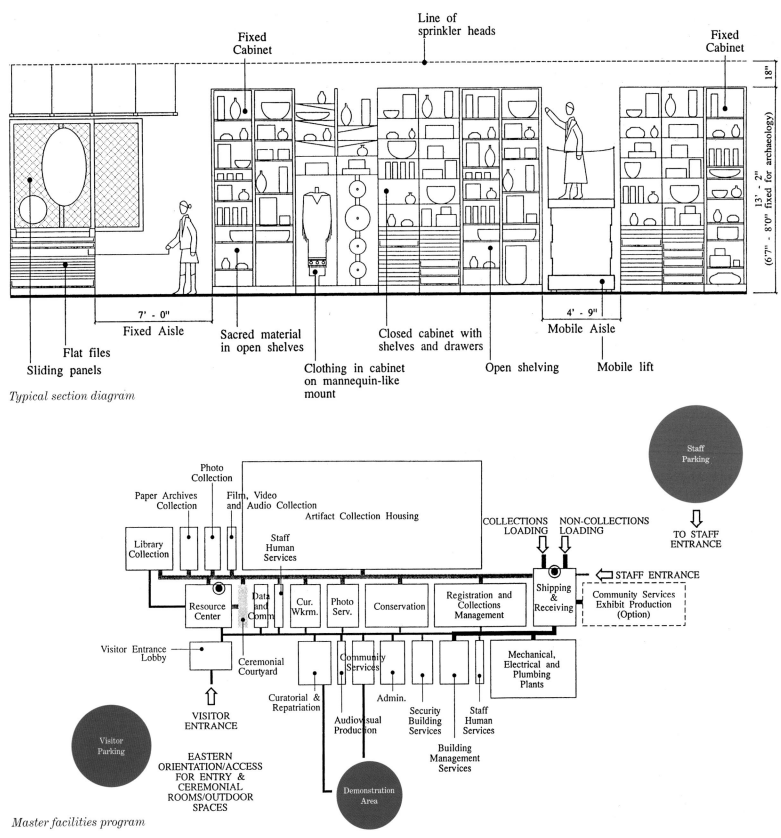

Line of sprinkler heads

Fixed Cabinet

Fixed Cabinet

18"

13' - 2"
(6'7" - 8'0" fixed for archaeology)

7' - 0"
Fixed Aisle

4' - 9"
Mobile Aisle

Flat files

Sliding panels

Sacred material in open shelves

Clothing in cabinet on mannequin-like mount

Closed cabinet with shelves and drawers

Open shelving

Mobile lift

Typical section diagram

Paper Archives Collection

Photo Collection

Film, Video and Audio Collection

Artifact Collection Housing

Staff Human Services

Library Collection

Resource Center

Data and Comm.

Cur. Wkrm.

Photo Serv.

Conservation

Registration and Collections Management

COLLECTIONS LOADING

NON-COLLECTIONS LOADING

Shipping & Receiving

STAFF ENTRANCE

Staff Parking

TO STAFF ENTRANCE

Community Services Exhibit Production (Option)

Visitor Entrance Lobby

Ceremonial Courtyard

Curatorial & Repatriation

Community Services

Admin.

Security Building Services

Staff Human Services

Mechanical, Electrical and Plumbing Plants

Audiovisual Production

Building Management Services

Demonstration Area

VISITOR ENTRANCE

Visitor Parking

EASTERN ORIENTATION/ACCESS FOR ENTRY & CEREMONIAL ROOMS/OUTDOOR SPACES

Master facilities program

23 Expo '92 Pavilion
Competition Entry for United States Pavilion

Seville, Spain, 1989

World expositions, by design, create a competitive visual environment in which almost anything goes. The crux of the design problem for a United States pavilion is how to create economical interior space with an architectural exterior that will create sufficient impact to compete within this overwrought kind of environment. Why not try a classic American billboard? One economical design with such an impact would be a generic loft— a "decorated shed"—sporting a fragment of a big flag as a sign.

VSBA's design for the U.S. Pavilion at Expo '92 represents an architectural solution that promotes symbolism, communication, interaction, and civic amenity rather than architectural articulation as abstract expressionism. The most effective way to express the pluralism and diversity that is basic to American democracy is to make the pavilion a simple structure in which the exhibitors can achieve full and diverse expression behind the symbol of national unity—the American flag. The combination of engineering tour de force—a cantilevered space-frame facade that can contain a theater line—and explicit symbolism can represent an appropriate balance between technique and message in the postindustrial yet Jasper Johns age we live in.

The more functionally specific and environmentally sensitive areas of the theater, restaurant, museum, and administration are concentrated in a multistory part of the loft structure at the west side; the major part of the building contains a hypostyle exhibit hall on grade. All the public space except for the theater is placed at grade so that people can enter and exit the pavilion along the total of its 120-meter frontage.

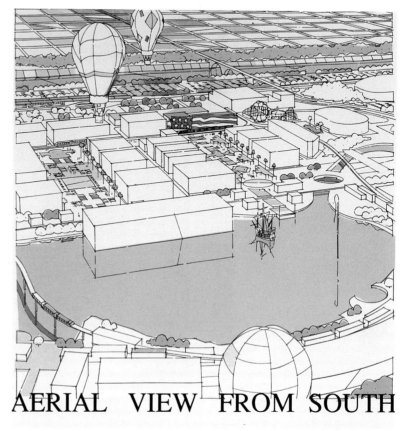

AERIAL VIEW FROM SOUTH

Aerial view from south

Main elevation

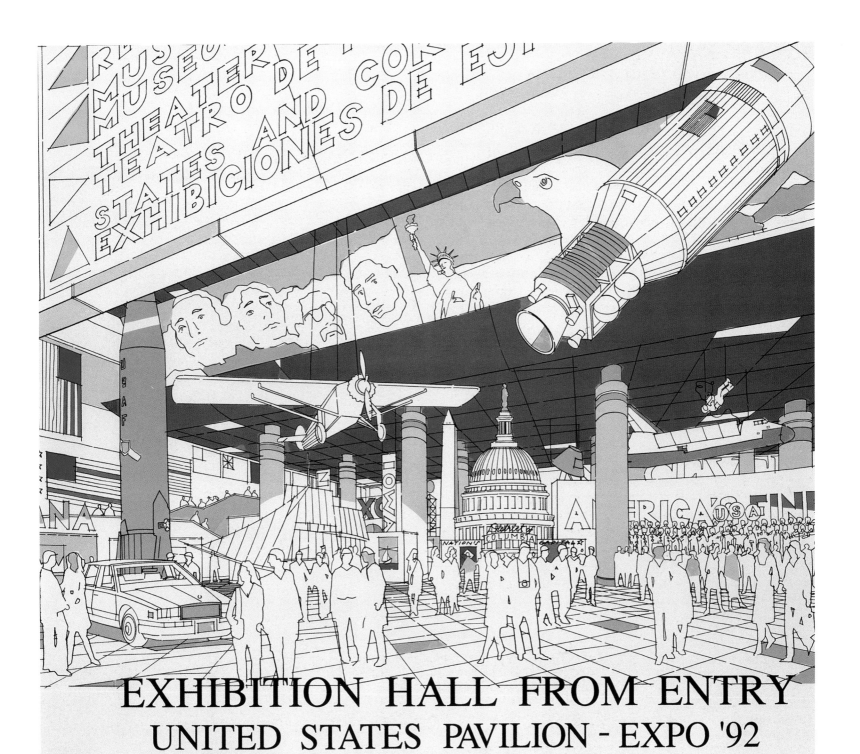

EXHIBITION HALL FROM ENTRY

UNITED STATES PAVILION - EXPO '92

SEVILLE, SPAIN

VENTURI, RAUCH AND SCOTT BROWN
APRIL 1989

Perspective view of exhibition hall from entry

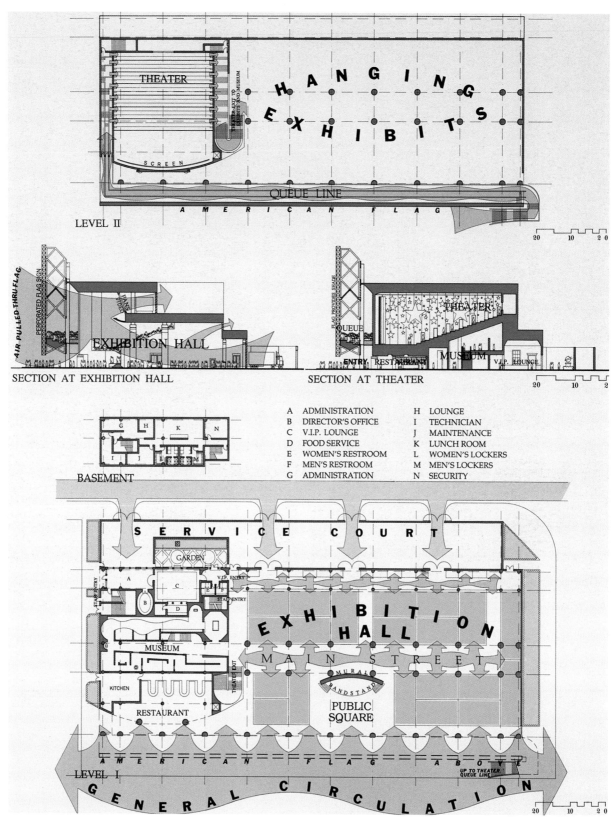

LEVEL II

THEATER

SCREEN

HANGING
EXHIBITS

QUEUE LINE

AMERICAN FLAG

20 10 2 0

SECTION AT EXHIBITION HALL

AIR PULLED THRU FLAG

PERFORATED FLAG SIGN

EXHIBITION HALL

SECTION AT THEATER

FLAG PROVIDES SHADE

QUEUE

THEATER

ENTRY RESTAURANT MUSEUM V.I.P. LOUNGE

20 10 2

BASEMENT

A	ADMINISTRATION	H	LOUNGE
B	DIRECTOR'S OFFICE	I	TECHNICIAN
C	V.I.P. LOUNGE	J	MAINTENANCE
D	FOOD SERVICE	K	LUNCH ROOM
E	WOMEN'S RESTROOM	L	WOMEN'S LOCKERS
F	MEN'S RESTROOM	M	MEN'S LOCKERS
G	ADMINISTRATION	N	SECURITY

SERVICE COURT

GARDEN

V.I.P. ENTRY

EXHIBITION HALL

MAIN STREET

MUSEUM

KITCHEN

RESTAURANT

MURAL
BANDSTAND

PUBLIC
SQUARE

AMERICAN FLAG ABOVE

UP TO THEATER
QUEUE LINE

LEVEL I

GENERAL CIRCULATION

20 10 2 0

Plans and sections

Model view

Principal in charge: Robert Venturi
Project manager: Steven Izenour
With: Michael Ablon, John Bastian,
Catherine Bird, Josh Brandfonbrener,
John Forney, Don Jones,
Timothy Kearney, Pablo Meninato,
Marc Pinard, Matthew Schottelkotte

24 Stedelijk Museum Addition
Competition Entry

Amsterdam, The Netherlands, 1992

A design for the extension of the Stedelijk Museum serves several goals. First, it acknowledges in the character and quality of the design the distinction of the original museum, both as an important institution in the world of art and as a building in a place.

The addition creates a whole on the inside, which accommodates the varied and complex program of the new wing and relates it to the activities in the old building. The proposed settings for art are in themselves art but work as background for art, too. These generic spaces, subtly and flexibly lit, lend themselves over time to different ways of arranging art and circulating among artworks as well as forming auxiliary spaces for sitting down and looking out.

The building complex is civic as well as institutional. Its scale relates to the city as a whole, and its form and symbolism are inviting and attractive to many different people. Architectural harmony between the old and the new is achieved through the design of new elements that are both analogous to and contrasting with the old. For instance, the brick and the masonry trim of the new building match the materials and colors of the old; the patterns in the new are in some ways analogous to and in other ways contrasting with the patterns of the old; and the architectural forms and vocabularies of old and new vary, but the heights of their exterior walls correspond.

Further Purposes

The original museum and the addition together form an architectural whole. The new wing is a fragment that inflects toward the old building. The addition would not make sense functionally or formally if it were to stand alone; it bows architecturally to the original building.

The urban neighborhood is the context and basis for the design of this building. Each side of the building relates to the environment immediately around it: the west facade, for instance, emphatically accommodates the new main entrance to the complex, but it also acknowledges the commercial character of Van Baerlestraat and the particular quality of the facade of the Stedelijk Museum on that street; the patterned park front forms a backdrop to the park and sculpture court. The new-old "interior facade" identifies the new entry hall.

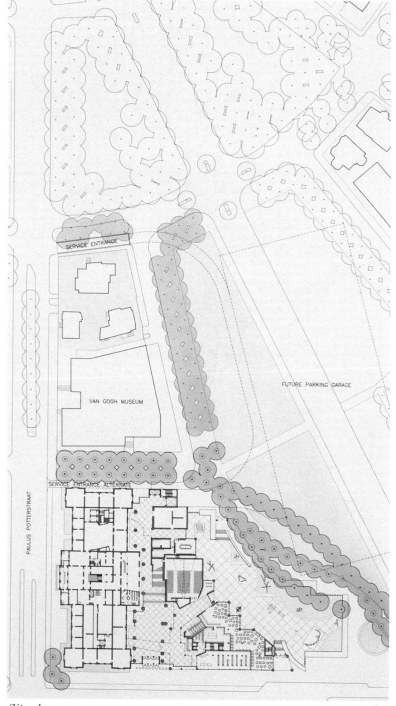

Site plan

View of Great Hall

Principals in charge: Robert Venturi,
Denise Scott Brown, Steven Izenour
Project manager: Nancy Rogo Trainer
With: Hidenao Abe, Jason Brody,
Stephanie Christoff, Ronald Evitts,
John Forney, Tom Jones, Timothy
Kearney, James Kolker, Amy Noble

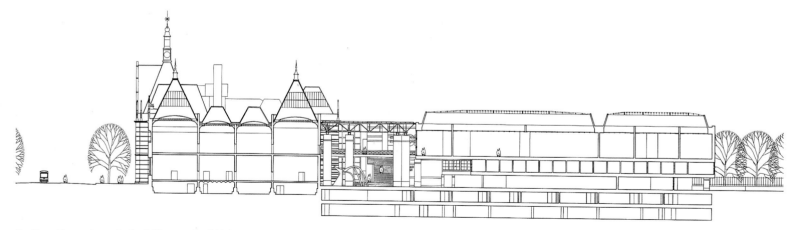

Section through main building and addition

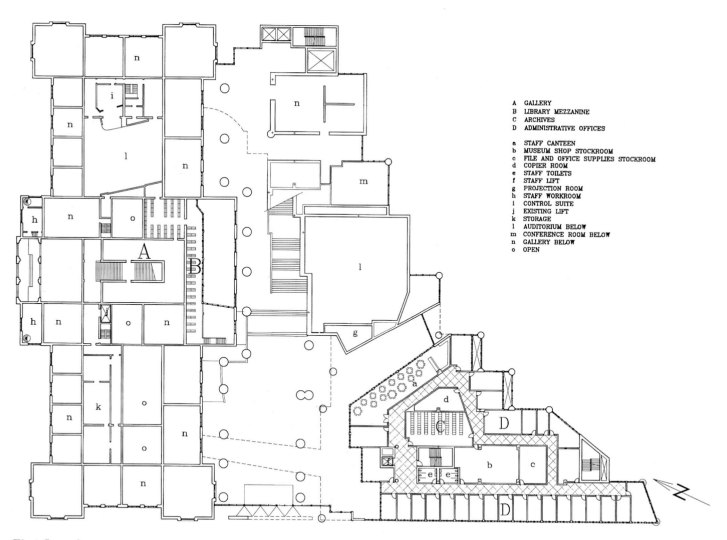

A   GALLERY
B   LIBRARY MEZZANINE
C   ARCHIVES
D   ADMINISTRATIVE OFFICES

a   STAFF CANTEEN
b   MUSEUM SHOP STOCKROOM
c   FILE AND OFFICE SUPPLIES STOCKROOM
d   COPIER ROOM
e   STAFF TOILETS
f   STAFF LIFT
g   PROJECTION ROOM
h   STAFF WORKROOM
i   CONTROL SUITE
j   EXISTING LIFT
k   STORAGE
l   AUDITORIUM BELOW
m   CONFERENCE ROOM BELOW
n   GALLERY BELOW
o   OPEN

First-floor plan

New entrance facade (sketch by Robert Venturi)

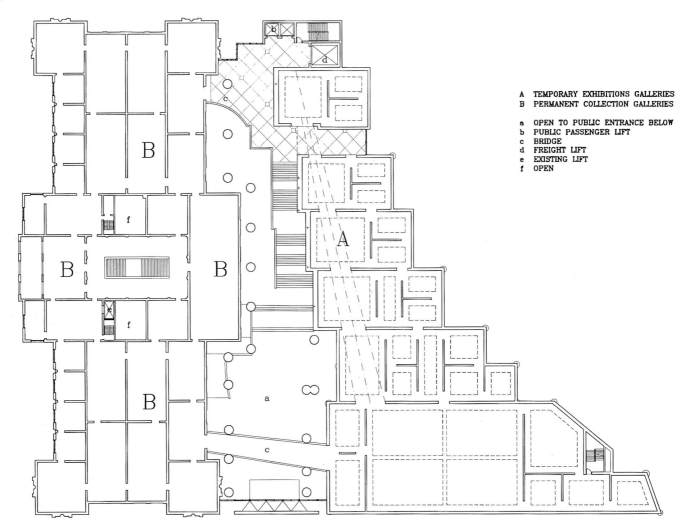

A   TEMPORARY EXHIBITIONS GALLERIES
B   PERMANENT COLLECTION GALLERIES

a   OPEN TO PUBLIC ENTRANCE BELOW
b   PUBLIC PASSENGER LIFT
c   BRIDGE
d   FREIGHT LIFT
e   EXISTING LIFT
f   OPEN

Gallery-floor plan

The display of art is the raison d'être of this building, but it is also essential to acknowledge the civic function of receiving people. This is accomplished in the Great Hall, which acts as a civic gesture. Although it is inside the building, this hall is figuratively an outside space, in terms of its size and scale and in the quality derived from its "open" ends. It is expressed not as a part of the building but as a space between buildings; visitors circulate through almost as they would on the sidewalks of surrounding streets or along walks in the park. It is both a residual space between buildings and a positive space functioning as a central hall. It is also an entrance; it draws visitors ceremoniously toward the art, either via a ramp to the original wing or up the civic-scaled stair to the new wing.

The extension acknowledges the civic setting of the Museumplein and the monumental buildings around it, including the Concertgebouw Hall and the Rijksmuseum. The inflected shape of the new wing and the configuration of the sculpture garden reinforce the diagonal order of the Museumplein. Urban context is again asserted as the museum "in the thick of things" announces its current shows by means of a grand "art board" over the main entrance. This series of painted metal panels, civic in content, commercial in scale, has a dramatic impact on the street. The images on this surface could be LED pixel–generated.

Finally, the museum's support spaces work within the hierarchy of the complex whole and for the extensive and varied activities typical of museums today. These spaces support museum activities behind the scenes, in the mezzanine and basement of the new building and the modified spaces of the original building; they contribute vitality on the south side of the Grand Hall, activity along Van Baerlestraat, and amenity at the edge of the sculpture garden.

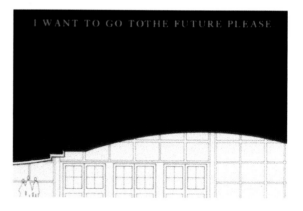

Entrance "art boards"

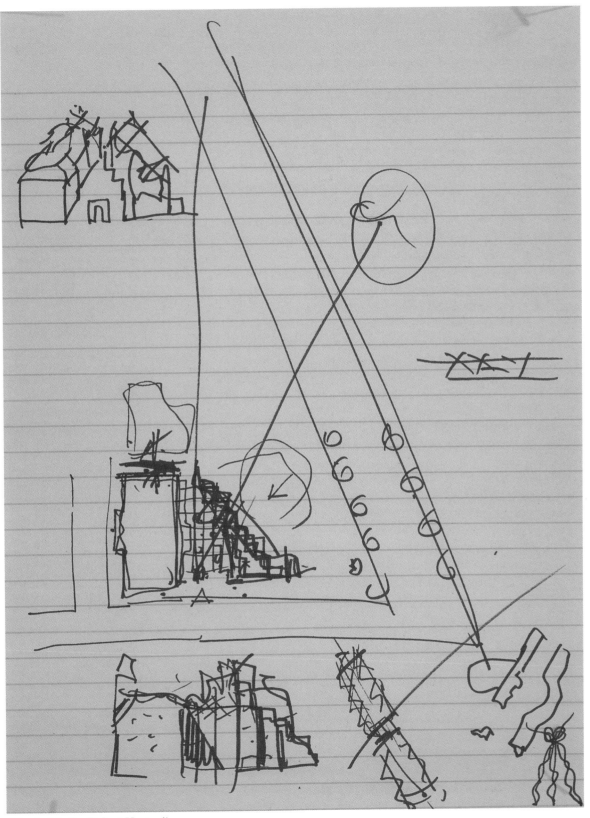

Site sketch (by Robert Venturi)

25 Museum of Contemporary Art, San Diego

Additions, Renovations, and Restorations

La Jolla, California, 1986–1996

The project for San Diego's Museum of Contemporary Art involved demolishing, renovating, restoring, and adding to parts of the original museum complex to accommodate the program of a modern museum and make a new civic building for La Jolla.

On the outside, a rich and varied urban context was to be acknowledged and the gently civic precinct of the La Jolla museum was to be accommodated: in the front, sublime historic buildings by Irving Gill; in the back, a natural landscape and the infinite space of the Pacific Ocean. Within the site, the facade of Gill's Ellen Browning Scripps house—entombed within the complex of 1960s extensions to the then La Jolla Art Center—had to be excavated, exposed, and restored. The house is an acknowledged masterpiece of American architecture.

The new interiors are essentially a setting for the exhibition of art. They consist of spaces neutral in character and varied in configurations that accommodate, as well, flexibility for lighting and circulation. Windows discreetly placed among the galleries facing west permit occasional views of the garden in the foreground and the ocean beyond.

But the museum program for today embraces significant spaces other than those dedicated to art; making up approximately two-thirds of the area of the building are educational, communal, social, administrative, storage, and mechanical and maintenance spaces, including a library, auditorium, shop, and cafe with kitchen. And there is a central space, the Axline Court, that in its image identifies this civic institution as a whole. Its architectural fanfare—spatial and ornamental—is appropriate just once within the otherwise recessive interior designed to cradle works of art.

Context and Scale

The architecture of the new building works to harmonize with that of the old buildings of the precinct by means of analogy and contrast. Its symbolic and formal vocabulary is analogous to Gill's in its abstract-cubist forms, multiple arched openings, and rhythmic columned pergolas. The greater scale of these forms and their iconographic dimension are in contrast with Gill's more domestically scaled and aesthetically abstract buildings. The new building's accommodation to context helps to enhance the already beautiful setting by making it more of a whole. And it is the element of scale—large scale combined with small scale to accommodate perception by the individual up close and by

Irving Gill, Scripps house, La Jolla, 1916

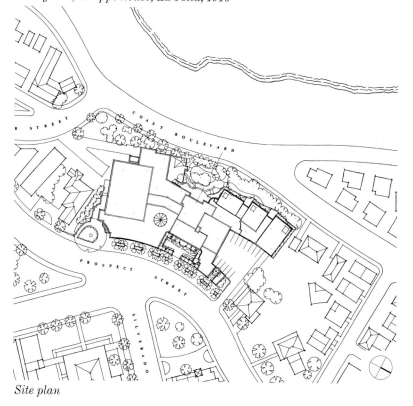

Site plan

Entrance court with museum café

Irving Gill, Women's Club, La Jolla, 1914 (right) with view toward San Diego MoCA (left)

General view from Prospect Street

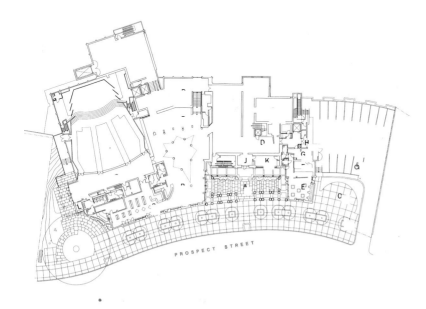

PROSPECT STREET

Main-floor plan

the community at a distance—and the element of iconography—embracing symbolism and graphics—that make this building relevant for a civic institution in late-twentieth-century La Jolla. The facade is also characterized by its rhythmic composition, in which the even pattern of the line of palm trees along the sidewalk plays contrapuntally against the uneven rhythms and varying scales of the arches and columns. By its position right at the line of the sidewalk this facade reflects the slight curve of Prospect Avenue and becomes an urban as well as a civic building in the La Jolla of our time.

A significant element of this civic-urban front facade is its signage, with graphics that are varied and bold—in their color, scale, and lighting—and inherent to the composition. These graphic elements combine with the symbolic and representative forms to constitute the iconography essential to a late-twentieth-century building.

The relation of the newly revealed facade of the Scripps House to the newly designed facade of the whole is significant: the new facade works as a civic statement analogous to its context but also as a frame—as a context itself—for the earlier facade. And as a frame the new works to enhance the old by acknowledging its significance and reinforcing its character—the latter by creating contrast and encouraging comparison in scale where the big civic scale of the new makes explicit the small residential scale of the old. Simultaneously, the intimate quality of the forecourt

Museum court

Axline Court

provides an immediate context that the surrounding and enclosing new facade promotes. It is hoped that the old facade will become a precious jewel protected via enclosure and enhanced via the space and scale of its new context.

The slight variations in the hues among the stucco facades of the complex are significant. The slightly pinkish-white hue of the original Gill facade (as well as the green of the window frames, mullions, and doors) corresponds to the original hue as interpreted from surface scrapings. The slightly grayish-white hue of the new front facade works subtly to reinforce the difference between the old and the new and yet reinforces representation of the old in the new so that the new appears almost like a black-and-white photograph. The scenographic-representative quality of the new parts of the front facade is substantiated by the construction of their walls: conventional stucco-faced masonry rather than the technologically progressive concrete lift-slabs of the walls of the original building.

The rear facade of this complex consists mostly of the varied forms added in the 1960s that accommodate the idea prevalent at the time of designing from the inside out. This picturesque effect of the design has been maintained, and the contrast between the urban front (designed from the outside in as well as vice versa) and the almost rural back has been thereby enhanced—thus acknowledging a valid "Queen Anne front and Mary Anne behind."

The most significant architectural contributions to the rear facade and its setting consist of the graphics that adorn the complex configuration of retaining walls and the external mural. It is fortuitous that the mural has a window in it and an uneven border that perceptually integrate it with the building, and that it is reproduced via a billboard-graphic technique that also makes it changeable—and that it is by Ed Ruscha. It adorns a face of the old auditorium wing, perpendicular to the ocean at the scale of a billboard and at home at the edge of the Pacific Ocean. And it finely and eloquently and iconographically expresses the contrast between the front and the back of this building that evolved over time between urban and rural, and local and universal contexts.

Principal in charge: Robert Venturi
Project managers: John Hunter, Daniel McCoubrey, Ann Trowbridge, Jim Williamson
With: Denise Scott Brown, Hidenao Abe, John Bastian, Laura Campbell, Stephanie Christoff, Claudia Cueto, Ronald Evitts, Christine Gorby, Don Jones, Kimberley Jones, Timothy Kearney, Brian LaBau, Susan Lockwood, Thomas Purdy, Alex Stolyarik, Nancy Rogo Trainer
In association with:
David Raphael Singer Architect

Ocean facade with mural by Ed Ruscha

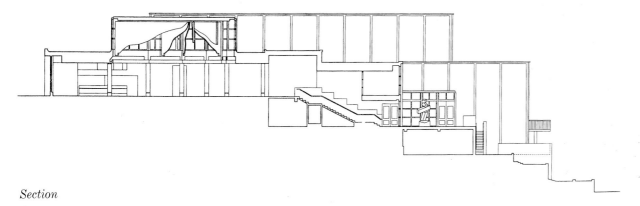

Section

26 Junipero Serra Shrine
Competition Entry

Los Angeles, California, 1996

This is essentially a design for a holy shrine in a Los Angeles cloverleaf. It is a shrine that relates to its regional and urban context and unites with its immediate natural setting to create a whole—perceptual and symbolic. Its curving walls and curving paths, geometric and organic in their configurations, create a harmony of motif within the greater context and the immediate setting that is analogous and contrasting, lyrical and dissonant. The geometrically curving walls also reflect the surrounding street configurations, while the organically curving paths reflect the natural contours of the site itself. At the same time these segmental walls are geometrical fragments of large-scale circles that by implication extend beyond the site. And the undulating profiles of the tops of these curving walls suggest, and thereby symbolize, the mountains beyond. The diverse iconography incised on these grand-scale walls and within the chapel promotes individual scale that is comfortable up close and civic scale that is perceived from a distance. (It is important to remember that iconography is an element that predominates in Roman Catholic architecture from Byzantine times to the present.)

Contemplative Place and Urban Setting

Here is a shrine as an exterior contemplative place in a busy urban setting that accommodates followers of Serra, frequenters of the local neighborhood, and people beyond. Within the shrine is the chapel, with an interior space that embraces spiritual dimensions—atmospheric via the admission of natural light and iconographic via the mural on the wall—and thus accommodates both contemplation and celebration. And here is a chapel both integral in terms of motif with the shrine as a whole—via its curving parapeted walls—and contrasting in terms of space with the shrine as an atrium—via its spatial enclosure.

Here in the end is a place to be felt and read, to appeal to grown-ups and children, to create an aura and tell a story— historic and spiritual—within the tradition of Roman Catholic ecclesiastical architecture; a place whose symbolism and iconography acknowledge the richness of multiculturalism and accommodate the embrace of Catholicism; a place whose design in the end juxtaposes form and symbol, aura and iconography, architecture and landscape to create a holy precinct that is unified in a Los Angeles cityscape.

Views of model

Principals in charge: Robert Venturi, Denise Scott Brown
Project manager: Timothy Kearney
With: Sara Loe, Amy Noble, Felisa Opper, Brian Wurst

General view with Los Angeles City Hall tower in background

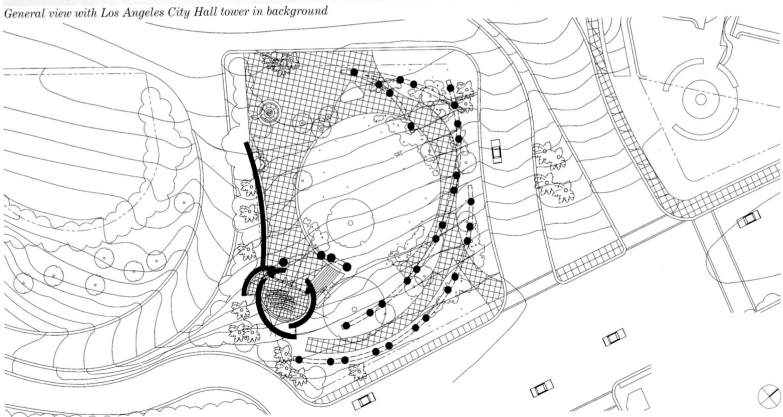

Site plan

27 Whitehall Ferry Terminal

New York, New York, 1992–1996

The Whitehall Ferry Terminal project represents the winning design in an invited competition sponsored by the Economic Development Corporation of New York City. A significant element of the design is its clock facing the water. The clock is a sign, a representation of a clock; it is not a real mechanical clock but an electronic depiction of a clock with "hands" that move around the face via the media of LED pixels that sparkle day and night.

After public condemnation of the aesthetics of the design by the president of the borough of Staten Island, and after a reduction of the budget by a new city administration, a new design was required. The second design, besides eliminating the old clock and the great vault, accommodates more complex program requirements for existing underground circulation and above-grade pedestrian and bus circulation as well as an entirely new requirement, a car-on-ferry system.

In the second version of the design the plan of the plaza and building accommodates the expanded circulation systems demanded by the lower-budget new program by means of geometric distortion: the section of the building is lowered and simplified except for an upsweep toward the north to frame the immediate view of lower Manhattan from inside and a false facade toward the south and the bay; this upsweep can be equated, admittedly, with an electronic billboard. The wavy curves of the parapetted profile of this facade also contrast with the rectangular composition of the urban "backdrop" in the manner of an electronic LED signboard whose moving and changing images promote content—ornamental and informational—and whose truly modern technology permits bold perception from afar across the bay.

It is important to note the timing of this changing imagery. When a ferry, going or coming, is at a relatively great distance, a bold-scale symbolic image suggesting a waving American flag is projected to be constantly identified with this civic monument. When a ferry is relatively close, small-scale images that are informational and local in their reference predominate.

This second design met with disdain from the borough president equal to that shown toward the first design. Does this individual hate civic gestures like the Eiffel Tower, the Statue of Liberty, or Geneva's Jet d'Eau, which present fanfare via symbolism, technology, and scale to promote civic imagery and civic identity remembered all over the world?

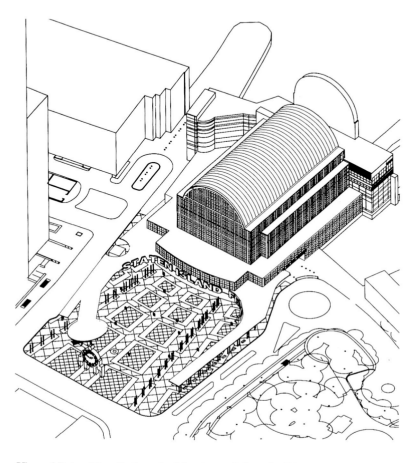

View of Peter Minuit plaza looking toward ferry building (1992 scheme)

The Symbolic Clock

In the old days the presence of the inevitable clock as part of the exterior architectural design of the railroad terminal was decorative and functional, since many approaching passengers did not own watches. Today a clock in such a context is hardly functional because virtually everyone wears a watch: the clock is therefore symbolic and decorative and civic because of its obsolescence, as well as its signification and its size.

In its shape, the Whitehall clock both reflects (from Manhattan's standpoint) and generates (from Staten Island's standpoint) the form of the barrel vault that floats behind it.

View from across the harbor (1992 scheme)

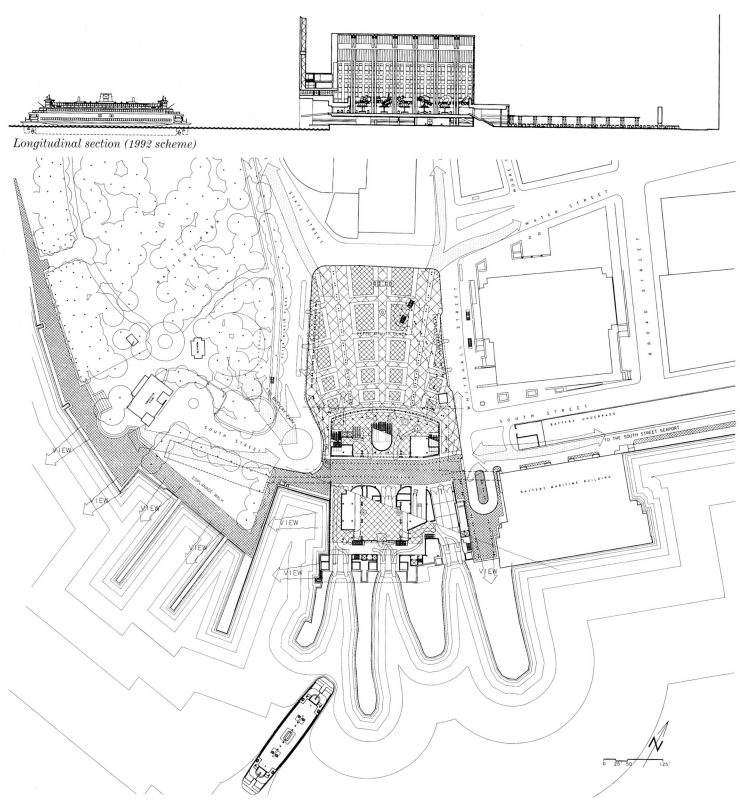

Longitudinal section (1992 scheme)

Site plan (1992 scheme)

Rendering of main hall with LED sign board (1992 scheme)

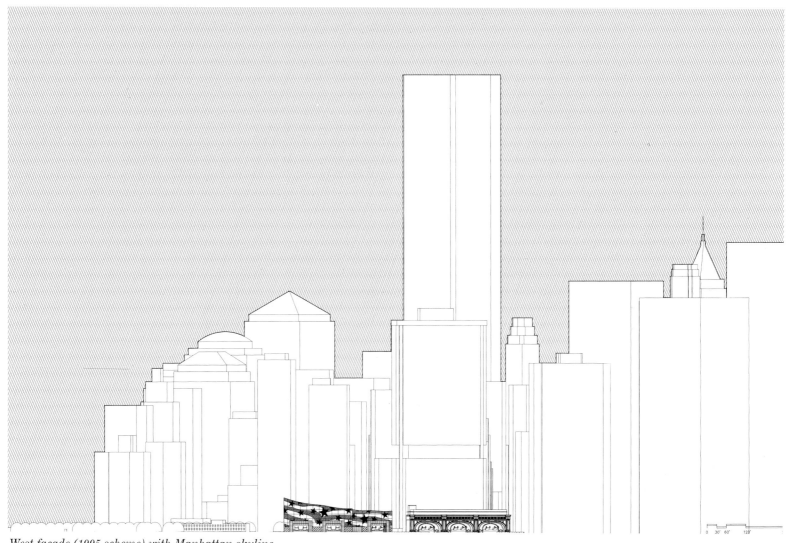

West facade (1995 scheme) with Manhattan skyline

And the grand vault represents a gesture toward the past when architecture of the urban infrastructure was civic in its scale and symbolism. The Jumbotron inside this vault represents the technology of today—and contributes an iconographic dimension that complements the spatial dimension within the waiting hall. But it is important to emphasize the formal as well as the symbolic significance of the clock. The circular form works as a vivid contrast to the rectangular forms of the skyscrapers, which create the famous skyline behind the clock and constitute its context from the water.

So why is this clock as a sign considered banal or oppressive by its opponents when it so aptly complements the Manhattan skyline formally and symbolically and compliments the borough of Staten Island? It looks good in Manhattan and from Staten Island while working vividly as a sign readable from afar and as a symbol whose hyper twentieth-century image corresponds to the bold nineteenth-century imagery of the Statue of Liberty across the bay.

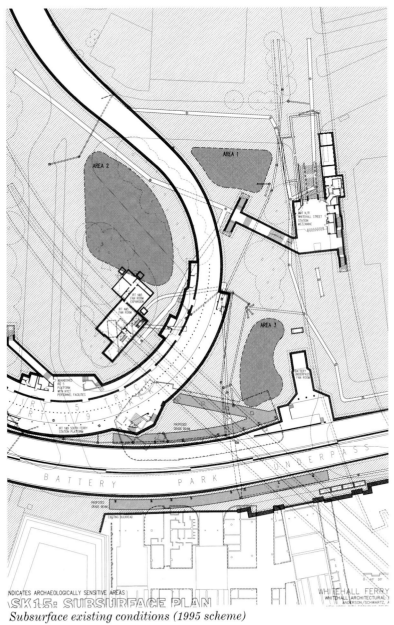

SK15: SUBSURFACE PLAN

Subsurface existing conditions (1995 scheme)

View from main lobby toward Manhattan (1995 scheme)

TASK 15: SECOND FLOOR PLAN

Second-floor plan (1995 scheme)

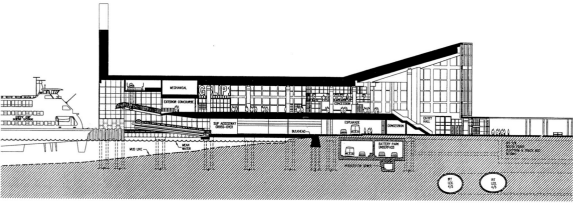

Principals in charge: Robert Venturi,
Denise Scott Brown
Project manager: Ronald Evitts
With: John Bastian, Catherine Bird,
Josh Brandfonbrener, Jason Brody,
Stephanie Christoff, John Forney,
John Izenour, Steven Izenour,
Timothy Kearney, Amy Noble,
Felisa Opper, David Singer,
David Vaughan, Ingalill Wahlroos
In association with: Anderson/Schwartz
Architects; TAMS Consultants, Inc.

Day view from harbor and section through main lobby (1995 scheme)

Views from harbor, night and day, with LED signboard showing changing images (1995 scheme)

28 Battery Park Band Pavilion
Competition Entry

New York, New York, 1989

These designs for a band pavilion in Battery Park embrace two approaches: one has historical-stylistic reference—playful, whimsical, and in an abstracted representational form; the other is also representational but in a literal, not a stylistic, sense. The latter is somewhat like the representational sculpture of Claes Oldenburg but is also architectural and provides shelter. Children, we hope, would love these and so would adults—those who would admit it.

Principal in charge: Robert Venturi
Project manager: Steven Izenour

Chrysler Building pavilion (sketch by Robert Venturi)

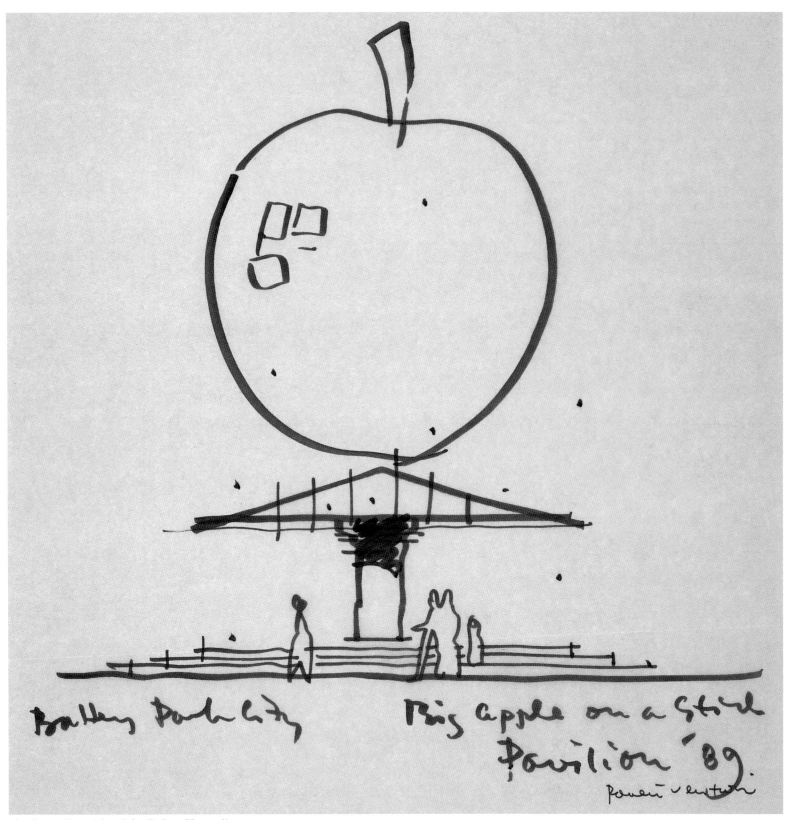

Apple pavilion (sketch by Robert Venturi)

29 Celebration Bank
The Walt Disney Company

Celebration, Florida, 1993–1996

The major design challenge for a small corner bank building in Celebration, Florida (Disney's planned new town) was to create a civic presence and scale for a small building. The flush neoclassical vocabulary is symbolic of a traditional bank; the detailing and massing are appropriate for a modest building.

The large order on the main facade is scaled to relate to the town as a whole; more circumstantial elements occur within the grand order. The plan is organized to provide a top-lit central space and central circulation for a civic building on an irregular site.

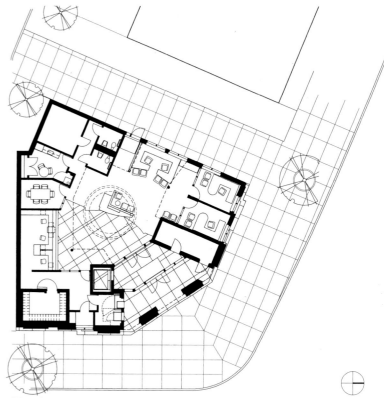

Site plan

Principal in charge: Robert Venturi
Project manager: Timothy Kearney
With: Claudia Cueto, Steven Izenour, Amy Noble, Brian Wurst
In association with: HKS

Central cupola

Street view

Celebration Bank **191**

30 Fire Station
Reedy Creek Emergency Services Headquarters, The Walt Disney Company

Walt Disney World Resort, Florida, 1992–1993

The Fire Station is the first back-of-house support facility visible to park visitors at the Disney World Resort in Orlando. It accommodates a state-of-the-art fire rescue center that includes living quarters, administrative offices, and an emergency communications center, as well as spaces for school groups and visiting firefighters.

The image of the building has been carefully designed to represent the traditional American firehouse; patterns and colors referring to red bricks and dalmations exaggerated in intensity and scale adorn the front in porcelain-enamel panels. Functionally it is a modern, single-story facility. The sweeping curve of the front facade acknowledges and accommodates the curve of the drive where the fire trucks exit from the complex expeditiously.

Principal in charge: Robert Venturi
Project manager: Timothy Kearney
With: Steven Izenour, Eva Lew, Amy Noble
In association with: Schenkel/Shultz Architecture/Interior Design

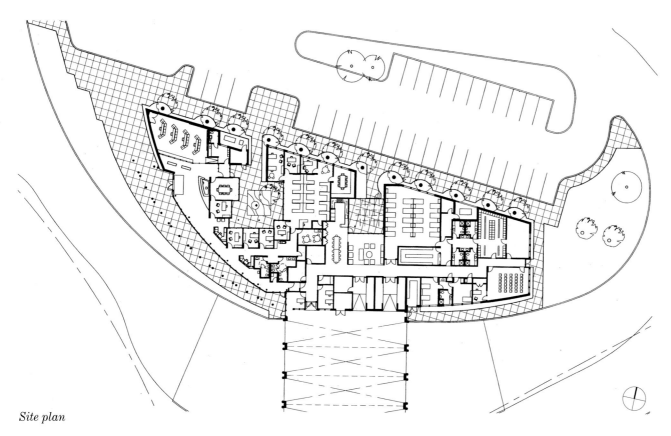

Site plan

General view

31 Trenton Fire Station Extension

Trenton, New Jersey, 1996–1999

In a fire station form must distinctly follow function, but the civic-aesthetic dimension is also important. So the architectural design for the Trenton Fire Station Extension directly accommodates and frankly expresses on the outside a big garage with industrial-like auxiliary spaces; yet it independently fulfills the civic-aesthetic dimension via applied iconography. This iconography embraces graphics and symbol juxtaposed on form; it is independent of the form and integral to it at the same time. As signage it identifies, informs, and ornaments all at once.

The frieze across the front of the new wing, consisting of Roman lettering, works to unify the irregular composition of the functional garagelike facade. At the new pedestrian entrance is architectural fanfare: a traditional statue of a fireman and a representation of a large-scale helmet are the central accent for the whole composition. The entrance also purposely allows a view through the building, thereby spatially uniting the front and the back.

There is good precedent for lettering on building facades going back to Roman times. The boldness and color of this literally Roman lettering is appropriate for the late twentieth century with its hype sensibility and the requirement that words be legible while the observer is driving by.

The old building is to be carefully restored and the new building is to harmonize with the old via architectural elements that are both analogous to and contrasting with those of the old.

Principal in charge: Robert Venturi
Associate in charge: Timothy Kearney
Project manager: Brian Wurst
With: Sara Loe, Daniel McCoubrey, Amy Noble, Nathalie Peeters, Andrew Thurlow
In association with: Vaughn Organization

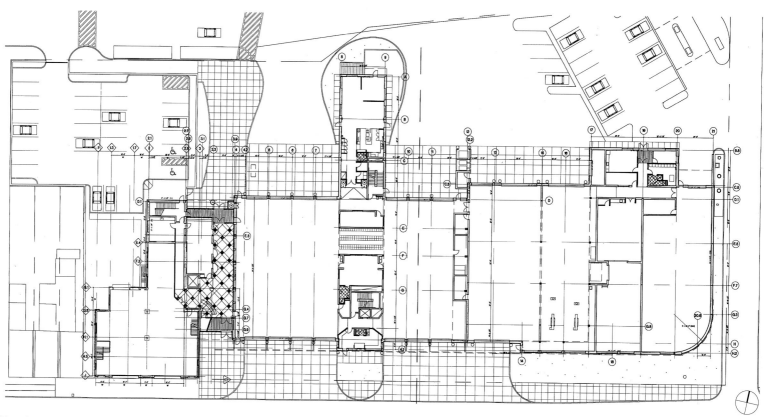

Site plan

Rendering of concourse

Streetfront elevation

32 Philadelphia Orchestra Hall

Philadelphia, Pennsylvania, 1987–1996

The Philadelphia Orchestra Hall was not to be at the edge of downtown on an open plaza or in the midst of parking—common locations for such halls in the last decades—and thus would never be spectacular architectural sculpture to be seen as a whole from a distance. Instead, its location within the egalitarian gridiron plan of Philadelphia presents a particular challenge. Given its relatively small size, it risks being dwarfed by larger but less important structures; because it sits on the street, not on a plaza or at the termination of a boulevard, the irregular and dramatic shape of the hall within cannot be reflected on the exterior, except above the roofline. In not "expressing" the interior on the outside VSBA departed from recent concert hall design directions and returned to an older tradition of halls and houses like those of La Scala in Milan and Philadelphia's Academy of Music itself, whose exterior forms are essentially rectangular as they define directional space along a street (or on a piazza) rather than sit as a point in space that is open.

In this kind of hall the acoustically shaped hall at the core is wrapped by a rectangular exterior layer that accommodates the line of the streets; the irregular residual spaces between the outer walls and the interior hall become the foyers and access lobbies—ceremonially important areas whose dynamic shapes direct concertgoers toward the hall and promote tension and interest within the layered composition as a whole. The south facade diverges exceptionally from the rectangular configuration of the plan as it curves slightly to accommodate space for the flow for auto, taxi, and bus drop-off and for access to the integral parking garage beyond.

One of the goals of this design was explicitly and conscientiously to meet the established budget, which was exceedingly low despite very expensive requirements deriving from municipal codes and acoustic determinants. We accomplished this via coordination with construction managers and by asserting that the exterior aesthetic would be that of a Pennsylvania Friends' meetinghouse rather than that of a palatial Baroque opera house.

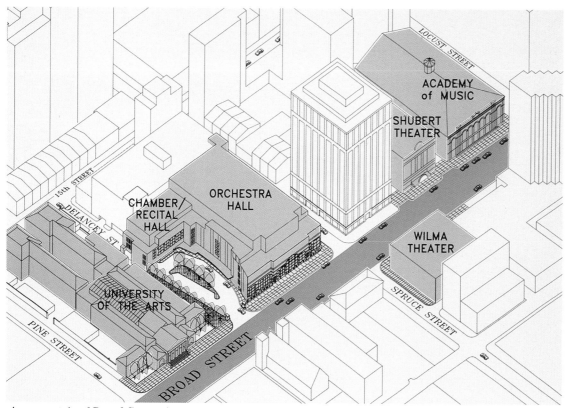

Axonometric of Broad Street site

Principals in charge: Robert Venturi, Denise Scott Brown
Project managers: Ian Adamson, Timothy Kearney
With: Michael Ablon, Josh Brandfonbrener, Mark Burgess, Rodney Collins, Stephen Glascock, Michael Guarino, Michael Haverland, Steven Izenour, Don Jones, Pablo Meninato, Adam Meyers, Catherine Murray Bird, Amy Noble, Willis Pember, Michael Peters, James Winkler

Rendering of Broad Street facade (1990 scheme)

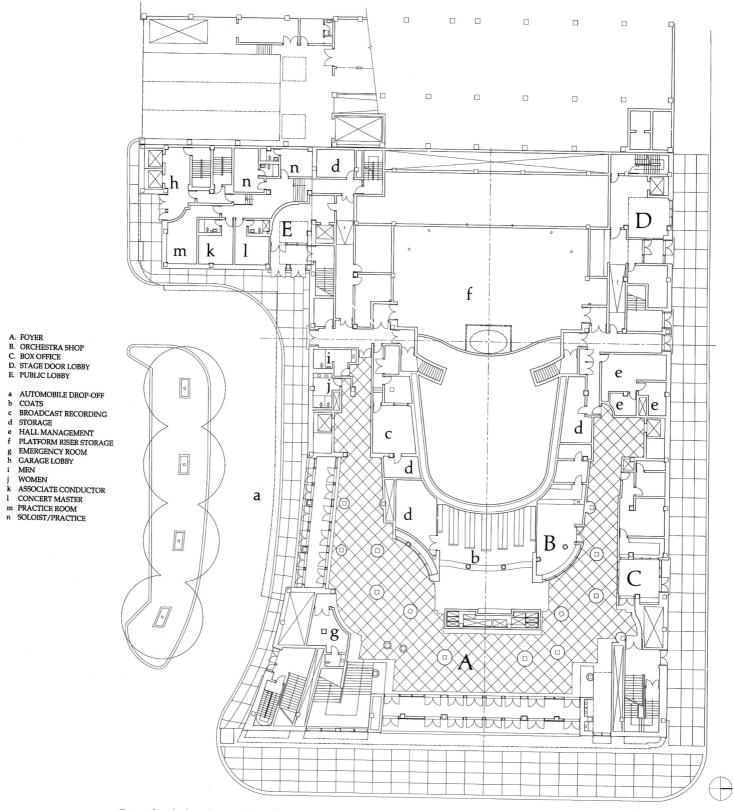

A. FOYER
B. ORCHESTRA SHOP
C. BOX OFFICE
D. STAGE DOOR LOBBY
E. PUBLIC LOBBY

a AUTOMOBILE DROP-OFF
b COATS
c BROADCAST RECORDING
d STORAGE
e HALL MANAGEMENT
f PLATFORM RISER STORAGE
g EMERGENCY ROOM
h GARAGE LOBBY
i MEN
j WOMEN
k ASSOCIATE CONDUCTOR
l CONCERT MASTER
m PRACTICE ROOM
n SOLOIST/PRACTICE

Street-level plan (1990 scheme)

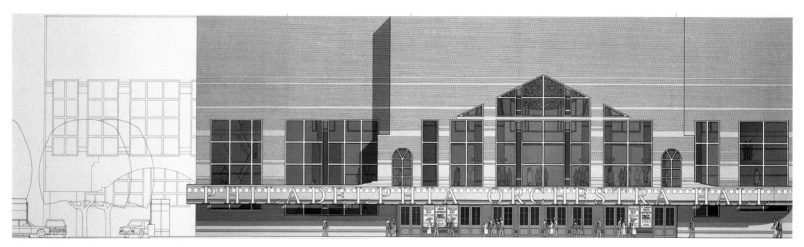

Broad Street elevation (1990 scheme)

Monumentality and Symbols

For this relatively small building to achieve an appropriate civic presence along Broad Street, elements of scale, iconography, and symbolism are employed. The first involves the rhythmic configuration of large windows on the front facade; these are monumental in relation to those of neighboring high-rise buildings. At night the grand and brightly lit windows through which activity is visible contribute to an inviting and gala effect on Broad Street. The monumentality of this facade derives also from symbolic elements—from the frieze of bold graphics and from the reference via the configuration of the large windows to the shape of the Classical pediment of the significant building next door, the University of the Arts, the Greek Revival work by John Haviland.

Inside, this concert hall is a hall—a chamber, a room—rather than a theater or an opera house. It works within the tradition of the halls of palaces where chamber and symphonic music evolved. The architectural-spatial effect of the hall derives essentially from the design and integral lighting of the faces of balconies, which surround both the audience and the orchestra and therefore reinforce the idea of the room as a whole. A clerestory of windowlike elements around the top of the hall accommodates acoustical flexibility and further symbolizes this space as a room rather than as a theater.

From Masonry Facade to Glass Front

Redesign of the facade was requested to accommodate the wishes of a particular donor and his adviser. At this point we were permitted to increase the budget for the facade of the hall and incidentally to accommodate, via its new design, its special new context—that of the civic and gala Avenue of the Arts, which South Broad Street had subsequently been designated.

Because of these circumstances the front facade of the Philadelphia Orchestra Hall evolved from that of a masonry wall—defined via window openings, surface patterns, and graphics—to that of a glass wall whose aluminum-surfaced structural grid is rhythmically complex as it depicts windows as well as grid and is brightly varicolored as it contrasts with the side walls, which remain surfaces of brick. Along the base of the facade is a range of backlit poster boards and a colorful LED frieze with moving informational graphics that contribute sparkling color, intimate scale, and interest at eye level along the sidewalk interrupted only by the entrance doors. Above this level floats an ornamental frieze consisting of abstracted and stylized musical notes on a staff made of stainless-steel sheets that reflect light at night. At night the facade explicitly emits rather than reflects light; also, its symbolic dimension is engaged by certain segments of the gridded glass that contain spandrel glass (only ambiguously evident by day but distinctly perceptible as opaque at night). In addition, certain panels of the wall are of stained glass rather than transparent glass, and certain linear elements of the grid are diagonal. These all configure to suggest—not represent—the columnar pedimented facade associated with civic and monumental architecture. Here is an image Miesian and Mondrianesque in its effect—but at the same time abstract and symbolic—accommodating the hype sensibility of our time, day and night, and embracing an expanded market for cultural institutions.

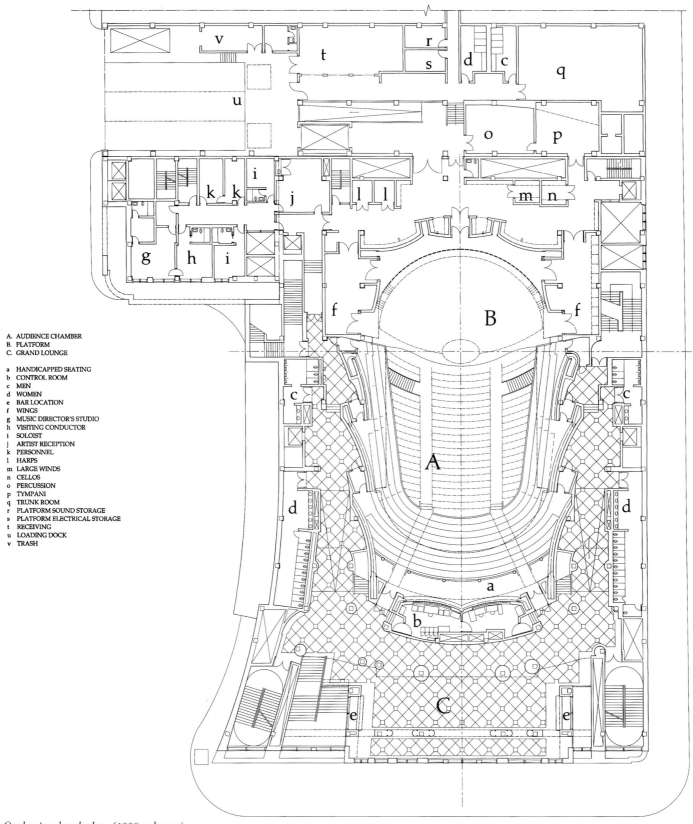

A. AUDIENCE CHAMBER
B. PLATFORM
C. GRAND LOUNGE

a   HANDICAPPED SEATING
b   CONTROL ROOM
c   MEN
d   WOMEN
e   BAR LOCATION
f   WINGS
g   MUSIC DIRECTOR'S STUDIO
h   VISITING CONDUCTOR
i   SOLOIST
j   ARTIST RECEPTION
k   PERSONNEL
l   HARPS
m   LARGE WINDS
n   CELLOS
o   PERCUSSION
p   TYMPANI
q   TRUNK ROOM
r   PLATFORM SOUND STORAGE
s   PLATFORM ELECTRICAL STORAGE
t   RECEIVING
u   LOADING DOCK
v   TRASH

Orchestra-level plan (1990 scheme)

Computer rendering of orchestra hall (1990 scheme)

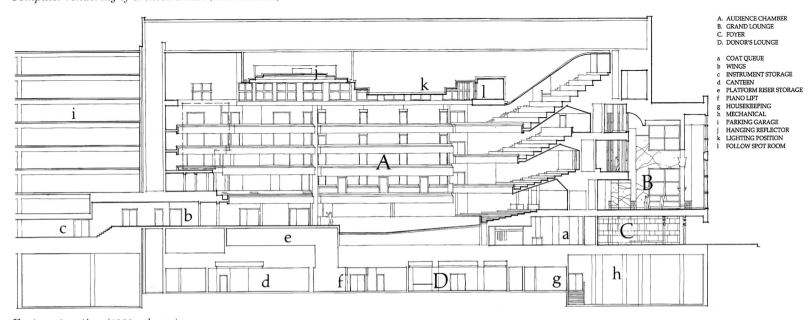

A. AUDIENCE CHAMBER
B. GRAND LOUNGE
C. FOYER
D. DONOR'S LOUNGE

a COAT QUEUE
b WINGS
c INSTRUMENT STORAGE
d CANTEEN
e PLATFORM RISER STORAGE
f PIANO LIFT
g HOUSEKEEPING
h MECHANICAL
i PARKING GARAGE
j HANGING REFLECTOR
k LIGHTING POSITION
l FOLLOW SPOT ROOM

East-west section (1989 scheme)

Rendering of facade at night (1995 scheme)

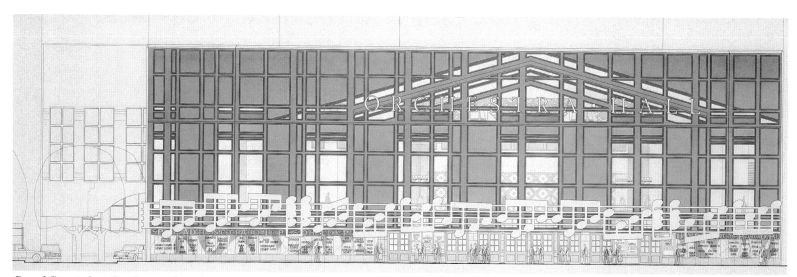

Broad Street elevation (1995 scheme)

Facade detail (1995 scheme)

33 Hôtel du Département de la Haute-Garonne

Toulouse, France, 1992–1999

The Hôtel du Département, like any provincial or state capitol, must combine repetitive office units with monumental forms and spaces appropriate for the official and ceremonial functions of government. Yet the hierarchical combination of uses must suggest a formal and symbolic whole.

This building must project a vivid civic image for the region and at the same time mesh with the fabric of the old city of Toulouse from its site on the edge. For this reason this building in its design is really a complex. It is activated by an important pedestrian street that connects a historic entrance to the city at an important bridge crossing the Canal du Midi with the diagonally opposite corner of the site, which faces a new commercial development, the Compans Cassarelli, to the southwest. In this way, the parts of the building are articulated while the whole promotes a civic scale and provides a sense of entrance at both ends of the site. It provides a great public space for the Haute-Garonne in the form of a crescent located along the pedestrian street and at the heart of the site. This space works as a focal point for the departmental offices and also as a counterpoint to the pedestrian street on one hand and the green park beyond.

A small park opposite the Salle du Conseil Général provides a partial vista of the building from Avenue Honoré Serres. A large park facing the Canal du Midi enhances the neighborhood and provides a setting for the building along the canal; the great curved section of the building may be seen as a reflection of the curve of the Garonne as it flows toward the sea. Covered glass bridges span the pedestrian street connecting the two wings of the building at two locations. They offer dramatic views from within the complex and, by their form and silhouette, serve as symbolic gateways to the civic crescent.

The entrance at the corner of Avenue Honoré Serres and Boulevard de la Marquette contains a representation of a great doorway set in a plain brick wall in the tradition of historic Toulouse buildings. Before this gate stand two-dimensional representations of the two monumental columns originally located near this spot at the edge of the old city, as evidenced in old photographs.

Limestone is the exterior material on the outer surfaces of the building. Generously scaled windows create some hierarchy among the floors as they ascend the facade. The facades of the interior court contain the same windows, and are of brick so the "street" evokes the rosy aura of the historic streets of Toulouse. Important forms such as those of the Hall d'Honneur and the Salle du Conseil Général are sheathed in glass curtain walls. The bridges and the colonnades of the street and crescent represent and celebrate historic architectural elements of the Haute-Garonne but do not reproduce them literally.

The image and the unity of this building as a whole allow its individual parts to acknowledge formal and symbolic variety. The building is architecturally Modern and admits technological expression in its glass and paneled walls; at the same time it contains historical references in the types of windows used and in the way they are set within masonry walls. Its unity proclaims its civic importance while its variety acknowledges the rich variety evident today in the streets of Toulouse, the result of an architectural evolution over centuries.

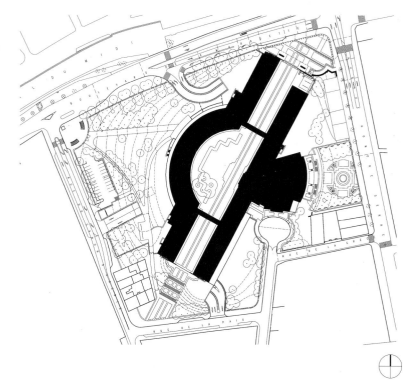

Site plan

Partial north facade with Canal du Midi

Interior of Assembly Hall

Exterior of Assembly Hall

Principals in charge: Robert Venturi, Denise Scott Brown
Project director: David Vaughan
Project manager: John Bastian
With: Hidenao Abe, Catherine Bird, Jason Brody, Laura Campbell, John Chase, Heather Clark, Ronald Evitts, John Folan, John Forney, Ion Ghika, Joseph Herrin, Daniel Horowitz, John Hunter, Timothy Kearney, Jeffrey Krieger, Eva Lew, Susan Lockwood, Nathalie Peeters, Alex Stolyarik, Brian Wurst
In association with: Hermet, Blanc, Lagausie, Mommens Architectes; Anderson/Schwartz Architects

Court exterior

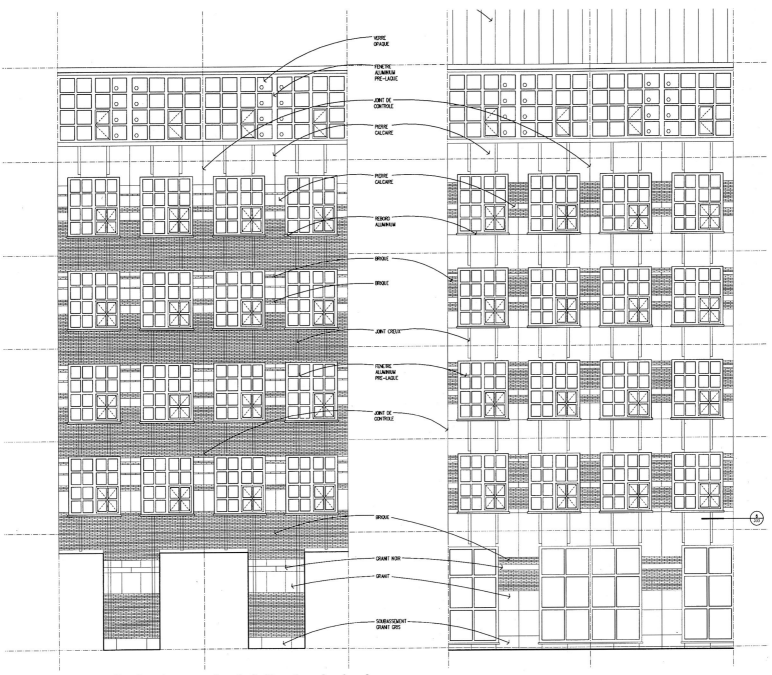

VERRE
OPAQUE

FENETRE
ALUMINIUM
PRE-LAQUE

JOINT DE
CONTROLE

PIERRE
CALCAIRE

PIERRE
CALCAIRE

REBORD
ALUMINIUM

BRIQUE

BRIQUE

JOINT CREUX

FENETRE
ALUMINIUM
PRE-LAQUE

JOINT DE
CONTROLE

BRIQUE

GRANIT NOIR

GRANIT

SOUBASSEMENT
GRANIT GRIS

East wing facade studies: interior street facade (left) and garden facade

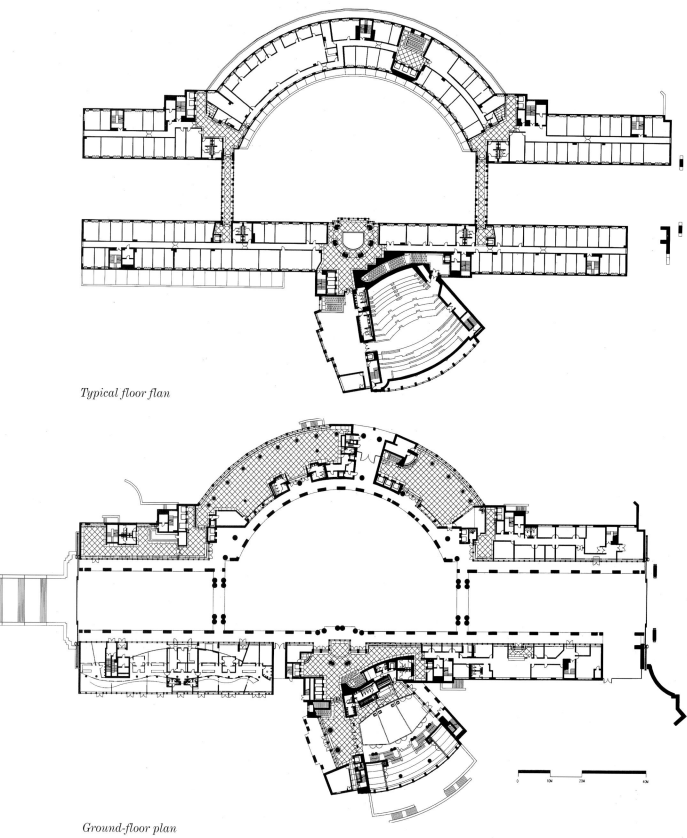

Typical floor plan

Ground-floor plan

Rendering of Assembly Hall

34 Berlin U.S. Embassy
Competition Entry

Berlin, Germany, 1995

The competition entry for the United States embassy in Berlin involves four components that are crucial—urban context, cultural reference, interior flexibility, and expressed hospitality—combined with acute security. The urban context—civic, historic, and symbolic—is extremely significant, since the building is to face on three sides the Brandenburg Gate and Pariser Platz, which its main entrance opens onto; Ebertstrasse, facing the Tiergarten; and Behrensstrasse, across which is anticipated the Memorial to the Jewish War Dead.

Rhythm and Context

The facade on the Pariser Platz aims at harmony via analogy—essentially via the configuration of rhythmic window openings hierarchically tiered in a limestone wall. These elements of the facade conform in an abstract way to what is architecturally anticipated in the rebuilding of the square. But this wall and its rhythmic composition are interrupted with a vertical break that opens into an entrance courtyard that signifies hospitality. The elements visible beyond and within the courtyard create contrasts within the contextual whole—the treetops protruding from a larger courtyard beyond and the LED screen that can be glimpsed within the court, like the rich lining of a coat with mosaiclike pixels that project changing images of symbolic, narrative, and informational references to American culture. These layers of natural treetops and iconographic screen—as tantalizingly glimpsed—combine with the facade as a whole to create harmony at the front through analogy and contrast.

The LED screen in the court specifically acknowledges and depicts a range of American culture from pop to fine art, from Fats Waller to Raggedy Ann dolls to the Bill of Rights, as well as information on sports and news and cultural announcements. This iconographic element is especially relevant in terms of its advanced aesthetic and advanced technology. And the interior ceremonial spaces immediately beyond the entrance contain murals whose traditional media correspond to those of WPA post offices and Baroque palaces.

The facades to the side and the rear, also composed of lime-stone, adapt to their contexts (the Tiergarten and the anticipated memorial representing civic-natural and civic-symbolic urban spaces) and also reflect the generic configuration of the interior of the building, which consists of flexible office space. This

Perspective view of forecourt with Brandenburg Gate in the background

Principals in charge: Robert Venturi, Denise Scott Brown, Steven Izenour
Project manager: John Bastian
With: Hidenao Abe, Catherine Bird, Tony Bracali, Angelina Chong, Heather Clark, Diane Golomb, Michael Haverland, Daniel Horowitz, Timothy Kearney, Adam Meyers, Amy Noble, Nathalie Peeters, Thomas Purdy, Steven Stainbrook, Richard Stokes, Nancy Rogo Trainer, Linh Tran, James Wallace, Brian Wurst, Joy Yoder
In association with: Einhorn Yaffee Prescott; Andropogon Associates, Ltd.

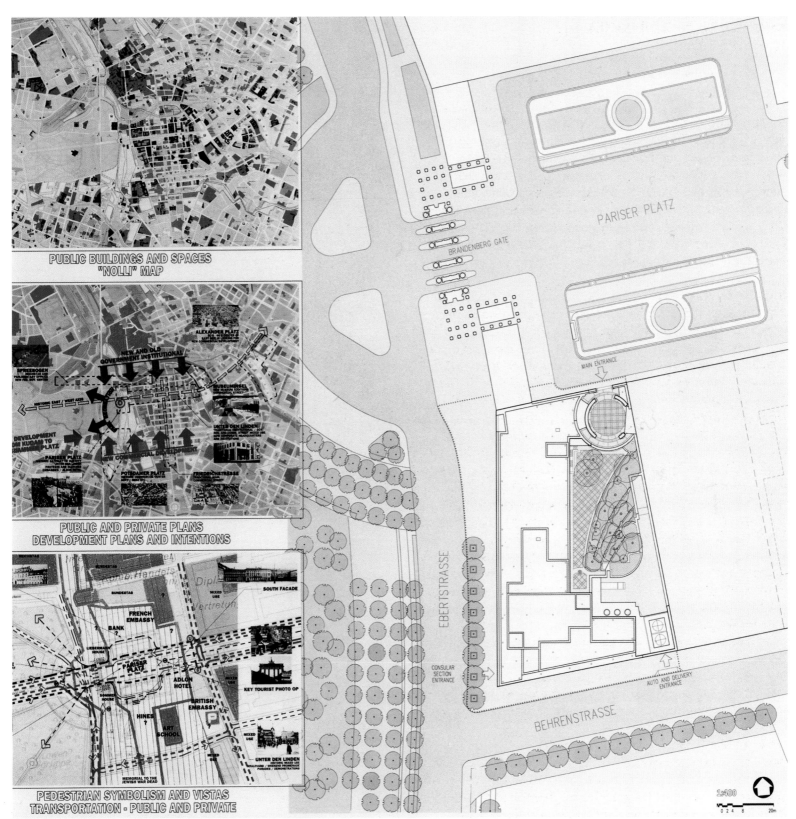

PUBLIC BUILDINGS AND SPACES
"NOLLI" MAP

PUBLIC AND PRIVATE PLANS
DEVELOPMENT PLANS AND INTENTIONS

PEDESTRIAN SYMBOLISM AND VISTAS
TRANSPORTATION - PUBLIC AND PRIVATE

PARISER PLATZ

BRANDENBERG GATE

MAIN ENTRANCE

EBERTSTRASSE

CONSULAR
SECTION
ENTRANCE

AUTO AND DELIVERY
ENTRANCE

BEHRENSTRASSE

1:400

0 2 4 8   20m

Site plan with studies of economic and traffic growth tendencies around Pariser Platz

adaptation and reflection result in a facade with a functional and consistent configuration of windows but with a juxtaposed irregular rhythmic system composed of applied, ornamental, colored aluminum elements suggesting pilasters. The uneven rhythm of these elements creates a crescendo as it approaches and articulates the secondary entrance, at the southern end of the facade, to the consular section of the embassy. These vertical elements work also as a "giant order" that promotes a gently monumental scale as it enhances a sense of a cohesive whole. These surface elements—consistently flush and purely ornamental—are also variously colored red, white, and blue, and via their color configurations they reinforce the rhythmic crescendos on the facades. Two elements—the setback creating a terrace for the ambassador's suite facing the Tiergarten and the service entrance at the rear—act as exceptions to the order and thereby create aesthetic tension.

Interior flexibility is achieved in this design by means of a conventional order, tried and tested: the generic office loft that promotes flexibility (spatial via flexible partitions and mechanical via lighting) and accessible ceiling space and achieves amenity with careful detailing of the parts and quality of the furniture. This system realistically balances the practical needs for change over time.

The design is determined by security requirements in significant spatial, structural, formal, and technical ways: circulation patterns that particularly affect the design of entering and exiting systems; mechanical-electronic systems; wall thickness; and wall-window ratios. The entrance design, with its transitional courtyard and vestibules, combines a practical security system through circulation configurations and electronic systems and at the same time promotes an effective expression of gracious hospitality through apparent openness and spatial amenity.

Much more could be written about the complexities of the program and design of this architectural project, but the most important thing is its realistic integration of generic planning that is spatial and technical, its expressions and meanings that are formal and iconographic, and its contextual integrity as a building within a sensitive cultural and historic setting. It is not signature but architecture—bridging expressively and technologically symbols and functions of yesterday, today, and, incidentally, tomorrow.

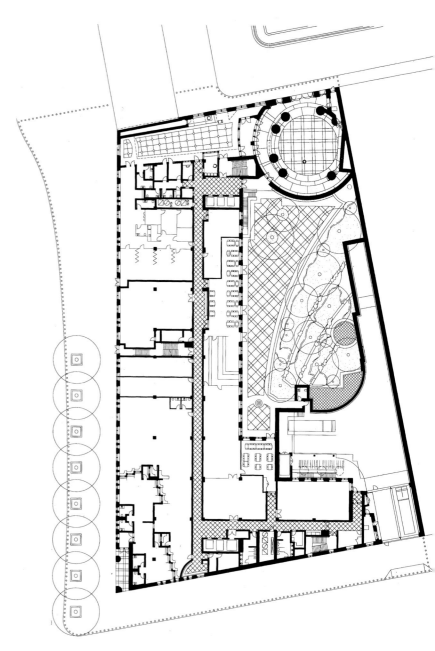

First-floor plan

View from Tiergarten with Brandenburg Gate

Perspective from Pariser Platz

Perspective of Lobby

View of entrance forecourt with LED display

Typical LED Display Content
1:100

No Place Like HOME

The Philadelphia Orchestra
WOLFGANG SAWALLISCH
MUSIC DIRECTOR

SCHUMANN   Symphony No. 2
SHOENBERG   Piano Concerto

BERLINER
PHILHARMONIE
SATURDAY OCTOBER 2

View of changing LED display in forecourt compared to the colonnade of Schinkel's Altes Museum

Perspective of main entrance from Pariser Platz

Michigan Stadium
"HALO"

Institutional Buildings

218   *Clinical Research Building,*
University of Pennsylvania

220   *Fisher and Bendheim Halls*

224   *Bard College Library Addition*

230   *Trabant Student Center*

234   *Gordon and Virginia MacDonald Medical*
Research Laboratories

238   *Gonda (Goldschmied) Neuroscience and*
Genetics Research Center

240   *George LaVie Schultz Laboratory*

244   *Medical Laboratory, Yale University*

246   *Roy and Diana Vagelos Laboratories*

248   *Residence Hall Complex,*
University of Cincinnati

252   *Frist Campus Center*

256   *Berry Library and Academic Wing*

259   *Center for International and Area Studies,*
Yale University

260   *Clinical Research Center,*
National Institutes of Health

35 Clinical Research Building
School of Medicine, University of Pennsylvania

Philadelphia, Pennsylvania, 1985–1990

For the University of Pennsylvania's School of Medicine we designed a scientific laboratory as a generic loft to accommodate spatial and mechanical flexibility for research and provide an unobtrusive background for concentration and communication within an academic community. Incidental interaction to promote collegiality among the users is enhanced via occasional meeting places or niches within the circulation system. The design of the outside (the main responsibility of VSBA) achieves aesthetic quality appropriate to an urban campus with consistent but complex rhythms that derive from repetitive bays and windows and from surface ornament within its brick and cast-stone surfaces. Exceptions to the order at the entrance and at the ends and top of the building enhance the whole. Up top is also an explicit sign, a representation of the shield of the university. The shield connects through scale with downtown Philadelphia at a distance and identifies the university.

Principal in charge: Robert Venturi
Project managers: Ian Adamson, Michael Peters
Project architects: Eric van Aukee, James Kolker
With: John Bastian, Catherine Bird, John Forney, James King, Amy Klee, Robert Marker, Charles Renfro, Ann Trowbridge, James Winkler, Christian Wise
In association with: Payette Associates Inc.

View of University of Pennsylvania area with Clinical Research Building sign in background

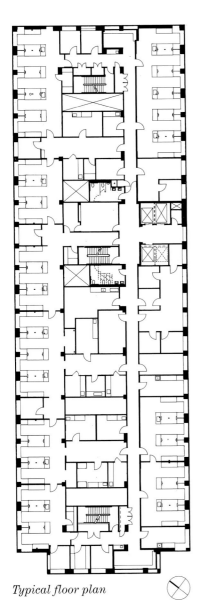

Typical floor plan

View of building with downtown Philadelphia in background

36 Fisher and Bendheim Halls
Department of Economics and Center of International Studies, Princeton University

Princeton, New Jersey, 1986–1990

The building containing Fisher and Bendheim Halls houses the Department of Economics and the Center of International Studies at Princeton. These two departments are adjacent to each other rather than one above the other so that each can maintain more effectively its own entrance and identity—Fisher for economics, and Bendheim for international studies. The former faces Prospect Street, while the latter is located within the campus off Scudder Plaza. While the Center of International Studies accommodates offices and seminar rooms, the Department of Economics accommodates series of faculty and administration offices above grade, and student carrels and teaching and computer spaces below grade. The departmental library with its mezzanine seminar room works as a central meeting place within the hierarchy of spaces and scales inside the building; the halls and corridors also contain eddies for incidental meetings that enhance a sense of community.

Outside, Fisher and Bendheim Halls sit in a diverse part of the campus. Toward the east and south is Prospect Street, which is lined with eating clubs that are in a variety of styles and almost domestic in scale. To the north and west sit institutional buildings varied in their architectural quality but related via their proximity and academic functions. The new building is attached to Corwin Hall and is connected to Robertson Hall via a tunnel to the west.

The slablike form of Fisher and Bendheim Halls accommodates the three-story series of offices inside, which in turn promote, with their repetitive window configurations, a rhythmic quality in the facades outside. The slab terminates at its southern end in the two-story bay window, which establishes a hierarchy of scale outside and promotes a sense of the building as a whole; it also works to identify the Fisher entrance at the lower level. At the northern end the slab expands to accommodate particular interior requirements of the Center of International Studies and thus distinguishes this end of the building from the other, and accommodates and identifies its entrance.

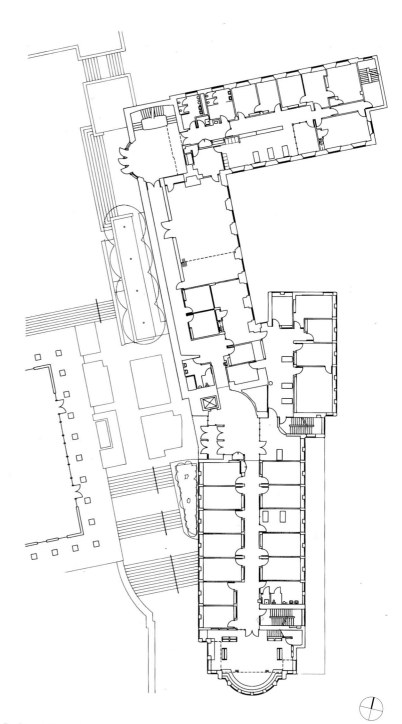

Podium floor plan

Entrance facade of Bendheim Hall

Form, Space, Symbolism

In its formal and spatial context this building both directs space via the stairway between the plaza and the street and terminates the complex of academic buildings at the west end of Prospect Street. In its surface design and symbolic context it combines contrast and analogy: its brick is like that of Corwin Hall, and its brick in combination with limestone trim is like that of '79 Hall and other buildings in the southeastern precinct of the Princeton campus. In its limestone-trimmed strip windows, big bay window, and ornamental elements the building adapts the Gothic-Elizabethan vocabulary of '79 Hall visible across Washington Road, which is associated with Princeton campus architecture as a whole, but the adaptation consists of stylistic abstraction, of representation, rather than of replication of a style.

An essential quality of the architecture is the play between order and disorder, system and circumstance, consistency and exception in form and symbolism. The building promotes, on one hand, order that is generic and comforting and that emanates from the basic quality of its academic program; on the other hand, exceptions to that order reflect and accommodate valid contradictions within a complex whole.

In the end the tension among these forces makes for valid art.

Principal in charge: Robert Venturi
Project managers: David Schaaf, Venita Van Hamme Brown
Project architect: Edward Chuchla
With: Steven Izenour, David Perkes, Michael Peters, Matthew Schottelkotte, Ann Trowbridge, Malcolm Woollen

View of building

Library in Fisher Building

Southeast corner

37 Bard College Library Addition
Charles P. Stevenson Jr. Library Addition, Bard College

Annandale-on-Hudson, New York, 1989–1994

The addition to the Hoffman Library at Bard College presents a true challenge. It is an addition to a Classical temple, which is perhaps an oxymoron because the Classical temple is the ultimate architectural whole—almost by definition it cannot be added to.

And there are other challenges: from the plateau of the upper campus the addition is seen at eye level where it peeks around the corner of Hoffman and is proclaimed by the new tempietto; from playing fields on the lower campus it is seen from below against the hill. It has to look good from both viewpoints. Also, in addition to the relationship to Hoffman, which is the temple as a whole, there is the relationship to the Kellogg Wing attached to the rear facade of Hoffman.

In the design of the recessive and flexible loft of the addition, we acknowledge convention over originality in the design of a generic setting where things can happen not yet dreamed of in philosophy. Out of this should derive serenity and tension in architecture as background.

But finally, in this place for working and meeting at tables, in carrels, at seminars, in offices, in niches and window seats we have broken the generic order of the adaptable loft. An exceptional specific space that penetrates the building vertically presents an exception to the order at the entrance, where the visitor identifies with the community as a whole and looks onto the world outside to come back to the image of the Classical temple as it is framed by the great window. This oblique image perhaps represents a basis for and symbol of Western culture within this multicultural place of books and computers.

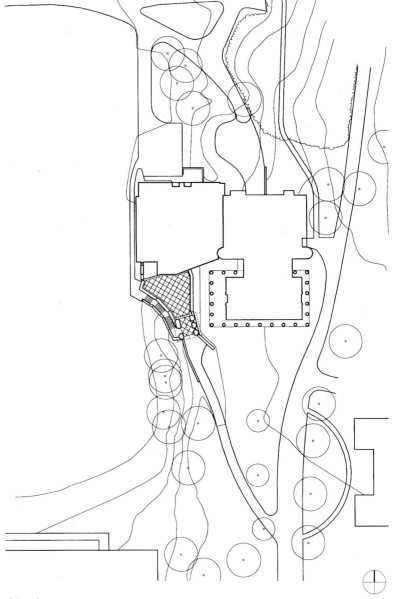

Site plan

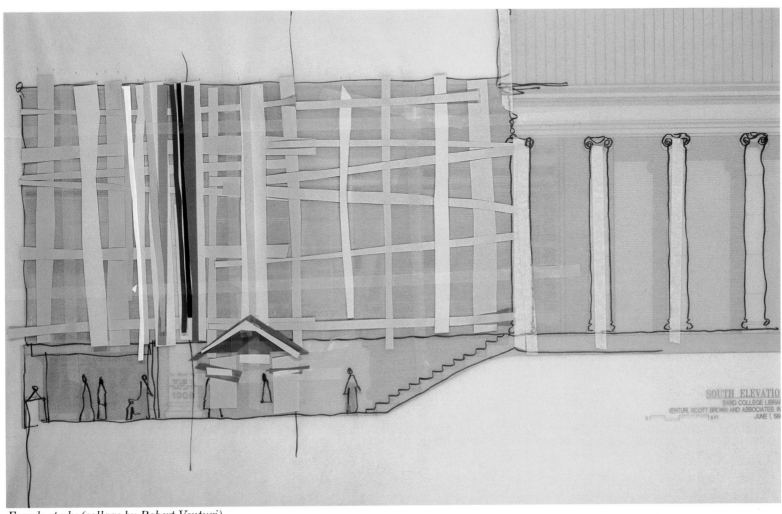

Facade study (collage by Robert Venturi)

General view

Principal in charge: Robert Venturi
Associate in charge: Ann Trowbridge
Project managers: Edward Barnhart,
Thomas Purdy
With: Ronald Evitts, John Forney, Timothy Kearney, Matthew Schottelkotte,
Nancy Rogo Trainer

General view

View from portico of old library

Stair leading from sports field to level of old library

Analogy and Contrast

VSBA considered additional issues in the design of this library complex as a whole. The restoration of Hoffman Hall, which acknowledges its historic and aesthetic significance, and its renovation, which accommodates its evolving program inside, are essential parts of this project. The same is true of the renovation of the Kellogg Wing beyond.

The addition is designed as an architectural whole, but it is also a fragment as its billowing facade inflects toward Hoffman. That is to say, the new building would not make sense standing alone.

The harmony between the addition and Hoffman Hall derives both from analogous and contrasting elements within the design of the addition. Its main compositional element on the front is rhythm—but a contrapuntal rhythm created by a crescendo of Modern pilasters that involve dissonant—maybe jazzy, perhaps mannerist—versions of the sedate rhythm of the rows of Classical columns that distinguish the old building.

While the old building includes columns that are Ionic, the new building includes pilasters that are Miesian—or ironic. While the new facade starts as a skeletal frame, it ends as a wall punctured by windows as it evolves toward the corner. The facade also expresses the interior order of the building—the generic loft—which is analogous to that of the Kellogg Wing. It derives from a tradition that includes the New England mill and the Renaissance palazzo, and it permits flexibility inside both spatial and mechanical.

The new wing creates a setting that is recessive, a background for work and for mess that accompanies work, a non-distracting place that accommodates concentration and communication as essential elements of academic life, where students focus and meet both explicitly and incidentally, where books are stored in the center and explored next to windows.

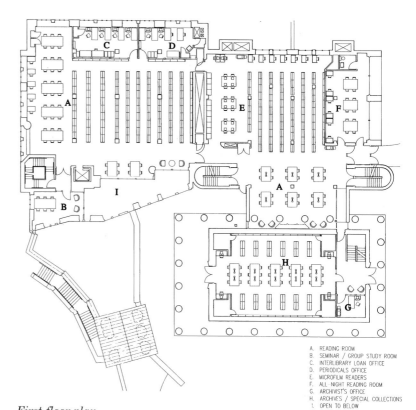

First-floor plan

A. READING ROOM
B. SEMINAR / GROUP STUDY ROOM
C. INTERLIBRARY LOAN OFFICE
D. PERIODICALS OFFICE
E. MICROFILM READERS
F. ALL-NIGHT READING ROOM
G. ARCHIVIST'S OFFICE
H. ARCHIVES / SPECIAL COLLECTIONS
I. OPEN TO BELOW

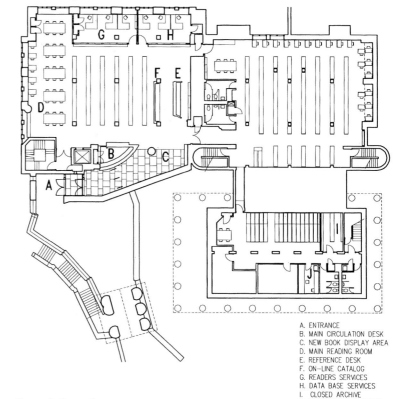

A. ENTRANCE
B. MAIN CIRCULATION DESK
C. NEW BOOK DISPLAY AREA
D. MAIN READING ROOM
E. REFERENCE DESK
F. ON-LINE CATALOG
G. READERS SERVICES
H. DATA BASE SERVICES
I. CLOSED ARCHIVE
J. ARCHIVAL WORK SPACE

Ground-floor plan

Entrance hall

View from reading room towards old library

Reading room

38 Trabant Student Center
University of Delaware

Newark, Delaware, 1992–1996

This Trabant Student Center is designed to be an integral part of the pedestrian circulation system of the whole campus and town. Its arcade-facade is bold in scale as it relates to this whole but also, via its details, small in scale to relate to individuals. Thus it has a civic presence as a kind of amenable shortcut with interesting and useful things along it and opportunities for meeting within a community—it is a place as well as a building.

A structure like this is inevitably awkward as a whole. Many uses must be accommodated on two floors, so it is by nature big and deep, but also low, without sloping roofs, and without windows in its rear facades. It can easily look like a warehouse or a shopping mall. To avoid this, the bulk of the building has been concentrated within the interior of the block it sits in, and, most important, the fabric of existing buildings along the perimeter of the block has been maintained. Charming little buildings, mostly houses, toward the south and west, help preserve the existing quality of this part of town and its historic aura. At the same time they hide the bulk of the rear of the Student Center.

The interior of this building accommodates specific elements of the program, including meeting, dining, working, and service spaces, but includes as well an essential function within the program that is less specific but extremely important. It accommodates, indeed encourages, chance or incidental meetings among students and faculty members, and thereby communication, via occasional niches for sitting along corridors and via the side aisle along the arcade-gallery.

The arcade-gallery, as it corresponds to a dominant pedestrian circulation route of the campus, is emphatic but varied in its architectural quality. On the east are the niche and aisle spaces and also the extended ramps required to accompany the stairs in the arcade. The space on the inner side of the arcade is active with commercial-like signs proclaiming a variety of eating places, a book store, kiosks, and other service uses. Above these "shops" is a series of meeting rooms that look out through windows onto the gallery.

Reinforcing the gala effect of the gallery are bannerlike signs that are more or less decorative or informational. Parts of them contain computer-video graphics. Spanning this gallery are decorative arches formed by repetitive floating neon tubes, which vividly articulate the place as a whole.

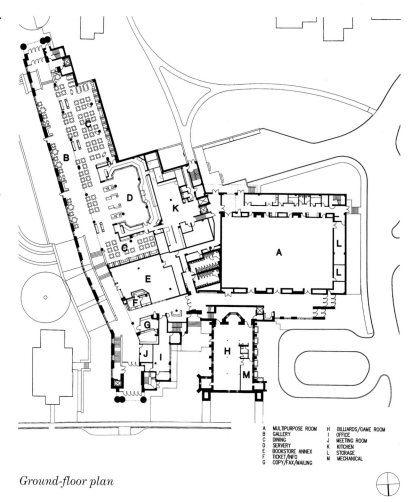

A	MULTIPURPOSE ROOM	H	BILLIARDS/GAME ROOM
B	GALLERY	I	OFFICE
C	DINING	J	MEETING ROOM
D	SERVERY	K	KITCHEN
E	BOOKSTORE ANNEX	L	STORAGE
F	TICKET/INFO	M	MECHANICAL
G	COPY/FAX/MAILING		

Ground-floor plan

Principal in charge: Robert Venturi
Project managers: James Kolker, Nancy Rogo Trainer, James Wallace
With: Denise Scott Brown, Stephanie Christoff, Joseph Herrin, Jeff Hirsch, Elizabeth Hitchcock, Steven Izenour, Timothy Kearney, Adam Meyers, Felisa Opper, Alex Stolyarik, David Vaughan, Jon Wagner, Ingalill Wahlroos, Brian Wurst

Night view from park

View from College Street

View into the gallery by night

Ground floor (sketch by Robert Venturi)

View from park

View into the gallery by day

PIZZA DELI SNACKS ICE CREAM FRIES GRILL PASTA SALADS CAMPUS SHOP INFO SERVICES

Section through gallery

39 Gordon and Virginia MacDonald Medical Research Laboratories

School of Medicine, University of California at Los Angeles

Los Angeles, California, 1986–1991

The MacDonald Medical Research Laboratories building, which is in the UCLA School of Medicine precinct, affects its setting through its presence and at the same time is affected by it in its design. It also is designed to complement the originally anticipated Gonda (Goldschmied) Research Center, which actually started construction later and which will create by its presence a green forecourt. Unfortunately but inevitably, the MacDonald building is now seen "out of context."

The building itself, because it is designed from the inside out, consists of generic loft space, which permits flexibility for interior work space and for mechanical systems and which projects a consistent, unobtrusive background for working. Inside spaces for work and for people are placed around three sides of the perimeter of the building where the windows are, while bulk mechanical and support space is in the central core. The anticipated corridors have windows in two places on each floor so that there is exterior light and window seats at those ends of the corridors for incidental meetings to promote a sense of community appropriate for an academic research laboratory. Along the front of the building on each of the floors are window configurations appropriate for offices rather than laboratories; this variation is reflected in the rhythmic compositions of the exterior facade.

Rhythm and Ornament

The glory of a facade of a loft—whether this be on a palazzo or a New England industrial loft—is its rhythm. And this rhythm is usually consistent, if complex, in its kinds of compositions. The rhythmic composition at UCLA is consistent, but with exceptions: slight variations distinguishing laboratories from offices inside, window-seat areas, and the special quality of the corner rooms that terminate the facades. These subtleties are sensed more than seen, and they create for the facades a quality of tension that makes them vital.

The other feature of the facade, besides rhythm manifest in bays and windows, is ornament—ornament derived from combinations of different materials and from combinations of different colors within the same materials. This means that the architectural quality of the exterior of this kind of building depends on an overall repetitive pattern, rhythmic at a small scale and contrapuntal to the rhythm of the bays and windows. In the colors and symbolism of these patterns is reference to the building's

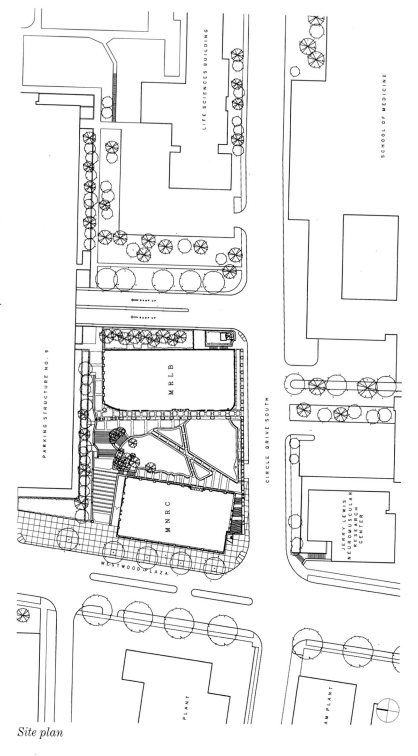

Site plan

Principal in charge: Robert Venturi
Project managers: Ronald Evitts,
James Williamson
With: Denise Scott Brown,
Kairos Chen, Catherine Cosentino,
Susan Hoadley, Steven Izenour,
Don Jones, Jeffrey Krieger,
Steven Wiesenthal, Joan Pierpoline,
Charles Renfro, Scott Osbourne
In association with:
Payette Associates Inc.;
Ronald McCoy, Architect

View from Westwood Plaza

Back of building

context—both immediate, since the MacDonald building is analogous to the brick structures around it in the School of Medicine precinct, which have random patterns, and less immediate, since it is analogous to the brick surfaces of the original complex of buildings in the central part of the campus built in the late 1920s in a Lombardian Romanesque style. The limestone trim of the new building also refers in an abstract way to that of these historic revival buildings, which typify the older part of the UCLA campus.

The light limestone base on the front of the MacDonald building works to relate it to the anticipated building across the court, to identify that court, and at the same time to brighten the court. The

"high-reader" ornamental column on Westwood Boulevard, the grand ramp, and the big arch of the building beyond contribute a complementary large scale to the composition in which these elements are local and also part of the overall system of the campus.

Context in architecture refers not only to the physical formal-spatial configuration around a building, but also to the aura of the place as a whole. This building makes visual sense in terms of its local context (the dense and potentially more dense School of Medicine at UCLA) and at the same time in terms of the whole campus with its Italian-Spanish atmosphere deriving from the style of major older buildings and the colors of newer ones.

Views of entrance and main facade

40 Gonda (Goldschmied) Neuroscience and Genetics Research Center

School of Medicine, University of California at Los Angeles

Los Angeles, California, 1993–1998

Principal in charge: Robert Venturi
Associate in charge: Thomas Purdy
Project manager: Eva Lew
Project architect: Sara Loe
With: Denise Scott Brown,
Adam Meyers, Mindy No
In association with: Lee, Burkhart, Liu, Inc.

The design of the Gonda (Goldschmied) Research Center—like that of the Gordon and Virginia MacDonald Medical Research Laboratories—is based on that of a generic loft, which accommodates spatial and mechanical flexibility and is appropriate to the dynamics of science-laboratory programs. Along the windowed outer walls of a typical floor, east and west, are the structural and spatial bays appropriate for varieties of lab and office functions and configurations; within the interior space, between and parallel to these two zones, are mechanical and support spaces and circulation corridors. Exceptions within this specific but flexible floor system occur on the two lower floors, which accommodate the vivarium, special mechanical and storage facilities, administrative offices, meeting rooms, social and dining spaces, and the entrance lobby.

The exterior design of this building is important in relation to its general context—the UCLA campus as a whole—to its immediate setting at the main entrance to the campus on Westwood Boulevard, within the School of Medicine complex, and, most intimately, to the immediate complex it will complete in terms of its position across the court from the MacDonald Laboratories.

A Note on the Interior

A laboratory building in an academic community is a place for concentration and communication; the design of the interior must accommodate these two varieties of activities in different combinations and with ease. The laboratory spaces and offices as settings for concentration are to be recessive as well as flexible in their design so that they encourage concentration among individuals or groups and accommodate mess that derives from creative process. But each typical floor is also to include space as place as well as space as setting. This is to accommodate incidental communication—interaction that is incidental rather than planned.

This kind of place we have designated as also architecturally not too explicit—as not a room but rather as an eddy within the circulation system on each floor. It is a kind of extended window seat with niches at the south end of the corridor where there is abundant natural light, modulated by horizontal louvers inside, that attracts users. This interior space is an exception within the repetitive order of the generic loft and an oblique enhancement of that architectural order.

Ornament and Abstraction

A generic loft building like the MacDonald Laboratories across the court cannot depend on sculptural articulation within its architectural form for its exterior effect; it relies instead on surface ornament for its severe enclosing form. This ornamental element, along with the rhythm of its bays and the proportion of its window openings, is what must establish its aesthetic quality as an academic building in an academic setting. The red brick surfaces of the Gonda (Goldschmied) Research Center are analogous to those of other buildings in the School of Medicine precinct.

As a whole the research center relates to the MacDonald Laboratories simply by replicating its surface ornament, but with a twist: elements of the original pattern are simplified and somewhat amplified to enhance the scale of the new building, which unlike the MacDonald building does not face an intimate campus court but defines an edge of the campus within a larger urban space, that of Westwood Boulevard. The ornament at the base of the facade on Westwood is therefore bold in its abstract reference to historical ornamentation on buildings at the center of the campus. But it also contains small-scale elements that may be perceived by individuals walking close by along the sidewalk.

A particular challenge involving architectural context derives from the form of the new building, which is similar in proportion to the MacDonald Laboratories but smaller in size so that it might perceptually seem a kind of underdeveloped twin and encourage thereby an ambiguity that could be disturbing. VSBA solved the problem by adjusting the layout of the mechanical equipment on the roof and thereby modifying the shape of the building on top—so that it is higher than the MacDonald building on the west and the same height on the east. This asymmetrical profile also permits more light to enter the courtyard from above.

Finally, the exception within the interior system—the interaction space at the south end of the building—has implications on the outside. The exception is acknowledged in differences in the geometry of the form (points in plan reflect the interior nooks for conversing), in the materials (glass and spandrel glass), and in the pattern of the surface. All work dramatically to form a contrast with the body of the building and act as a kind of fanfare that enhances the image of the building on the southern approach to the campus.

West elevation

View of model

Typical floor plan (MacDonald Medical Research Laboratories below)

41 George LaVie Schultz Laboratory
Department of Biology, Princeton University

Princeton, New Jersey, 1988–1993

General view with Lewis Thomas Laboratory (right)

The Schultz Laboratory building works as an extension of Guyot Hall at its rear; at the front it maintains, indeed enhances, the identity and quality of College Walk by reinforcing the directional character, friendly scale, and sense of rhythm that characterize this important pedestrian way on the Princeton campus.

The new building also creates a contrapuntal cross-axis that acknowledges a programmatic connection between Schultz Laboratory and Lewis Thomas Laboratory. This kind of cross-circulation between microbiology and biology must be real and symbolic at the same time; it must thereby connote at this end of College Walk a local sense of community.

Lewis Thomas Laboratory for Molecular Biology (1983–1986)

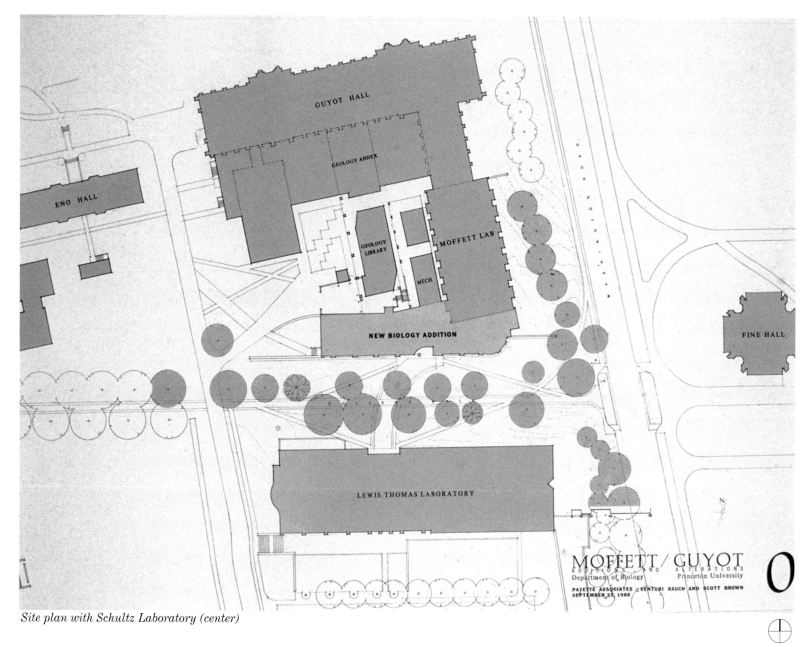

Site plan with Schultz Laboratory (center)

Most important, the design of the Schultz Laboratory promotes a generic spatial and structural system that accommodates flexibility among individual laboratory units and classrooms inside and the mechanical systems that serve them. It also includes exceptions within the architectural system that encourage incidental meetings among scientists and students. This system and its exceptions create a whole that is an appropriate setting for academic work. The Schultz Laboratory also manifests a composition of consistent if complex rhythms on the facade of the building that are appropriate in the academic setting.

Principal in charge: Robert Venturi
Project manager: Michael Peters
With: Ian Adamson, Josh Brandfonbrener, Ronald Evitts, Douglas Kochel, Brian LaBau, Mark Schlenker, David Singer, Kenneth Wood
In association with: Payette Associates Inc.

Corner View

Hallway

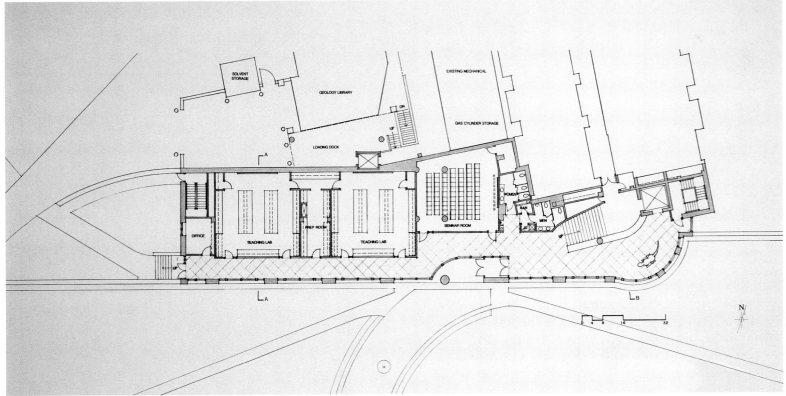

Ground-floor plan

42 Medical Laboratory
Project for the Center for the Study of Human Disease, School of Medicine, Yale University

New Haven, Connecticut, 1991

The functional-aesthetic basis of Yale's new medical research laboratory is the loft building. The new laboratory does not represent a rhetorical, articulated, architectural gesture, but a generic kind of architecture that accommodates flexibility—in its interior spaces for laboratories, offices, meeting places, and mechanical services that change over time—and that promotes the elemental qualities of rhythm, scale, and ornament on the outside.

The primary way of accommodating flexibility in an institutional building involves consistency—consistency deriving from typical structural bays and generosity of scale. These qualities of the generic loft promote a background for work as well as for change—a background that accommodates either clutter or spareness, that neither intrudes nor distracts. But as scientists need a serene setting for concentrating in this building— in laboratories at the perimeter of the building where there is natural light—they also need, as members of an academic community, places to communicate in, incidentally or otherwise— provided here at the ends of corridors and in one corner of the building. Central bays of this loft structure accommodate mechanical space; along the north face of typical floors are series of lower-height offices in a split-level section that promotes economy of space.

Principal in charge: Robert Venturi
Project managers: Ian Adamson, John Bastian
With: Jason Brody, Brian LaBau, Susan Lockwood, Amy Noble
In association with:
Payette Associates Inc.

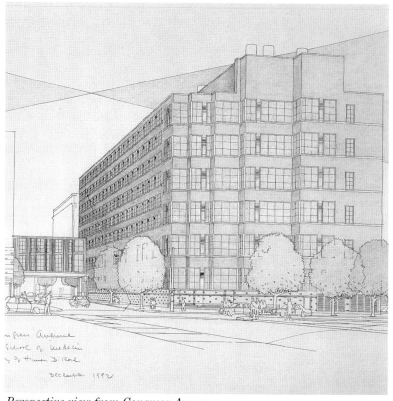

Perspective view from Congress Avenue

1 Office
2 Conference
3 Administrative Support
4 Fellows
5 Atrium Lounge/Conference
6 Restroom
7 Building Support
8 Elevator Lobby
9 Lounge
10 Break Room
11 Pantry
12 Laboratory
13 Laboratory Entry Alcove
14 Fume Hood Alcove
15 Optics
16 Special Procedure/Equipment
17 Environmental Room
18 Darkroom
19 Equipment
20 Tissue Culture
21 Glass Wash

Typical laboratory-floor plan

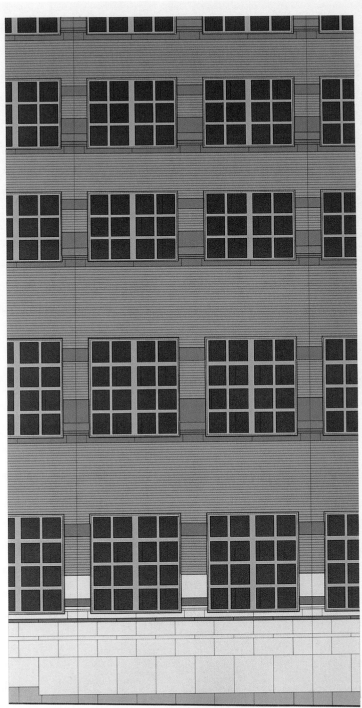

Partial Typical Elevation Study
Labs for Clinical Science
Yale University School of Medicine
May '92

$3/8" = 1'-0$

Facade study

Section

Order and Exceptions to the Rule

The generic loft with an order and quality that derive from consistency and generosity has to accommodate as well exceptions to the rule if it is to acknowledge flexibility and complexity—the complexity that is part of the modern laboratory program. This means that the rhythm—the rhythm that dominates the facades of this kind of building and derives from the repetitive order of bays inside and series of windows outside—has to acknowledge contradiction, or rather contradictions that exemplify the variations within the overall order of generous lab spaces, cozy offices, and residual nooks and crannies. Such variations show up in the facade as inconsistencies or contradictions of form; scale and rhythm can be lyrically subtle or emphatically dissonant. The Yale Laboratory, for instance, deviates from the generic rectangular quality of its overall form on the west end facade, where receding multiple corners— permitted by a peculiarity of the site boundary—enhance the amenity of the principal meeting place on each floor inside. The windows of this space also contrast in size and scale as well as rhythm with those of the adjacent offices. A similar variation in window size and rhythm occurs where the bridge element intersects the building above the main entrance. Such valid inconsistencies in the overall order create a tension within the order of the building, and that is what can make good architecture.

43 Roy and Diana Vagelos Laboratories
Institute for Advanced Study of Science and Technology, University of Pennsylvania

Philadelphia, Pennsylvania, 1990–1997

The laboratory building for the Institute for Advanced Study of Science and Technology at the University of Pennsylvania is located in the historic center of the Penn campus. It accommodates the Philadelphia gridded street pattern through its position within the science precinct, where it is attached to the existing chemistry building and thereby enhances a sense of academic community. The new building is designed to act toward the west within its immediate architectural context as a background for the great library by Frank Furness along Thirty-fourth Street.

Background Building

The new building is a generic loft: inside it accommodates flexibility, spatial and mechanical, and creates a setting for concentrating and communicating; outside it offers facades composed of consistent rhythms that reflect structural bays and repetitive windows. Ornamental patterns in surface brick and brownstone also enhance contrasts among scales. But exceptions in the inherent consistencies promote tension within the aesthetic of the building. At the southern end of the street the facade inflects and branches out to acknowledge the facade of the old building it is attached to. At the northern end the interior program accommodates spaces for planned and incidental meetings within an academic community and effectively breaks the rhythm and scale of the facade with large windows. The top of the facade promotes varied rhythms via windows and louvers, which accommodate the central mechanical equipment system.

This new laboratory building enhances its setting through harmonies deriving from contrast and analogy. It articulates Smith Walk by diverting its path and vista subtly and dynamically toward the apse of the Furness building rather than toward the indeterminate part of that building it actually faces. The rhythmic aesthetic of the new loft creates a background for the fanfare that is Furness's Library.

Principal in charge: Robert Venturi
Associate in charge: David Marohn
Project managers: Tom Beck, Eva Lew
With: Denise Scott Brown, Andrew Benner, Claudia Cueto, Christine Gorby, Daniel Horowitz, Mindy No, Michael Peters
In association with:
Payette Associates Inc.

View from Locust Walk

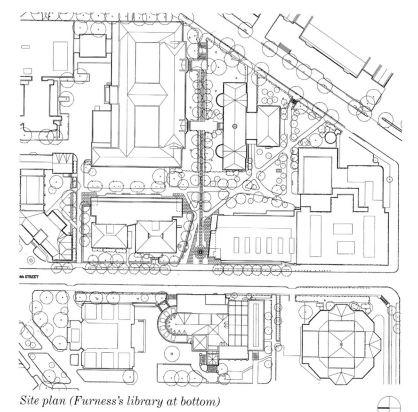

Site plan (Furness's library at bottom)

Section

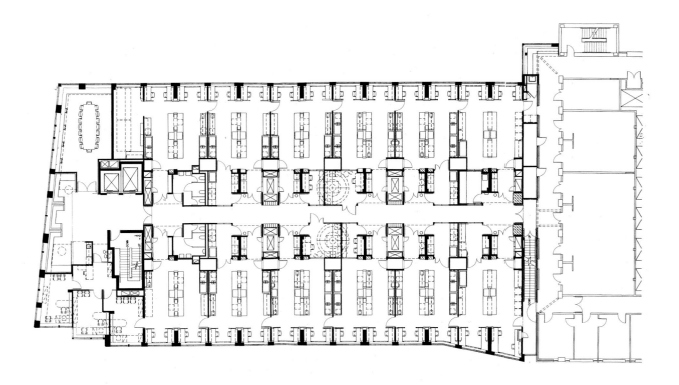

Typical floor plan

44 Residence Hall Complex
Project for Student Apartments, University of Cincinnati

Cincinnati, Ohio, 1994–1996

The program for the residence hall project included living quarters for students; secondary spaces including lounges, computer centers, workout rooms, and so on; and dining facilities and kitchen, a teaching-learning facility, and a faculty apartment. Its design was originally accepted and then later rejected. VSBA's justification for the design was presented by Robert Venturi; incidentally, it indicates not only our intentions but the university's critique.

"On Context in Architectural Composition"

As a preamble, let me mention that I believe I was the first to enunciate the now ordinary architectural concept of context, when, in 1950, I presented my master's thesis and called it "Context in Architectural Composition." This was at a time when Modernism in its confidently revolutionary stance didn't care a bit about acknowledging setting, formal or historical—either the effect of it or the effect on it—except perhaps in the work of Alvar Aalto. The role of context has been paramount in our design ever since—especially in our campus design, which constitutes the main body of our architectural and master-planning work. I shall attempt to describe how the design of the residence hall promotes contextual harmony via analogy and contrast.

Principal in charge: Robert Venturi
Project manager: Ann Trowbridge
Project architect: James Wallace
With: Denise Scott Brown,
Tony Bracali, Laura Campbell,
Nathalie Peeters, Thomas Purdy
In association with: KZF

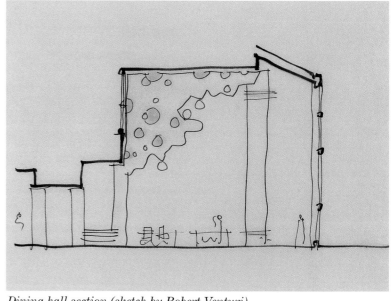

Dining-hall section (sketch by Robert Venturi)

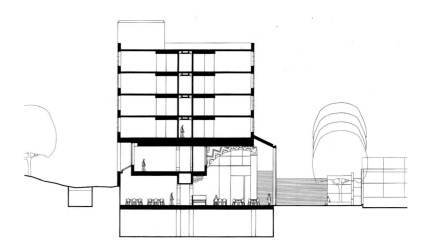

Section

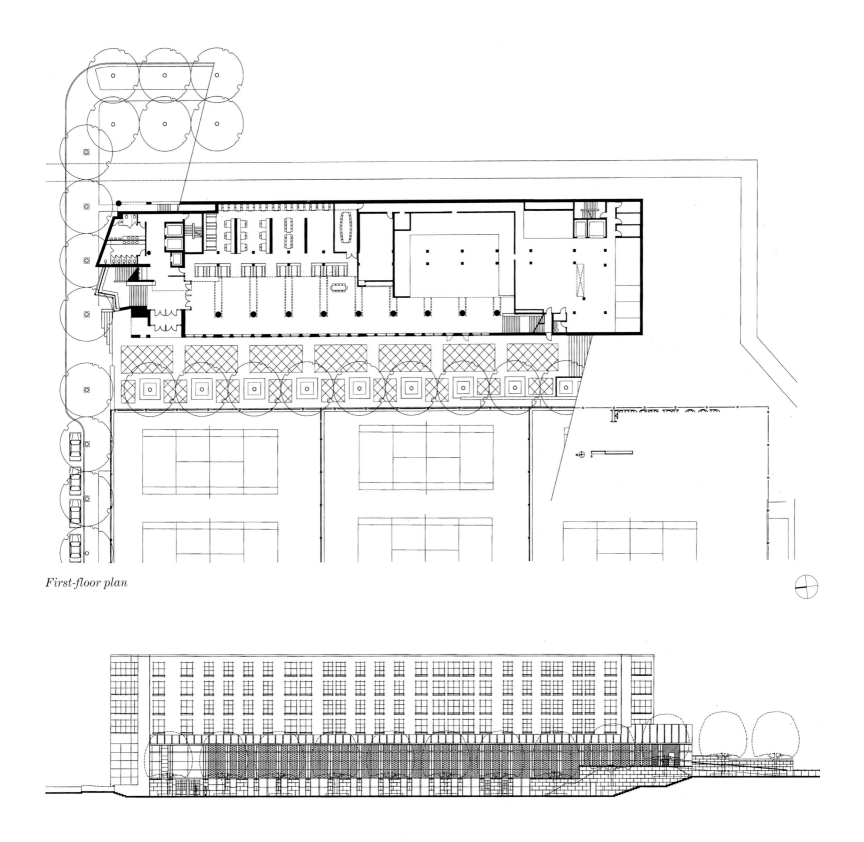

First-floor plan

East elevation

Residence Hall Complex **249**

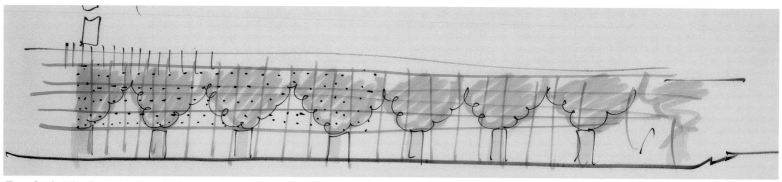

Facade sketch of ground-floor hall, west elevation.

This building, in its form and aesthetic, is a slab—unabashedly a generic slab—that acknowledges its program with ease and economy. The program, naturally, accommodates repetitive living quarters and acknowledges its setting, which directs exterior space rather than defines a point in space, thereby enhancing the spatial integrity of Jefferson Avenue, which it sits along, and delineating the edge of the campus.

Two more things about the slab are important. We should not succumb to the cycle of taste that makes us reject the architecture of the recent past that includes Modern slabs in the way our predecessors fatuously despised Victorian. But we should also acknowledge the differences between our slab and, for instance, the residence hall slabs up Jefferson Avenue. The Modernist slab in its purist order wallows in minimalist simplicity and modular consistency; our slab in its complex and contradictory order accommodates exceptions to the rule that promote aesthetic tension. These exceptions are exemplified in the following elements: the irregular relationships within the rhythmic pattern of generously scaled windows along the main facades; the varying quality of the base of the slab as it accommodates the porchlike entrance to the faculty apartment and the eye-level clerestory windows of the private dining spaces along Jefferson Street; the irregular shape of the north end elevation as it distorts toward the view to the northwest from within and at the same time accommodates its context as it inflects toward the entrance to the campus outside.

Perhaps the most incorrect thing about this Modernesque slab is the shed-roofed extension along its western face. At its base it sticks out instead of in! And the frit pattern that is to modulate the penetration of western light along the high glass wall of this shed extension (with an exact configuration to be determined in design development) may also be seen as incorrect. And integrating the dining, living, and learning center community areas essentially within the bulk of the slab, rather than articulating them as bulges or separate units beyond the slab contributes to the tense complexity within the form of this slab—and also makes significantly for a land-economic building. A slab embracing not one dominant modular defined use is the main thing that makes this slab unorthodox.

Manifest in this slab-cum-decorated-shed are other dimensions, aesthetic and programmatic, exterior and interior. Its form directs space along the campus side of the site as well as along the street side and thereby articulates a pedestrian promenade between the linear form of the building on one side and the linear configuration of tennis courts on the other. So this slab sits not importantly on a Ville Radieuse superblock but rather directs space while encouraging activity and enhancing existing context within its precinct.

The decorative and iconographic element, unique for the architecture of our time—indeed, for the architecture of the last seventy years—is unusual in another way: it promotes detail at eye level and thereby enriches the viewer's perception of the architecture both on the approach and on circulating around and within it. Almost all Modern and current architecture looks good in a model on a conference table because its sexy, "original" character derives from an overall sculptural effect. But this kind of architecture looks good from eye level and close up, where its sexy original detail is juxtaposed on generic form—although it doesn't necessarily make for a great model.

A last question is the issue of a bottom, middle, and top in the architectural expression of a building. This building has a bottom and a top but no middle because the interior configuration of spaces deriving from the program does not call for three segments layered vertically. A bottom pertains to the more public, high, and community-oriented spaces, and a top contains the more private living spaces. Putting a top on the top just doesn't make sense. And by the way, a flat roof does not imply mean—the palace of Versailles has a flat roof.

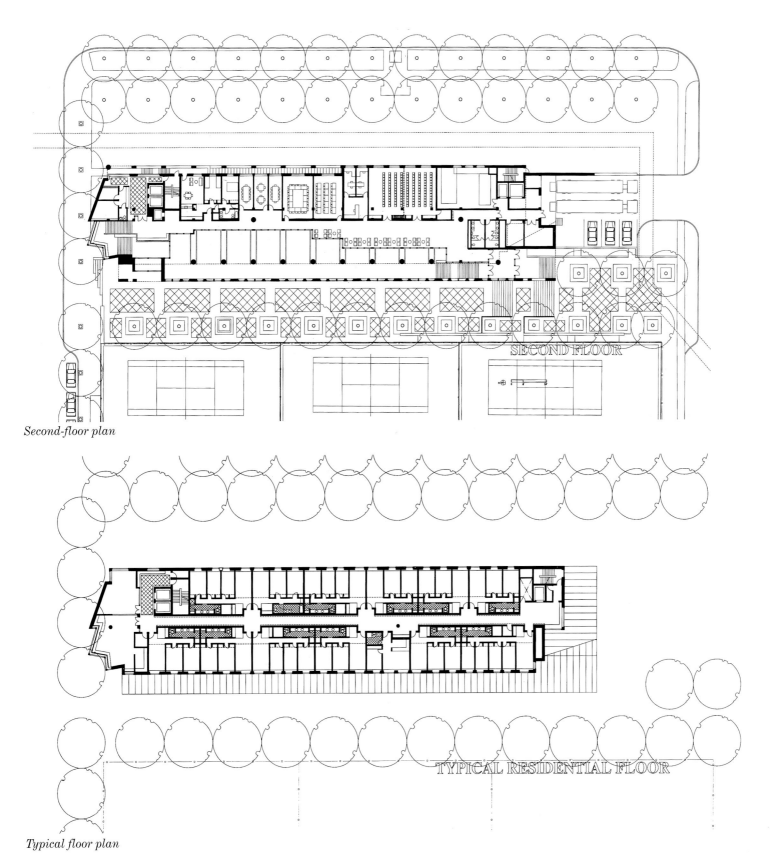

Second-floor plan

Typical floor plan

45 Frist Campus Center
Princeton University

Princeton, New Jersey, 1996–1999

The Frist Campus Center is sited in what, with recent and anticipated development, has become the central part of the Princeton campus. The location along Washington Road works well for service access. Incorporated within the new campus center complex is the old Palmer Physics Building, which was erected in 1909 in the Elizabethan style and which represents a particularly adaptable form of generic loft building that will enrich the architectural quality of the whole.

Two particular challenges are offered by this site and this building. The first is the immediate context, in which the explicitly symmetrical north facade of the Palmer Building is perceptually cut in half by the later Woolworth Music Building; this truncation makes for aesthetic discomfort and perceptual debasement. The second challenge is the single entrance atop a flight of steps at the center of this facade; the configuration, though gracious, connotes that Palmer is a private departmental building for a specialized use for a select group of people. This implication was fine when Palmer was an institutional physics building, but it is inappropriate for an institutional communal building. The main idea of this new complex is without a doubt communal, and so its entrance system must suggest generous scale and spatial openness, a place where pedestrians flow into the building as it connects with the open space before it and with the circulation paths around and approaching it. The entrance must attain the hierarchical quality and importance—if not the form—of the famous Gothic-style arches at Princeton, where visitors enter more than a building—they enter an important beyond.

Entrance Arcade

Entrance to the building from the north is through an existing series of basement window openings, which are approached via laterally extended steps. This sequence is architecturally discreet because it intrudes only minimally upon the physical fabric of the old building and is visible only from close-up. An additional architectural element makes this sliced-in-half mono-entranced physics building an imageful campus-civic building from the north approach: an apparent entrance arcade is juxtaposed as a layer on the facade at ground level. The inherent and consistent openness, generous scale, and gracious rhythms of this apparent arcade are inviting; the real and necessarily more restricted entry doors are behind it. Precedents for the architectural arcade at the base of a communal building are offered by the arcaded buildings surrounding Piazza San Marco, with a civic-urban context, and by the base of a rural building, like Hardwick Hall, which has an extended columned porch. But the Princeton "arcade"—two-dimensional and unroofed—derives from architectural layering in which the fabric of the old facade is not touched physically but is changed perceptually. And this perceptual juxtaposition—this representation of a facade—can embrace the old and the new. At the entrance to the arcade is a surprise—the semi-enclosed space between arcade and building is a kind of paved forecourt teeming with variety at all scales and levels: cluttered iconography that makes the backs of the arcade piers into light boxes and boards for various kinds of information, campus-communal posters, notices, and the like. Thus the element of explicit communication is engaged on the exterior of the campus center.

Entrance elevation

Principal in charge: Robert Venturi
Project manager: James Wallace
Project architects: Elizabeth Hitchcock,
Felisa Opper, Jennifer Kinkead,
Peter DiCarlo
With: Denise Scott Brown, John Bastian, Tony Bracali, Linna Choi, Angelina Chong, Seth Cohen, Claudia Cueto, Meredith Elbaum, Mark Kocent, Eva Lew, Sara Loe, Catherine Moy, Julie Munzner, Amy Noble, Cynthia Padilla, Matthew Seltzer, Ian Smith, Ann Trowbridge, Brian Wurst,
Steven van Dyck, David Vaughan
In association with:
Andropogon Associates, Ltd.

Perspective view from Washington Street toward entrance and across campus

Views of wall screening entrance to student center (full-scale mock-up)

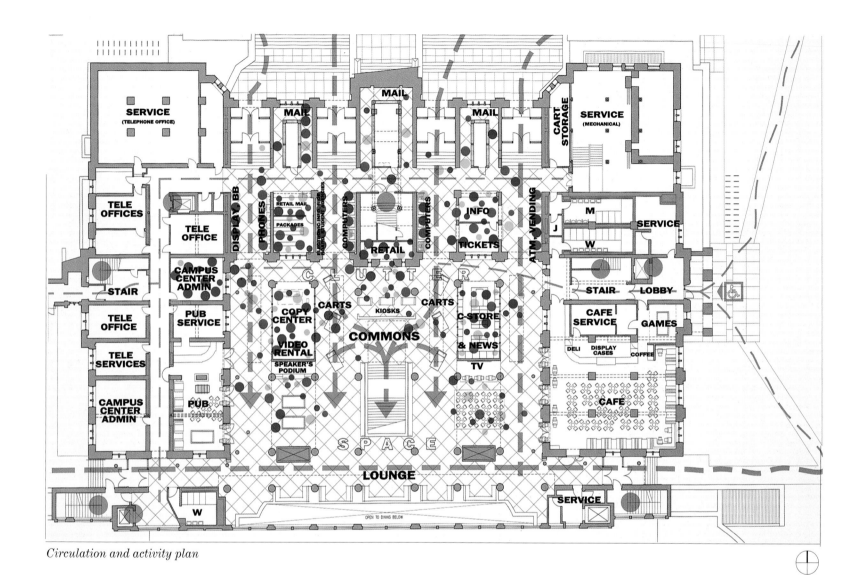

Circulation and activity plan

Interior Street System

In the interior upper floors is acknowledged the historic and elegant loftlike quality of this classroom/laboratory building of generic, minimally changed spaces for new academic, office, and library uses. In the basement a mazelike street system within the brick bearing walls accommodates combinations of quasi-commercial uses and information media. It evolves toward the south side with new multilevel flowing spaces dedicated to the more communal uses in a kind of court with a great glass wall facing the facade of Guyot Hall outside; off of this high space are niches for incidental meetings and various dining areas. This space is like a piazza that can accommodate unanticipated uses.

Rendering of south facade

View into main lounge

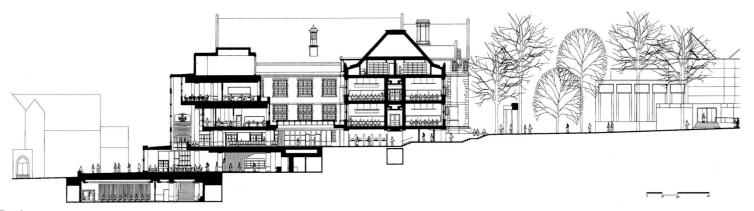

Section

46 Berry Library and Academic Wing
Dartmouth College

Hanover, New Hampshire, 1997–

The Berry Library is an extension to Baker Library at Dartmouth College. A further extension within this complex is to be designated an academic classroom building that will also accommodate a program for academic computing. The combination of these programs will enrich the academic experience.

The plan of the complex evolved as part of VSBA's master plan for the northern campus. The front facade of the library will terminate the dominant exterior space known as Berry Row. This facade is also to complement that of Baker Library and to identify and direct an important pedestrian circulation route connecting the east and west parts of the campus via its linear extension and its arcade, symbolic and actual.

The aesthetic of the linear facade is based on counterpoint that derives from juxtaposition and rhythm, from layers with complex rhythmic surface compositions—consistent and exceptional, lyrical and dissonant. The layers themselves are the result of combinations of repetitive windows in the inner and upper layer and combinations of repetitive openings in the outer and lower arcade. This arcade is both functional and symbolic as it accommodates an explicit pedestrian route and an important series of entrances to the building. The symbolic arcade facade will contain graphic iconography and will contribute a human dimension to the composition and also juxtapose its own kind of rhythm.

At the same time the facade reflects the interior of the complex as a generic loft. This approach is especially appropriate for the interior spaces of a library and an academic classroom complex where spatial and mechanical-electronic flexibility is necessary for constantly evolving programs. Penetrating the loft space on the main floor is a "main street"—a permanent circulation route connecting the new and old buildings; along the "street" are varying uses that accommodate information services and promote a sense of community. This consistent route will also work to provide orientation and identity within the kind of maze that inevitably characterizes a contemporary library.

The symbolic quality of the facade as a whole, with its brick surfaces, white window frames, and rhythmic compositions, is referentially but not literally Georgian and therefore analogously harmonious within its context as a connection to Baker Library and as a part within the Dartmouth whole. It thereby works to create harmony between the old and the new via analogy and contrast within its compositional elements, both abstract and symbolic.

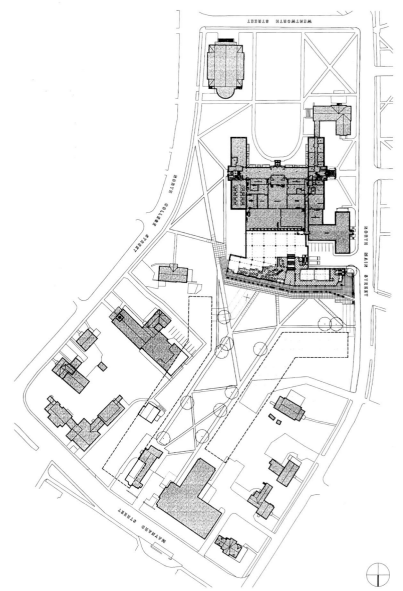

Site plan

Rendering of front facade

Side view with arcade

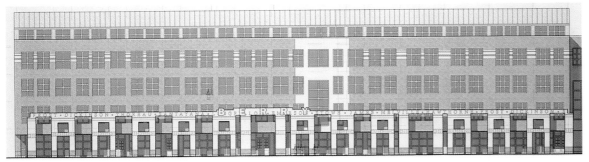

North elevation

Principals in charge: Robert Venturi, Denise Scott Brown
Associate in charge: Daniel McCoubrey
Project manager: James Kolker
With: Stephanie Christoff, Jeff Hirsch, Diane Hosler, John Jones, Tse-Chiang Leng, Matthew Seltzer, Howard Traub
In association with: Shepley, Bulfinch, Richardson and Abbott

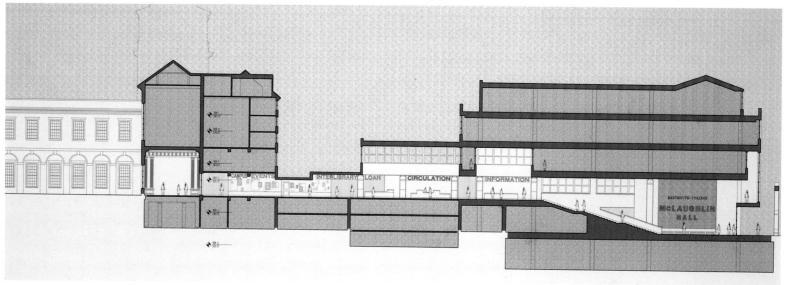

Section through existing and proposed new building

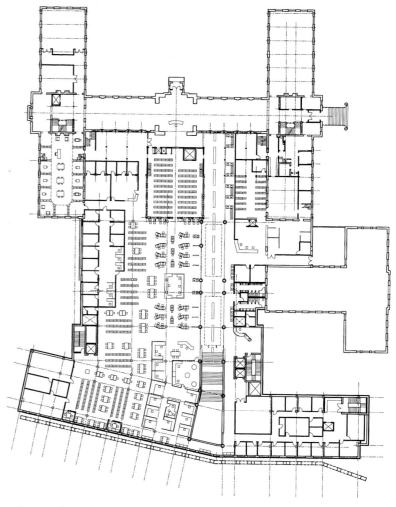

Second-floor plan

47 Center for International and Area Studies

Yale University

Principal in charge: Robert Venturi
Project managers: Edward Chuchla,
David Vaughan

New Haven, Connecticut, 1991

The relatively small Center for International and Area Studies on the Yale University campus was to house a very important institute. Its site was to be within a block facing Hill House Avenue, a street of important historic mansions that mostly house university functions, so the building on the outside has to look at home in an almost residential setting and yet contain a scale that reflects its academic importance. Thus it must be a small building with generous scale.

We accomplished this goal by employing hierarchy within the composition both inside and outside—a device with a long tradition exemplified in the Italian palazzo with the second floor as piano nobile. In this way the building was to relate to the big houses around it and at the same time acknowledge its institutional importance. These exterior determinants fit nicely with the interior needs. The hierarchy of spaces—communal and assembly spaces, teaching and private office spaces—defines a place with an overall unity while accommodating overall diversity. It is designed as a workplace and a community at the same time.

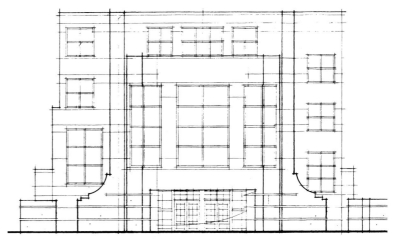

Facade

Site plan

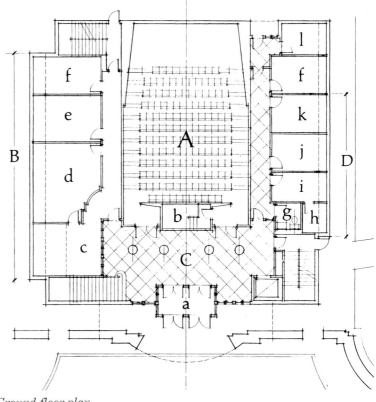

Ground-floor plan

48 Clinical Research Center
Competition Entry, National Institutes of Health

Bethesda, Maryland, 1996

The medical complex for the National Institutes of Health presented a complicated program for a very big building within a campuslike environment facing a residential suburban community. The design that evolved combined the main working elements of the program in layers—layers of medical research laboratories, nursing services, and clinical patient rooms with circulation along and between the layers and frequent connections among the layers for interaction and communication. The laboratory layer space is like a generic loft and therefore flexible in terms of spatial layout and mechanical services. Along its length on one side are windows. Within the other layers space and utilities are of necessity more permanently organized. The layer composition on the clinic side of the building is zigzag in plan to diminish the length of the complex both visually—upon viewing—and perceptually—upon circulating. Within the linear circulation system are nichelike spaces, often near windows, for sitting and talking, which enhance amenity for the patients and their visitors and encourage incidental communication among the staff.

The ground floor contains complex, more public uses; at its side is a complex configuration of vehicular and bus drop-off places. This busy activity is largely hidden from the front—that is, from the residential neighborhood the building faces. This quality of hiding is achieved via the landscape design, which creates another layer, a stylized hill in the manner of a picturesque English Romantic garden or a traditional Japanese garden. This hill, however, is two-dimensional and scenographic; its back is a retaining wall along the extended drop-off area.

This complex building, which accommodates its complex program via interacting spatial/formal layers, both architectural and landscape-composed, presents an amenable face to the community. But it was evidently not picturesquely complex and contradictory enough, and so the VSBA team lost the competition.

Principals in charge: Robert Venturi, Denise Scott Brown
Project managers: Ann Trowbridge, David Vaughan, James Wallace
With: Hidenao Abe, Tony Bracali, Angelina Chong, Heather Clark, Diane Golomb, Steven Izenour, Eva Lew, Nathalie Peeters, Howard Traub, Kenneth Wood
In association with:
Payette Associates Inc.,
Andropogon Associates, Ltd.

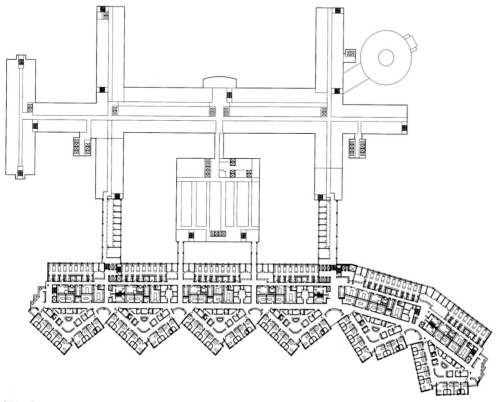

Site plan

View of model

Perspective view

Commercial Buildings

264   *Gas Station, The Walt Disney Company*

266   *Frank G. Wells Building,*
      The Walt Disney Company

270   *Hotel Mielparque Resort Complex*

280   *Rural Wine Center and Label*

49 Gas Station
The Walt Disney Company

Orlando, Florida, 1993–1994

The prototypical gas-station design for Walt Disney assumes
that the logo or name of the particular gas company is secondary
to the image of the gas station as a generic roadside element.
The solution projects a conventional canopy-and-pump structure
connected at a bold scale to a convenience store with large
graphics spelling "food" or "eats" in a translucent frit applied
to the inside of the glass curtain wall. Two optional solutions for
the roadside "high-reader" are monumental—the thirty-foot-
high, three-dimensional letters spelling "gas" or the seventy-five-
foot high "gas pump" sign.

Elevation study

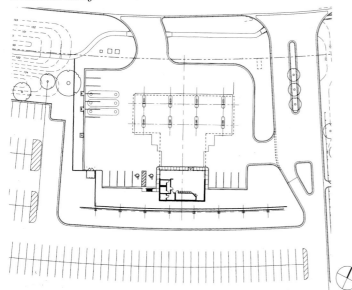

Site plan

Principal in charge: Steven Izenour
Project manager: Timothy Kearney
With: Robert Venturi, Laura
Campbell, Amy Noble, Felisa
Opper, Steven Stainbrook
In association with: BNM Construction

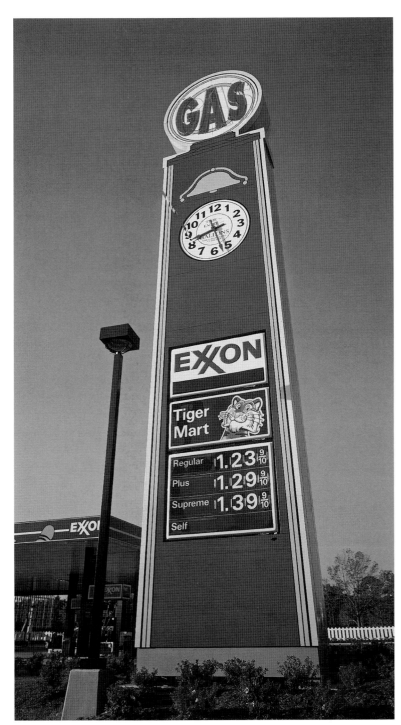

Gas station with symbolic pump

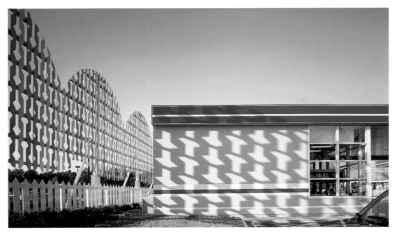

Views of gas station with symbolic trees

50 Frank G. Wells Building
The Walt Disney Company

Burbank, California, 1994–1997

The Frank G. Wells Building is a five-story office building adjacent to the main Alameda gate on Disney's Burbank studio lot. It is a large building designed to be sympathetic to the distinguished low-scale Kem Weber buildings that make up the fabric of the campus and to the grand Team Disney Building that it faces. It is laid out as a loft building with standard office depths surrounding an interior courtyard. At the entry, the modest plaster surfaces of the building are replaced by porcelain enamel panels. Initial designs included a sixty-five-foot, two-dimensional Mickey Mouse that grew out of the building at the front entrance. The final design integrates within the colored and patterned panels an image that designates entrance and represents a moving-picture reel; its strip of film creates an overhang. Once again the architectural expression derives from coherent rhythmic content and applied fanfare.

Principal in charge: Robert Venturi
Project manager: Timothy Kearney
With: Denise Scott Brown, Tony Bracali, Linna Choi, Heather Clark, Claudia Cueto, Elizabeth Hitchcock, Steven Izenour, Sara Loe, Meredith McCree, Adam Meyers, Julie Munzner, Amy Noble, Nathalie Peeters, Thomas Purdy, Brian Wurst
In association with: HKS

Typical floor plan

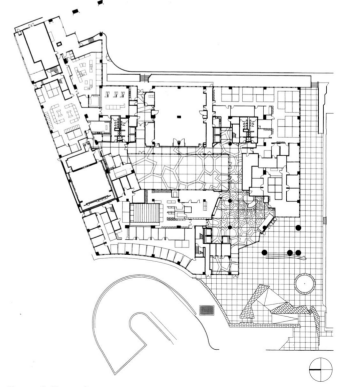

Ground-floor plan

Entrance facade opposite Team Disney Building (by Michael Graves)

Entrance

Lobby

Proposed exhibit in themed working section

268 COMMERCIAL BUILDINGS

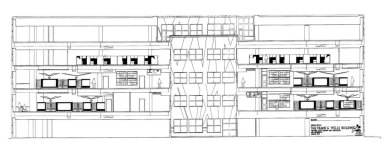

Section

Courtyard

51 Hotel Mielparque Resort Complex

Nikko, Kirifuri, Japan, 1992–1997

The architecture of the Kirifuri resort complex is essentially scenographic. Its generic forms are adorned with signs and the conventionally ordinary is made aesthetically extraordinary. The program consists of four major elements: natural landscape, a bridge, the hotel, and an athletic building.

The landscape consists of a forest and clearings. It is a setting for the buildings but also an important ecological heritage to be supported and enjoyed via trails and outlooks. The bridge—vehicular and pedestrian—crosses a ravine near the entrance to the site and acts as a sign.

The hotel contains guest rooms of Western and traditional Japanese design. Other facilities include a public bath with hot-spring spa, conference facilities, two dining facilities, a bar-café, a central lobby, interior tennis courts, and interior below-grade parking. The athletic building contains a large indoor swimming pool, locker and dressing-room facilities, a lounge, a gallery with commercial space, wet and dry dining spaces, and various other spa facilities.

Architecture and Landscape

The hotel complex is designed to be perceived as a series of modest buildings set against the texture of the wooded site. In form, the whole is complex and small in scale; symbolically, it suggests a rural village, particularly in its vehicular approach, which evokes a village street.

It is significant that car arrival is within, not at the edge of, the complex. Beyond the entrance lies a second pedestrian "street": the hotel lobby. Off this linear space are restaurants, a café, conference rooms, and commercial areas; along it are series of signs, decorative and symbolic two-dimensional depictions of historical, traditional, contemporary, ordinary, and conventional elements of an ordinary village. These colorful abstracted signs are placed perpendicular to the axis of the "street." The scenography of the "street" reflects the traditions and celebrates the spirit of Japanese urban and village life, making the hotel lobby a lively and gala place for adults and children.

Aerial view

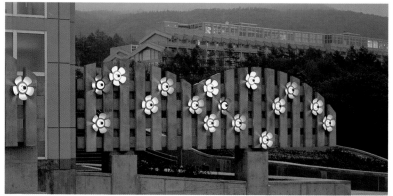

View from spa toward hotel complex

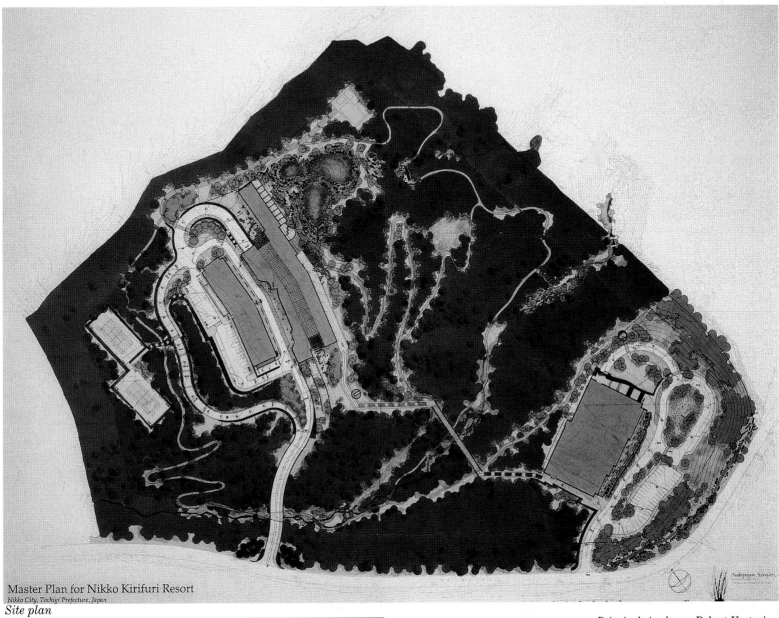

Master Plan for Nikko Kirifuri Resort
Nikko City, Tochigi Prefecture, Japan
Site plan

Access road to hotel complex

Principals in charge: Robert Venturi,
Denise Scott Brown
Associate in charge: David Marohn
With: Hidenao Abe, Edward Barnhart,
Jason Brody, Angelina Chong,
Stephanie Christoff, Claudia Cueto,
Elizabeth Hitchcock, Daniel Horowitz,
Steven Izenour, Timothy Kearney,
Eva Lew, Jeffrey Lewis, Meredith
McCree, David Vaughan, Jon Wagner
In association with:
Marunouchi Architects and Engineers

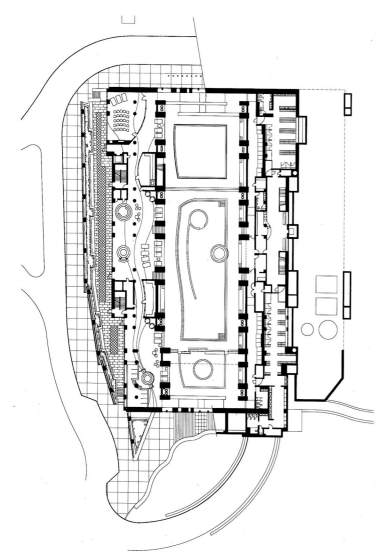

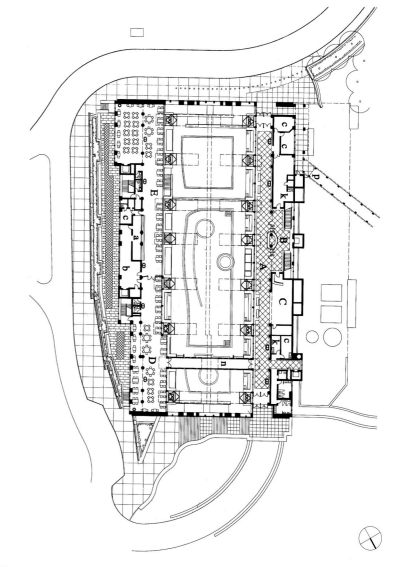

Lower-level (left) and upper-level plans of spa complex

Spa with "autumn" leaves

Spa with "spring" leaves

Spa building

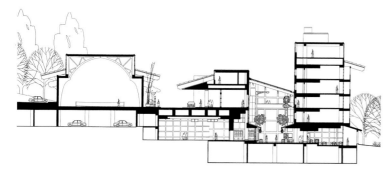

Section through hotel complex and village street

Outside, the architectural forms of the hotel subtly suggest traditional rural architecture in their proportions. Symbolic ornamental elements applied to the buildings suggest traditional roof forms and overhangs when perceived from eye level. Appliqué patterns on some wall surfaces suggest exposed wood-frame construction (as well as Mondrian compositions). It is intended that Kirifuri's architecture-for-recreation express the vigor and wit that are a part of Japanese public life today, and at the same time that the design of the hotel and athletic building be marketable to and loved by the public.

The attitude toward ecology and the environment embraces the renewal of the natural landscape, with its dynamic topography, rich forest, and misty atmosphere, as both background and stimulus for the design of the complex. Among our goals were to see the ecological-environmental characteristics of Kirifuri as determinants of its built forms; to design strategies to ensure that the particular values of this place will be sustained and enhanced; to derive land use and design guidelines for landscape and architecture from patterns and processes inherent in the landscape; to use advanced biotechnical methods creatively to handle precipitation runoff, paving, and other significant elements; to demonstrate the significance and quality of ecological systems in Kirifuri via carefully engineered trails. This approach involves acknowledging cultural and historical dimensions within the context as well as natural dimensions—dimensions local and universal, historical and communal. It includes Nikko as a functioning community and as a renowned religious and architectural place.

The design of the bridge juxtaposes upon the two faces of reinforced-concrete structure (derived from contemporary engineering technology) decorative planes that represent a symbolic abstraction of a traditional Japanese bridge. These planes are composed of aluminum members whose color is recessive within their natural setting.

The athletic building's interior contains a particularly significant space for a swimming pool. The interior structure admits shafts of ambient natural light through clerestory windows during the day. The light is modulated by lacelike space frames that span the major space. These frames are composed of standard steel elements that are connected to form truss configurations. Attached to the steel members are decorative planar forms suggestive of leaves; in combination with the space frame, they convey the sense of a forest clearing and refer to the forest that is famous in Nikko. Looking south, the surfaces of the "leaves" are bright green to suggest summer; looking north, they are warm yellow to suggest autumn. During the day the "leaves" modulate natural light to create an aura; at night they reflect artificial light and sparkle.

Spa building by night

Spa building by day

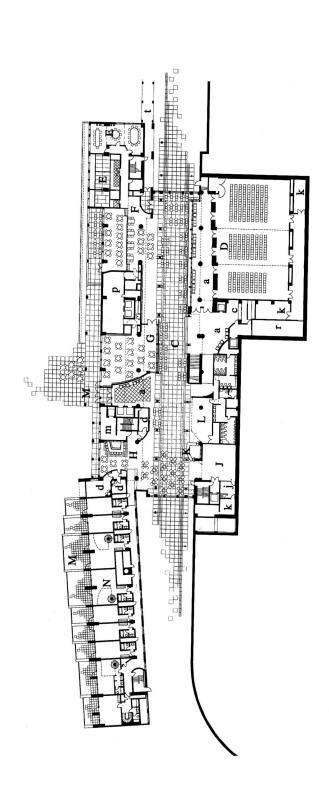

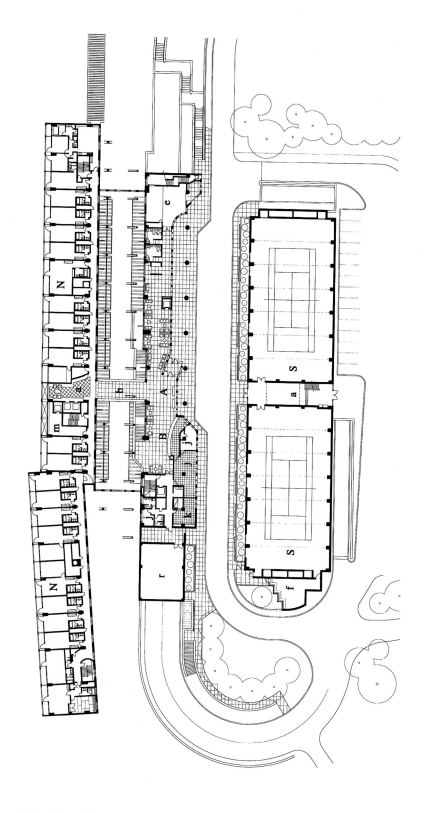

Village-street level

Typical hotel floor

Hotel entrance with symbolic eaves and front yards

Rear view of hotel complex

Flower motif for village street

Views of village street

Village street

52 Rural Wine Center and Label
Ernest and Julio Gallo Winery

Dry Creek Valley, California, 1989

VSBA designed a pavilion as a center for entertaining for the
Ernest and Julio Gallo Winery within their vineyards in a
beautiful valley in northern California. It is a series of rooms
for varying sizes and kinds of entertaining, with views through
arcades toward the valley in front and onto enclosed gardens
to the side. The approach to the building is from across the
vineyard, where its rhythmic facade can be seen against a hill;
the building complex is entered via car between hill and
building—the enclosed spatial experience contrasts with the
recent crossing of the open vineyards and also the imminent
viewing of them. Terraces above the building connect via a
pedestrian bridge to the hill and its upper gazebo. In the center
of the main facade sits a big sculptural bunch of grapes; their
bold symbolic image works as an accent within the complex
rhythms of the arcades and windows. We thought a little bit
about the Villa Aldobrandini and its topography at Frascati.

Principal in charge: Robert Venturi
Project manager: David Marohn
With: Maurice Weintraub

Gallo label

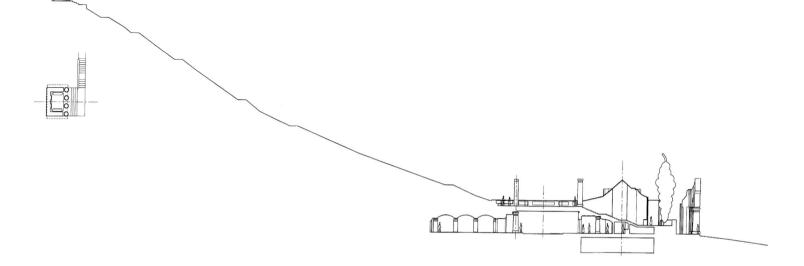

Section through complex

General view (sketch by Robert Venturi)

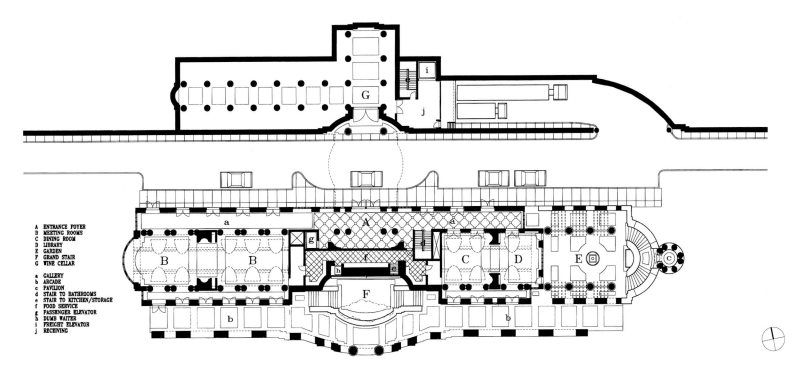

A   ENTRANCE FOYER
B   MEETING ROOMS
C   DINING ROOM
D   LIBRARY
E   GARDEN
F   GRAND STAIR
G   WINE CELLAR

a   GALLERY
b   ARCADE
c   PAVILION
d   STAIR TO BATHROOMS
e   STAIR TO KITCHEN/STORAGE
f   FOOD SERVICE
g   PASSENGER ELEVATOR
h   DUMB WAITER
i   FREIGHT ELEVATOR
j   RECEIVING

Plan

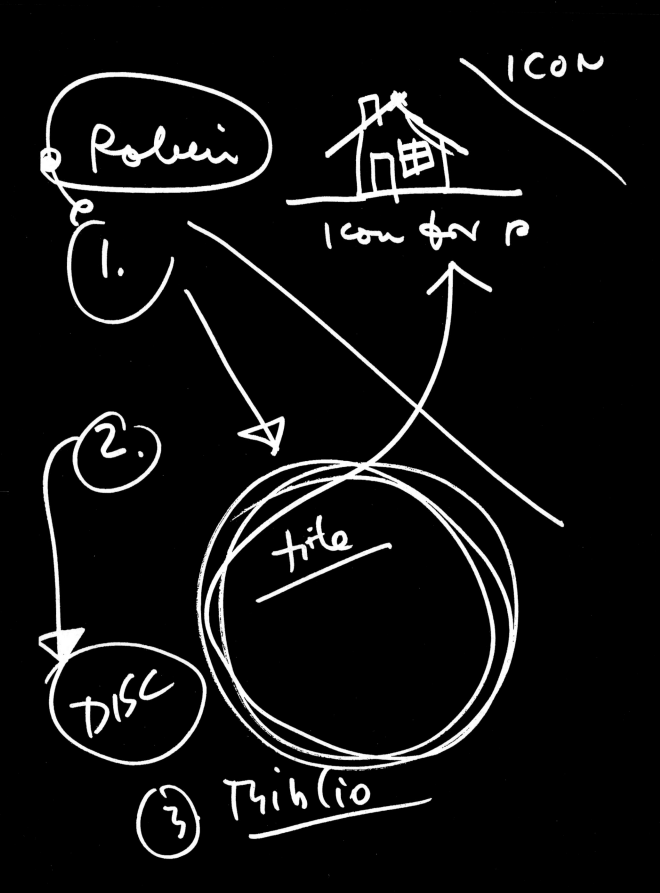

ICON

Robin

Icon for P

1.

2.

title

DISC

3 Thiblio

Houses

284 *House on Long Island*

286 *Project for a House in Tuxedo Park*

288 *House on Long Island Sound*

291 *Pearl Houses*

292 *House on the Coast of Maine*

296 *Project for a House in Chester County*

298 *Houses for Mitsui Home Co.*

53 House on Long Island

East Hampton, New York, 1985–1990

VSBA designed a summer house to satisfy the desires and needs of a family with two children. It is secluded within a beautiful wooded area in the sandy soil of the site.

On the outside the house refers to Shingle Style resort architecture in its generous scale, ample porch, double-hung sash, dominant roof, and, of course, abundance of natural cedar shingles on roof and walls. Because there is no dominant view from the site, the house is almost the same all around: it is rather like a pavilion without distinctions between back and front or particular accommodation for a front entrance. The sloping roof forms create a feeling of shelter among the trees. These dominant forms along with the big window on the east side create a large scale that contrasts with the variety of smaller elements, sometimes circumstantially located within the composition—windows, doors, porch, and so on, around the base of the house.

Inside, the ground-floor spaces all look into the woods. The space on this floor flows around a central core that integrates fireplace and stairs—and sometimes up into the floors above. The bedrooms beneath the sloping roofs have an atticlike feel. The small bedrooms for the children on the third floor contain built-in furniture rather like that in boats; in both cases the furniture conforms to an exterior-determined shape.

General view

Principals in charge: Robert Venturi, David Vaughan
Project managers: Fran Reed, Perry Kulper

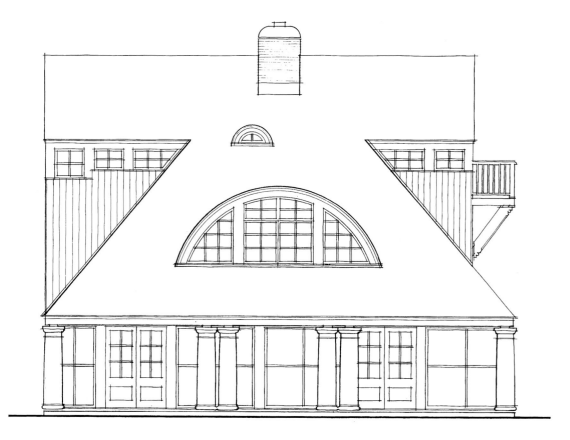

Entrance elevation

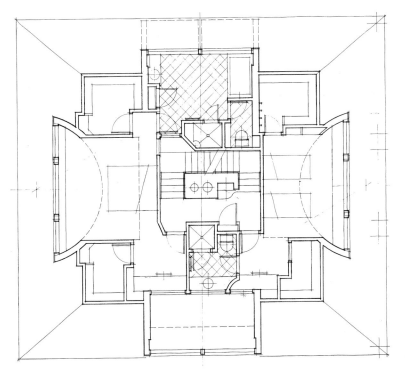

Second-floor plan

Section

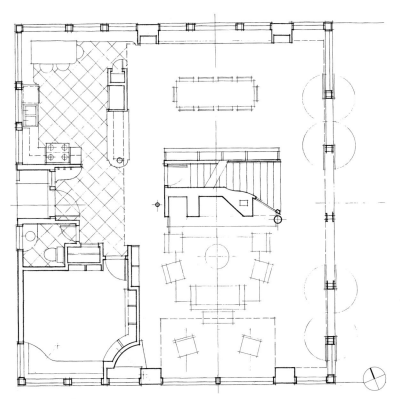

First-floor plan

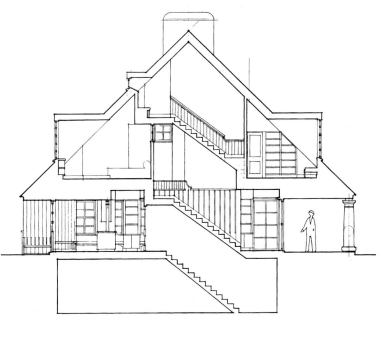

Section

54 Project for a House in Tuxedo Park

Tuxedo Park, New York, 1987–1988

We designed a weekend and summer house in—and at home in—Tuxedo Park. The town is architecturally distinguished; Bruce Price created inspiring examples of domestic Shingle Style architecture there in the 1880s. The house combines asymmetrical wings and a turret in the picturesque manner, but these elements are suggested—are vestigial or embryonic—in the manner of late H. H. Richardson. In combination these varied elements create a tense whole.

Principal in charge: Robert Venturi
Project manager: Daniel McCoubrey
With: Steven Wiesenthal

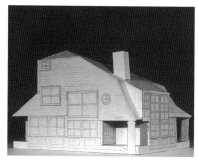

View of model

South elevation

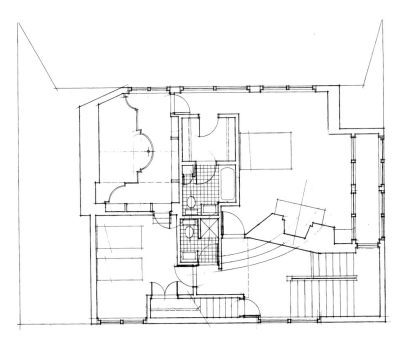

Second-floor plan

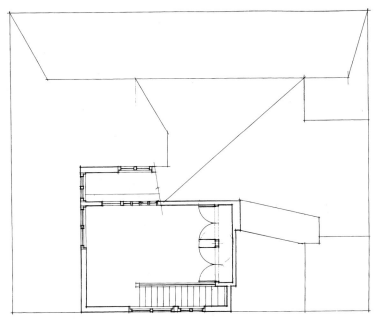

Third-floor plan

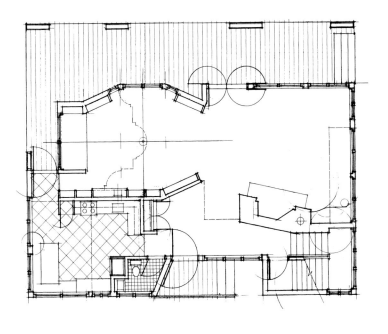

First-floor plan

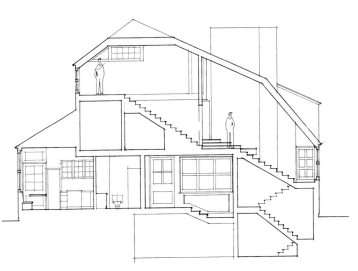

Section looking east

55 House on Long Island Sound

North Shore, Long Island, New York, 1983–1985

The remarkable site for a house we designed on the North Shore of Long Island—a private peninsula in Long Island Sound—has water on three sides; the views include the Connecticut shore and the New York skyline and are graced almost constantly by the movement of boats of all kinds in mid-distance. The foreground consists of pure lawn rimmed and protected by boulders.

The house is bold in scale to acknowledge its monumental and elemental setting; up close, however, its details make it friendly and appealing. The house also connotes elemental shelter within the open natural setting, manifest in the dominant gambrel roof, which encompasses the whole, and the protective shadowed recesses within the sweeping porches.

A Variation on the Shingle Style

The character of the architecture of this house derives from its stylistic references to the Shingle Style, which defined rural Long Island in the last half of the nineteenth century. The typical Shingle Style house had generous proportions and quiet dignity that accommodated gracious country living and combined subtle luxury and quiet taste. The weathered silver-gray cedar shingles of the roof and walls of VSBA's house make it recessive and at home in its natural setting of sea and sky; the traditional white trim of its windows and porches adds sparkle to the whole effect. The pool house outside is a miniature version of the big house and makes for a play of scale within this architectural complex.

Inside, the major rooms are upstairs to maximize the views on all three sides and to exploit the quality of space and the height advantage under the roof slopes; on the ground floor are the family recreation room, directly accessible from the porch and the outside; the indoor exercise pool; and the garage and other service spaces. The stairway up to the main floor is gracious in width and incline and in its flowing spatial quality; it has lots of natural light at the top. The space upstairs is generously open and flowing, punctuated by friendly and cozy nooks with built-in window seats, bookshelves, and cabinets. The curving wall opposite the generous fireplace contains a continuous window seat with a spectacular view behind. This room accommodates the effect of the season or the day; residents orient themselves cozily by focusing on the fireplace or expansively by embracing the sweep of the view. The bedrooms toward the rear are spacious and comfortable; each focuses on a sea view, and one has a balcony.

Porch

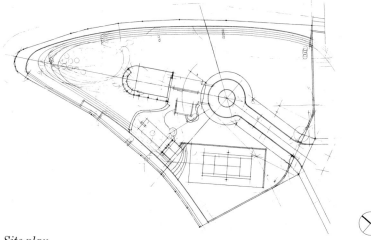

Site plan

This house can perhaps be perceived as at once generous and cozy in its quality inside and out, and luxurious in a subtle way. There is a great deal of attention to detail both as accommodation to convenience and comfort and as element of art for the eye.

Access to house

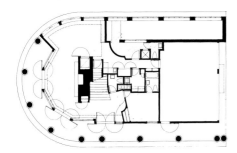

First-floor plan   Second-floor plan

Principal in charge: Robert Venturi
Project managers: Perry Kulper,
John Pringle, Fran Reed
With: James Kolker, Frederic Schwartz

Fireplace

56 Pearl Houses

Breakers West, Florida, 1985–1989

Principal in charge: Robert Venturi
Project managers: Perry Kulper,
Willis Pember

VSBA was asked to create a prototype design with distinct variations for a series of houses to be offered by the Warren Pearl Development Corporation at Breakers West, a private community in Florida. This particular design would provide buyers with a series of options that would be marketable and could accommodate various program needs. The options would include choices between one and two stories, different numbers of bedrooms and bathrooms, variable window placements, different fireplace and entrance designs, and various detailing elements.

This approach to developer housing works against the Modernist view that the exterior design derives solely from and expresses literally interior functional-spatial configurations. The prototype acknowledges referential elements of design and accommodates the developers' marketing need for programmatic and symbolic variety, and yet it accommodates as well a degree of constructive consistency.

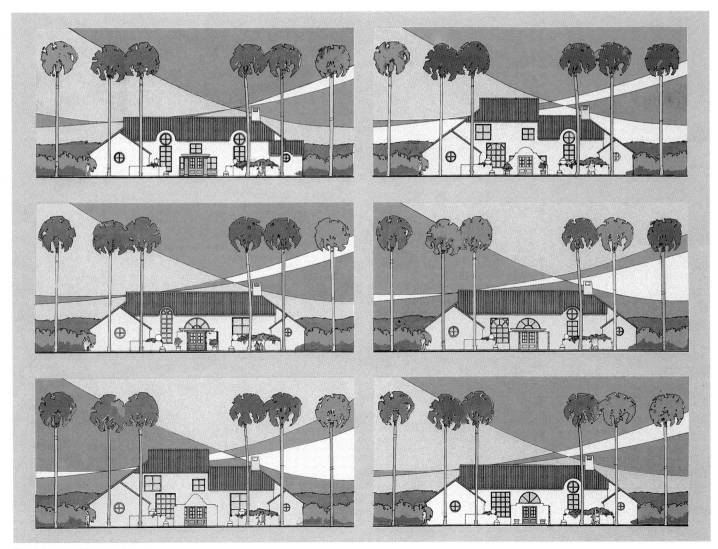

Prototype options

57 House on the Coast of Maine

1986–1989

VSBA designed this Maine house both as background and as accommodation to background—that is, as a restful and generous background for family living and as an accommodation, harmonious and analogous, to its natural background. The house is for a family of four on vacation; the site is on a cliff with the sea on one side, woods on the other, and a view down the coast. The community beyond is cherished for its shingled architectural tradition.

The plan is consistent: it is essentially one room wide on the ground floor, and views to both sides present the protected and scenic characters of the site. But within this major order are exceptions and variations, formal and spatial, among windows, openings, dormers, porches, and balconies. This makes for built-in and cozy nooks and crannies inside, as well as the spatial openness that children will enjoy as they grow, and also friendly picturesqueness outside. The ends of the long house have special functions: the east end exploits the view down the coast; the west end accommodates the family entrance.

The vocabulary of the house is abstracted Shingle Style. Its picturesque parts are melded within a whole, and it refers to the old days. The assembly of furnishings is eclectic, easy, and comfortable.

Principal in charge: Robert Venturi
Project manager: Roc Caivano
With: James Kolker, Gabrielle London, Maurice Weintraub
In association with: Dian Boone

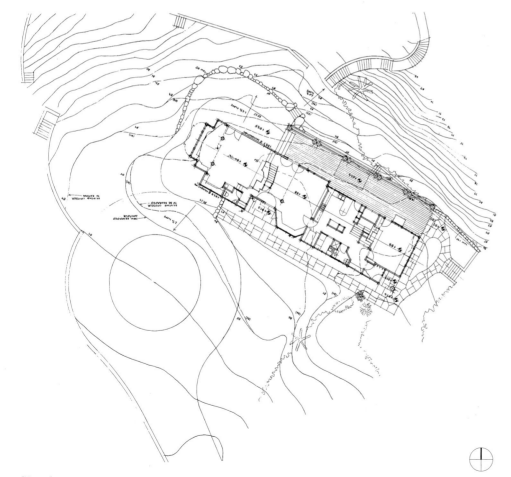

Site plan

View from southeast

View from southwest

Side elevation

View from library balcony

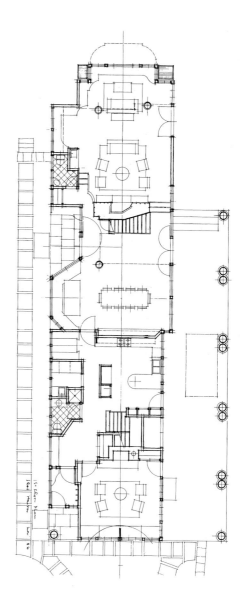

First-floor plan

Porch

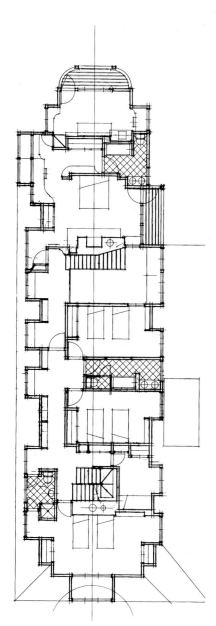

Second-floor plan

Hall

Sitting room

58 Project for a House in Chester County

Devon, Pennsylvania, 1993–1995

The Chester County house was to be located on a family farm close to Philadelphia, at the edge of a large field sloping to the south and closely bounded by a large dense wood. We designed the house as a modern interpretation of the classic eighteenth-century Pennsylvania farmhouse. It is essentially one room wide, and each major room has views on each side into the woods and down to the fields. The scale, appropriately, is bigger than that of a real farmhouse; its essentially shed roof facing the fields emphasizes the scenographic-aesthetic effect from the fields. The front, seen from a distance against the woods and visually representing a farmhouse, is different from the back, which is seen from close-up in the woods as essentially designed from the inside out.

All of these configurations make for complex spatial relationships inside—especially in the living-dining room. The kitchen is designed so that cook, family, and guests can socialize and dine together.

Principal in charge: Robert Venturi
Project manager: Timothy Kearney
With: Susan Lockwood

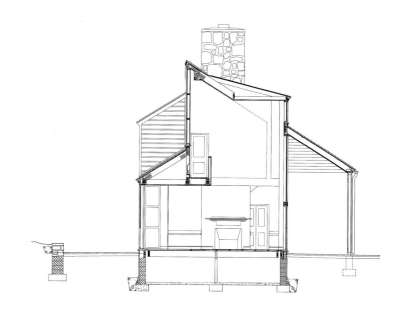

Section

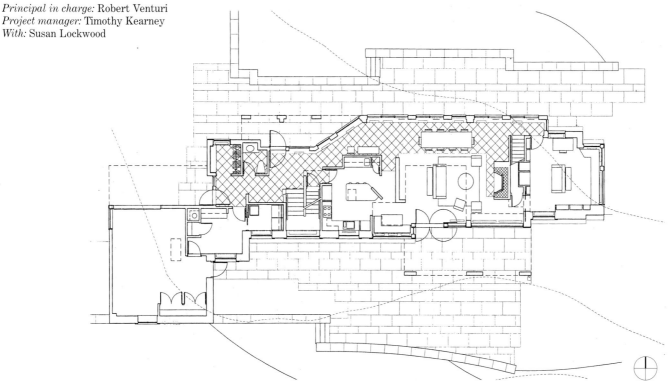

First-floor plan

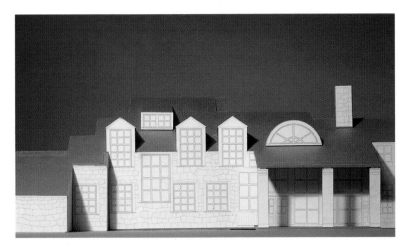
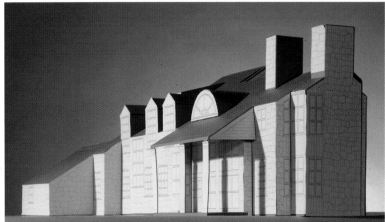
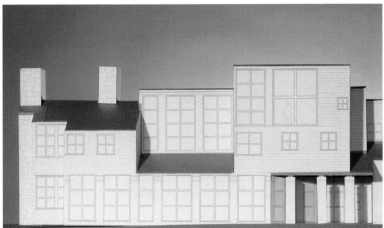

Views of model

Garden elevation

59 Houses for Mitsui Home Co.
Project for Prototypical Suburban Homes

Japan, 1990

VSBA's prototypical houses for Mitsui Home Co. offered optional designs, each option accommodating varying programmatic needs and site restrictions. It was intended that each design type would be constructed as a model for potential purchasers.

The designs acknowledge program requirements and space restrictions characteristic of the Japanese market and of the urban-suburban context. They are artful in their accommodating and varying cultural dimensions. Despite the small size, the houses project bold scale in their design, which is in accord with the hype sensibility that is universally of our time.

Principals in charge: Robert Venturi, Steven Izenour
Project manager: John Forney

View of model of House C

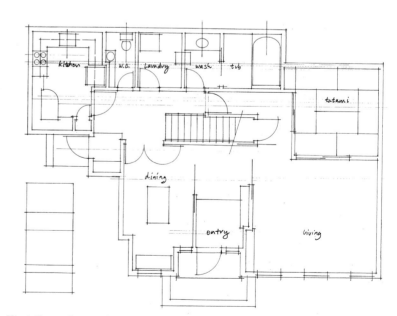

First-floor plan and front elevation of House A

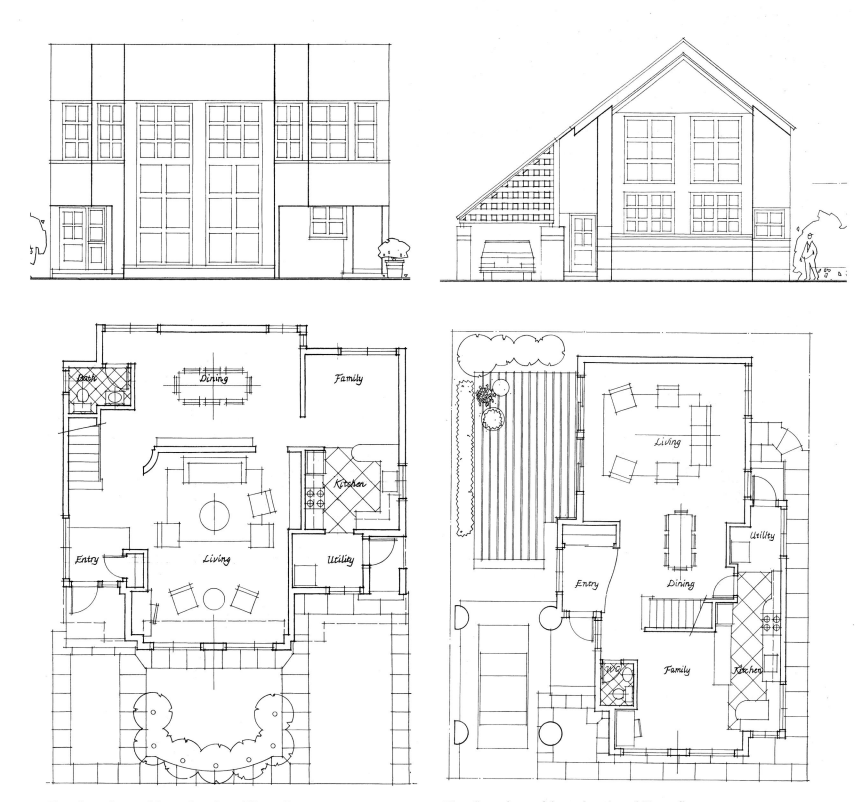

First-floor plan and front elevation of House B

First-floor plan and front elevation of House C

- Lighting
- lighting differentiation
- open vs - - -
- kiosk
- continuity
- circulation
- info - video
- · · · · not
- law of info : info system :

- consultant
- Scheduling - night vs day
- cont : kiosks
- Re021 lle vs booths built in

- Store kiosks
- Day light
- Curtains. molding circulation

Booths : →

Renovations

302   *Tarble Student Center*

304   *Mass MoCA*

306   *Furness Building*

310   *Thayer School of Engineering*

312   *Memorial Hall*

60 Tarble Student Center
Renovation, Swarthmore College

Swarthmore, Pennsylvania, 1984–1985

When Swarthmore College needed a student center for its campus, VSBA was asked to design a new building. Instead, we recommended, after careful analysis, the adaptation of an existing building, Clothier Hall, because of its central location and its adaptability, since it was a building whose original uses were no longer vital to the life and ways of the campus.

The design solution provides the various spaces for the uses of a student center while preserving, protecting, and maintaining the interior's irreplaceable beauty as an example of Collegiate Gothic architecture of the 1920s. The insertion of a freestanding structure adds a new level of use in what was originally an auditorium. The basement and first floor house the bookshop, lounges, and other services. The upper level is used for dances and activities such as theater productions and assemblies. It is fun to be up in the hammerbeam trusses of this space, now adapted for theatrical and other forms of lighting.

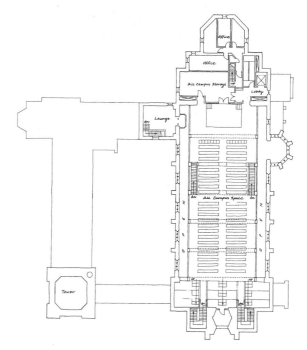

Upper-level plan

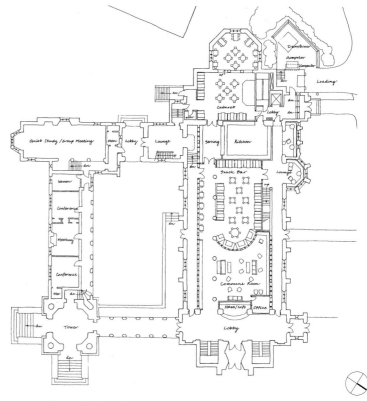

Ground-floor plan

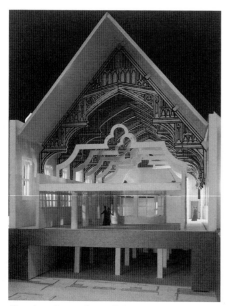

Section through model

View of addition from ground floor

View of upper-level addition

Principal in charge: Robert Venturi
Project managers: Daniel McCoubrey,
David Marohn
With: Eric van Aukee, Timur Galen,
Steven Izenour, Gabrielle London,
Robert Marker, John Pringle,
Sherri Williamson

61 Mass MoCA

Feasibility Study for the Massachusetts Museum of Contemporary Art

North Adams, Massachusetts, 1988–1989

The Massachusetts Museum of Contemporary Art, or Mass MoCA, was to occupy over seven hundred thousand square feet of now abandoned nineteenth-century textile mill buildings—generic/flexible lofts—in North Adams, Massachusetts. The museum would focus on the exhibition of several major art collections of the 1960s and later. It would also house an important collection of contemporary architectural drawings, models, and artifacts.

Thomas Krens, the project's initiator, envisioned Mass MoCA as a "museum like no other." It would comprise an integrated mix of galleries, an inn, restaurant and retail spaces, orientation and theater spaces, staff workshops, and children's activity spaces organized within and around the existing mill buildings, courtyards, and dramatic bridges and tunnels.

The project would be a major spur to economic growth for North Adams and an international center of contemporary art. Proposals included coordination of the museum plans with development projects and art installations off site and the initiation of a major "biennale" exhibition to compare to that of Venice. Mass MoCA would satisfy the critical need for large-scale display areas for contemporary sculpture, which are unavailable in many urban museums, particularly for in-depth display of an artist's work in an appropriate context—not too different from this generation's industrial lofts in Soho or other similar places.

The sign above the industrial stack would be read from the adjacent expressway and identify the place in a witty way—representational and graphic.

General view

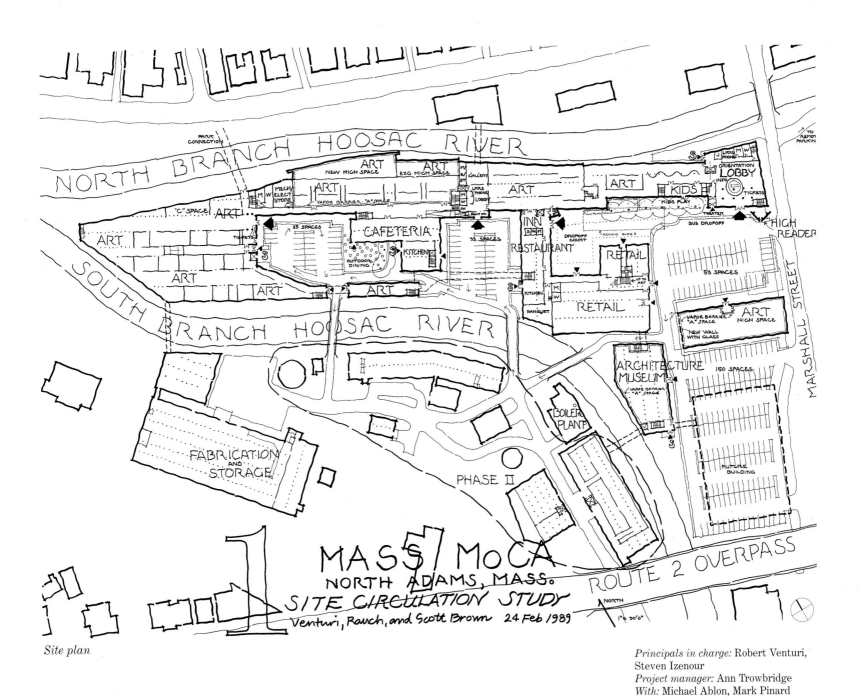

NORTH BRANCH HOOSAC RIVER

SOUTH BRANCH HOOSAC RIVER

ART · NEW HIGH SPACE
ART · EXG HIGH SPACE
GALLERY
ART
ART
KIDS
ORIENTATION LOBBY
INFO
TICKETS
ART
ART
MECH/ELECT/STORE
"C" SPACE
VAPOR BARRIER "A" SPACE
25 SPACES
CAFETERIA
KITCHEN
OUTDOOR DINING
TICKETS
INN
55 SPACES
RESTAURANT
DROPOFF COURT
REMOVE BLDG.
RETAIL
KIDS PLAY
THEATER
BUS DROPOFF
HIGH READER
ART
ART
ART
ART
KITCHEN
BANQUET
RETAIL
53 SPACES
VAPOR BARRIER "A" SPACE
NEW WALL WITH GLASS
ART · HIGH SPACE
MARSHALL STREET
ARCHITECTURE MUSEUM
VAPOR BARRIER "A" SPACE
150 SPACES
BOILER PLANT
FABRICATION AND STORAGE
PHASE II
FUTURE BUILDING

1 MASS / MoCA
NORTH ADAMS, MASS.
SITE CIRCULATION STUDY
Venturi, Rauch, and Scott Brown   24 Feb 1989

ROUTE 2 OVERPASS

NORTH   1" = 30'0"

Site plan

Principals in charge: Robert Venturi, Steven Izenour
Project manager: Ann Trowbridge
With: Michael Ablon, Mark Pinard
In association with: Skidmore, Owings & Merrill, New York; Frank O. Gehry and Associates; Bruner/Cott and Associates

62 Furness Building
Restoration and Renovation for the Fisher Fine Arts Library, University of Pennsylvania

Philadelphia, Pennsylvania, 1985–1991

The Furness library, which originally served as Penn's main library, was designed in 1888 by Frank Furness and is widely regarded as one of his masterpieces. It was Furness who first acknowledged in this building the dual character of the library: he separated the monumental civic space for reading from the expandable utilitarian space for book storage—what came to be known as stacks. We restored Furness's building to house the Fisher Fine Arts Library of the University of Pennsylvania and other archival and teaching spaces.

The restoration began with a master-plan study guided by a building committee composed of architecture, art history, and historic preservation faculty and library staff. The study focused on historical documentation, assessment of building conditions, and evolving a program of restoration and reorganization of uses. The resulting plan reasserts the logic of the original library plan and allows for growth of the Fisher Fine Arts Library and the Architectural Archives while meeting studio, teaching, and faculty office space needs for the Graduate School of Fine Arts.

Construction was done in three phases, beginning with exterior restoration in 1987. Renovations and exterior restoration of the bookstack building followed, including installation of modern environmental control, sprinkler, electrical, data, and security systems. The third phase involved restoration of the great interior spaces. The leaded-glass skylight of the Main Reading Room was restored while the 1922 midlevel floor insertion was removed, reestablishing a noble space perhaps unsurpassed in the United States. Re-created historical lighting fixtures and custom furnishings, designed to recall lost Furness pieces, were installed in time for the centennial celebration of the completion of the building, February 7, 1991.

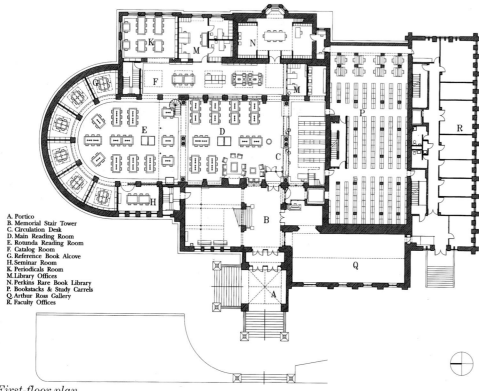

A. Portico
B. Memorial Stair Tower
C. Circulation Desk
D. Main Reading Room
E. Rotunda Reading Room
F. Catalog Room
G. Reference Book Alcove
H. Seminar Room
K. Periodicals Room
M. Library Offices
N. Perkins Rare Book Library
P. Bookstacks & Study Carrels
Q. Arthur Ross Gallery
R. Faculty Offices

First-floor plan

Reading room after restoration

Reading room before restoration

Principal in charge: Robert Venturi
Associate in charge: David Marohn
Project manager: Brett Crawford
With: Denise Scott Brown,
Chris Appleford, David Franke,
Richard Mohler, Thomas Purdy,
Mark Schlenker, Mark Stankard,
Richard Stokes, Nancy Rogo Trainer
In association with:
Marianna Thomas Architects;
CLIO Group, Inc.

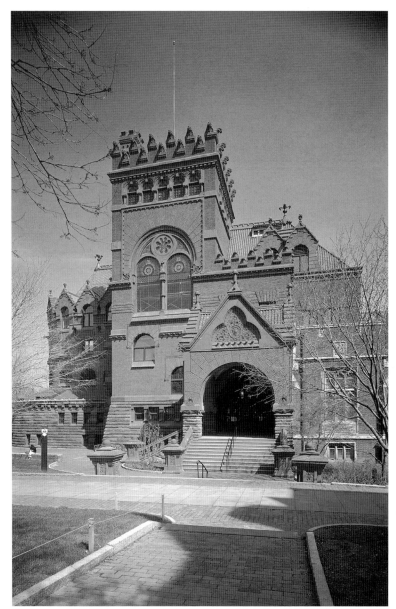

Entrance facade

Fireplace

Studio

63 Thayer School of Engineering
Additions and Renovations, Dartmouth College

Hanover, New Hampshire, 1986–1990

At the Thayer School of Engineering Building at Dartmouth College, located in a part of the campus dominated by distinguished Georgian Revival brick buildings of the 1920s and 1930s, VSBA's work consisted of additions and renovations. The additions maintain harmony and enhance their setting with their analogous architectural vocabulary. The addition on the front contains a new entry with a monumental meeting room above conforming quite literally in its vocabulary to the existing Georgian-style buildings. The new laboratory wing at the back recalls the tradition of the generic and generous New England mill building with its even rhythmic bay system evident on an unadorned brick exterior.

Inside, the rear extension accommodates the classic laboratory system, which is flexible both spatially and mechanically. This new wing, as it relates to the configuration of the old building, also creates a central meeting place. Three walls of this meeting space consist of original exterior facades of the old building, thus making for a kind of academic community space that encourages communication as students and faculty pass through and interact there. The new courtyard as a place to communicate contrasts with the spaces for concentration in the laboratories, new and old.

Principal in charge: Robert Venturi
Project managers: Roc Caivano,
Thomas Beck
With: Ian Adamson, John Bastian,
Catherine Bird, Catherine Cosentino,
John Forney, David Franke,
Susan Gallagher, Sharon McGinnis,
David Perkes, Mark Stankard,
James Winkler
In association with:
Payette Associates Inc.

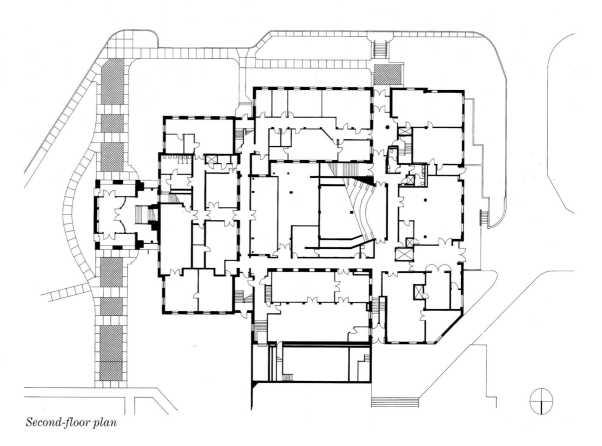

Second-floor plan

Rear view

Front addition with main entrance

Second-floor community space

Second-floor community space

64 Memorial Hall
Restoration and Renovation of Memorial Hall, including Annenberg Hall and Loker Commons, Harvard University

Cambridge, Massachusetts, 1992–1996

Memorial Hall is America's supreme example of Ruskinian Gothic. Our team of architects and consultants has restored the Great Hall, now named Annenberg Hall, with its hammerbeam trusses and stained-glass windows—the latter supremely exemplifying nineteenth-century craft and contributing aura via the penetration of exterior light through colored glass. This ground-floor space has reverted to its original use as a great dining hall—in our era to be limited to freshmen. It has thereby become an institutional space par excellence. Also included in the spaces that have been virtually literally restored are the hall memorializing the fallen alumni of the North during the Civil War and Sanders

Auditorium, renowned for the quality of its acoustics. What makes literal restoration virtual rather than literal is the need to accommodate various code restrictions and necessary programmatic changes.

Aura and Sparkle: Notes on Loker Commons
The basement of Memorial Hall has been renovated to become Loker Commons—the central meeting place for the whole academic community, a flexible space to lounge and eat in and for communication of all sorts, a non-institutional kind of place for hanging out. The design of this commons incorporates little

Interior of Annenberg Hall

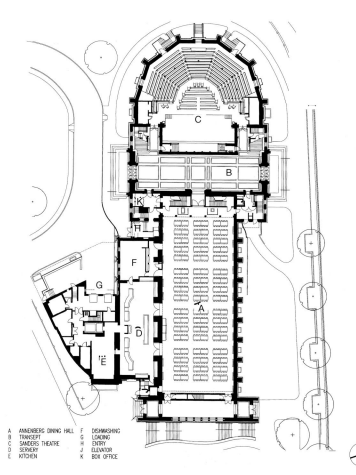

A	ANNENBERG DINING HALL	F	DISHWASHING
B	TRANSEPT	G	LOADING
C	SANDERS THEATRE	H	ENTRY
D	SERVERY	J	ELEVATOR
E	KITCHEN	K	BOX OFFICE

Ground-floor plan

Section

Rear view

Loker Commons

Principal in charge: Robert Venturi
Project manager: Daniel McCoubrey
Project architect: Richard Stokes
With: Hidenao Abe, Jeff Hirsch,
Joseph Herrin, Kimberley Jones,
Brian LaBau, Mindy No,
Alex Stolyarik, James Wallace,
Steven Wiesenthal
In association with:
Robert G. Neiley Architects;
Bruner/Cott and Associates, Inc.

architectural imagery because its architectural quality essentially derives not from light reflecting off surfaces and articulated details but from light sources themselves that create sparkle and accents within a recessive aura. The architectural surfaces and the furniture are neutral in hue and dark in value, so that the small amount of ambient light derived from ceiling fixtures tends to be barely reflected off surfaces but to focus on people to make them into accents.

An exception occurs at the series of old-fashioned bulletin boards for varieties of tacked-on notices; these surfaces, spotlit from above, reflect light as they also articulate circulation through the space. Another exception occurs in a parallel zone behind the bulletin boards, where during the day an existing row of small high windows admits ambient light into a series of peripheral niches that contain booths accommodating those who enjoy being on the periphery. The other side of the room is lined with food counters and constitutes another parallel zone, this one brightly lit from above.

But the essential effect in this interior derives from sparkling interplay between two kinds of light sources. The first is a row of parallel colored fluorescent tubes arranged on the ceiling to articulate decoratively a major circulation route. The second consists of two electronic sources: an *LED* board as a frieze with moving images along and above the food counter, which viewers note incidentally, and an *LED* board as a screen that terminates the circulation route, which is a specific focus.

These electronic elements promoting flexible imagery—graphic, narrative, abstract, and/or symbolic—work as sources of ornament that appeal to the hype sensibility of our time and

Annenberg Hall with stained-glass window

Loker Commons elevation study

Views of Loker Commons with changing LED panel

also as sources of information, dynamically complex and multi-cultural. Their setting in a meeting place incidentally adapted from a conventional basement—not arty/architectural but generically flexible—adapts to a kind of grunge aesthetic for this generation. Here architecture becomes non-architecture.

Something that is hard to do in architecture is to create aura and sparkle in space inside a building—as opposed to ambient light inside a building that derives from reflection from architectural surfaces. This kind of light in space is essential for the basement of Memorial Hall, which included no restorative element in its design.

Can it be said that the sparkle of pixels in Loker Commons downstairs corresponds to the glory of vitraux in Annenberg Hall upstairs, that twentieth-century electronic technology meets nine-teenth-century historicist craft, that informational iconography corresponds to traditional iconography? In the basement of Memorial Hall contemporary electronics succeeds revivalist craft.

It is important to note that signs are wonderful but troublesome elements because, unlike abstract ornament, they require an ingredient of content and, ironically, while our information age projects lots of graphic imagery, it is still hard to organize multi-culturally correct content. However, we think this dimension/medium can be enriching and valid and—via changing electronic signage—essential to the ethos of this place. It can also recall the civic-cultural graphic tradition within architecture—Classical and medieval—that has enriched architectural settings in the past and that, in its Victorian and Romantic manifestation, is an essential part of the distinguished architectural setting upstairs.

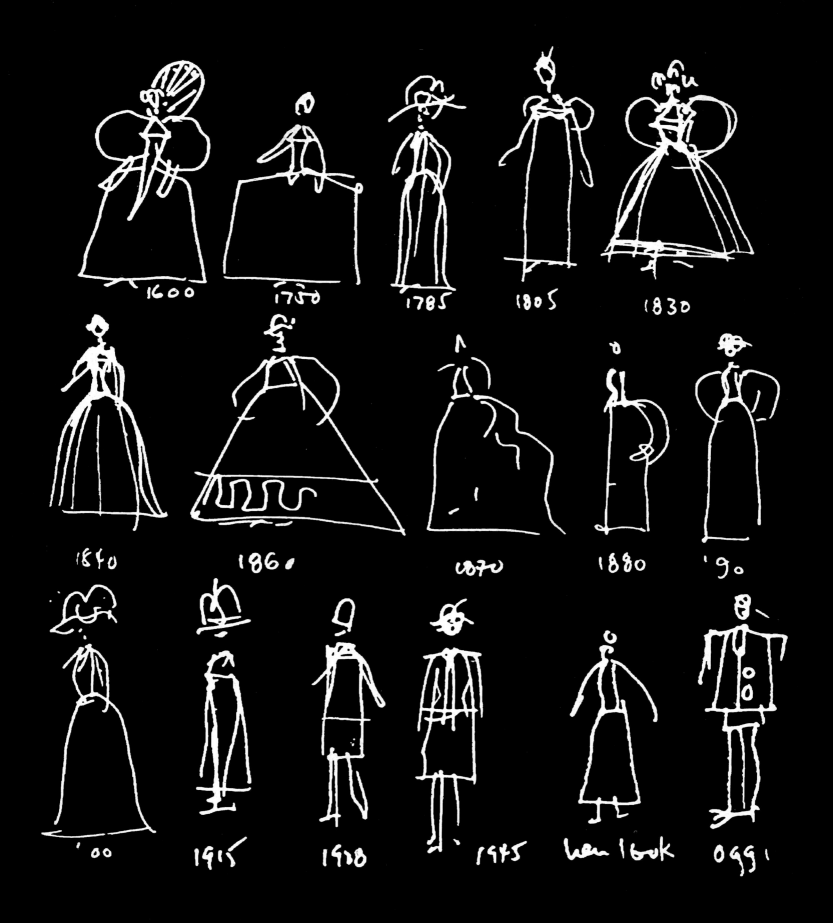

1600   1750   1785   1805   1830

1840   1860   1870   1880   '90

'00   1915   1920   1945   New Look   Oggi

Exhibitions
Interior Design
Decorative Arts

318 *ICA Exhibition*

320 *Venturi Shops*

322 *Alessi Biblioteca*

323 *Sainsbury Wing Furniture*

324 *PMA West Foyer*

326 *Princeton Club of New York*

328 *Hotel Mielparque Resort Complex*

329 *Designs for Kitchen Units*

330 *Flatware for Swid Powell and Reed and Barton*

330 *Candlesticks for Swid Powell*

331 *Cuckoo Clock for Alessi*

332 *Place Settings for Swid Powell*

334 *Fabrics for Designtex*

336 *Rugs for V'Soske*

338 *Jewelry for Munari*

340 *Campidoglio Tray for Alessi*

341 *Memorial Lunette*

65 ICA Exhibition
Exhibition on the Work of VSBA at the Institute of Contemporary Art, University of Pennsylvania

Philadelphia, Pennsylvania, 1992–1993

The design of an exhibition on our work acknowledges some of the difficulties inherent in architectural exhibitions. By their nature, architectural exhibitions deal with secondary sources—drawings, photos, models. While these elements might be artful in themselves, they are not what architecture is all about—the perception of three-dimensional buildings involving space, structure, and symbolism.

The design of this exhibition employed three traditional elements—original sketches, photography (via large slide projections), and models—and then included a fourth: graphics that describe an architecture of ideas in words. Big- and small-scale white vinyl graphics were sprinkled on black walls in a manner both decorative and content-driven; this concept extended the opportunity to deal explicitly with content—with discussion and intellectual and architectural oppositions. The models and drawings—highlighted within an otherwise dark ambience—provided a small-scale visual counterpoint to the graphics and the big-scale frieze of slide projections.

It is important to note that the images of the slides were a series of very large projections that changed every half-minute on a high wall, which made for an evolving kind of mural-frieze.

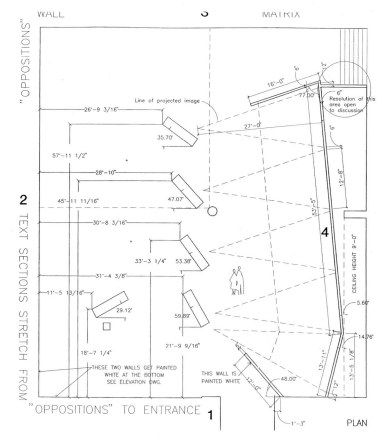

Plan

General view

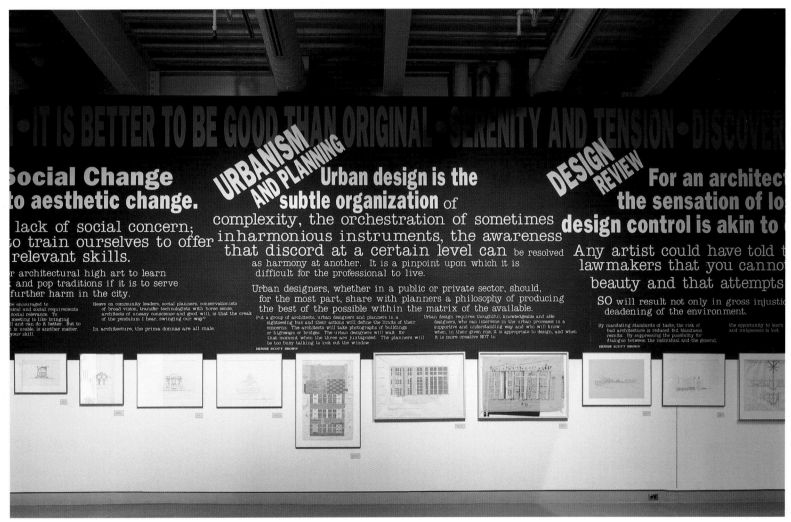

The wall text reads:

• IT IS BETTER TO BE GOOD THAN ORIGINAL • SERENITY AND TENSION • DISCOVER

Social Change to aesthetic change.

lack of social concern; to train ourselves to offer relevant skills.

r architectural high art to learn and pop traditions if it is to serve further harm in the city.

URBANISM AND PLANNING Urban design is the subtle organization of complexity, the orchestration of sometimes inharmonious instruments, the awareness that discord at a certain level can be resolved as harmony at another. It is a pinpoint upon which it is difficult for the professional to live.

Urban designers, whether in a public or private sector, should, for the most part, share with planners a philosophy of producing the best of the possible within the matrix of the available.

DESIGN REVIEW For an architect the sensation of lo design control is akin to

Any artist could have told t lawmakers that you canno beauty and that attempts

SO will result not only in gross injustic deadening of the environment.

General view

View with Grand's Restaurant sign (1961) and Guild House aerial (1963)

Principal in charge: Robert Venturi
Project manager: Steven Izenour
With: Denise Scott Brown,
Stephanie Christoff, David Dashiell,
John Forney, Tom Jones, Amy Noble

66 Venturi Shops

Exhibition of Japanese Objects, Philadelphia Museum of Art

Philadelphia, Pennsylvania, 1995

These objects from the collection of Denise Scott Brown and Robert Venturi are manifestations of the Japanese custom of giving gifts. Most derive from small shops and markets the architects found so interesting that a Japanese friend renamed them "Venturi shops."

The exhibition itself combines very diverse objects seemingly haphazardly to demonstrate their variety and range. On the walls are graphic inscriptions that describe sources and express fascination.

Japonisme?

We have written of our initial responses as American architects to Japanese art and culture, historical and contemporary. We have thus added our perspective and interpretations to those of Western artists and architects of the past who explicitly acknowledged influences in their writings or made them apparent in their work.

Some of these architects focused on their particular views of the generic and pure shrines in Kyoto, which excluded context beyond that of the gardens the shrines are in, not acknowledging the markets typically across the way that are a significant part of a whole. Those markets teem with complex and contradictory varieties and juxtapositions and embrace dimensions sensuous and lyrical in terms of color, pattern, and scale. We instead saw historic Kyoto as an exemplification of Japanese art and architecture that included shrines in gardens and markets in streets and figures in colorfully patterned kimonos visualized all over. The simple shrines were made sublime by the juxta-position of complex context.

And then there are the objects that make up the market. These objects fascinate because they exhibit at once skill, pride, and wit, rare and precious elements in our time. In a Western country might be found combinations of any two but seldom all three at once. The element of care is important too. In Japan, God and workers are in the details.

Principal in charge: Robert Venturi
Project manager: Stephanie Christoff
With: Denise Scott Brown,
Felisa Opper

Venturi Shops

Exhibition installation

67 Alessi Biblioteca

Lago d'Orta, Italy, 1984

Alessi Bibliotèca

The Alessi Biblioteca is a kind of new lining within an old building—an old rustic building of great quality characteristic of its locale in northern Italy. The client requested a domestic library two stories in height with Empire-style references in the architectural vocabulary. The references are abstracted, stylized, and exaggerated in scale in their representations in furniture and architecture.

Principal in charge: Robert Venturi
Project managers: James Bradberry, Maurice Weintraub

68 Sainsbury Wing Furniture
National Gallery

London, England, 1990

 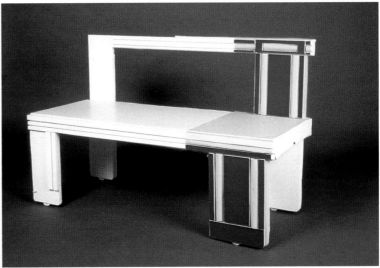

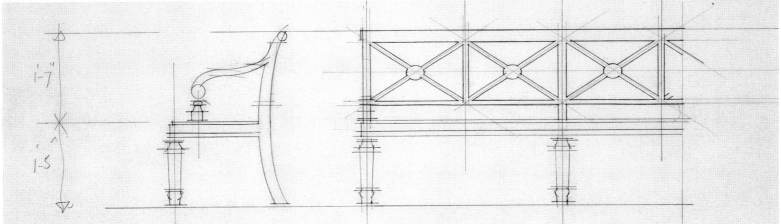

Prototypes and drawings of tables and benches

Our designs for furniture for the Sainsbury Wing of the National Gallery acknowledge historical precedent—as does the design of most of the architectural spaces they were intended for. These spaces—most of them context for paintings from specific historical periods—promote harmony between objects and setting via analogy rather than contrast, via historical-symbolic reference rather than abstract-expressionist contrast. But the reference of the furniture itself, like the architecture it is in, is abstracted and therefore does not involve literal historical replication.

Unfortunately, the client wanted an English designer to design the furniture. His design is based on thematic adaptations of elements of the architectural design (see pp. 122–39).

Principal in charge: Robert Venturi

69 PMA West Foyer
Philadelphia Museum of Art

Philadelphia, Pennsylvania, 1986–1989

The West Foyer has become the main entrance to the Philadelphia Museum of Art because of its automobile access and proximity to parking. The goals of the interior renovation were to facilitate the admission and circulation of large crowds, to improve the transmission of information, to upgrade amenities for visitors, and to provide improved lighting. These goals were to be met within the context of the existing beautiful but severe masonry lobby and within the spirit of the lively and colorful Greek ornament characteristic of the museum's exterior.

Desks for admissions, membership, and information were replaced by a single central desk surrounding a tall kiosk. The desk and kiosk are made of white oak with a combination of natural and brightly colored enamel finishes. The kiosk incorporates graphics on the front that provide membership and admissions information, and an electronic sign on the back that provides changing information about tours and events. The kiosk also contains lighting that is projected onto the ceiling, which itself was repainted with colors that accent the decorative moldings of the coffers. The kiosk is topped by a fanfare of profiles of three griffins depicted in blue neon; they were derived from the bronze griffins (actually lightning rods) that adorn the museum's roof. The griffin, which the museum has adopted as its symbol, was the mythological guardian of Greek treasures.

New benches of similar material and finish incorporate Greek motifs and provide seating at the perimeter of the room. Panels on the walls provide further graphic information, and a soft pattern painted on the walls adds a guarded richness to the whole effect, in which amenity and information come together.

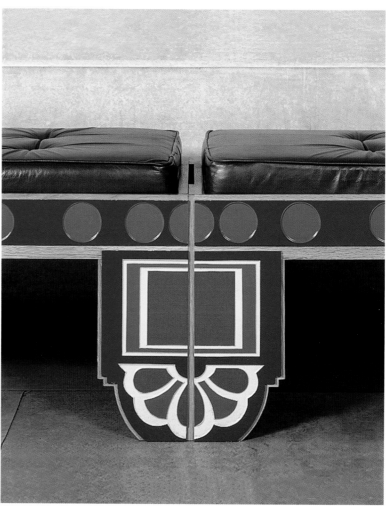

Bench detail

Principal in charge: Robert Venturi
Project manager: Ann Trowbridge
With: Willis Pember

Information desk

70 Princeton Club of New York
Renovations

New York, New York, 1989–1990

This renovation of the Modernist building of the Princeton Club of New York includes the redesign of several major rooms, including the Woodrow Wilson Dining Room and the Tiger Bar and Grill. The new scheme for the former space of the dining room is derived from wood wall paneling; the conventional but bold beaded-board striations become a major decorative element of the design through their shadowed articulations and color combinations. Orange and black, the school colors, are prominent. More patterns are manifest in the carpet and upholstery, which are bold and delicate in their combinations of scale. The furniture itself is purposefully conventional but carefully chosen. The low ceiling is perceptually alleviated by three-dimensional articulation within it, which accommodates ambient lighting systems. Lighting is most significant in the dining room, and the ambient effect is contrasted by the sparkle of wall sconces, which are specially designed and stylized representations of traditional sconces.

The atmosphere of the Tiger Bar and Grill is very different. Its aesthetic effect derives from the clutter of photographs and trophies ornamenting the walls, juxtapositions of various patterns in dark fields, and low light levels highlighted by sparkling light sources and mirrored reflections at the bar.

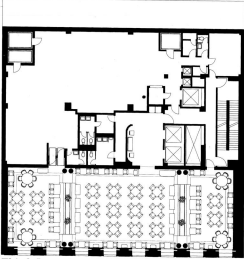

Third-floor plan

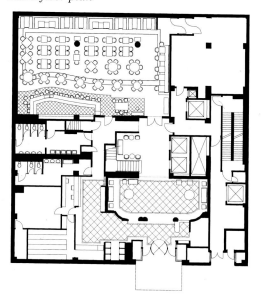

Ground-floor plan

Dining room

Principal in charge: Robert Venturi
Associate in charge: Ann Trowbridge
Project managers: Jeffrey Krieger,
Mark Wieand
With: Eric van Aukee, Catherine Bird,
John Forney, Michael Haverland,
Don Jones, Timothy Kearney, Brian
LaBau, Thomas Purdy, Richard Stokes,
Nancy Rogo Trainer, Maurice Weintraub
In association with:
Anderson/Schwartz Architects

Tiger Bar and Grill

71 Hotel Mielparque Resort Complex
Patterns for Interior Decoration of Hotel Rooms

Nikko, Japan, 1997

The interior design of the guest rooms of the Mielparque Nikko Kirifuri Resort Hotel consists of juxtapositions of various classic and generic kinds of furniture of the Modern period, eschewing consistency and unity and promoting richness and variety via scale and forms. The different fabrics, carpets, and wallpapers were specially designed by VSBA; they derive from large-scale abstractions of historical peasant fabrics, traditionally executed in blue hues and light values that create an aura inside reflecting that of the misty climate outside.

Principal in charge: Robert Venturi
Project manager: Claudia Cueto
With: Denise Scott Brown, Stephanie Christoff, Jeffrey Lewis

Typical hotel room with Saarinen chair and VSBA fabrics

72 Designs for Kitchen Units
Prototypical Domestic Kitchen Units, Hanssem Co.

Seoul, Korea, 1990–1991

Principal in charge: Robert Venturi
Project manager: Maurice Weintraub
With: Felisa Opper

The prototypical domestic kitchen complexes we designed are destined for the American and Japanese markets and accommodate ways of living today. The collaboration of the president of the company and his staff was very important in the creation of these designs.

Each of the optional layouts of the kitchens acknowledges the architectural role of the kitchen as part of the living room, where the cook as parent and/or host can partake in the life of the living room. This family-social connection is enhanced by the kitchen counter's placement: the cook faces the living room as he or she works.

Optional ornamented surfaces and colors for the cabinetry are included in these designs. Also, varying kinds of cabinets were designed for more conventional kitchen layouts. Some of the variations are in accord with the bold sensibility of today.

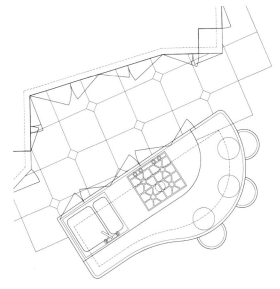

Floor plan

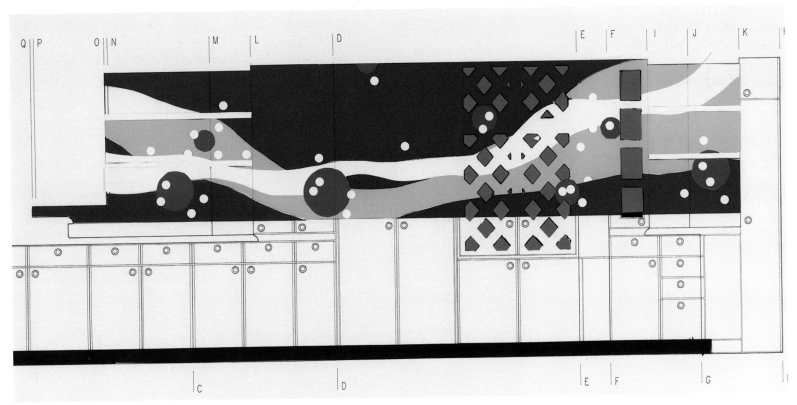

Kitchen Prototype

73 Flatware for Swid Powell and Reed and Barton

1991

Each of the pieces of VSBA's flatware service is a stylized and abstracted representation of one of the three Classical orders in architecture—decorative and witty, it is hoped, but not crazy. We think of these elements of a Classical architectural vocabulary as a most vivid image of a universal element.

Principal in charge: Robert Venturi
Project manager: Maurice Weintraub
With: Felisa Opper

Swid Powell/Reed and Barton flatware

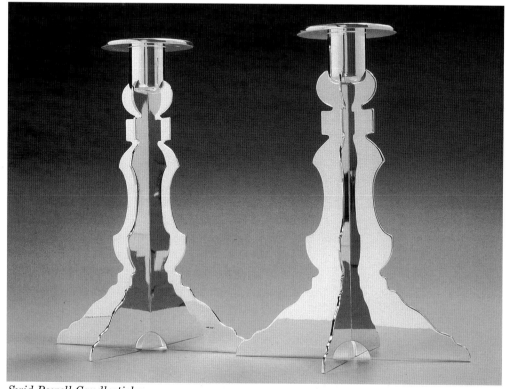

Swid Powell Candlesticks

74 Candlesticks for Swid Powell

1991

Our candlestick holders evoke eighteenth-century Classical references via their juxtaposed metal plates/silhouettes.

Principal in charge: Robert Venturi
Project manager: Maurice Weintraub
With: Felisa Opper

75 Cuckoo Clock for Alessi

1988

Alessi clock

We designed the clock as a playful abstraction of a familiar and beloved element of our culture. Its scale is larger and its colors are more vivid than usual. The materials are lacquered wood, and the cuckoo melody is bellows-operated.

Principal in charge: Robert Venturi
Project manager: Maurice Weintraub

76 Place Settings for Swid Powell

Flower Pattern, Classical Pattern, Line and Dots Pattern

1993

Flower pattern

VSBA's set of dishes for Swid Powell have a pattern of sketchy flowers that looks bold and pretty—and tense.

Principal in charge: Robert Venturi
Project manager: Jeannie Adams
With: Felisa Opper

Various patterns in blue remind viewers, via sketchy abstraction, of classic styles of dishes. The patterns are also Classical in their reference.

Principal in charge: Robert Venturi
Project manager: Maurice Weintraub
With: Felisa Opper

Classical pattern

We thought this might be the beginning of a dalmatian phase.

Principal in charge: Robert Venturi
Project manager: Maurice Weintraub
With: Felisa Opper

Lines and Dots pattern

77 Fabrics for Designtex

1990

We designed a series of fabrics for upholstery under the guidance of Designtex that involves varying color combinations within each pattern type, varying symbolic sources for each of the pattern types—including Japanese patterns from kimonos—and varying juxtapositions of stripes and dots, geometric and naturalistic patterns, and contrasting textures within some of the patterns. The designs are meant to be perceptually intriguing but also recessive—background elements within their intended contexts that are not intrusive or tiring over time.

Principal in charge: Robert Venturi
Project manager: Maurice Weintraub
With: Denise Scott Brown,
Jeannie Adams

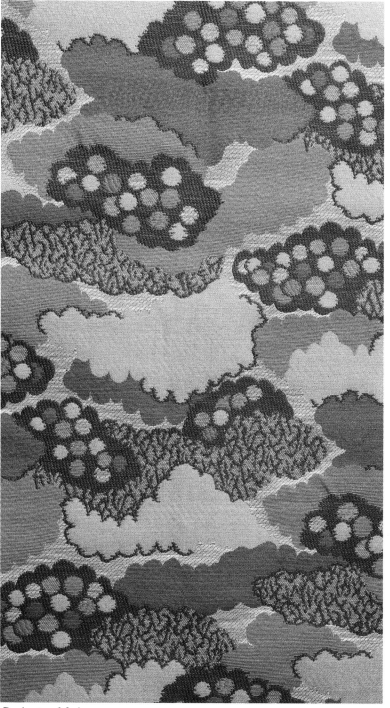

Designtex fabric

Designtex fabric

78 Rugs for V'Soske

New York, New York, 1993

Principal in charge: Robert Venturi
Project manager: Maurice Weintraub
With: Denise Scott Brown,
Jeannie Adams

V'Soske rug

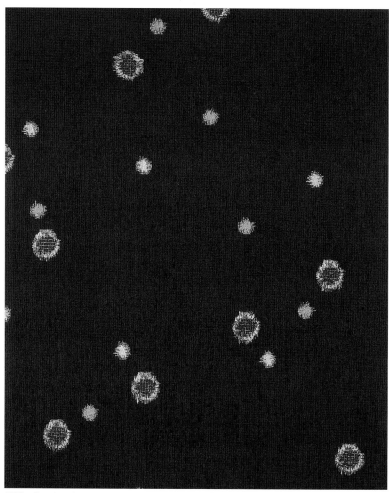

V'Soske rug

The patterns and textures of VSBA's V'Soske rugs represent abstractions of the patterns and textures of fabrics of silk kimonos that might be found in the Japanese equivalent of thrift shops. Their varying degrees of abstraction derive from changes in scale—the patterns of the rugs are bigger than those of the textiles that inspired them—and, of course, from the transposition of use, material, and context; in this sense our designs fall within the tradition of pop art.

Symbolically, these designs derive from a fascination with aspects of Japanese art—a fascination that acknowledges the tradition in which Western artists interpret and adapt Japanese art and architecture—although we are admittedly focusing on a humble manifestation of Japanese art. Two of the rugs conform to orthodox Modern tradition in art: their designs are literally and figuratively flat and they look flat in the quality of the original patterns and the representation of the patterns; they conform thereby to the nature of their material and to their function.

But the third rug does not conform to this context: it is a flat representation of complexly patterned fabric that is gathered into random three-dimensional folds. Representation of the shades and shadows of the folds makes it read three-dimensionally even though it is a flat rug on a floor.

V'Soske rug

79 Jewelry for Munari

1985

Necklace

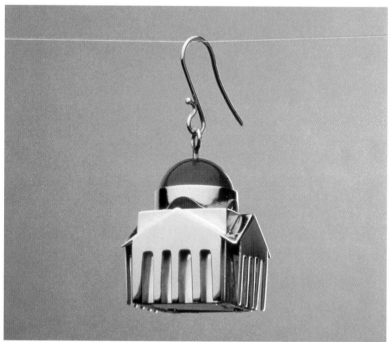

Earring

Ring

Each of the pieces of jewelry we designed embraces representation combined with abstraction and via that juxtaposition creates aesthetic tension and a kind of playfulness often found in toys.

Principal in charge: Robert Venturi
Project managers: James Bradberry, Maurice Weintraub

Necklace

80 Campidoglio Tray for Alessi

1980–1985

Campidoglio tray

Our Alessi tray reminds us of an architect's most beloved piazza—Michelangelo's Capitoline Hill. The tray is made of polished stainless steel with a gold-plated pattern.

Principal in charge: Robert Venturi

81 Memorial Lunette

1983

Memorial lunette

This sculpture-as-fragment was commissioned by David van Zanten as a memorial to his wife, Ann Lorenz van Zanten, the distinguished art historian and loving young mother killed in a terrorist attack on the rue de Rosiers in Paris in 1982. It represents a fragment: an abstraction of a part of a Luca della Robbia terra-cotta lunette. Its inscription, from Ernest Renan's *Vie de Jèsus*, was chosen by David van Zanten. It was to ornament the top of an opening in the hall of the St. Louis Art Museum in Ann van Zanten's home town.

Principal in charge: Robert Venturi

Detail study

THERE WAS:

a heroic architecture combining:
- Minimal - abstract composition,
- Functional - derived form,
- Industrial - derived vocabulary,
- Original - sculptural expression.

HERE IS:

a realist architecture juxtaposing: Symbolic meaning (rather than abstract expression) deriving from ornamental/ iconographic appliqué upon conventional (not original) generic form where functions are accommodated (rather than function is followed) and shelter is explicit and technologies are electronic!

VIVA Decorative Iconography upon generic Architecture:

as in ancient Egyptian, Byzantine, gothic and Renaissance architecture — for an age that is post-industrial and electronic — for the "Information Age"

VIVA Buildings that look like buildings!

RV '98

On Artful Artlessness

Denise Scott Brown and Robert Venturi
in conversation with Mary McLeod and
Stanislaus von Moos

1. *The Las Vegas Strip as an automobile environment, c. 1970*

On Artful Artlessness

Las Vegas—Today

MMcL: One thing that struck me reading Bob's recent book[1] was the reassessment of Las Vegas. You didn't sound as happy with Las Vegas today. One sensed that its "Disneyfication" had affected the vital, crude vernacular culture that you valued in an earlier era.

RV: When we wrote recently about latter-day Las Vegas, it's important to realize we were not talking about Fremont Street, the downtown Las Vegas, but the Las Vegas that is outside the center of town—that is, where the original Strip used to be. Since we were there two years ago, Fremont Street as a Main Street has been transformed into a very up-to-date, state-of-the-art electronic environment that, of course, did not exist in the late sixties. What we learned then about a classic strip environment involved simple lessons, such as what happens to architecture when it is designed to be seen from a fast-moving car. Generally, architecture before Las Vegas was made to be seen at a speed of about four miles an hour, at a walking pace, or maybe at ten miles an hour from a carriage. But Las Vegas has—or had—an architecture based on being seen from the side of the road as you were going relatively fast (figs. 1, 4). And so it had vitality as well as vulgarity—the architecture and its iconography tempted you to stop and be drawn into it. Now, it's been kind of . . .

MMcL: Disneyfied?

RV: Yes, but before we get to the Disney part, I'd like to say it's been made less naughty and more correct. Gentrified is the word. Now it's no longer just a place for gamblers to come and play around, or, if you weren't a gambler, a place where you could pretend to be daring—pretend you were one of those cowboy types of the Old West. Now the market has been expanded so that you go there for a wholesome holiday with your family. And it's no longer a place that relates to a moving car; it's a place where you walk from one building to another, despite the enormous heat in the summer (figs. 2, 3). So it has become scenographic instead of signographic. And this may be why it doesn't have the originality and the whammo power it used to have. By becoming pedestrian (in two senses of the word) and gentrified, it's more a kind of Disneyland, despite the spectacularity of aspects of it. Again, I'm not talking about the Fremont Street of today, which we haven't seen, and I imagine we could learn a lot from now.

DSB: The Strip is much more crowded and built up now. It's like a long Piazza Navona, and the thirty-five-mile-an-hour drive through the desert doesn't apply anymore. We were talking then about attracting a car and responding to the driver's reaction time, whereas today the Strip must draw the pedestrian in from the road. The timing and structure of movement have changed, given the new density.

The scale of enterprises has changed too. On the sixties Strip, large, individually owned hotels were separated by small motels

2. *Excalibur Hotel, Las Vegas, c. 1990*

3. *The Las Vegas Strip as a pedestrian environment, c. 1990*

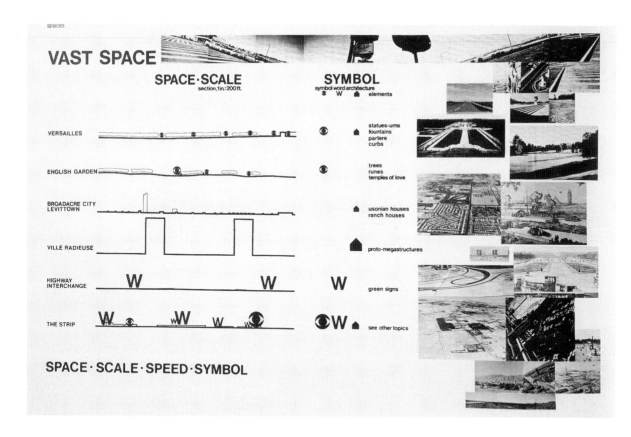

4. The scale of signs along commercial streets in relation to traffic speeds, showing changes from the medieval town to Las Vegas (from Robert Venturi, Denise Scott Brown, and Steven Izenour, Learning from Las Vegas, *1972)*

and diners and a few gasoline stations. Now maybe twelve big companies are there. The scale is much, much bigger—it's the scale of mass America, much bigger than the gambler's Strip was. They're building at a global scale. And behind the velvet glove, behind all the whimsy, is the iron hand of very large-scale corporate America. Disney too is different now from what it was.

Recycling the Billboard

SvM: Maybe that's why a project like the Stardust Hotel, or other projects you've done for Disney (see pp. 19, 49), try to retrieve some of the old days of Las Vegas and bring them to Disney World and Disneyland. It creates an interesting . . .

DSB: Inversion.

SvM: Inversion! Yes. In more general terms, you are attracted to aspects of "pop" reality that are in the process of becoming history. It is at that moment that you pick up on them and make them into "motifs," subjecting them to aesthetic recycling.

DSB: Yes. In fact, when we hit Las Vegas, the Strip was already coming under the influence of gigantism and gentrification. As Bob says, we architects are always behind. Also, to be read as a symbol, an object needs a certain history behind it.

RV: Right.

Learning from Corporate America?

MMcL: Both of you have argued eloquently about learning from what *is;* yet I sense an ongoing critique of large-scale capitalism. It seems much more problematic to you than the smaller-scale, laissez-faire entrepreneurial capitalism that you saw as characterizing Las Vegas in the late sixties. I'm wondering if there's something that might also be learned from this large-scale capitalism— its mass culture. In some ways, it seems as if your work incorporating LEDs might relate to that.

DSB: Large-scale corporate architecture is usually architect-designed, and we're not really interested in examining corporate architects' culture. We learn more from a more naive level of form-making. It's like Beethoven borrowing folk songs for a string quartet.

RV: One way to answer your questions is to say that, in our opinion, what is there now does not have the vitality of what was there before. It has an amazing spectacularity but it doesn't have the vitality. In the end, it's not as thrilling. And we don't think we can learn as much from it.

Pop Sources for University Buildings?

MMcL: This raises the question of how your sources have changed over the years. Are there aspects of your earlier work that you

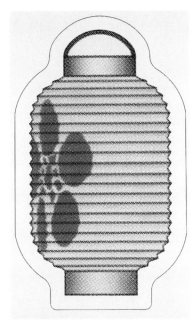

5. VSBA, Hotel Mielparque
Resort Complex, Nikko, Kirifuri,
Japan, 1992–97. Decorative sign
for the "village street"

6. Commercial
building in Tokyo,
Japan

now reject, or earlier sources that no longer hold your interest? How have large institutional buildings changed the nature of imagery in your work of the last fifteen years?

RV: The jobs we get are not Las Vegan, not commercial, often not connected with the street. The point is that in most of our work, which is institutional—for universities and colleges and museums—you don't bring in pop imagery, which can be inappropriate and distracting. It does not fit in with the aura of the place, with the context. It's true that now that we are doing a hotel for the first time, we are relating symbolically and aesthetically to the everyday commercial ethos (fig. 5; see pp. 270–79). But we wouldn't dream of doing that for a university building. And in our institutional architecture we evoke the ordinary through its generic qualities—in terms of form, space, and symbolism—not commercial imagery.

DSB: Except for a student center (see pp. 230–33). One of the important new sources for our work at the moment is Japan, especially Tokyo—again, not the large urban-renewal projects of high-design architects but the more naive everyday architecture, built between 1950 and 1960, that absorbs influences from America but uses them in ways no polite architect ever would (fig. 6).

The Extraordinariness of Being Ordinary

MMcL: A question about your own roles as innovators. Even though you have never valued originality per se, many view your projects, especially the early ones, as highly original—even iconoclastic. Even though you support the "everyday" and the "ordinary," hasn't your own professional positioning—manifestos, cartoon diagrams, aphorisms, a kind of pleasurable "naughtiness" —been self-consciously avant-garde? Would you agree that your support of the "ordinary" has a strong undercurrent of iconoclasm? I'm curious how both of you reconcile your interest in the everyday and the ordinary, on the one hand, with your interest in invention, on the other. Or is it an inherent contradiction?

DSB: We've been strongly aware of this paradox from the beginning. When revolution is the norm, the ordinary becomes revolutionary. Modern architecture proclaimed itself to be a revolution, but by the time we were writing, it was an old revolution. And you fight an old revolution with a new ordinariness. Yet the ordinary is what revolutionaries usually revolt against; that's where the paradox lies.

MMcL: But what about the manner in which you propagate the ordinary? Would you have any problem in saying that there's a kind of self-conscious iconoclasm about your role in the profession, that there's an avant-gardism about being ordinary?

DSB: Yes.

RV: But it's incidental. We're not trying to be avant-garde. A while back I was on a panel with Peter Eisenman, and out of the blue—it wasn't really related to the discussion—he leaned over and said, "Come on, Bob, you must admit, when you wrote *Complexity and Contradiction*, you were trying to shock." I said, "No, Peter, I was only trying to make sense."

DSB: Peter is the one who tries to shock. But don't be misled into thinking the anti-hero is not a hero.

RV: In this era, to be unheroic is heroic. To be conventional is unconventional. There is a wonderful quotation from Nathaniel Hawthorne that goes something like this: "You cannot be a hero in an unheroic age." I think this idea again relates to Modernism. There are times in history when revolution makes sense, when being a revolutionary makes sense. But pseudo-revolutions are horrible, and at this time, the evolutionary way is probably the real way of being visionary. I think that there is still on the part of architects the desire to be original—that old Romantic ideal of the architect as an original genius. Yet probably the greatest art is conventional; you can reach greater heights by combining the original with the not original. The idea of being new with every building is simply nonsense. It's harder to be good than it is to be original.

The Commercial Vernacular

SvM: From your writings, it seems that you are interested primarily in the facade, and in what is applied to it as decoration or "iconography." But you also say you spend as much time on the "shed" as you do on the "decoration." And more recently, you refer to the "generic" in architecture.

RV: One similarity between our approach and that of the early Modernists is they were adapting, to a great extent, a vernacular vocabulary—that of industrial generic architecture, of the American factory. Essentially, and ironically, the International Style vocabulary of Modernism derived from Central Europeans being thrilled by American grain elevators and factories (fig. 7). They looked exotic to them, and became essentially the symbolic basis of their architecture—European architects didn't say it that way, but that is what they were doing. They adopted the symbolism of the generic factory building as a reference for the vocabulary of their architecture.

We are finding that we are thrilled by another form of American vernacular, not the industrial but the commercial vernacular. Yet before Walter Gropius came here and taught at Harvard and made the industrial vernacular respectable—as Mies van der Rohe did at I.I.T. when he (decoratively?) applied standard I-beams to the

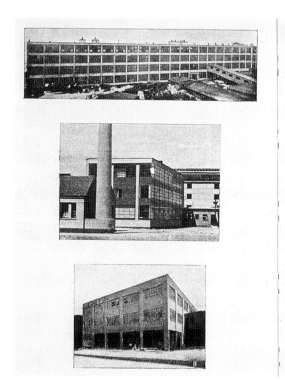

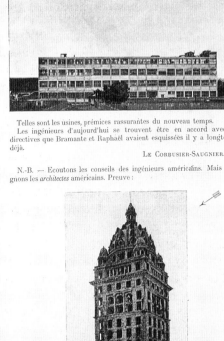

Telles sont les usines, prémices rassurantes du nouveau temps.
Les ingénieurs d'aujourd'hui se trouvent être en accord avec
directives que Bramante et Raphaël avaient esquissées il y a longte
déjà.

LE CORBUSIER-SAUGNIER.

N.-B. — Écoutons les conseils des ingénieurs américains. Mais
gnons les *architectes* américains. Preuve:

8. VSBA, *Lewis Thomas Laboratory for Molecular Biology, Princeton University, Princeton, New Jersey, 1983–86*

7. *American industrial building as inspiration for European Modern architecture: two pages from Le Corbusier's article in* L'Esprit Nouveau; *reprinted in* Vers une architecture *(1923)*

outside surfaces of his high-rises—industrial architecture was scorned, as commercial vernacular continues to be scorned today, especially if an Italo-American like me promotes it, or a woman like Denise. There has to be some seemingly more educated foreigner involved.

DSB: Rem Koolhaas!

RV: Rem Koolhaas has to come over and say the commercial vernacular is okay, because Marcel Duchamp and Salvador Dalí had said so too.

Fanfare and Drum Beat; or, Is "Generic" Generic?

SvM: In most of your writings, you seem to imply that the "generic" is something given, something that you can take from a catalog, as it were. Yet looking at your work, it seems that the generic has to be reinvented with every project ad hoc. It seems to be part of a vocabulary that is constantly redefined and that, in its complexity, involves both "fanfare" and "drumbeat," as Bob once said.

DSB: That's true, and I think we give as much loving attention in most of our buildings to the shed, to the generic, as to the fanfare. We try to understand the generic archetype or prototype that the building is tending toward.

RV: To say it another way, the generic is part of the art of what we're doing. Therefore, the generic must be as artful as the decoration and the message (fig. 8).

DSB: Although we may try to make the shed seem artless, it's artfully artless.

RV: The creative component might be more in your original choice of what you use, rather than in its original creation. You still have to make creative decisions, even if you go to a catalog and use a patent building.

MMcL: Then is the building really a loft anymore, or, to put it another way, is the "shed" really "generic"? By giving it a kind of modest demeanor, you make it look generic in some ways, but that belies the level of design involved.

DSB: I don't believe "generic" indicates a low level of design, but in any case, for a building to outlast present uses, it needs certain regularities. It needs a regular, rhythmic beat of support systems, and a carefully considered spacing of supports, to allow for its present functions and for changes in those functions. Its service spaces, utilities, and usable spaces must relate in certain ways if it is to serve future generations of users. If the building meets these requirements, it will probably be generic, like a mill or loft building.

RV: Modernism assumed that function is static, and that form follows function. If you use the generic, you're acknowledging that function is not static. Function is going to change, even before a building is completed, or even while you're designing the building. In that sense, too, we're evolving from Modernism. For us, this means that form accommodates functions, not that form follows function.

SvM: So we are back to Mies!

DSB: Yes, we learned a lot from Mies.

RV: But it's Mies with signs.

Universalism and Control

SvM: To continue with "generic" building: is the generic loft going to be the next International Style?

RV: Yes. In my opinion, it is.

SvM: But doesn't that bring us back to the "universal values" of Modernism?

RV: That's true. "Universalism" might return or remain in aspects of architecture where it does make sense, for instance, where it accommodates varying functions and evolving technical/mechanical/electronic elements over time. However, what's applied to that basic infrastructure is not universal—the iconographic appliqué is most significant. The symbolic or decorative can be specifically multicultural or contextual. So we are going back to an original aspect of Modernism in only one sense.

DSB: We never left that aspect of it.

RV: Right, we never left it. We are Modernists, after all, not Postmodern Modernists! If we were to redo the station building in Lucerne by Calatrava, it wouldn't have all those sentimental and obsolete structural decorations on the facade. It would be a loft building with iconography—with explicit ornament and maybe pictures on it.

Now the issue of control. The problem is that, in the end, the architect doesn't have much control. Nowadays, civic buildings are at least partly designed by committees. Even more important are the implications of community participation—which, theoretically, is a good thing. Anyway, America is becoming a place where the architect is losing control. And in some ways, maybe that's good, because the architect as dictatorial expert made lots of mistakes too!

Also, when you get as old as I am and go back to your earlier buildings, you see that they are often not being maintained well. Furthermore, contemporary buildings tend to be clad in cheap finishes, because you can't afford good materials when 40 percent of the budget has to go into mechanical equipment. The Pantheon is still there, although a lot of its iconography has been removed, because the Greeks could afford good, solid materials and they could put 100 percent into architectural construction and ornamentation. If you're an architect today, you have less control than

9. VSBA, *Sainsbury Wing,*
addition to the National
Gallery, London, 1986–91.
Detail of stair

10. *Interior of a house by
Frank Furness (from* The
Book of American Interiors
by C. W. Elliot)

if you were a watercolorist—no one goes and adds more paint to a finished watercolor.

But the idea of changing iconography via electronic means is not necessarily bad. It can be wonderful where content can evolve dynamically over time. In this case, the architect's loss of "control" is not necessarily a bad thing. And it's something that is in the air anyhow.

SvM: That surprises me. I am under the impression that the kind of architecture you do really needs the control of an architect, the architect who is responsible for everything, from A to Z. In the Sainsbury Wing, the fact that the furniture is not designed by you is dramatic for me (fig. 9).

RV: Traumatic!

SvM: I'm relieved you said it. If the Sainsbury Wing really were a generic loft, then perhaps we wouldn't mind what furniture was in it. But since it is really a perfectly designed object, consistent with all its inconsistencies, it needs control down to the level of detail.

DSB: You have chosen one of the most extreme examples: a museum where every inch is designed to suit a permanent collection of some of the world's most precious paintings. Lab buildings designed by us allow for continual change inside. A museum is different, and *that* museum is the most permanent of all our museums. But the lighting is changeable, and the actual gallery spaces are more loftlike than those of the existing museum.

RV: Let me add something here about Frank Lloyd Wright. You

know that Wright designed the andirons, the chairs, virtually everything in the house. He ultimately tried to design even the frocks of the women who would inhabit his houses. That involved extreme control, well beyond what we would want.

We are architects who are not aiming at a highly unified composition. We are the opposite of Frank Lloyd Wright. Wright aimed at a motival unity, where everything explicitly related to everything else. He was reacting against a kind of Victorian living-room aesthetic, with all sorts of stuff coexisting in there. We, in turn, are learning to be non-motival. We're getting back to the Victorian interior, with its rich combinations of different things all in one room (fig. 10).

DSB: Eclecticism!

RV: Yes, eclecticism. In that respect, we're learning a lot from Tokyo.

Electronics and Design

SvM: In your recent work, you like to use neon signs and electronic pixel boards: in Loker Commons, the "underground" of Harvard's Memorial Hall; at the University of Delaware; and, on a spectacular scale, in your design for the Staten Island Ferry Terminal (see pp. 180–87). Even for a very formal building, such as the proposed U.S. Embassy in Berlin, you envisioned the placement of large pixel boards in strategic locations (see pp. 210–15).

Can you tell us how your interest in the media affects your design? As early as 1967, with your Football Hall of Fame, you introduced electronics into "high" design (fig. 11). Here, as in most projects that involve media spectacles, architecture is a mere support for messages that are basically non-architectural. There appears to be no conceptual link between the building carrying the media-board and what appears on the board as a message. The architecture is fairly traditional or "generic."

At the same time, I realize that you are involved with the media world on a more conceptual level as well. In a certain sense, your interests in eclecticism as a design strategy and in pluralism as reflecting our cultural predicament relate to the explosion of imagery in the late twentieth century.

DSB: The effect of these multimedia facades is decorative. Architects are looking for valid ways to enliven their buildings. Before Modernism, they saw lettering on buildings as decorative and were less concerned about its content.

When we were adding to Oberlin's Art Museum, we enjoyed the Roman frieze on the entrance loggia of the existing building that says something like "Art Is the Inspiration of the People." But when we came across Cass Gilbert's original working drawings, we found the frieze there said something like "A Sign Here in This

Type of This Size." Now when we put inscriptions on drawings, we use a similar phrase in Roman type, in Latin. We have it in the computer. So the content and the decorative element are not necessarily the same. But there is a problem: a sign that is easy to put up can be easily taken down. We lost the antenna atop Guild House, and we had to fight to keep the sign above the entrance.

Electronics as Zeitgeist

MMcL: I have another question concerning electronics. On the one hand, you seem to propose electronics, media, communication, information, as inherent to the zeitgeist; you see an electronic, LED architecture as the appropriate solution for the age. On the other hand, you have stressed the pluralistic cultures that make up today's society, the particular parameters of a program, the specificities of site, and their importance for design. I wonder how you reconcile a concept such as zeitgeist—which implies that an idea may have universal validity in a historical moment—with your interest in diversity and pluralism.

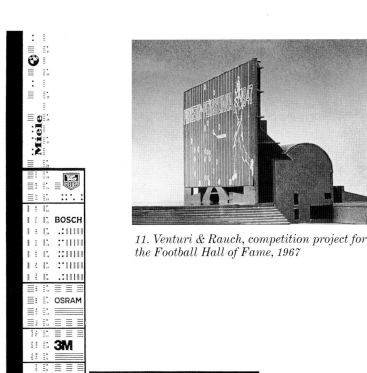

11. Venturi & Rauch, competition project for the Football Hall of Fame, 1967

12. Jean Nouvel, Media Park, Cologne, Germany, 1991. Northwest elevation

RV: I think there are two ways to look at it. On the one hand, there are many zeitgeists in our time, rather than a single zeitgeist. On the other hand, you can say that there *is* a zeitgeist for our era, but that that zeitgeist is full of complexity and contradiction and variety, compared to earlier periods when "culture" was maintained by an elite in a relatively limited area. In any case, the technical iconography that we're now talking about is one that is moving and changing. Since it is not carved in stone, it doesn't present the dangers that I think some people perceive in this kind of stuff—that it can promote fascist content, for instance. Our electronics and our graphics are changeable, and that allows for variety and the opportunity for many kinds of messages.

SvM: So there are many zeitgeists today, and one either chooses one party within this hodgepodge of zeitgeists, or alternatively, one chooses a point of view outside of it that includes them all.

RV: I think if you're a good artist, you can connect with different zeitgeists in different contexts. Or, as I said before, perhaps there is a zeitgeist that is extremely accommodating and varied within a general culture. Maybe that's a contradiction in terms; if there's a zeitgeist that is terribly disunified, it's no longer a zeitgeist. So you can take your choice: multiculturalism may create several zeitgeists, or it may result in a single zeitgeist that accommodates cultural variety.

The Media Facade

SvM: Returning to electronics, multiculturalism, and the zeitgeist, you said that if you were to build a railway station, you would implement a sort of a media facade, with various kinds of messages sprinkled over it, and would not use structural symbolism—you referred to Calatrava and the Lucerne railway station as an example. Many younger architects would certainly agree with you, at least with regard to the "media facade." Piano and Rogers, after all, used your Football Hall of Fame project as a reference for their Centre Pompidou project as early as 1971. And many people took off from there, including Rem Koolhaas, Jean Nouvel, Herzog and de Meuron, and others (fig. 12). For instance, Herzog and de Meuron's project for the Bibliothèque Nationale in Paris and its media facade relates to Labrouste via your work.

MMcL: Another example might be Rem Koolhaas's competition project for a media center in Karlsruhe.

SvM: How do you feel about these more recent developments?

RV: I don't keep up very much with recent trends. But I would say that the difference between the kind of architecture done by those architects and the kind of architecture we're advocating or doing involves the degree of abstraction. I think those people are still abstraction fanatics with significant dashes of industrial symbolism. They are essentially old-fashioned Modernists—or Modern Revivalists.

SvM: Could you live with the idea that some are not abstract? Some actually include figurative imagery in design.

RV: I don't see much of it.

DSB: We're looking mainly at Americans and know little about recent European architecture. Eisenman et al. aren't doing representation; they're doing abstraction—or abstract expressionism.

RV: The work in MoMA's "Light Construction" exhibition[2] was essentially abstraction. Different kinds of surfaces invoked space and aura in subtle and tasteful configurations but without alluding to the hype sensibility of today. It's still another form of abstraction.

DSB: But those are not the architects Stan is talking about. He's talking about people who use electronic imagery.

MMcL: The people overlap. Although Herzog and de Meuron were in that exhibition with "abstract" work, other projects by them are explicitly iconographic.

SvM: In the late eighties Herzog and de Meuron did a project for a Greek church in which they proposed that images taken from Byzantine wall paintings be encrusted in the stone with the help of a complicated photo-mechanical process. In another project, which was actually built, the glass facade is turned into a flower pattern (fig. 13). It's not something that you could mistake for a project by VSBA, to be sure. But in terms of its approach, in the non-architectural means of decoration, it's comparable.

13. Herzog and de Meuron, Ricola Warehouse, near Mulhouse, France, 1992–93. Translucent facade with flower pattern

The Flag on the Bay; or, the Issue of Content

MMcL: That brings up the issue of the content of media versus simply the usage of media.

DSB: The trouble we had with our second Whitehall Ferry Terminal design points up the difficulties surrounding this entire issue. There's the prejudice against signage—the political repercussions of this prejudice ultimately caused us to resign from the project. Then there's the conflict between civic and commercial. Even *we* felt the terminal's electronic facade should project an American flag for forty or fifty minutes, with only ten or twenty minutes allotted to changing, possibly commercial, messages. There's a real contradiction between the medium and the message: to say that, despite the fact that it's changeable, you should keep the image still, because it's civic (figs. 14, 15).

RV: Not exactly still—the flag actually "waves."

DSB: It waves, yes.

RV: We want this facade to have an identity appropriate to a civic work of art. And in order to have an identity as strong as that of the Statue of Liberty, there has to be a certain consistency. But the surface can give passengers changing information as the ferry approaches. Once you're far away from it, it should project the consistent image of the waving flag. The whole issue of the content is an interesting one. The architect should be responsible on a general level—but not on the level of detailed information. The American flag is an example of a general statement.

DSB: How can you achieve that, when the whole LED system is set up for change? By using LEDs, you are essentially making the message changeable; it can be programmed any way at all. Then you say it may not be reprogrammed for fifty minutes of every hour.

The Issue of Control

RV: The question of control exists always in architecture, and more so than ever now, when architecture depends increasingly on maintenance and mechanical systems that change. But this has always been the situation. You're at the mercy of what follows. Christianity could have knocked down the Pantheon and built a church there.

DSB: At Loker Commons the content of the signs could be programmed entirely by, say, the extreme right wing, and we could patiently wait for democracy to reassert itself. But in a big civic building such as the Whitehall Ferry Terminal, we have problems with the changeability of signs. The building is located opposite the biggest open space in the city—the bay and harbor—and can be seen from miles away. It should be strong enough to join the Statue of Liberty and the Brooklyn Bridge as one of the three major elements in the harbor.

14, 15. VSBA with Anderson/Schwartz, Whitehall Ferry Terminal, New York, New York, 1992–96. Second project: terminal with alternating images, 1995

For these reasons, we're concerned that the flag sign could be switched off most of the time—and maybe there will be no flag at all, because people think it's an unsuitable symbol. We think it's *the* most suitable symbol, and would like to see it on fifty minutes of every hour, to make it really civic. But we don't have a way of controlling that. So the more a building becomes civic, the more the changeability of the sign may be a problem.

Yet the main reason we use signage is admittedly for decoration, and the decoration could, in most buildings, be as fleeting as its electronics. Another way to describe our position is by imagining an ancient stone temple decorated with flowers. The flowers may last one day and the temple two thousand years. In civic architecture, you've got to provide for the flowers *and* the temple.

SvM: What if the people, rather than seeing the decoration as ornament, either find the decoration ugly and thus not ornamental, or read it iconographically as symbol? I imagine that many people would read the giant clock that you originally proposed for the Ferry Building as a symbol of, for instance, the time control exerted by Manhattan over the rest of the bay. It takes aesthetic refinement to see the decorative quality of a giant clock in that context, to focus on its metasymbolic or meta-informational qualities (fig. 16).

DSB: But people love Big Ben on the Thames and the Colgate clock on the Hudson.

Electronics and/or Iconography?

MMcL: You brought up an interesting point when you said that you're concerned with iconography and that many architects who use electronic imagery aren't. One of the issues your work raises is the relationship between electronic media and iconography. Iconography implies there's a particular content you want to communicate, but the use of electronic media suggests that content can be variable. Isn't there a conflict between advocating iconography and using electronic media?

DSB: Bob seems to believe that it's no different from that of the tension between permanence and change in any building. That may be so, but LEDs are at the far end of the spectrum of change, and at the other end is, say, the Parthenon.

RV: It is. In the Bibliothèque Ste. Geneviève, Labrouste engraved the facade with the names of the authors whose books are stacked in that library, and they're there forever. On the other hand, now we could do it in such a way that you could remove some of those names and substitute others. There are dangers in that, but there are also opportunities. The architecture can stay more vital, in some ways.

Today's Media Boom

SvM: But then the "media" isn't just electronics and pixel boards. It's a question not just of technology but of general culture and the economy of signs, involving consumption and production of images at an ever increasing speed, in architecture like everywhere else. And isn't the expressionist urge in the arts and architecture of today *also* a response to the media's need to consume and produce new images every morning?

MMcL: I am the last to defend this sort of expressionist bravura, but couldn't one say—and here I'm playing the devil's advocate—that this media explosion has created a new form of Victor Hugo's "Ceci tuera cela": that electronics are killing architecture, and that TV, the web, the net, the fax machine can all convey information better than architecture? Why should architecture want to compete with those media? Perhaps it should focus on what it can do, and on what verbal or more specific representational messages can't do. Might not architecture's power come less from its ability to convey information than from its nature as a more general cultural sign whose meaning doesn't necessarily translate readily to words?

But perhaps there is a more fundamental problem at stake here: that architecture's traditional role as a public form of communication, as a means of commemoration or celebration, as a form of expression of values beyond the mere necessity of shelter, is being challenged by the sheer pervasiveness of these new communicative vehicles.

RV: One way or another, I would say—and I wrote a little essay entitled "Cela est devenu ceci"[3]—that hype is a fact of life now. It's a condition that's here; I call it "the sensibility of hype." And I think that architects are not accommodating it. They forget the Russian Constructivists of the twenties, when graphics and color played a major iconographic role in architecture.

Applying the industrial vocabulary as an abstract expressionist aesthetic—what I call industrial *rocaille*—to these forms is to me sacrilegious. Ironically, they are making a formalist joke out of what was a puritanical approach to a truly functional/industrial process.

DSB: They're doing Pomo design using Modernism as a historical style.

RV: Exactly! They are like Puritan ladies dancing the cancan with a lot of rouge on their lips. Instead, accept multimedia, combine multimedia. Look at the sculpture and scenography of the Baroque—I guess you can say that's hype!

The Uses of History and the Art of Drawing

SvM: And yet what architects look at today is early Modernism and not the Baroque.

DSB: I feel that many architects have returned to early Modernism because they don't know enough about historical architecture to do Pomo, either well or badly. And they don't draw well enough either.

But when they returned to Modernism, they applied it in a Pomo way, using it as decoration, as others might have used any historical style. In that sense, I see a parallel with the Art Deco architects who were faced with Modernism—in particular, Cubism and the International Style—and reacted by incorporating some of those elements into their Beaux-Arts language. The result was Art Moderne or Art Deco. Now we admire its skill and refinement, but initially we considered it the worst enemy of Modern architecture, worse than traditional architecture. Art Deco is Beaux-Arts architects' reaction to Modernism, and "Decon" is Modern architects' reaction to Postmodernism (figs. 17, 18).

RV: Mod-Deco . . .

DSB: Art Decon. We learned from Art Deco too—from the way it flattened Cubism. Our chairs—for example, the Knoll Art Deco and Sheraton chairs—employ the Deco principle of flattening, using Deco-esque and Georgian, Adams-esque decoration.

Postmodernism

SvM: In earlier conversations, you have referred disparagingly to "the Postmodernists." But you yourselves are Postmodernists, after all!

DSB: No.

SvM: Why? And what then is Postmodernism? Who are the Postmodernists, if you're not?

DSB: We have always claimed that we are Modernists, in any rational definition of Modernism, because it is our point of departure. We subscribe to a set of ways of building that stem from the Modern movement, and we think of ourselves as functionalists. We have approached Modernism as loyal supporters who change it to keep it relevant.

RV: We have been adapting an existing American vernacular to a Modernist way of thinking.

16. Whitehall Ferry Terminal. First project: terminal with symbolic clock, 1992

17. *Issue of* Architectural Review *on Deconstructivist architecture*

18. *Art Deco district, Miami Beach, Florida*

SvM: So you are claiming that you are Modernists by using a "low" vernacular language and transforming it into "high" architectural forms?

DSB: No—no more than the Modernists would have claimed that their transformation defined *their* Modernism.

RV: We represent a valid evolution of Modernism.

DSB: We think that some people learned the wrong lessons from what we wrote, and applied our ideas inappropriately. They jumped on the history bandwagon, assuming license rather than taking liberties, borrowing irrelevantly from the building next door or from a theater building for an office tower, from an office building for a house—these are the ones I call Postmodernists. Also the social component of Modernism was ignored by the Postmodernists but not by us.

RV: A while back Herbert Muschamp wrote that *Complexity and Contradiction in Architecture* "gave license" to architects to design in historical styles. What a misinterpretation of a work where history was employed as analogy for analysis, not as a source for designing! Basically, we're mannerist architects, although it may sound pretentious to say so. As such, we're hard to categorize. We use the past in our designs, but we purposely use it incorrectly.

SvM: What would you have chosen as a designation a hundred years ago? Eclecticism? Neoclassicism? The term "mannerism" didn't exist then.

RV: "Transitional," I guess. We love Arts and Crafts and Lutyens and Art Nouveau.

The Issue of Material Truth

SvM: Speaking of Arts and Crafts, two lines of tradition seem to be apparent in your recent work: on the one hand, Arts and Crafts—the interest in traditional materials such as tile, brick, and wood (the Shingle Style house was after all part of Arts and Crafts)—and on the other, an abstract, non-sensual way of dealing with such materials, which brings up again the issue of "representation."

There is, in other words, an Arts and Crafts "love" for simple and traditional materials, as in your houses by the sea and your recent buildings at Princeton (see pp. 220–23, 240–43, 252–55). But there is also the long-span stone lintel over the entrance to the Sainsbury Wing, for example. Here we have a rather abstract, conceptual—mannerist?—way of using material, one that arranges materials in surprising configurations.

MMcL: Maybe there is even a third tendency, in which material almost becomes, to quote Peter Eisenman, cardboard—in which it becomes so flat that its materiality is denied.

DSB: It's the billboard.

RV: With a billboard, of course, you don't worry about how it is constructed. We are anti-Modernists as far as that is concerned. Although, actually, look at the Villa Savoye!

For example, the Sainsbury Wing is a distorted billboard and, at the same time, a continuation of the main facade (fig. 19). And then there are the huge openings, which are terribly incorrect. But they are there for the sake of certain contextual realities. At the same time, we had to superimpose the late twentieth century on the facade—

19. *Sainsbury Wing (at left), with National Gallery*

DSB: —through relationships of scale—

RV: —and scale pertaining to population. Originally, two hundred, maybe one hundred, aristocratic gentlemen visited the old building each day. Perhaps ten thousand visit the new one each day.

Returning to the issue of "material truth," when you walk behind those pillars of the entrance, you can see that the limestone on the front is a thin appliqué. So, in detail, the facade's non-structural quality is expressed.

MMcL: But there is another side to your work that I might call Ruskinian: the pattern-making. We see it in the MacDonald laboratories (fig. 20; see pp. 243–37), the Bard library (see pp. 224–29), and the Princeton laboratories. And while it is true that all these facades seem like "false skin" or appliqué, at the same time they are working with the visual qualities of brick and tile and with the pattern-making that these permit.

RV: We use traditional materials for several reasons. One is contextual: to make the building seem at home where it is. That's contextual "analogy" rather than "contrast." The other reason is, frankly, that traditional technologies are safer in terms of maintenance and life span, and that conventional materials are usually cheaper. We aren't out for the thrill of using new materials, although we'll use them—cautiously—if it makes sense.

Béton brut buildings are often greasy where people's hands touch them; they're hard to maintain—there are all sorts of problems. Modernism adored being advanced technologically and we can empathize with that thrill, but it isn't our thing. Our thing is representation and context.

"Pattern Language" and Functionalism

MMcL: Is it accurate to speak of Ruskin at all? I mention him because there is a quality beyond the ordinary in your use of materials, a pleasure in materials. What interests you in patterns? Is it formal liveliness, a delight in aesthetic manipulation?

RV: The material issue is theoretical. We are not architects who love material as such. I'm not a mechanical person—someone who enjoys repairing the house on Saturdays. I couldn't be a bricklayer. But we do work with the traditional compositional elements of pattern and rhythm essentially as they did in the past.

The first time we really used pattern was at the Oberlin museum (fig. 21). There, and later in other places—usually on loft-like buildings—we used it as a way of saying, "We're not doing Richardson Towers." We are not going to articulate form, "express" the mechanical systems, etc. We are making a box that is a loft, that is generic. We're saying, "It's a shoe box, and that's it," because it is flexible inside and economical and generally sensible. But when you get close to it, there will be things to show that it is an institutional building—that there *is* art to it *and* detail to interest you. And there are also changing rhythms. We love rhythm—we "got rhythm."

Context and Contextualism

SvM: Your work is, in many ways, synonymous with a concern for "context." Yet some of your more recent projects have caused you trouble with preservationists; referring to the University of Pennsylvania, you speak of the "preservation game" and of an increasing tendency toward "embalming sentiment."[4] Has the current enthusiasm for context and the propensity for the picturesque—toward the imitation of traditional details, street patterns, and building heights—put a deadlock on architectural vitality?

DSB: First, we disagree with the Postmodernists in that we define context as something broader than the immediate physical surroundings; there are also cultural, social, and political contexts.

Of course, the physical context is relevant, but while Pomo appropriates elements from the building next door, we're more inclined to learn from the overall architecture of a town or area, or from the aspect of context that is relevant for perhaps a cultural or historical reason.

We have always felt that you may acknowledge the context on one level and diverge from it on another—to deal with other aspects of context, such as the givens of conventional building systems today. For me, the person who doesn't consider context at all is a boor; the person who considers *only* context is a bore.

RV: Concerning the more general issue of context, just yesterday Herbert Muschamp, in the *New York Times*, referred to the horrible, boring contextual approach that Rem Koolhaas (in his book *S,M,L,XL*) is wonderfully abandoning by proposing the juxtaposition of very small and very big buildings.[5] When Muschamp refers negatively to so-called contextualism, he maybe has us in mind. I remember that when I was working on my thesis at Princeton, in 1950, I came across the word "context" in an article on Gestalt psychology in a journal in the Psychology Department library and said, "Eureka! Here I have something to work from!"

What happened is what happens so often. You have an idea, the idea gets misinterpreted, and either you are mad because they forgot it was your idea or you are relieved because they have misunderstood it. The point is, to acknowledge context does not necessarily involve accommodation to context. It can also involve contrast. My great teacher Jean Labatut said you can achieve harmony through contrast as well as through analogy. You can have a gray suit and a gray necktie—that's analogous harmony. But a gray suit and a red necktie can also be harmonious. We tend to put a gray suit with a red necktie with gray dots, or with a gray necktie with red dots. The Piazza San Marco is a great civic place, and it's harmonious with its juxtapositions of a Gothic Doge's Palace, a Byzantine Duomo, and a Renaissance library. It involves contrast in a harmonious way.

There is yet another related issue: architectural vocabulary. In architecture, Modernism saw itself as a universal vocabulary, appropriate for all time and all places. Yet there can be other vocabularies that acknowledge context and that vary from place to place. Contextualism, I feel, should not be a question of copying, of replication. It should be a question of combining the universal with the local or multicultural.

Harmony via Contrast, Abstraction, Variation . . .

MMcL: I see two strategies of reference at work in your designs. One uses flat images involving explicit visual reference to historical precedent or a building, whether for contextual or thematic purposes. The other uses massing and siting to generate references and relate to an existing context. An example is Gordon Wu Hall at Princeton (fig. 22). Its massing is not only sympathetic to the immediate context but also seems to allude to other buildings on campus, even if there are other elements in Wu Hall—flat images such as the huge "Renaissance" marble insert above the entrance—that undoubtedly startle people. Are there certain situations, such as campuses, where your primary objective is to respect and enhance what is there, whereas in other situations you are more willing to shake the fabric a little to make people think—or to introduce a different set of concerns?

20. VSBA, Gordon and Virginia MacDonald Medical Research Laboratories, University of California at Los Angeles, 1986–91

21. Venturi, Rauch & Scott Brown, addition to Allen Memorial Art Museum, Oberlin, Ohio, 1976. Detail

22. VSBA, Gordon Wu Hall, Princeton University, New Jersey, 1980

23. *Political rally in front of the Sainsbury Wing*

RV: Very much. We do emphasize symbolic-iconographic qualities, and the marble screen over the entrance to Wu Hall shows how we connect with history via symbolic representation and we therefore become a bit ambiguous in our reference. But we also connect with context via space and form. For instance, the long shape of the building is partly determined by the interior need for a dining hall as a kind of refectory, and at the same time, the building's massing is linear in order to produce an exterior directional space along the pedestrian route that leads from one part of the campus to another.

SvM: By being so contextual, it seems to underplay its originality.

DSB: The prime example of contextualism is the Sainsbury Wing. It does something different on each side based upon adjacent conditions. And yet that's not the whole story by any means, because it's also a Modern box with a transparent skin that is visible behind the stone skin of the Classical facade. This makes the stone outer skin a billboard bearing a variety of messages, including some about Classical architecture in the computer age.

Architecture as Mother?

SvM: Denise, I believe you once referred to the Sainsbury Wing as a kind of mother, that it embodies the gentle, caring gesture of a good mother. It was in a lecture, and you showed a picture with a crowd in front of the building at some political march (fig. 23). Do you see this architecture as expressive of female qualities—as opposed to, let's say, the "macho" rationality of Modernism? Is that what you had in mind?

DSB: Yes and no. No, in the sense that the stereotyping of male and female characteristics is unacceptable. On the other hand, if you're prepared to say that all males have qualities we term "female" and all females have qualities defined as "male," then yes. Trafalgar Square is one of London's sites for serious demonstrations—as opposed to Hyde Park, which is mostly for humorous rhetoric. The picture shows people demonstrating against the October War. It was taken just after the building was opened. For me, the building provides shelter on the outside as well as on the inside. It's sheltering that crowd, rising above it as a protective, civic form.

The building does have a nurturing quality and we're thrilled about that. But if you say, "It's a great big mother," it has good *and* bad connotations, and this suggests something of the strong feelings architects in London had against the building.

Mother and Architecture

RV: Vincent Scully makes a lot of my mother's house and of the picture with my mother sitting at the front door opening[6] (fig. 25).

MMcL: Do you know Robert Somol's interpretation of your mother's house?

DSB: No.

MMcL: At Columbia, a few years ago, he gave a long talk on

24. *Le Corbusier and Pierre Jeanneret,*
Villa Stein-de Monzie, Garches (near Paris), 1927

25. *Venturi & Short, Vanna Venturi House,*
Chestnut Hill, Pennsylvania, 1961

your mother's house, and more generally on your firm's work vis-à-vis this issue of "mother."[7] He compared your mother's house to the Villa Stein at Garches and said that in the mother's house, the symbolism of the car is replaced by that of the mother (fig. 24).

RV: Wow!

MMcL: I am curious to know how conscious or unconscious this was from your perspective. Did you consciously put your mother instead of a car in front of the house?

RV: In fact, I didn't think about it. It's my mother's house, so I included my mother for scale.

It's sad, though, that at the Venice Biennale a few years ago, when they included a mural of the house and I had the arch outlined in neon—I love those Catholic churches where the Madonna has a neon halo—they left out my mother![8]

DSB: So who has the problem with the mother: the one who put her in or the ones who took her out?

On Feminism and Academia

MMcL: Denise, you've appeared rather prominently in some recent feminist conferences, and it seems, after all these years, that feminism has now gained a kind of fashionability in architectural circles. I'm curious about your reaction to this shift. For example, what did you think of the conference held at the University of Pennsylvania, "Inherited Ideologies," and the subsequent book, *The Sex of Architecture?*[9]

DSB: First, there are now several generations of women in architecture. It's wonderful that I'm not the only one, and haven't been for fifteen years or so; there are women with years of involvement in the field! Then there's also a kind of ebullience around feminism in architecture. The atmosphere at the conference reminded me of when Bob and I were upending Modernist ideology—it was fun! I felt that "Inherited Ideologies" was a better name than "The Sex of Architecture," because rethinking Modern architectural ideology from a new viewpoint is what they were doing.

There is a group of younger women who seem to feel that the battle has been won. I fear that when they suddenly hit the glass ceiling and find prejudice, they'll think it's their fault. I was surprised that most women at the "Inherited Ideologies" conference were academics. Perhaps it's easier to establish oneself as a woman in academe than in practice. This may be partly because woman professors have the flexibility of schedule that only a principal can have in architectural practice—even if, for both, it's mainly illusory!

But women academics—like all academics in architecture today—face the problems of divorcing theory from practice, of getting away from their roots in *doing*. I myself am bored with philosophy unrelated to action. I feel that architectural academics risk losing an important tie to action and becoming in some ways trivial. And despite all the doctorates, I don't see many who practice scholarly skills. At the conference, surmise was presented as fact, rhetoric as philosophy. This is not only among women; it's a rather general flaw in present architectural scholarship.

MMcL: Given this, I was curious if there was anyone's work at the conference that was especially interesting to you, or provocative.

DSB: Not very many. When most speakers discussed the design of housing for women, they typically looked at how architects design houses for upper-class women—for instance, how Rietveld designed a house for Truus Schröder. They didn't consider how suburbia could be designed for women, or how merchant builders have tried to do the same thing. Their focus was still the narrow one of architects dealing with a certain class.

For me, one of the most interesting presentations was by Ghislaine Hermanuz. But even though she dealt with plans of houses to suit different groups, she didn't broaden her concern to include the urban residential neighborhood and the adaptation of existing housing, which is where I think most solutions will need to be found.

On the Dichotomy between Doing and Thinking

MMcL: Speaking more generally, are there any new social thinkers or artistic figures that have had a particular impact on your work of the last ten years?

DSB: We're keeping afloat a business of fifty people and we're very busy with work, so we don't have a lot of time and we don't read very much.

RV: In order to be architects today, we have to spend so much time running around. Being good—that's easy. Proving we're good is hard. So it's very hard for architects to be intellectual in the traditional sense nowadays. When we get home, we listen to the TV and fall asleep—or I do the crossword puzzle. And that's why there is this dichotomy between practitioners and teachers. They're separate. When I was young, they were together. Lou Kahn ran an international office and he taught. At that time, I had a little office and I taught, too. Now, you have the other extreme. You are either a practitioner or a theoretician.

These days I read *The Nation* but I don't read the latest thing on architecture. I don't read Walter Benjamin.

DSB: We wish it weren't that way. But I think it's part of a life cycle.

SvM: At least you take the time to write.

MMcL: Bob, I remember that you once mentioned that one reason you have such a strong sympathy for Aalto is the fact that he wrote very little. I found that comment amusing, coming from one of the most articulate architects practicing in America. And I can see why both of you hang yourself with words—you're so good at them.

Notes

This text is excerpted from two interviews held at the Venturi, Scott Brown & Associates office in Philadelphia, Pennsylvania, on March 4, 1996, and December 12, 1996. Mary McLeod and Stanislaus von Moos would like to thank Stephen Frankel and Lynette Widder for their help in preparing this interview for publication.

1. Robert Venturi, *Iconography and Electronics upon a Generic Architecture: A View from the Drafting Room* (Cambridge, Mass.: MIT Press, 1996).

2. Terence Riley, *Light Construction* (exhibition catalog, New York: Museum of Modern Art, 1995).

3. Robert Venturi, "'Ceci tuera cela' Is Now 'Cela est devenu ceci': Some Thoughts Concerning Architecture and Media," *Iconography and Electronics*, 275–78; originally published as "Ceci Deviendra Cela" in *Lotus* 75 (February 1993): 127.

4. Robert Venturi, "The Preservation Game at Penn: An Emotional Response," *Iconography and Electronics*, 145–48.

5. Herbert Muschamp, "Rem Koolhaas Sizes up the Future," *New York Times*, March 3, 1996. Review of Rem Koolhaas and Bruce Mau, *S,M,L,XL* (New York: The Monacelli Press, 1995).

6. Vincent Scully, "The Failure of the Hero Architect," *Metropolitan Home*, November 1988. See also Scully, "Robert Venturi's Gentle Architecture," in *The Architecture of Robert Venturi*, ed. Christopher Mead (Albuquerque: University of New Mexico Press, 1989), 8–33.

7. See Robert E. Somol, "Les Liaisons Dangereuses, or My Mother the House," in *Fetish: The Princeton Architectural Journal* 4 (New York: Princeton Architectural Press, 1992), 50–71.

8. *La presenza del passato: Prima mostra internazionale di architettura* (Venice: Edizioni La Biennale di Venezia, 1980).

9. "Inherited Ideologies: A Re-Examination," conference, University of Pennsylvania, March 31 and April 1, 1995. Selected papers from that conference are published in *The Sex of Architecture*, ed. Diana Agrest, Patricia Conway, and Karen Weisman (New York: Abrams, 1996).

Bibliography

A complete bibliography is available at www.vsba.com.

Memphis Center City Development Plan

D. LaBadie. "Jack Tucker." *Memphis Commercial Appeal*, September 23, 1984, F1, F2.

D. LaBadie. "Planner Measuring Social Need." *Memphis Commercial Appeal*, January 17, 1985.

D. Scott Brown. "From Memphis down the Mississippi to the World." Foreword to *Memphis: 1948–1958* (exhibition catalog, Memphis: Memphis Brooks Museum of Art, 1986).

J. Branston. "Downtown's Changing Face." *Memphis Commercial Appeal Mid-South Magazine*, August 3, 1986, 6–12, 14.

D. Scott Brown. "Peabody Place and Beale Street, Memphis." In D. Scott Brown, *Architectural Design Profile: "Urban Concepts"* 60 (January–February 1990).

D. Scott Brown. "Memphis: A Housing Strategy." In *Venturi, Scott Brown and Associates: On Houses and Housing* (London: Academy Editions; New York: St. Martin's Press, 1992), 122–29.

Berlin Tomorrow Competition

D. Scott Brown and R. Venturi. "Berlin When the Wall Comes Down." In V. M. Lampugnani and M. Mönninger, *Berlin Morgen. Ideen für das Herz einer Grossstadt* (Frankfurt: Deutsche Architektur Museum, 1991), 148–53.

N. DiBattista. "Berlino domani. Idee per il cuore di una metropoli." *Domus*, March 1991, 54–63.

Denver Civic Center

"Civic Center Cultural Complex." *Denver Art Museum Annual Report 1991–1992*, 3.

B. Hornby. "Agenda Could Move Downtown into Reality." *Denver Post*, February 27, 1992.

B. Hornby. "Jumpstarting Downtown Denver's Batteries." *Denver Post*, March 8, 1992.

M. Voelz Chandler. "3 Neighbors Formulate Cultural Vision." *Rocky Mountain News*, April 22, 1992, 24.

C. Ford, ed. "Growing the Circle: Arc a Scott Brown Master Stroke at Civic Center." *Urban Design Forum*, September–October 1992, 1, 6–7.

M. Voelz Chandler. "Is There No Escape from Stalag 13th?" *Rocky Mountain News*, November 7, 1993, 50A.

T. Noel. "Celebrity Architects Blemish Civic Center." *Denver Post*, November 13, 1993, 7B.

A. Gabor. *Einstein's Wife* (New York: Viking Press, 1995), 156–231.

Columbus Gateway Study

"Winners of the Journal's Architectural Drawings Contest." *AIA Journal*, September 1982, 33–65.

Dartmouth College Campus

A. deForest. "Future Look." *Dartmouth Alumni Magazine*, May 1990, 20–29.

R. Adams. "College Eyes Northward Development." *Dartmouth Life*, December 15, 1991, 2.

Benjamin Franklin Bridge Lighting

R. Cohn. "Installation of Bridge Lights Set." *Philadelphia Inquirer*, June 16, 1987, 1B, 3B.

T. Hine. "The Art of the Lighted Bridge." *Philadelphia Inquirer*, September 19, 1987, 1D, 9D.

T. Hine. "Putting Night Lights on Franklin Bridge." *Philadelphia Inquirer*, September 30, 1987, 1C, 3C.

S. Izenour and G. C. Izenour. "Animated Electric Light Enlivens Benjamin Franklin Bridge." *Architectural Lighting*, January 1988, 22–29.

S. Pollock. "Suspended Animation." *Lighting Dimensions*, January–February 1988, 14.

"A Dazzling Light Show Animates a Bridge." *New York Times*, February 11, 1988, C3.

M. H. McNamara, ed. "Awards of Merit: The 1988 Awards for Design Excellence." *CitySITES: "Columns,"* summer 1988, 6–7.

"Special Feature: Venturi, Scott Brown and Associates." *A+U (Architecture and Urbanism)*, June 1990, 100–102.

P. B. Bach. *Public Art in Philadelphia* (Philadelphia: Temple University Press, 1992).

Christopher Columbus Monument

T. Hine. "A Phila. Salute to Columbus." *Philadelphia Inquirer*, December 22, 1991, 1F–6F.

"Tony DePaul Erecting Columbus Monument at Penns Landing." *PCA Construction News, Eastern Pennsylvania Edition*, July 29, 1992, 1.

B. Forgey. "Columbus and the Sailing-the-Ocean Blues." *Washington Post*, October 12, 1992.

"A Celebration of Exploration." *Philadelphia Inquirer*, October 13, 1992, B1.

"Waterjet System Helps Create a Lasting Monument." *Fabricator*, September–October 1993, 36–37.

S. Tuzi. "Robert Venturi." *Materia* 15 (1994): 12–17.

"Honor Award: Christopher Columbus Monument." *Pennsylvania Architect*, spring 1994, 17.

Sainsbury Wing

"Here We Go Round the Square Again." *Art & Design*, March 1986, 40–41.

"Robert Venturi: Learning from Trafalgar Square?" *Art & Design*, March 1986, 6–7, back cover.

M. Gildea. "The Politics of Art: Blame it on Venturi." *In Style*, summer 1986, 78, 86–87.

A. Forty. "Robert Venturi and Denise Scott Brown on the National Gallery Extension." *Artscribe International*, September–October 1986, 32–34.

"Notes and Comments: National Gallery Extension VI." *International Journal of Museum Management and Curatorship* 6 (1987): 211–17.

J. Lubbock. "The Family Mausoleum." *New Statesman*, April 1987, 22–23.

"Gallery Plan Wins Prince's Approval." *Daily Telegraph*, April 15, 1987, 1.

C. Knevitt. "Gallery Extension Praised for Originality." *Times* (London), April 15, 1987.

C. Knevitt. "Marriage of the Arts." *Times* (London), April 15, 1987.

P. Goldberger. "Architecture: Design for National Gallery in London." *New York Times*, April 16, 1987, C21.

I. Latham. "Learning from London." *Building Design*, April 17, 1987, 2–3.

S. Jenkins. "British Renaissance Reborn." *Sunday Times* (London), April 18, 1987, 25.

T. Hine. "How a Philadelphia Firm Met a Challenge in London." *Philadelphia Inquirer*, April 19, 1987, 10G.

I. Latham. "London Calling." *Building Design*, May 1, 1987, 16.

M. Pawley. "Il trionfo dell'anatra." *Casabella*, June 1987, 39–41.

S. von Moos. "Ampliamento della National Gallery, Londra." *Domus*, June 1987, 25–31.

J. McEwen. "Britain's Best and Brightest." *Art in America*, July 1987, 31–41.

H. P. Svendler Nielsen. "The Venturis in Europe." *Skala*, August 1987, 26–29.

J. Abrams. "Contemplation and Congregation in the Popular Urban Art Museum." *Lotus International* 55 (1988): 85–117.

M. Bar-Hillel. "U.S. Designs on London." *Sunday Telegraph*, April 3, 1988, 21.

S. von Moos. "Ampliacion de la National Gallery, Londres." *Arquitectura*, May–June 1988, 150–51.

C. Amery. "The Master Builders." *Financial Times*, June 11, 1988.

E. Louie. "Museums as Architectural Showpieces." *New York Times*, June 16, 1988, C3.

C. Norberg-Schulz. "The Two Faces of Post-Modernism." *Architectural Design*, July–August 1988, 11–15.

E. Posner. "The Museum as Bazaar." *Atlantic Monthly*, August 1988, 67–70.

G. London. "London Observed." *Transition*, fall 1988, 72–79.

H. Honour. "The Battle Over Post-Modern Buildings." *New York Review of Books*, September 29, 1988, 27–33.

L. Durning. "Venturi's Architecture of Diplomacy." *New Art Examiner*, October 1988, 34–36.

H. P. Svendler Nielsen. "Venturi, Rauch and Scott Brown." *Arkitekten*, October 1988, 221–33.

P. Goldberger. "80's Design: Wallowing in Opulence and Luxury." *New York Times*, November 13, 1988, H1, H32.

B. Hatton. "The Prince and the Architects." *Ottagono*, March 1989, 15–24.

J. S. Russell. "Living on Borrowed Light." *Architectural Record*, May 1989, 150–53.

"Venturi, Rauch & Scott Brown's Working Drawings for the National Gallery Sainsbury Wing." *Architecture Today*, September 1989, 54–55.

V. Gregotti, ed. *Casabella: Indici 1982–1988 (2) Argomenti Luoghi Libri*, 1990, 27, 59.

H. Honour. "La batalla del posmoderno." *A & V* 21 (1990): 12–19.

J. Morris. "Venturi, Scott Brown and Associates, Inc.: Invited Work." *The Royal Scottish Academy 164th Annual Exhibition Catalogue of Painting, Sculpture, and Architecture* (Musselburgh, Scotland, 1990), 22–23.

"We Are Architects Who Love Classical . . ." *Materia* 4 (1990): 18–31.

K. Powell. "A Welcome Invasion from the Other Side of the Atlantic." *Daily Telegraph*, March 3, 1990.

J. Nuttall. "The Sainsbury Wing: An Extension to the National Gallery, London." *Planning*, May 1990, 28–35.

M. Pawley. "Tales of an American Architect in London." *Building*, July 6, 1990, 33.

J. Russell. "A Fine Scottish Hand." *New York Times Magazine*, July 22, 1990, 22–26, 42, 45.

M. Pawley. "Sticks and Stones." *Time Out 20/20*, August 1990, 34–38.

"Robert Venturi." *Plus: Architecture + Interior Design*, August 1990, 115–73.

"London Goes Post-Modern." *Times* (London), December 21, 1990, 13.

C. Amery. "The Architecture of Post-War Galleries." In *Palaces of Art: Art Galleries in Britain, 1790–1990* (exhibition catalog, Dulwich: Dulwich Picture Gallery, 1991), 176–85.

C. Amery. *A Celebration of Art & Architecture: The National Gallery Sainsbury Wing* (London: National Gallery Publications, 1991).

"New Museology: The Third Annual Academy Forum." *Art & Design: "New Museology"* 6, no. 7–8 (1991): 9–37.

G. Baker. "The Sainsbury Wing at the National Gallery by Venturi, Scott Brown and Associates." *Architectural Design Profile No. 94: "New Museums"* 61 (November–December 1991): 16–19.

C. Jencks. "National Gallery/Sainsbury Wing: Interview with Robert Venturi, David Vaughan." *Architectural Digest Profile No. 91: "Post-Modern Triumphs in London"* 61 (May–June 1991): 48–57.

S. Lavin. "Outside with the Venturis." *Architectural Design Profile No. 94: "New Museums"* 61 (November–December 1991): 14–15.

"Europe '91: A Festival of Arts." *New York Times*, March 24, 1991, 14–16.

H. Porter. "More Post Office than Post-Modern." *Independent on Sunday*, March 24, 1991, 8.

"The Sainsbury Wing of the National Gallery, London." *Zodiac*, March–August 1991, 90–125.

M. Filler. "An American in London." *House & Garden*, April 1991, 126–29, 206.

M. Pawley. "What London Learnt from Las Vegas." *Blueprint*, May 1991, cover, 20–23.

S. Jenkins. "Triumph for a Modern Master." *Times* (London), May 4, 1991.

G. Stamp. "The Battle of Trafalgar Square." *Times* (London), May 4, 1991.

H. Pearman. "Designed to Steal the Show." *Sunday Times* (London), May 12, 1991, 10–11.

S. von Moos. "Fisiologia y caligrafia." *Arquitectura Viva*, May–June 1991, 10–17.

N. Penny and A. Reeve. "New Colours for Crivelli." *Independent Magazine*, June 7, 1991, 1–2.

C. Bremner. "Prophesier of Modern History." *Times Saturday Review*, June 22, 1991, 10–12.

R. Cork. "Step by Step to the Grand Stare." *Times Saturday Review*, June 22, 1991, 10–11.

R. Miller. "Playing to the Gallery." *Sunday Times Magazine*, June 23, 1991, 16–17, 19–20, 22, 24.

R. Dorment. "After All the Flak, a Clear View of Art." *Daily Telegraph*, June 25, 1991, 14.

I. Gale. "On a New Wing and a Prayer." *Independent*, June 25, 1991.

"Happy When Bob's Your Carbuncle." *Building Design*, June 26, 1991.

M. Kimmelman. "National Gallery Wing Set to Open in London." *New York Times*, June 26, 1991, C11, C14.

J. Gowan. "The Duck Stops Here." *Building Design*, June 28, 1991, 9, 12–13.

D. May. "Unexpected Treasure." *Elan*, June 28, 1991, 29.

R. Chesshyre. "The Miracle in Trafalgar Square." *Telegraph Magazine*, June 29, 1991, 22–29.

R. Maxwell. "Both Serious and Popular: Venturi's Sainsbury Wing." *Architecture Today*, July 1991, 30–41.

R. Moore. "Public Face and Public Place." *Architectural Review*, July 1991, 30–36.

"Son of Carbuncle Opens Its Doors." *Design*, July 1991.

C. McGuigan. "The Thinking Man of Design." *Newsweek*, July 1, 1991, 60–61.

B. Russell. "The Softer Touch." *Newstatesman Society*, July 5, 1991, 28–29.

J. McEwen. "Everything Just Right in Place and Time." *Sunday Telegraph*, July 7, 1991, xv.

"The Much Loved Friend?" Television review. *Observer*, July 7, 1991.

"The Much-Loved Friend?" Television review. *Guardian*, July 8, 1991.

"Gallery Architects Dismiss Criticism." *Daily Telegraph*, July 9, 1991, 4.

M. Hoelterhoff. "National Gallery's Disputed New Wing." *Wall Street Journal*, July 9, 1991.

C. Jencks. "As Relaxed with Mies as with Brunelleschi." *Financial Times*, July 9, 1991, 15.

W. Packer. "New Lease of Life for Renaissance Masterpieces." *Financial Times*, July 9, 1991, 15.

M. Steyn. "Royal Long Shot Falls Well Short." *Evening Standard*, July 9, 1991, 37.

T. Hine. "New Wing Vindicates Prince Charles." *Philadelphia Inquirer*, July 10, 1991, D1, D7.

T. Weasel. "Up & Down the City Road." *Independent*, July 13, 1991, 9–10.

A. L. Huxtable. "Why the Critics Got It Wrong." *Daily Telegraph*, July 25, 1991.

J. M. Dixon. "Learning from London." *Progressive Architecture*, August 1991, 80–85.

M. Rabino. "Alla National Gallery il futuro ha un'ala in più." *La Stampa*, August 1991.

R. Torday. "Gallery of Horror." *Connoisseur*, August 1991, 114–15.

C. P. Reynolds. "Lunching with the Muses." *New York Times*, August 11, 1991, 16, 29.

D. Jenkins, D. Hawkes, M. Pawley, and D. Cruickshank. "Capital Gains." *Architectural Journal*, August 20–21, 1991.

D. Hawkes. "Lighting Art Gallery, Venturi, Scott Brown and Associates." *Architectural Journal*, August 21–28, 1991.

B. Maguire. "Frontis." *RIBA Journal*, September 1991, 6–12.

M. Pawley. "PS." *RIBA Journal*, September 1991, 73.

G. Pigafetta. "Venturi a Trafalgar." *Casabella*, September 1991, 34–35.

M. Champenois. "La Bataille de Trafalgar Square." *Le Monde*, September 14, 1991, B1, B15, B18.

F. Irace. "Londra: Sainsbury Wing, Sackler Galleries." *Abitare*, October 1991, 223–28.

T. Lynham and S. Stallard. "Robert Venturi y Denise Scott Brown: Desde la polemica." *Diseño Interior*, October 1991, 70–73.

M. Palmer. "Recorrido por las Salas Sainsbury." *Diseño Interior*, October 1991, 92–93, 98–99.

M. Pawley. "Viewpoint." *Architectural Record*, October 1991, 75.

J. S. Russell. "To Mannerism Born." *Architectural Record*, October 1991, 71–79.

R. Kimball. "Clipper-Class Classicism: Robert Venturi's London Adventure." *New Criterion*, December 1991, 42–45.

M. Filler. "Architecture." *New York Times Book Review*, December 1, 1991, 77.

P. Barrière. "L'harmonie dans le paradoxe." *Cree*, December 1991–January 1992, 104–9, 179.

P. Fumagall. "Sainsbury Wing of the National Gallery, London: Venturi, Scott Brown and Associates." *Museo d'arte e architettura* (Milano: Museo Cantonale d'Arte Lugano, 1992), 110–18.

H. Moriyama. "The Charm of London's New Galleries." *Nikkei Architecture*, January–June 1992, 196–99 (in Japanese).

A. Tzonis and L. Lefaivre. "Venturi, Scott Brown and Associates, Inc.: The National Gallery, Sainsbury Wing." In *Architecture in Europe: Memory and Invention since 1968* (New York: Rizzoli, 1992), 272–75.

"Best of 1991 Design: Addition to National Gallery, London." *Time*, January 6, 1992, 82.

S. Castiglione. "Diseñar a partir de la memoria: La ampliación de la National Gallery de Londres." *Arquitectura & Diseño*, March 1992, 1, 2, 8.

D. Dillon. "Context and Craft." *Architecture*, March 1992, 48–52.

M. Linder. "Contingency and Circumstance in Architecture: Venturi and Scott Brown's Sainsbury Wing." *A+U (Architecture and Urbanism)*, May 1992, 11–41.

P. Goldberger. "Pushing Classicism to Extremes." *New York Times*, May 17, 1992, 33.

C. Temin. "London's National Is Grander than Ever." *Boston Sunday Globe*, June 28, 1992, B1, B9, B10.

"Showcase 1992: British Slate Goes to the New Wing of London's National Gallery." *Stone World*, July 1992, 66.

C. Dibar and S. Castiglione. "Robert Venturi/Denise Scott Brown: Aprendendo Com a Complexidade." *Arquitetura e Urbanismo*, October–November 1992, 62–71.

P. Heyer. *American Architecture: Ideas and Ideologies in the Late Twentieth Century* (New York: Van Nostrand Reinhold, 1993), 240–42.

S. von Moos. "Venturi, die Kunstgeschichte und das 'Princeton System.' Zum neuer Erweiterungsbau der National Gallery in London (1986–1991)." In *Künstlerischer Austausch/Artistic Exchange. Akten des XXVIII. Internationalen Kongresses für Kunstgeschichte Berlin, 15.–20. Juli 1992*, ed. Thomas W. Gaehtgens (Berlin: Akademie Verlag, 1993), 15–34.

A. Bugatti. "Quando la forza è l'immagine." *Costruire*, February 1994, 104–6.

C. Vaccaro. "La Strada Secondo Robert Venturi e Denise Scott Brown (interview)." *Arredo Urbano* 52 (March 1994): 72–85.

S. Duncan. "In the Best Possible Light." *Metropolis*, April 1994, 58–63.

"Venturi, Scott Brown & Ass.: Recent Work." *Archithese*, November–December 1995, 16–19.

Seattle Art Museum

T. Tang. "Robert Venturi: Of Ducks and Sheds." *The Weekly*, October 10–16, 1984, 33–35.

R. Hackett. "Architects Have Mixed Reaction to Art Museum Plans." *Seattle Post-Intelligencer*, September 11, 1986, C7.

S. Lavin. "Artistic Statements." *Interiors*, November 1987, 131–37, 166.

R. Maxwell. "Due Musei negli USA di Venturi-Rauch-Scott Brown." *Casabella*, November 1987, 33–37.

"New Seattle Art Museum Model by Robert Venturi Was Unveiled." *A+U (Architecture and Urbanism)*, November 1987, 6–7.

J. Abrams. "Contemplation and Congregation in the Popular Urban Art Museum." *Lotus International* 55 (1988): 85–117.

E. Posner. "The Museum as Bazaar." *Atlantic Monthly*, August 1988, 67–70.

V. M. Lampugnani. "Seattle Art Museum." *Domus*, November 1988, 36–40.

V. Gregotti, ed. *Casabella: Indici 1982–1988 (2) Argomenti Luoghi Libri*, 1990, 72.

T. Egan. "Museum by Venturi Opens In Seattle." *New York Times*, December 10, 1991, C15.

T. Egan. "Venturi's New Seattle Art Museum Opens." *New York Times*, December 10, 1991, B1, B8.

T. Hine. "A Comfortable New Seattle Art Museum." *Philadelphia Inquirer*, February 9, 1992, H1, H5.

P. Goldberger. "An Art Museum Lifts Seattle's Cultural Profile." *New York Times*, February 16, 1992, 34H.

K. Andersen. "Pioneer's Vindication: The Founder of Postmodern Architecture Adds the Seattle Art Museum to His String of Triumphs." *Time*, February 17, 1992, 82–83.

D. Bonetti. "Architects Pursue a Lofty Vision." *San Francisco Examiner*, February 20, 1992, C1, C4.

A. Belluzzi. "Venturi, Scott Brown e Associati a Seattle." *Abitare*, April 1992, 182–87.

H. Dudar. "A Welcoming New Museum for the City on the Sound." *Smithsonian*, April 1992, 47–56.

R. Kimball. "Elitist Anti-Elitism: Robert Venturi Does Seattle." *New Criterion*, April 1992, 4–9.

S. Castiglione. "Museo de arte en Seattle: La Obra Mas Reciente del Estudio Venturi-Scott Brown y Asociados." *Arquitectura & Diseño*, June 1992, 1, 2, 8.

P. Nicolin. "Il contesto come collage/The Context as Collage: The Decorative Response of Robert Venturi in Seattle." *Lotus International* 74 (November 1992): 86–97.

C. Norberg-Schulz. "The Transformation of What Is Known." In *Images in Stone: International Award Architecture in Stone* (Milan: Electa, 1993), 56–59.

E. Scigliano. "Clash of the Titans: When 'Hammering Man' Strode into Seattle, Culture and Subculture Collided." *New York Times*, October 10, 1993, 6.

A. Banerji and M. Elmitt. *Between Lines: From Doodles to Composition* (Waterloo, Ontario: Escart P, 1994), cover, 3, 188, 189.

"Venturi, Scott Brown & Ass.: Recent Work." *Archithese*, November–December 1995, 20–21.

Children's Museum, Houston

P. Peters. "A Temple for Tots." *Cite*, spring 1991, 5.

A. Holmes. "Museum a Challenge for Venturi." *Houston Chronicle*, June 3, 1991, 1D, 6D.

A. Holmes. "Venturi's Statement: Architect Watches His Houston Project Take Shape." *Houston Chronicle*, August 16, 1992, 15, 30.

D. Sabota. "Notable Architects Return to Houston with New Landmark Building Projects." *Houston Business Journal*, October 26, 1992, 4A.

D. Dillon. "Good Design Can Be Kid Stuff." *Dallas Morning News*, November 22, 1992, 1C, 8C.

L. Bullivant. "The Children's Museum." *Abitare*, March 1993, 165–67.

G. Moorhead. "Caryakids At Play." *Architectural Record*, March 1993, 78–83.

D. Dillon. "Decorated Shed." *Architecture*, April 1993, 46–51.

E. Gunts. "Architecture for Kids." *Architecture*, April 1993, 43–45.

D. Turner. "Little Caesar's Palace." *Cite*, spring–summer 1993, 29–35.

G. Bensi. "Citazioni per gioco." *Costruire*, June 1993, 146–49.

T. Peeters. "For the Young and the Young-at-Heart." *Texas Highways*, July 1993, 46–51.

W. Winters. "New Texas Museums." *Texas Architect* 7–8 (1993): 36–43.

P. Goldberger. "For Children, Pop Goes the Museum." *New York Times*, August 22, 1993, H30.

"PC or Not PC." *Architects' Journal*, October 6, 1993, 10.

D. Dillon. "The Children's Museum of Houston Lets Robert Venturi Take Some of the Starch out of Classicism: Kid Stuff." *Elle Decor*, October–November 1993, 124.

R. K. Lewis. "Serious Play: Children's Museum of Houston." *Museum News*, November–December 1993, 36–38.

"Museo del Niño de Houston." In *Museos y arquitectura: Nuevas perspectivas* (Madrid: Ministerio de Obras Públicas, Transportes y Medio Ambiente, 1994), 126–31.

S. Tuzi. "Robert Venturi." *Materia* 15 (1994): 12–17.

D. R. Armando. "Venturi, ahora para los más chicos." *La Nacion Arquitectura* (Buenos Aires), July 20, 1994, section 5, 1–2.

"Venturi, Scott Brown & Ass.: Recent Work." *Archithese*, November–December 1995, 24.

National Museum of the American Indian

B. Gamarekian. "Venturi Firm Is Chosen for Indian Museum Project." *New York Times*, April 10, 1991.

"Creating a Museum for the 21st Century." *Native Peoples Magazine* 5, no. 2 (winter 1992): 38–41.

A. Gabor. *Einstein's Wife* (New York: Viking Press, 1995), 156–231.

Expo '92 Pavilion

M. Wigley. "The Decorated Gap." *Ottagono*, March 1989, 36–55.

J. Cenicacelaya. *Arquitectonica*, October 1989, 25–96.

J. Morris. "Venturi, Scott Brown and Associates, Inc.: Invited Work." *The Royal Scottish Academy 164th Annual Exhibition Catalogue of Painting, Sculpture, and Architecture* (Musselburgh, Scotland, 1990), 22–23.

Stedelijk Museum Addition

A. Wortmann. "Het Stedelijk Museum: projectontwikkelaarscachet of undergroundkunst." *Archis*, February 1993, 2–5.

C. de Bruijn. "Amsterdam alla Venturi." *Costruire*, March 1993, 67.

M. van Nieuwenhuyzen. "Uitbreiding Stedelijk Museum." *Stedelijk Museum Bulletin*, March 1993.

Museum of Contemporary Art, San Diego

K. Kaiser and R. L. Pincus. "LJMCA Looks to Venturi." *San Diego Union*, July 24, 1986, C1, C7.

K. Kaiser. "There's a Method to Venturi's Vagueness in La Jolla." *San Diego Union*, May 31, 1987, F2.

M. Granberry. "Top Architect Tapped for Tough Museum Task." *Los Angeles Times*, June 10, 1987, section VI, 1, 6

"Pencil Points." *Progressive Architecture*, July 1987, 26.

L. Allen. "President's Message." *Women in Architecture/Articulations*, May 1988, 3.

H. Harper. "La Jolla Museum of Art Unveils Venturi's Design for Expansion." *Los Angeles Times*, May 5, 1988, section VI, 1, 10.

T. Perry. "Museum Launches Expansion." *New York Times*, July 15, 1994, F14.

P. Jensen. "The Venturi Effect." *San Diego Home/Garden*, July 1988, 15.

E. Posner. "The Museum as Bazaar." *Atlantic Monthly*, August 1988, 67–70.

"President's Report," "Director's Report." *San Diego Museum of Contemporary Art Biennial Report 1988 and 1989*, 3–4, 5–6.

J. S. Russell. "Living on Borrowed Light." *Architectural Record*, May 1989, 150–53.

R. J. Onorato. "Collecting in Context." *On the Road: Selections from the Permanent Collection of the San Diego Museum of Contemporary Art* (Seattle: Marquand Books, 1990), 10–40.

"Renovation and Additions to the Museum of Contemporary Art, San Diego, California, U.S.A." *Zodiac*, March 1996, 126–33.

P. Goldberger. "Refashioning the Old, with All Due Respect." *New York Times*, May 5, 1996, 40.

K. D. Stein. "Irving Gill Reconsidered." *Architectural Record*, August 1996, 88–93.

Whitehall Ferry Terminal

H. Muschamp. "6 Visions of a New Ferry Terminal." *New York Times*, November 5, 1992, C17, C22.

H. Muschamp. "For Staten Island, a Ferry Terminal Rooted in the Past." *New York Times*, November 22, 1992, H32.

A. Hess. *Viva Las Vegas* (San Francisco: Chronicle Books, 1993).

P. Hall. "Marking Time." *I.D.*, January–February 1993, 19.

U. Lambsdorff. "Manhattan: Time is Money." *Ambiente*, January–February 1993, 20.

M. McDonough. "Learning from Sony." *Avenue*, April 1993, 8.

A. Kishimoto. "Whitehall Ferry Project." *Eciffo*, summer 1993, 50.

"Whitehall Ferry Terminal: Gateway to New York." *Building Journal Hongkong China*, June 1993, 45.

"Whitehall Ferry Terminal Competition." *Compe & Contest* 31 (November 1993): 1, 21–24.

"Whitehall Ferry Terminal, New York." *Domus*, January 1994, 28–31.

M. McDonough. "Currents: Design's Future." *New York Times*, June 9, 1994.

J. Melvin. "Challenging Insularity." *Building Design*, July 1, 1994, 12–17.

"Venturi, Scott Brown & Ass.: Recent Work." *Archithese*, November–December 1995, 32–33.

Battery Park Band Pavilion

"Edible Architecture: Delicious Designs." *Sotheby's Auction Catalogue*, December 14, 1989, items 36–40.

Celebration Bank

B. Dunlop. "Designs on the Future." *Architectural Record*, January 1996, 66.

Fire Station, The Walt Disney Company

B. Dunlop. "Fire Cracker." *Architectural Record*, May 1994, 94–97.

"(Still) Learning from Las Vegas." *New Yorker*, May 23, 1994, 38.

"Reedy Creek Emergency Services Headquarters." *Korean Architects*, September 1994, 32–35.

W. Moonan. "Three-Alarm Spots and Dots at Disney." *New York Times*, September 15, 1994, C3.

B. Dunlop. *Building a Dream: The Art of Disney Architecture* (New York, Harry N. Abrams, 1996).

"Fire Station at Orlando, Florida." Domus, November 1996, 26–27.

Philadelphia Orchestra Hall

T. Hine. "Orchestra Chooses Venturi." *Philadelphia Inquirer*, July 21, 1987, 1A, 4A.

L. Fleeson and T. Hine. "Two Designers and How They Won the Hall." *Philadelphia Inquirer*, July 26, 1987, 1I, 12I.

D. Webster. "Orchestra Hall Plans Unveiled." *Philadelphia Inquirer*, June 28, 1989, 1A, 14A.

T. Hine. "Unveiling the Orchestra Hall." *Philadelphia Inquirer*, July 2, 1989, 1E, 6E.

"A New House for the Fabulous Philadelphians." *Architectural Record*, August 1989.

B. Suner. "Venturi et Scott Brown à Philadelphie." *L'Architecture d'aujourd'hui*, April 1990, 175–77.

P. Goldberger. "In Philadelphia, 3 Arts Centers, 2 or One?" *New York Times*, May 2, 1990, C15.

"Robert Venturi." *Plus: Architecture + Interior Design*, August 1990, 115–73.

"Philadelphia Orchestra Hall." *Zodiac*, September 1990, 74–109.

M. A. Heckscher. "A Shared Vision for the Future of Philadelphia." *The Shingle*, summer 1991, 28–30.

P. Meninato. "Armonia en Filadelfia." *Arquitectura & Diseño*, March 1992, 4, 6.

Y. Mikami. "New Blood into the Tradition of Horse-shoe Type: Philadelphia Orchestra Hall." In *Space Design Series: Theaters & Concert Halls*, ed. Toru Funakoshi (Tokyo: Shin-Nihon-Hoki Publishers, 1994), 232–33.

"Venturi, Scott Brown & Ass.: Recent Work." *Archithese*, November– December 1995, 22–23.

Hôtel du Département de la Haute-Garonne

A. Buisson. "Une grande maison de brique vue par un Américain." *Grand Toulouse*, June 4, 1992, 16.

J. Melvin. "Challenging Insularity." *Building Design*, July 1, 1994, 12–17.

Berlin U.S. Embassy

"Venturi, Scott Brown & Ass.: Recent Work." *Archithese*, November– December 1995, 34–35.

"Building Security: Berlin's New Embassy: Safeguarding a Symbol." *Architectural Record*, March 1996, 36–43.

R. Kroloff. "A New Embassy in Berlin." *Architecture*, April 1996, 131–37.

Clinical Research Building, University of Pennsylvania

M. Wagner. "Plum Jobs." *Interiors*, January 1988, 40.

M. Wigley. "The Decorated Gap." *Ottagono*, March 1989, 36–55.

T. Hine. "A Study in Constrasts at Penn." *Philadelphia Inquirer*, January 21, 1990, 1I, 6I.

J. Selwyn. "Building Boasts Novel Design, Research." *Daily Pennsylvanian*, January 25, 1990, 1, 9.

"For Medicine: A Seal of Approval." *Pennsylvania Gazette*, February–March 1990, 98.

B. Gabby. "About Face." *Architecture*, April 1990, 113–14, 141–43.

P. Arcidi. "Inquiry: Laboratories." *Progressive Architecture*, August 1990, 102.

"Space, Light, and Close Colleagues." *Penn Medicine*, winter 1990, 25–27.

J. Collins Jr. with I. Adamson. "Trends in Laboratory Design." *Architectural Record* Review, 1991–92, 64–67.

B. J. Novitski. "CADD Consequences." *Architecture*, May 1992, 109–12.

Fisher and Bendheim Halls

M. A. Branch. "Three for One." *Progressive Architecture*, August 1991, 88–91.

"Venturi, Scott Brown and Associates, Inc., University Buildings at UCLA, Los Angeles, and in Princeton, New Jersey." *Zodiac*, March–August 1992, 65–71, 76–95.

"Silver Medal Winner, Fisher and Bendheim Hall." *Pennsylvania Architect*, winter 1992, 16–18.

"Venturi, Scott Brown & Ass.: Recent Work." *Archithese*, November– December 1995, 30–31.

Bard College Library Addition

H. Muschamp. "Democratic Decorations at Bard College." *New York Times*, October 31, 1993, 42H.

VSBA. "The Charles P. Stevenson, Jr., Library, Bard College, Annandale-on-Hudson, New York." *Zodiac*, November 1993, 218–35.

M. L. Bierman. "Arcadian Acropolis." *Architecture*, February 1994, 78–84.

VSBA. "Color Confessions of Contemporary Architects." *Daidalos*, March 15, 1994, 38–39.

J. Melvin. "Challenging Insularity." *Building Design*, July 1, 1994, 12–17.

"Venturi, Scott Brown & Ass.: Recent Work." *Archithese*, November– December 1995, 27–29.

Trabant Student Center

L. Hardy. "Defending His Design." *News Journal* (Wilmington, Del.), June 23, 1994, B1.

"Editorial: Flap over UD Hall Renovation Misguided, Unfair to Designer." *News Journal* (Wilmington, Del.), June 27, 1994.

"University of Delaware Student Center, Newark, Delaware, U.S.A." *Zodiac*, March 1996, 134–37.

G. Soulsman. "A Building for the Future." *News Journal* (Wilmington, Del.), April 29, 1996, C1, C2.

Gordon and Virginia MacDonald Medical Research Laboratories

M. Wigley. "The Decorated Gap." *Ottagono*, March 1989, 36–55.

P. Portoghesi. "The Decoration." *Materia* 9 (1992): 3–39.

"Venturi, Scott Brown and Associates, Inc., University Buildings at UCLA, Los Angeles, and in Princeton, New Jersey." *Zodiac*, March–August 1992, 65–71, 76–95.

B. Binét and V. Beck. "MacDonald Laboratories Assure Scientific Collaboration." *UCLA Magazine*, winter 1992, 56.

A. Vidler. "Architectural Awakenings." *UCLA Magazine*, summer 1994, 41–44.

"Venturi, Scott Brown & Ass.: Recent Work." *Archithese*, November– December 1995, 25–26.

Medical Laboratory, Yale University

C. A. Nicholas. "A New Building for a New Medicine: The Center for the Study of Human Diseases." In *A New Medicine for a New Century* (New Haven: Yale School of Medicine, Office of Development, 1993), 7–12.

Clinical Research Center, National Institutes of Health

B. McKee. "NIH's Newest Experiment." *Architecture*, March 1996, 131–39.

Gas Station, The Walt Disney Company

"Gas Station at Orlando, Florida." *Domus*, November 1996, 26–27.

Project for a House in Tuxedo Park

V. Geibel. "Trending toward the Gothic." *On the Avenue*, November 1988, 8–11.

House on Long Island Sound

"Steven Izenour of Venturi, Rauch & Scott Brown." *GA (Global Architecture) Houses* 16 (1984): 140–47.

H. Klotz, ed. "Steven Izenour." *Architectural Design: Revision of the Modern*, March–April 1985, 48–49.

"House on Long Island Sound." *A+U (Architecture and Urbanism)*, July 1985, 18–24.

D. D. Boles. "Ecumenical Honor Awards." *Progressive Architecture*, May 1987, 29, 32, 34.

"House in Long Island." *GA (Global Architecture) Houses* 28: *Project 1990*, March 1990, 102.

"Special Feature: Venturi, Scott Brown and Associates." *A+U (Architecture and Urbanism)*, June 1990, 39–130.

G. DeGiorgi, A. Mutoni, and M. Pazzaglini. "Robert Venturi, Denise Scott Brown and Ass., Inc., House in Long Island, NY." *Metamorfosi*, November 1990, 30–32.

S. Stephens. "In the Coastal Vernacular." *Architectural Digest*, December 1990, 112–19.

S. Stephens. "Architettura: La nave di Robert Venturi." *Architectural Digest: Le piu belle case del mondo*, December 1991, 170–75, 207.

"Venturi, Scott Brown & Ass.: Recent Work." *Archithese*, November–December 1995, 38–39.

Pearl Houses

P. L. Brown. "Venturi à la Carte: A Signature Series in Florida." *New York Times*, March 9, 1989, C1, C6.

C. McGuigan. "High Style in the 'Burbs." *Newsweek*, March 27, 1989.

P. L. Brown. "Famed Architect Tries Hand at Developing Housing." *Island Packet*, July 23, 1989, 4C.

H. Muschamp. "Venturi to Order." *House & Garden*, August 1989, 104–8, 141.

House on the Coast of Maine

P. Goldberger. "Architecture: Robert Venturi: The Shingle Style Recast for the Nineties in Maine." *Architectural Digest*, July 1992, 141–48.

Project for a House in Chester County

"Venturi, Scott Brown & Associates." *Materia* 25 (1997): 12–17.

Houses for Mitsui Home Co.

"Judges' Comments," "Discussion: Diversity in Houses," "Ethos and Place in a Non-Universal Architecture of Institutions" (lecture by Robert Venturi, February 27, 1990, Tokyo). *Mitsui Home International Residential Design Competition, 1989* (Tokyo: Mitsui Home Co., 1990), 32, 34–50, 51–102.

Tarble Student Center

"Tarble Student Center, Swarthmore College, Swarthmore, Pennsylvania." *Architectural Record*, March 1987, 106–11.

"Special Feature: Venturi, Scott Brown and Associates." *A+U (Architecture and Urbanism)*, June 1990, 86–89.

Mass MoCA

C. Boneti. "Sprague Electric Company/North Adams from Mill to Museum." *ART New England*, September 1989.

N. Brooke Mandel. "Mass MoCA: A Museum in Search of Itself." *Metropolis*, January–February 1992, 54–59.

L. Fleeson. "From Mill to Museum." *Philadelphia Inquirer*, February 20, 1990, 1D, 8D.

Furness Building

M. F. Schmertz. "Furness Expurgated." *Architectural Record*, June 1988, 69.

F. Richards. "Restoring a Masterpiece." *CitySITES*, fall 1988, 4–5.

J. S. Russell. "Living on Borrowed Light." *Architectural Record*, May 1989, 150–53.

G. E. Thomas, M. J. Lewis, and J. A. Cohen. "Furness and Taste." *Frank Furness: The Complete Works* (New York: Princeton Architectural Press, 1991), 5–6.

P. Arcidi. "Mending a 'Difficult Whole.'" *Progressive Architecture*, May 1991, 81–89.

"Merit Awards: Venturi, Scott Brown; Wesley Wei." *Philadelphia Architect*, June 1991, 6.

P. Goldberger. "In Philadelphia, a Victorian Extravaganza Lives." *New York Times*, June 2, 1991, 32.

T. Hine. "Spreading the Word of Furness' Singular Art." *Philadelphia Inquirer*, August 25, 1991, 1C, 6C.

P. Goldberger. "A Victorian Extravaganza." *Pennsylvania Gazette*, October 1991, 27–30.

J. O'Gorman. "A Masterpiece Restored." *Interiors*, January 1992, 94–95.

J. Loomis. "La conservazione: Il futuro del passato/Conservation: The Future of the Past." *Casabella*, January–February 1992, 82.

C. Dibar and S. Castiglione. "Robert Venturi/Denise Scott Brown: Aprendendo Com a Complexidade." *Arquitetura e Urbanismo*, October–November 1992, 62–71.

"Learning from Philadelphia." *Abitare*, November 1992, 146–52, 204.

M. L. Bierman. "Celebrating Pluralism" (1993 AIA Award winners). *Architecture*, May 1993, 100.

"Venturi, Scott Brown & Ass.: Recent Work." *Archithese*, November–December 1995, 36–37.

E. Bosley. *University of Pennsylvania Library: Frank Furness* (London: Phaidon, 1996).

Thayer School of Engineering

"Doble lenguaje." *A & V* 21 (1990): 46–48.

J. S. Russell. "Two of a Kind." *Architectural Record*, May 1991, 78–87.

Memorial Hall

D. Bradley Ruder. "Gift Establishes Student Commons in Memorial Hall." *Harvard University Gazette*, September 25, 1992, 1, 14–17.

D. Bradley Ruder. "Memorial Hall: Center of Attention for Architects, Engineers, Planners." *Harvard University Gazette*, April 9, 1993, 1, 12–13.

Memorial Hall, Harvard University (special edition, Cambridge: Harvard University, June 1993), 44.

R. Campbell. "Harvard's Great Room." *Boston Sunday Globe*, January 28, 1996, 29, 39.

ICA Exhibition

T. Hine. "Putting Architecture into Words at the ICA." *Philadelphia Inquirer*, February 28, 1993, 1H.

H. Steinberg. "Venturi, Scott Brown & Associates at the ICA." *Philadelphia Architect*, April 1993, 4.

A. Stein and A. Miksitz. Review of "About Architecture: An Installation by Venturi, Scott Brown and Associates." *Architronic: The Electronic Journal of Architecture*, May 1993, 4.

Venturi Shops

M. Geran. "Designers' Choices: Robert Venturi and Denise Scott Brown." *Interior Design*, December 1994, 55.

"Rethinking What is 'Japanese' From the Viewpoint of a Western Eye." *Nikkei Design*, April 1995, 55.

Alessi Biblioteca
G. Odoni. "Le Architetture Diverse." *Casa Vogue*, October 1988, 184–85.
J. Giovannini. "The House of Houses." *Metropolitan Home*, November 1988, 142–43.
"Special Feature: Venturi, Scott Brown and Associates." *A+U (Architecture and Urbanism)*, June 1990, 95.

PMA West Foyer
J. S. Boggs. "Planning for the Future." *Philadelphia Art Museum 105th Annual Report 1980–1981*, 1981, 11.
S. Stephens. "Currents: Philadelphia Museum's Energetic Desk." *New York Times*, February 2, 1989, C3.
D. Rice. "Examining Exhibits." *Museum News*, November–December 1989, 46–50.
D. B. Brownlee. *Making a Modern Classic: The Architecture of the Philadelphia Museum of Art* (Philadelphia: Philadelphia Museum of Art, 1997), 114–17.

Princeton Club of New York
J. Nasatir. "Princeton Club." *Interior Design*, September 1990, 174–77.
K. Maserjian. "Venturi, Scott Brown: Tiger Bar and Grill at the Princeton Club." Interior Design, October 1992, 184–87.

Designs for Kitchen Units
N. Y. Yang and J. Kim. "Hanssem Kitchen Furniture." *Design*, August 1992, 98–101 (in Korean).

Cuckoo Clock for Alessi
"Special Feature. Venturi, Scott Brown and Associates." *A+U (Architecture and Urbanism)*, June 1990, 115.
Alessi: The Design Factory (London: Academy Editions, 1994), 95.

Fabrics for Designtex
P. Blake. "3 Directions in 3 Dimensions." *Interior Design*, March 1991, 120–25.
K. D. Stein. "Meier, Rossi, Scott Brown and Venturi Add Fabrics to Their Futures." *Architectural Record*, May 1991, 21.
L. Rachele Balinbin. "In Focus." *Perspectives*, summer 1991, 14.

Rugs for V'Soske
J. V. Iovine. "Splendors in the Grass." *New York Times Magazine*, October 30, 1994, 74–75.

Jewelry for Munari
"Special Feature: Venturi, Scott Brown and Associates." *A+U (Architecture and Urbanism)*, June 1990, 120.

Campidoglio Tray for Alessi
A. C. Papadakis, ed. "The Post-Modern Object." *Art & Design*, April 1987.
"Fauna de sobremesa." *ARDI*, May–June 1988, 129.
M. R. Paulis. "The Design of 'The Campidoglio' Tray." *Officina Alessi* (Crusinallo: Alessi, 1989), 31–34.
"Special Feature: Venturi, Scott Brown and Associates." *A+U (Architecture and Urbanism)*, June 1990, 117.
M. R. Paulis. "The Design of 'The Campidoglio' Tray." *Officina Alessi: La Tavola di Babele* (catalog, Crusinallo: Alessi, 1993), 69–72, 108.
Alessi: The Design Factory (London: Academy Editions, 1994), 43.

Photography Credits

Alessi: 322, 340
Atwater Kent Museum, Philadelphia: 20 right, 21 right
Ellen Perry Berkeley: 16 left
Tom Bernard: 43, 55 left, 303, 357 center, 357 right
Richard Bryant (Arcaid): 129 bottom center
Center for Furness Studies, Architectural Archives, University of Pennsylvania: 22 top
CLIO Group: 307 bottom
Mark Cohn: 18 right
Susan Dirk: 144 right
Paul Hester: 153
Koji Horiuchi: 270 bottom, 278
Timothy Hursley: 173, 174, 175, 176, 177
Steven Izenour: 358
Kawasumi Architectural Photograph Office: 270 top, 272, 273, 274, 275, 277, 279
Collection Kunsthaus Zurich: 34 right
Rollin LaFrance: 359 right
Courtesy Landesbildstelle Berlin, Karlsruhe, Germany: 62 left
Library Company of Philadelphia: 12 left
Julie Marquart: 10 top left, 10 bottom, 246, 253
Munari: 338, 339
Museum of Fine Arts, Boston: 61 left
Museum of Fine Arts, Houston: 36 right
Courtesy Museum of Modern Art, New York: 59 right
Norton Gallery and School of Art, West Palm Beach, Florida: 10 right
Panoptic Imaging: 183
PhotoKosuge: 63, 278
Pinacoteca di Brera, Milan: 44 left
Courtesy Princeton University Libraries: 42 left
Steve Rosenthal: 312, 313
Martha Seng: 140
Shinkenchiku-sha: 271
Timothy Soar: 128, 129 bottom left, 130 top right, 131 top left
Phillip Starling: 132, 134, 139
Strode Eckert Photographic: 146
Courtesy George E. Thomas: 22 bottom (William Sellers & Co.);
23 (illustration from *Harper's Weekly*, February 14, 1891)
Prints Collection, University of Virginia Library: 27 left
VSBA: 45 right, 147, 267, 268, 269, 328, 344, 345, 347 right, 355 right
Courtesy Roger Viollet: 43 left
V'Soske: 336, 337
Matt Wargo: 12 right, 32, 40 left, 46 top right, 115, 116, 117, 123, 125, 127, 129 bottom right, 130 top left, 130 bottom, 131 bottom left, 135, 136, 137, 141, 142, 143, 144 left, 149, 150, 151, 190, 191, 193, 205, 206, 218, 219, 221, 222, 223, 225, 226, 227, 229, 231, 232, 233, 235, 236, 237, 240, 241, 243, 265, 284, 288, 289, 290, 292, 293, 294, 295, 307 top, 308, 309, 311, 314, 315, 318, 319, 320, 321, 324, 325, 326, 327, 330, 331, 332, 333, 334, 335, 341, 348 right, 350 left, 356, 357 left
Yale University Library: 30 left